D0628055

Bill Dodson
1973

Collective
Bargaining
in
Government

COLLECTIVE
BARGAINING
IN
GOVERNMENT
Readings and Cases

J. JOSEPH LOEWENBERG

Temple University

MICHAEL H. MOSKOW

U.S. Department of Labor

PRENTICE-HALL, INC., *Englewood Cliffs, New Jersey*

To our wives, for their
patience and understanding

© 1972 by PRENTICE-HALL, INC., Englewood Cliffs, New Jersey

All rights reserved. No part of this book may be reproduced in any
form or by any means, without permission in writing from the
publisher. Printed in the United States of America

ISBN: 0-13-140483-0

Library of Congress Catalog Card No.: 78-162353

10 9 8 7 6 5 4 3

PRENTICE-HALL INTERNATIONAL, INC., London
PRENTICE-HALL OF AUSTRALIA, PTY. LTD., Sydney
PRENTICE-HALL OF CANADA, LTD., Toronto
PRENTICE-HALL OF INDIA PRIVATE LIMITED, New Delhi
PRENTICE-HALL OF JAPAN, INC., Tokyo

CONTENTS

CHAPTER 3   *Read for Tommorrow* :
THE PROCESS OF COLLECTIVE BARGAINING
IN PUBLIC EMPLOYMENT   **116**

CHAPTER 4
CASE STUDIES ON PUBLIC SECTOR BARGAINING   **145**

PREFACE

The most dramatic new development in the field of labor relations in the past ten years has been the spread of collective bargaining to the public sector. For the first time on any meaningful scale, employees of local, state, and federal governments have bargained collectively for improved wages and working conditions. Until the 1970 postal strike, local government employees—particularly teachers, sanitation workers, police, and firefighters—were the most active groups of public employees. Today the phenomenon is spreading among all levels of government and occupation categories. Public sector bargaining is clearly "where the action is."

This book should be of interest to students in several general fields of study: labor relations, labor economics, public administration, and political science. Public sector bargaining is of interest to the student of labor relations because it represents an extension of the institution of collective bargaining to another industry. The labor economist views it as a new factor in the distribution of resources. To the student of public administration or political science, the phenomenon modifies the traditional system of government.

The literature on collective bargaining in the public sector has mushroomed in recent years. The editors believe that this book will serve as a companion volume to another book they recently wrote.[1] They anticipate that the present volume of readings and cases will be used primarily as a supplementary book in general courses in labor relations, collective bargaining, public administration, and political science. It is also appropriate as a basic or supplementary text in a course devoted exclusively to public sector bargaining.

This book has several unique features that make it interesting as well as pedagogically useful.

    1. Twelve articles were written especially for this volume. Other selections

---

[1]Michael H. Moskow, J. Joseph Loewenberg, and Edward Clifford Koziara, *Collective Bargaining in Public Employment* (New York: Random House, 1970).

have been chosen because they represent classic statements or situations or because they represent the most current information on an interpretation of a subject.

2. Several topics have been presented to provide a variety of views. For instance, the problems of appropriate administrative agency or of the right of government employees to strike offer no single correct answer. The editors feel the reader should evaluate the arguments and counterarguments.

3. The book features a series of case studies, five of them in Section IV. These in-depth studies permit the reader to become involved in the material pertaining to a single case and to analyze and interpret this material with other members of the class.

4. The book is divided into seven sections, each devoted to a separate aspect of public sector bargaining.

The editors would like to thank the authors of the articles and the journals for giving permission to reprint this collection of articles and cases. They are especially grateful to the authors who wrote articles specifically for this volume.

Our thanks go also to Professor Harold W. Davey of Iowa State University, Professor David W. Belcher of San Diego State College, Dr. Dale Yoder of California State College at Long Beach, and Professor Neil Chamberlain of Columbia University, whose critical comments and constructive suggestions were greatly helpful to us.

J. Joseph Loewenberg
Michael H. Moskow

Collective
Bargaining
in
Government

CHAPTER 1

THE BACKGROUND DEVELOPMENTS

AND LEGAL STRUCTURE

OF PUBLIC SECTOR BARGAINING

Government is the most rapidly growing sector of our economy. Employment in this sector increased by 46 percent from 1960 to 1969 while employment in the remainder of the economy increased by only 26 percent in the same period. The percentage of our labor force employed by federal, state, and local governments increased from 9.6 percent in 1920 to 17.4 percent in 1969.

Although government is growing very rapidly, it has lagged behind the private sector in the development and spread of collective bargaining. The Wagner Act, which granted collective bargaining rights to most employees working in the private sector, was passed in 1935. It was not until 1962, however, that the federal government granted some form of collective bargaining to its own employees. Similarly, only one state, Wisconsin, had provided bargaining for employees of its local units of government by 1962.

The scene changed dramatically in the 1960s. Twenty-two states passed laws granting collective bargaining to local or state employees. President Nixon replaced Executive Order 10988 (1962) with Executive Order 11491 (1969) which updated and expanded the framework for federal employee bargaining. In 1970 the post office was transformed into an independent agency, simultaneously granting full collective bargaining rights on wages and working conditions to its employees.

This group of articles and source materials provides some historical perspective to the changing legal structure and the growth of collective bargaining in the public sector. After a section by the editors on the growth of employment in the public sector Cohany and Dewey analyze the trends in union membership among government employees. Chamberlain compares collective bargaining in the public sector with collective bargaining in the private sector thirty-five years ago. Excerpts from the Illinois task force report describes early collective bargaining experience among a group of state employees.

The rash of state laws passed in the 1960s put to rest the debates on the legality of public sector bargaining. These state laws, which are highly diverse, are described and analyzed by Goldberg in his article "Labor-Management Relations Laws in Public Service." Dole analyzes the legality of public sector bargaining in the absence of legislation, which is still applicable for the majority of the states.

TRENDS IN EMPLOYMENT IN THE PUBLIC SECTOR

J. Joseph Loewenberg
Michael H. Moskow

The emergence of collective bargaining in public employment occurred in an era of change in government employment and the environment in which government operated. Among the outstanding features of government employment in the last three decades have been growth and changing composition.

TOTAL GROWTH

The total number of government employees has increased greatly in the last thirty years, from 4.2 million employees in 1940 to 12.2 million employees in 1969 (see Table 1). The growth from year to year has not been steady, but the general trend has been unmistakably upward.

table 1　Government Employment in the United States

	Number of Government Employees. (in thousands)	Percentage Increase in Government Employment	Total Payroll Employment in the United States (in thousands)	Government Employment as a percentage of Total Payroll Employment
1920	2,603		27,088	9.6
1930	3,148	20.9	29,424	10.7
1940	4,202	33.5	32,376	13.0
1950	6,026	43.4	45,222	13.3
1960	8,353	38.6	54,234	15.4
1969	12,226	46.4	70,139	17.4

Source: U.S. Department of Labor, Bureau of Labor Statistics, Employment and Earnings, XVI, No. 8 (Washington, D.C., February 1970)

The 200 percent increase in employment between 1940 and 1969 makes government one of ⎯ne most rapidly expanding growth industries in the United States. In comparison, employment in manufacturing increased 87 percent and in services 320 percent in the same period. As a proportion of total payroll employment, government employment increased from 13.0 percent in 1940 to 17.4 percent in 1969. Thus about one of every six workers in the labor force in the United States is employed by the government.

The increase in public employment may be due to several factors. Among them are the following:

1. Population   A larger number of citizens require a larger amoung of public services, all other things being equal. The population of the United States grew by 53 percent between 1940 and 1969. Some of the increase in public employment may be attributed to the increase in population. An additional portion may be needed to deal with the concentration of population in urban areas. But population and its location cannot by themselves account for the total relative increase in the labor force working for government.

2. Complexity of Society and the Environment   Prosperity and technological advancement have brought a whole new range of problems for the United States. Some of these are primarily intensification of government's existing functions; for instance, the increase in auto and air transportation has demanded increasing attention and resources for highway and airport construction, airlane regulations, and so on. Other areas are new functions, resulting from the private sector's failure to provide service, such as mass urban transport, or to regulate its activities, such as pollution of the air and water.

3. Government Services   Government presumably serves the citizenry. But the kind and amount of services provided by government vary considerably over time. One reason for the change in the mix of government services may be due to changes in popular concepts of what government can and/or should provide. Thus many government programs well accepted in the 1960s were resisted in earlier years; some were not even thought of three decades earlier. Other programs, such as government's contribution to higher education, have been vastly expanded. Another reason may be the government's view of its own functions, quite apart from providing direct services to the people. The role of the United States in the world was quite different in 1969 than it was in 1940. Economic aid programs, military and support functions, and a much greater involvement in international relations have added new dimensions—and new employment demands—for government.

DISTRIBUTION OF PUBLIC EMPLOYMENT

While total government employment has expanded rapidly, the increase has not been equal for all levels of government. The increase has been especially dramatic at the local level (see Table 2). While federal employment increased 40 percent between 1950 and 1969, employment increased 147 percent in state governments and 120 percent in local governments during the same period. Viewed in a different way, the proportion of all government employees of state and local governments grew from 66.9 percent in 1950 to 77 percent in 1969.

The change in the distribution of employment by level of government reflects the changing emphasis of government services. Increasing attention to defense, education, health, and research has contributed to heavier employment patterns in those areas. Approximately 39 percent of all public employees in 1969 were engaged in education compared to 29 percent in 1940. Similarly, the percentage of civilian employees working in national defense and international relations rose in the same period from 5.7 percent to 11 percent of all public employees.

The federal system of government in the United States means that responsibility for public functions is carried out at different levels of government. This distributable 2   **Distribution of Public Employment by Level of Government**

Year	Total Government Employment*	Federal Employees*	% of total	State Employees*	% of total	Local Employees*	% of total
1940	4,474	1,128	25.2	†		†	
1950	6,402	2,117	33.1	1,057	16.5	3,228	50.4
1960	8,808	2,421	27.5	1,527	17.3	4,860	55.2
1970	12,685	2,969	23.4	2,614	20.6	7,102	56.0

*All figures in thousands.
†Not available.

Source: U.S. Bureau of the Census, *Statistical Abstract of the United States* (Washington, D.C.: Government Printing Office, annual)

tion of responsibility accounts for the differences in employment by functions among the different levels of government (see Table 3). All national defense, international relations, postal services, and space research are conducted at the federal level. Employees engaged in national defense and international relations overshadow all other functions of the federal government in terms of employment, accounting for 42 percent of all federal employees in 1970. The postal service with 25 percent represents the next largest group of employees. The federal government's role in other areas, such as education and highways, is limited largely to channeling funds, setting program standards, and conducting research. These functions are among those left largely to state and local governments. Education is far and above the major area of employment at the state and local levels, accounting

table 3   **Public Employment by Level of Government and by Function, October 1970**

Function	Employment, Full Time and Part Time (thousands)		
	All Governments (Civilian)	Federal Governments (Civilian)	State and Local Governments
Total	13,028	2,881	10,147
National defense and international relations	1,200	1,200	
Postal service	731	731	
Space research and technology	30	30	
Education	5,316	19	5,297
Highways	612	5	607
Health and hospitals	1,202	193	1,009
Police protection	538	30	508
Natural resources	404	221	183
Financial administration	334	94	240
General control	412	43	369
All other	2,249	317	1,934

Source: U. S. Bureau of the Census.

for over 50 percent of all employment at those levels. Further distinctions can be made among state and lower levels of government. State employment is largely in higher education, hospitals, highways, and natural resources. Local employment is concentrated in local schools, police and fire protection, hospitals, highways, local utilities, parks and recreation, and sanitation.

IMPLICATIONS

What are the implications of the trends in public employment? First, it is highly likely that public employment as a whole will continue to grow more rapidly than the total labor force. Many of the factors contributing to the past increase in public employment—population, urbanization, technology, changing concepts of government's role—will become more pressing in the future. Second, the focus of government functions may continue to change, thereby affecting the functional and occupational distribution of public employment. For instance, a curtailment of the country's defense commitments would presumably permit resources to be used elsewhere, such as for health and housing. The establishment of a public, nongovernment postal system also would affect the composition of public employment. Third, the relative growth in government employment is likely to vary among levels of government. Public views of federal-state and state-local relationships as well as policy decisions as to public expenditures will determine at which government level employment is likely to be added. Fourth, the trends noted above will accelerate government's competition with other employers for professional and nonprofessional white-collar employees. Fifth, government at all levels is already a major employer of minority groups, such as black persons and women. Continuing emphasis on equal employment policies as well as employment needs makes these trends likely to continue.

This brief review . . . should make apparent some of the pressures among public employees as well as some of their attraction for organized labor. While growth and changing composition of public employment do not explain the emergence of collective bargaining at all government levels in the 1960s, they contribute to the factors which made such emergence plausible and possible.

UNION MEMBERSHIP AMONG GOVERNMENT EMPLOYEES

Harry P. Cohany
Lucretia M. Dewey

In 1956, the year the Bureau of Labor Statistics started collecting data on union membership by industry, 915,000, or 5.1 percent of a total membership of

Harry P. Cohany is chief of the Division of Industrial Relations, Bureau of Labor Statistics, and Lucretia M. Dewey is an economist in the same division. Reprinted from the *Monthly Labor Review*, July 1970.

18.1 million were in government. In 1962, the number had grown to 1.2 million, or 7 percent of total membership, and by 1968, union membership among government employees had climbed to 2.2 million, 10.7 percent of total membership. During the period 1956-68, membership in all unions increased by 2.1 million of whom more than 1.2 million were in government. At the same time, gains in manufacturing and nonmanufacturing industries were only 379,000 and 487,000 respectively. While government unions scored gains of 135.5 percent, those in private industry were held to about 5 percent. All indications point to further advances in the public sector in 1969 and 1970 so that union membership as of mid-1970 is likely to exceed 2.6 million.

Not all elements of the labor movement shared in these gains. The major beneficiaries were unions affiliated with the AFL–CIO, which enrolled more than 1 million public servants during 1956-68, compared with 226,000 for those outside the Federation. In 1968, the last year for which data are presently available, 78 percent of the 2.2 million members in government were in AFL–CIO unions:

Membership (in thousands):	Total	AFL–CIO	Independent
1956	915	669	247
1960	1,070	824	247
1964	1,453	1,116	337
1968	2,155	1,682	473
Percent change:			
1956-60	16.9	23.2	....
1960-64	35.8	35.4	36.4
1964-68	48.3	50.7	40.4

These changes also are reflected in the growth figures for particular unions. Prior to 1960, only three government unions had 100,000 members or more; by 1968, there were six well above this size (table 1). Between 1956-68, unions in government did better than the average growth in membership. The American Federation of Government Employees (AFL–CIO) grew by 360 percent; the American Federation of Teachers (AFL–CIO) by 230 percent; and the American Federation of State, County and Municipal Employees (AFL–CIO) by 143 percent. Since 1968, the AFGE has reported a further increase of 30,000 members, reaching a total of 325,000, the AFT now claims 190,000, a gain of 25,000, and AFSCME rolls are up by 76,000 to a total of 440,000. In addition to those unions whose jurisdiction was confined to the public sector, significant breakthroughs among government employees were also scored by unions primarily active in private industry, such as the Service Employees (AFL-CIO), Machinists (AFL-CIO), Laborers (AFL-CIO), and a number of craft unions.

Comparison of membership at the various levels of government for 1968 show almost 1.4 million in Federal service (63 percent of the total), and 800,000 in State and local jurisdictions. During 1966-68, the rate of expansion in both major levels was about 25 percent.

In terms of union penetration, unions in the Federal service have fared far better than those in other jurisdictions. In 1968, one-half of all Federal employees were union members—a surprising statistic when compared with the situation in 1960. Although a large proportion of the membership was in a single department (the Post Office, which was better than 80 percent organized), major clusters were

table 1

Total Membership of Selected Unions with the Major Proportion of Their Membership in the Public Service, 1952-68*

Union	1952	1954	1956	1958	1960	1962	1964	1966	1968	Percent change, 1956-68+
UNIONS OF FEDERAL EMPLOYEES										
Total	452,242	526,033	533,433	545,709	535,277	667,021	793,458	933,035	1,100,087	106.2
ASCS County Office Employees, National Association of (Ind.)						12,888	14,098	14,300	14,130	8.6
Federal Employees Association (Ind.)	90,000	99,000	98,000	90,000	53,000	49,500	40,000	80,000	95,000	–3.1
Government Employees, American Federation of	48,000	62,000	64,000	60,000	70,322	106,042	138,642	199,823	194,725	360.5
Government Employees, National Association of (Ind.)							15,000			
Internal Revenue Association (Ind.)						27,125	27,000	24,130	26,360	–2.8
Letter Carriers, National Association of	95,000	103,000	108,000	110,000	138,000	150,114	167,913	189,628	210,000	94.4
Letter Carriers, National Rural Association of (Ind.)	34,570	36,355	35,900	36,723	38,321	35,852	42,300	40,340	41,192	14.7
Messengers, National Association of Special Delivery	2,000	2,000	2,000	1,987	2,000	1,500	1,500	2,073	2,605	30.3
Post Office Clerks‡	95,000	101,576	97,052	100,000	135,000	145,000	139,000	143,146	166,000	71.0
Post Office Craftsmen‡		40,000	40,100	38,500						
Post Office and General Services Maintenance Employees (Ind.)	10,000	7,549	7,700	7,700	7,400	8,000	8,424	9,237	13,175	71.1
Post Office Mail Handlers, Watchmen, Messengers, and Leaders; National Association of[10]	2,000	6,000	9,000	5,500	4,000	14,000	29,000	32,000	24,000	166.7
Post Office Motor Vehicle Employees, National Federation of	6,172	6,274	6,958	5,000	5,000	5,000	6,200	8,141	8,000	15.0
Postal and Federal Employees, National Alliance of (Ind.)		19,000	18,000	18,000	18,000	25,000	26,000	37,000	45,000	250.0
Postal Supervisors, National Association of (Ind.)	16,500	19,479	19,923	21,808	19,250	26,000	28,000	31,700	33,000	65.6
Postal Transport Association[11]	27,000	23,800	26,800	25,491						
Postal Union, National (Ind.)				25,000	32,000	43,000	62,000	70,000	80,000	220.0
Postmasters, National Association of (Ind.)							33,881	32,717	28,900	–14.7
Postmasters, National League of (Ind.)	26,000				12,984	14,400	14,500	18,000	18,000	38.6
UNIONS OF STATE AND LOCAL GOVERNMENT EMPLOYEES										
Total	211,000	226,468	285,000	343,772	361,156	339,856	450,197	521,277	662,120	132.3
Firefighters, International Association of	76,000	85,000	85,000	93,000	95,000	109,035	115,358	115,000	132,634	56.0
State, County, and Municipal Employees; American Federation of	85,000	96,328	150,000	200,000	210,000	220,000	234,839	281,277	364,486	143.0
Teachers, American Federation of	50,000	45,140	50,000	50,772	56,156	70,821	100,000	125,000	165,000	230.0

*Unions listed below have at least 50 percent of their membership in Government Service.
+Where 1956 figures are not shown, the base period is the first subsequent year for which figures are shown.
‡Post Office Clerks and Post Office Craftsmen merged to form United Federation of Postal Clerks (AFL–CIO) on July 1, 1961.

[10] Post Office Mail Handlers merged with Laborers' International Union of North America (AFL–CIO) on April 20, 1968.
[11] Postal Transport Association merged with United Federation of Postal Clerks (AFL–CIO) on July 1, 1961.

also found in a host of other agencies and installations covering professional, clerical, and blue-collar workers. Less than 10 percent of State and local employees was organized, although the number of those represented by associations or "near-unions" should be added to this figure to arrive at an overall assessment. For all of government, about one out of every five employees was a union member in 1968, a rate that has moved upward steadily throughout the last decade.

By State, government union membership varied greatly in 1968 from a low of 2,000 in Wyoming to a high of 309,000 in New York. However, union membership was concentrated in a few States. Of the total of 2.2 million, three States—California, New York, and Illinois—together accounted for about 1 out of 3 members. These three States, and Pennsylvania, Michigan, Ohio, Massachusetts, and the Maryland-D.C. area had over one-half of the total.

The States with the largest number of government union members are not always those in which unions have scored their greatest organizing successes. New York, California, and Illinois, which have the largest number of members, ranked 3rd, 34th, and 8th in terms of the proportion of government employees organized. Similarly, no strong relationship exists between the extent of organization among government employees and that among employees in nonagricultural establishments generally. West Virginia, for example, ranked first in terms of union membership in nonagricultural establishments, but only 45th in the extent of union membership among government workers. Ranked first among government employees, Rhode Island is only 22nd in rank in terms of total membership of nonfarm workers. One-fifth of the States rank in roughly the same positions in both categories. Thus, a relatively high degree of organization in private industry is not necessarily associated with similar gains in the public sector.

Of more than ordinary interest in looking at these figures are union successes in organizing white-collar workers, an area where only meager gains have been recorded in the past. The last BLS survey estimated 900,000 white-collar members in government enrollment. This figure has more than doubled since 1960 when it was estimated at 409,000. Between 1964 and 1968, white-collar membership in all unions increased by 590,000, of which 262,000 was accounted for by those in government. Massive additions to union ranks of professional and clerical employees in the public sector may well presage similar breakthroughs in private industry. At present, however, white-collar members constitute a greater proportion of all union members in government than they do in the private sector—nearly 42 percent in the former compared with 4 percent in manufacturing and 21 percent in nonmanufacturing.

	1960	1964	1968
Total white-collar membership (in thousands)	2,192	2,585	3,176
Estimated number in government unions (in thousands).	409	636	898
Percent in government unions	18.7	24.6	28.3
White-collar membership as a proportion of all members in government	38.2	43.8	41.7

It should be emphasized that all of the figures discussed refer to union *members* only. Not infrequently, the number of workers *represented* by unions far exceeds those on their books. Thus, union bargaining strength is in many jurisdictions far greater than is apparent from membership figures alone.

As noted, a complete evaluation of union gains would also have to take account of those organizations which are commonly referred to as "associations" or "near-unions." At the present time, however, no comprehensive figures for these groups exist. Various estimates place the total at between 2 and 2.5 million. The National Education Association, with more than 1 million classroom teachers, and the American Nurses Association, with 204,000 members, have been actively seeking recognition and engaging in collective bargaining, as have organizations of policemen, social workers, playground supervisors, university teaching assistants, and many other categories of State and local employees. A recent BLS survey of municipal public employee associations yielded 662 associations with about 265,000 members in 438 cities.[1] The Assembly of Government Employees, an association of State employee groups, claims that its affiliates represent more than 500,000 employees.[2] Recent contests between unions and associations leave no doubt that the latter groups are determined to stay. In a number of encounters in New York, California, and Oregon, among others, they decisively turned back union attempts to replace them.

FACTORS UNDERLYING GROWTH

What lies behind this unexpected thrust for public sector bargaining? It is a matter of profound interest to bewildered administrators and to the public at large. Unlike the depression in the 1930's and the subsequent breakthrough in union membership in mass production industries, no single factor can be offered to explain the recent growth.

Clearly, unions of government employees are not of recent origin, although organizing efforts by these unions have been markedly stepped up wince 1960, perhaps because of sheer persistence or a feeling that a turning point was near. Wage and fringe benefit gains by unions in private industry widely reported in the press, found a receptive audience among government workers; at the same time, the traditional "security" of government employment looked less and less appealing in a progressively inflationary economy characterized by tight labor markets. This was particularly the case with the steadily growing number who entered government service in recent years. Long-standing local wage relationships between private and public employees were upset to the all too apparent disadvantage of the latter. The usual methods by which public servants received wage increases were too cumbersome and uncertain, pointing up that new approaches were called for. It should be added that sophisticated techniques ("human relations," and so forth) used by private employers to thwart union organization had made little headway among public managers.

The rise in militancy among public employees can also be traced in some measure to the growing acquiescence in such actions by our society generally. The example of the civil rights movement, students, war protesters, and so on left its mark on teachers, hospital attendants, firemen, and others. Conduct of perhaps questionable legality had become accepted and, above all, had achieved results

---

[1] Teachers were not included in the survey.

[2] This figure, however, may also include employees represented by city or county associations affiliated with Statewide organizations.

where more conventional means had failed. In addition to material benefits, public employees, particularly professionals, were seeking a vehicle to participate in decisionmaking, from which they had previously been excluded.

A key turning point occurred in early 1962 with the issuance of President Kennedy's Executive Order 10988, which sanctioned union organization and had wide repercussions at non-Federal levels as well. After a string of union victories in several major cities, the momentum generated proved irresistible in jurisdictions in most parts of the country. Dramatic stoppages, such as the sanitation workers' walkout in Memphis, added impetus to union efforts. Legislative reapportionment, which entailed a shift from rural to urban representatives, may also have helped matters along in some situations.

In any case, the upsurge in union activity has brought in its wake a host of problems, some relating to interunion relationships. But its greatest impact has been on the public service and consequently on public policy.

EFFECTS ON POLICY

As unions in the public sector have grown, they have increasingly come into competition with those in the private sector which in the past have been unopposed in their role of union spokesman in the community. Those who seek labor's endorsement must now turn to several power centers, while those in these centers are carefully delineating their roles. This new state of affairs was recognized at the AFL–CIO's 1969 convention, when the federation added two presidents of government unions to its Executive Council.[3]

The prospect of further gains has also intensified rivalries among unions and between unions and associations in organizing compaigns. This competition for new members is likely to lead to jurisdictional conflicts between unions whose membership encompasses white-collar and blue-collar workers and those made up of a particular craft. Such conflicts often underlie the question of "unit determination" since depending on the expected election outcome, one group may opt for a smaller (craft) as against a broader (installationwide) unit in one situation while taking the opposite position in another. Even within national unions, sudden membership successes have exacerbated long-smouldering conflicts, frequently resulting in changes in top officers. Such unsettled internal affairs are likely to have repercussions in dealings with departments and agencies, at times in displays of militancy and escalation of bargaining demands.

Work stoppages and the attendant issue of dispute settlement are probably the most widely discussed issues in assessing union impact on the public service.[4] Since this issue has been the subject of a number of extensive investigations, attention should now shift to how to develop a workable labor relations system to insure industrial peace.

Civil service commissions and the merit system are bound to come in for a

---

[3]It was reliably reported that a third president of a government union would have been added to the Council had the postal unions been able to agree on a single candidate.

[4]For the incidence of such strikes, see "Work Stoppages in Government, 1958-68" (BLS Report 348). On this subject also see Anne M. Ross, "Public Employee Unions and the Right to Strike," *Monthly Labor Review,* March 1969, pp. 14-18.

drastic overhaul as the influence of unions expands. The functions of such commissions are likely to be confined to setting hiring standards, administering entrance and promotion examinations where stipulated, and protecting the merit system generally. Its customary role as the personnel arm of the government may be circumscribed if labor relations duties are assumed by new agencies specifically established for this purpose.

Personnel policies and their implementation, presently decreed unilaterally by agency heads, will increasingly become the subject matter of collective bargaining. The number of provisions included in agreements will grow in the years ahead as will the degree of detail describing specific working arrangements. In this context it is well to cite the clause in the Post Office agreement which reads: ". . . To the extent provisions of the Postal Manual which are in effect on the effective or renewal date of the agreement are in conflict with this agreement the provisions of this agreement will govern."[5]

The pressure of union wage demands will require a new look at present budget-making processes. It is clear that negotiated increases will have to be included in budget submittals lest agency heads find themselves unable to pay salaries which they have agreed to previously, or which will be agreed to during the budget year. This, of course, will also necessitate changes in existing ways of moving the budget through legislative bodies.

Public administration in the United States is presently in a period of transition. Basic philosophies will have to be reexamined and new ways of conducting the public's business will have to be found. While the precise nature of the changes likely to occur cannot be predicted, it may be appropriate to keep the following statement from the 1967 National Governors' Conference report in mind: "Neither the pillars of city halls nor the foundations of the civil service crumbled when conditions of employment were negotiated instead of being fixed unilaterally."[6]

PUBLIC VS. PRIVATE SECTOR BARGAINING

Neil W. Chamberlain

In matters of economics, it has become fashionable to speak of the "blurred line" between the public and private sectors. It is hard to know where one ends and the other begins. In matters of collective bargaining, on the other hand, the hard

Neil Chamberlain is Professor, Graduate School of Business, Columbia University. Reprinted from the *Proceedings* of the 5th Annual Orvil Dryfoos Conference on Public Affairs.

[5]U.S. Post Office agreement, February 9, 1968, p. 132, Article XXVI.

[6]See *Report of Task Force on State and Local Government Labor Relations* (Chicago, Ill., Public Personnel Association for the Executive Committee of the 1967 National Governors' Conference).

edge has been largely preserved. Whatever fuzziness may attach to the public or private nature of the operation, we still tend to use a binary sort to identify those who are public employees and those who are not. To those who are not (or at least to most of them), we apply one set of bargaining rules. To those who are public employees, we apply a different set.

Perhaps it overtaxes the imagination to speak of applying any set of rules to bargaining in the public service. Even if some jurisdictions have moved to codify practice, as in New York City, we can hardly say that governmental units in the United States, as a class, operate on industrial relations principles that are relatively uniform and understood. Instead, we have a wilderness of chiefly casual or undirected growth. There is no counterpart of the federal and state labor relations acts which provide a certain pattern in the private sphere. The federal Executive Order 10988 of 1962 does go some distance towards establishing a limited bargaining format for the classified civil service, but this embraces less than one-half of federal employees and confines bargaining to personnel policies and grievances, excluding all money matters and major benefits. In the states and municipalities there is only confusion or—if one is in a euphemistic mood—experimentation.

In some important respects one can compare collective bargaining in the public sector today with collective bargaining in the private sector 30 or 35 years ago. Problems which were a source of controversy and bitter dispute between unions and managers at that time, but which since have largely been worked out, have risen again to plague relations between unions and governments today. It is as though the law makers and law administrators can minister to others but not to themselves.

One of the most divisive issues in pre-World War II private bargaining was that of the managerial prerogative. Corporate officials intoned solemnly and repetitively that their legal obligation ran solely to the stockholders, and that they were in fact chosen by stockholder trustees to manage the company's assets in stockholder interests. How could they then consent to negotiate with an outside group, responsible to non-stockholder interests, concerning matters which affected so directly the profitability of the company? Even when the passage of time had conditioned managers to bargain with unions on wages, hours, and working conditions, they continued for a time to try to draw a line dividing subjects which were bargainable from those which were not. The latter were presumed to relate to the proper functioning of the business, and were the sole prerogative of management, of no concern to unions. The unions, for their part, refused to draw such a line. They argued that any aspect of corporate activity might conceivably affect their members so significantly that they in their turn would be abnegating their representative duty if they did not make it a subject for negotiation and for strike if ncesssary.

So bitterly did the conflict go that some top-flight executives of America's major corporations threatened to pull out of the system if they were forced to surrender on this matter of principle. But with the passage of time the conflict reduced to a skirmish, and what had been viewed as principle was seen as a matter of relative bargaining powers. There were no surrenders—only settlements. What had loomed as a threat to the maturation—and even to the survival—of private collective bargaining receded into the background. Now whenever the mothy issue is exhumed, as it occasionally still is, the sophisticated squirm uneasily as though good taste had been violated.

Except in the public sector. There the management prerogative issue is alive and shining, and battles are waged in its name. The name, to be sure, is changed—it is now spoken of as sovereignty—but the principle remains the same. In Hobbesian terms, government is identified as the sole possessor of final power, since it is responsive to the interests of all its constituents. To concede to any *special*-interest group a right to bargain for terms which the sovereignty believes contravenes the *public* interest is to deny the government's single responsibility. The government must remain in possession of the sole power to determine, on behalf of all, what shall be public policy. And public policy includes the determination of what proportion of tax revenues shall be allocated for the conduct of any service, whether it be police protection or sanitation or teaching. No union can be allowed to bargain up the rates for its members, through threat or pressure, thereby curtailing what the city can afford to do in other areas. The economic concept of opportunity cost demonstrates that if sanitation workers get more, the city must skimp in providing parks or manning fire stations. It is not for the sanitation workers to manipulate the government's budget; that is a matter for the legislators on behalf of the public as a whole. If sanitation workers are unhappy at the outcome, they are not bound to stay in service. The government makes its budget, determines its rates, and fills its jobs with those to whom the rates are satisfactory. The same line of reasoning applies to other conditions of employment.

Government employers are of course willing to listen to the arguments of their employees and to take those into account in fixing their personnel and wage policies. But union pressure tactics—the applications of private force—are out of place in dealing with a sovereignty.

Perhaps I have stated the issue more baldly and crudely than a constitutional lawyer would do, but this is the essence of the matter. The public service is held to be different from a private profit-making organization. If the latter may be defrocked of its managerial prerogatives without concern, the former must remain fully vested with sovereignty if society is to survive.

I submit that this argument is as specious as any of the older myths in industrial relations which we have relegated to some cobwebby historical attic. Is it essential that every act of government, however routine or however directly affecting the interests of some special group, however misguided or ill-conceived or convenient to itself, must be protected by the invisible shield of sovereignty? Certainly it is possible to distinguish between those acts of government which involve only an operating or administrative function and those which involve the policy-making or legislative function. If sovereignty is an attribute of the latter, it need not automatically be extended to the former. The managing of the public establishment can surely be differentiated from a determination of what the public establishment shall manage.

If we permit suppliers of equipment and materials to governments to negotiate over prices and delivery terms, are we denying governmental sovereignty any less than if we permit suppliers of services to do the same? Or in the case of services, is it that we are fearful of monopoly power or excessive bargaining strength? If that is the issue, then we are dealing with matters of relative bargaining power, just as in the private sector, so that principle is not involved. Or is it that public services are so essential that we cannot permit an interruption in them? If that is the nub of the problem, it speaks only for different procedures, not an absence of them. But these are issues to which I want to return later, so I will say no more about them now. I have mentioned them here only to strengthen my case that sovereignty as an excuse not to bargain in the public sector is no more a principle than management prerogative is in the private sector, that it is chiefly a source of comfort and convenience to government officials rather than a bedrock on which society rests.

Other issues which are viewed as relics in the private sector but as lively problems in the public domain are union recognition and exclusive representation rights. The bloody strikes in the little steel industry 30 years ago were aimed at forcing management to recognize the union as a representative institution, with which an agreement could—and should—be negotiated. The National Labor Relations Act which was passed in 1935 had set up an election procedure intended to resolve that issue, but so reluctant was management to admit that the union even existed that it sometimes required the force of a strike to secure what the law provided.

In the public sector the same reluctance is manifested today, as in the recent Memphis sanitation strike, the same affair in which Martin Luther King lost his life. Terms were not the issue there, only union recognition, beclouded it is true by the fact that it was a white government which was being asked to recognize a union composed largely of Negroes. But in the private sphere, color or no color, the recognition problem has long since been hurdled, while it still persists in some public jurisdictions.

Similarly with exclusive representation rights. That matter was laid to rest in private industry in the '30s. At first managements were willing, however reluctantly, to sign agreements with unions "for members only." This was the formula on which U.S. Steel finally came to terms with John L. Lewis, and it was considered a major union victory, despite the fact that it conferred less than the Wagner Act allowed. But by the end of that decade majority representation was an accepted principle. The union which won the backing of 51 percent of workers voting in an election was certified as the bargaining representative for all.

Many government officials remain reluctant to grant such status in public bargaining units. The "for members only" formula is the only one on which negotiations can take place even when the union is recognized. It is held that the government cannot compel a person to be represented by a union he does not want and in the control of which he does not participate—issues which were put to rest by government itself in labor legislation which it passed applying to others.

I do not mean to imply that all government units adhere to such views. Some have moved a long way towards modernizing their labor relations. But the public sector taken as a whole reveals a tangled underbrush of just such obsolete doctrines choking the path leading to improved collective bargaining.

One other comparable difficulty I will simply mention briefly. In the great upsurge of unionism in the '30s, labor negotiators sometimes complained that they could not locate the seat of corporate authority, with which they could effectively negotiate. Contracts were more often signed then with plants than companies, and a plant manager would sometimes maintain that he had no authority to commit the company, which might well have been the case. But the local union had difficulty in reaching a distant management, and if it did it might find itself being referred back to the plant management. Sometimes it took a strike to locate those with whom an agreement could be reached. By and large that sort of shadowboxing was as much a matter of artlessness as artfulness, of inexpertise rather than game-playing, and it is seldom any longer a factor in private negotiations. But it is still a problem in the public sector, especially in the cities, where a union may get shunted around among the conflicting or overlapping authorities of a department manager, a mayor, and a city council, and where it may still at times require a strike to identify who has the capacity to make an agreement.

I have so far been talking of respects in which collective bargaining in the public sector is slowly and awkwardly traversing the same ground that private collective bargaining covered some time ago, stubbing its toes on some of the same obstacles, without much apparent benefit from prior experience. But there are respects in which the two spheres are admittedly different, or are thought to be different, which introduce fresh problems of their own. These differences may indeed seem to render collective bargaining in the two sectors entirely non-comparable, rendering invalid those comparisons which I have just been making.

The first of these arises from the peculiar constraints imposed by the source of revenues of government as against business. When a business firm negotiates a new contract, the cost of the package can be covered from any or all of three sources: a reduction in its profits, greater efficiency (increased productivity), or higher prices on its products. A firm will bargain harder and grant less if these three sources are limited, and it will usually be more generous if these three sources are permissive. In the case of government, in contrast, it makes no profit and its productivity gains are limited since it deals primarily in services. Its primary source of revenue for the higher costs lies in raising its prices, which is to say its taxes. And that is a political act which it will take only with great reluctance. Thus one can expect that a government will tend to be niggardly with its employees to avoid the unhappy necessity of tax increases. The consequence is that, on the whole, the incomes of public employees have shared less in the general prosperity than have private incomes. It simply takes more pressure to raise the public remuneration level, given the different nature of the public employer.

There are some who are reluctant to confront this fact. They try to blunt the argument by pointing to the special advantages of public service, such as job security or longer vacations. There are always people who prefer such benefits to more money on private jobs, they say; if that were not the case, governments would have more difficulty getting people to work for them.

This argument can be faulted on two counts. Whatever special benefits may attach to certain types of public employment, the money side of the total package has not risen proportionately as much as in private employ, so that the relative position of civil servants has deteriorated. Second, the fact that people can be found for the jobs says nothing about the quality of those people—that too may be and probably has been deteriorating in recent years.

So I return to the special constraint lying on the public sector—that its revenues can be increased chiefly through taxes, leading public negotiators to tougher positions on the bargaining front. I am not unmindful of the fact that some unions themselves wield political influence, and have at times won what seem to be outsize increases presumably because of such influence, but these instances are not the common pattern, I am sure. In weighing certain public grumbling over higher taxes against a union membership's ambiguous pleasure over a fat settlement, most politicians would feel the scales were tipped to favor the former.

A second major dissimilarity between the public and private sectors lies in the availability of the strike. Despite the rash of walkouts of civil servants in the last few years, the doctrine remains that workers cannot strike against the government. Such state legislation as there is on public collective bargaining invariably affirms that dogma. In New York, when the Taylor Act replaced the Condon-Wadlin Act it did nothing to legalize strikes of public employees. On the contrary, it calls for fines to be levied against a striking union running for each day the strike continues. It does provide for fact-finding as to a fair settlement whenever union and government officials have reached an impasse, but it does not require either party to accept the recommendation, and there is no authorization of a strike even if one or both parties reject the recommendation.

The issue of strikes in the public service has been vigorously debated, and I will not review the arguments here. There are some who feel that no strikes against the government can be tolerated, and others who believe that strikes should be treated the same in the public as in the private sector—curtailed or controlled only when they create an emergency or threaten public health or safety, and otherwise permitted. Whatever one's views on the matter, the question of strikes against the government intrudes a special and thorny note which is absent from discussions of private collective bargaining. It is all tied up with the matter of sovereignty, and all very confused and confusing.

REPORT AND RECOMMENDATIONS

Governor's Advisory Commission
on Labor-Management Policy for Public Employees (Illinois)

CONDITIONS IN ILLINOIS

The need for appropriate legislation in Illinois is evidenced by the following facts: (1) Public employee activity directed toward improving conditions of employment and processing grievances is growing rapidly in many sectors and is already quite extensive. (2) Public officials lack guidelines to deal with the demands of these organizations for recognition and negotiations and are often in a quandary as to how to respond. Often they claim that they cannot lawfully engage in collective negotiations, grant exclusive recognition, or sign an agreement in the absence of specific legislative authorization. (3) Partly because of the uncertainties in public policy, conflicts and crises are occurring.

EXTENT OF EMPLOYEE ORGANIZATION

. . . Public employment in Illinois, excluding those on the federal payroll, numbers about 400,000, roughly 8 percent of the civilian labor force. It is diversified to an extraordinary degree both occupationally (from the least to the most skilled) and by employing authority. Illinois has more governmental units than any other state in the nation, approximately 6,400. The major categories of employment are:

	Number of Employees
Municipal	70,000
School	140,000
State, except universities and colleges	56,000
Universities and colleges	29,000
Counties, townships, special districts	100,000
	395,000

Municipal Employees

The 70,000 municipal employees are distributed among about 1,200 municipalities. More than 40,000 are employed by the City of Chicago. The responses to our questionnaires from 324 municipalities, including Chicago, covered about 54,000 employees. The following table provides certain salient facts about the 141 municipalities with more than 10 employees.[1]

Municipalities Classified by Number of Employees

	Over 500	150- 500	100- 149	50- 99	11- 49
Number of municipalities reporting	1	24	10	35	71
Number of employees	40,739	7,649	1,214	2,250	1,603
Have recognition agreement with employee organization(s)	—	5	1	8	7
Meet with employee representative	1	19	5	12	21
formally	—	3	1	3	9
informally	1	11	4	9	11
both	—	3	—	—	1
not stated	—	2	—	—	—
Number of agreements negotiated	—	10	2	7	7
Have arbitration	—	7	2	6	6
voluntary	—	2	—	3	3
advisory	—	4	1	1	1
binding	—	—	1	—	1
not stated	—	1	—	2	1
Have grievance procedure	1	19	8	19	25
formal	—	8	1	6	5
informal	1	8	4	11	15
both	—	1	—	1	—
not stated	—	2	3	1	5

[1]The returns from the 173 municipalities with 10 or fewer employees (a total of only 432 employees) are not included because it was often difficult to distinguish between collective and individual relationships.

Of the 141 reporting municipalities with more than 10 employees, only 21 stated that they had entered into formal recognition agreements and only 26 negotiated employment agreements, but 58 met with representatives of employee organizations and 72 had a formal or informal grievance procedure. Many of the larger cities recognized collective bargaining contracts with private employers in comparable activities (particularly the building trades) as the basis for setting wage rates. The occupational groups which participated in some form of collective discussions included the police (20), public works (16), firemen (14), clerical (8), waterworks (6), electricians (6), sanitation (4), common laborers (2), custodians (2), park (1), and department heads (1). Only 13 municipalities reported that they checked off dues for employee organizations.

School Employees

It is estimated that the approximately 1,500 school districts in the State employ about 140,000 employees, of whom about 100,000 are teachers. Responses to our questionnaires came from 640 districts employing 108,000 persons. Of this group, only 62 reported formal recognition agreements, but 155 negotiated collective employment agreements, 427 held meetings with representatives of employee organizations, and 372 had a formal or informal grievance procedure. The occupational groups which participated in some form of collective discussions included: teachers (396), custodians (152), cafeteria workers (66), clericals (58), and bus drivers (49). The employee organizations with whom reporting school boards dealt were: Illinois Education Association (217), American Federation of Teachers (28, including Chicago), other unidentified teachers organizations (70), the AFL-CIO Building Service Employees Union (25), other unidentified custodial organizations (44), and various secretarial and clerical organizations (29).

The following table provides selected data on school districts classified by number of employees:

State Employees

The number of State employees is about 55,500, of whom 44,000 are in the Code Departments. 1,500 are under the Police Merit System, and 10,000 are employees of constitutional officers not subject to the Personnel Code. The State-supported colleges and universities employ about 15,000 nonacademic employees (most of whom are under the University Civil Service System of Illinois) and about 13,800 academic employees.

In the Code System, several types of collective relationships were reported. One involves informal discussions between union representatives and department heads about general working conditions or policies, with the final decision left to the administration. A second involves the "prevailing rate" employees, craft workers whose rates are based on payments in private industry for comparable occupations. Labor organizations submit prevailing rate statements to the Department of Labor which in turn certifies the rates to the Department of Personnel, usually including the relevant contracts. The Department of Personnel in turn ex-

School Districts Classified by Number of Employees

	Over 500	250-499	Under 250
Number of districts	33	40	567
Number of employees	56,947	13,379	38,172
Have recognition agreement with employee organization(s)	14	10	38
Meet with employee representatives	30	37	360
formally	12	15	88
informally	9	12	193
both	6	5	41
not stated	3	5	38
Number of agreements negotiated	22	15	118
Have arbritration	13	9	83
voluntary	5	4	47
advisory	6	3	27
binding	1	—	6
not stated	1	2	3
Have grievance procedure	30	34	308
formal	12	13	61
informal	11	17	199
both	2	3	7
not stated	5	1	41

amines the rates and, if it has no questions, releases them to the operating agencies for implementation. If a question about the appropriateness of the rate exists, the Department of Personnel takes up the matter directly with the labor organization. Release dates for these rates have recently been confined to April 1 and October 1. The list of craft workers covered by this practice is extensive, ranging from construction workers to barbers and beauticians.

A third type of collective relations pertaining to Code employees is the equivalent of private sector bargaining. It involves two unions, the Teamsters and the Machinists, representing employees on the highways, in the State garages, a few chauffeurs, and waterways employees of the Department of Public Works and Buildings. The Director of Personnel acts as spokesman for the State, heading a committee of representatives of the operating agencies involved. Bargaining is over wages and working conditions. The result of the wage negotiation is reflected in Section 14.00 of the Pay Plan. Changes in working conditions are seldom recorded, although occasionally they are put in letter form.

Civil Service employees who comprise some 35,000 of the 44,000 in the Code Departments are able to raise grievances under the State's Civil Service grievance procedure. The employee may designate a union official, a lawyer, or any other person as his representative. The final stage of the grievance procedure is a hearing by a three-member committee appointed by the Director of Personnel from a panel of State employees and others. The recommendation of the committee is submitted to the Director of Personnel for final decision. The 1,500 employees under the Police Merit System are not unionized, but they too have a grievance procedure for individual employees, with a decision by the Director of the Department of Public Safety as the final step.

In the State-supported colleges and universities, formal collective negotiations, including signed agreements, are conducted for nonacademic employees, particularly maintenance and service employees. The crafts are paid on a "prevailing rate basis," and their agreements usually are not written. These negotiating practices take place within the University Civil Service System which provides a grievance procedure and an elaborate set of employment rules and conditions covering all nonacademic employees. A few academic employees are members of the American Federation of Teachers. A much larger number belong to the American Association of University Professors which functions as a professional organization concerned with salaries and terms of employment as well as academic policies but which does not engage in collective bargaining.

Other Public Employees

In addition to the State, municipal, and school employees, there are more than 100,000 public employees employed by the 102 counties, the 1,400 townships, and the 2,100 special districts (e.g., airport, drainage, housing, park, sanitary, etc.). Organization and collective bargaining practices vary widely in this highly miscellaneous category. The most developed relationship is that of the Chicago Transit Authority which engages in a private sector type of collective bargaining based on practices in effect when the transit system was privately operated. Less formal types of collective negotiations are found in various parks and sanitary districts.

No accurate information is available on the number of public employees belonging to unions or other employee organizations concerned with collective negotiations about wages, hours, and conditions of employment. Nor are there any satisfactory data on the extent and coverage of formal or informal collective negotiations. However, the following information reported to the Commission indicates that employee organization membership and collective relations are widespread.

1. The Building Service Employees International Union, AFL–CIO, claims over 20,000 members in State, county, and city agencies, park districts, school boards, public hospitals, toll road authorities, libraries, etc. In most cases, negotiations are informal and agreements are unwritten. It has a few written memoranda of understanding or signed agreements such as those with Morton High School and the University of Illinois in Urbana and Chicago.

2. The American Federation of State, County, and Municipal Employees, AFL–CIO, claims some 18,000 members in State hospitals, public aid offices, penal institutions, and universities. They are about equally divided between Cook County and downstate. Like the Building Service Employees Union, its negotiations are mostly informal, and agreements are not generally signed. Signed agreements are reported with agencies in some eighteen communities, including Joliet and Kankakee.

3. The Building and Construction Trades Unions, AFL–CIO, are estimated to represent over 1,000 craft employees in State institutions and a considerably larger, but difficult-to-estimate, number of employees in municipalities, park districts, school districts, etc. For example, the Structural Iron Workers report membership of 123 employees of the City of Chicago. Their members are usually compensated on a "prevailing rate" basis tied to contracts negotiated in private industry.

4. The International Brotherhood of Teamsters negotiates in behalf of all truck drivers and helpers employed by the State Highway Department and for smaller groups in the Mental Health and Labor Departments. In addition, the union represents drivers in the Cook County Highway Department and in other municipalities. It also has signed agreements with the University of Illinois in Chicago, the Chicago Transit Authority, and the Brookfield Zoo, and memoranda of understanding with the Chicago Board of Education, the Chicago Sanitary District, the Chicago Park District, the Chicago Public Library, and other units in Cook County.

5. The Illinois Nurses Association reports that it represents some 5,000 registered nurses in municipal and county public hospitals and in institutions of the State Department of Mental Health. It has signed agreements only in the Cook County and Reynolds hospitals.

6. The Fire Fighters Union, AFL–CIO, represents firemen in Chicago and many other smaller municipalities of the State. It negotiates over wages and terms of employment on an informal basis.

7. The American Federation of Teachers claims representation rights for some 30,000 Illinois teachers. It is the recognized negotiating agent and negotiates agreements for teachers in the Chicago primary and secondary schools, the Cook County Junior College system, East St. Louis, Belleville, Granite City, Joliet, Thornton, Stickney, Cahokia, and Niles Township, among others.

8. The Illinois Education Association has local chapters in a majority of the State's school districts. A substantial proportion of these chapters negotiate informally with their school boards on wages and other terms of employment. Comprehensive signed agreements (referred to as Level III agreements by the IEA) are reported in some 16 districts, including Batavia, Champaign, De Kalb, Downers Grove, East Alton, Elgin, and Geneva. Less extensive agreements are in effect in 14 other districts.

9. The Independent Union of Public Aid Employees is the recognized negotiating agent for some 4,200 employees of the Cook County Department of Public Aid. Most of its members are professional social workers.

10. The Illinois State Employees Association claims as members some 10,000 employees at all levels of State government. It is mainly a lobbying and consultative organization. It does not engage in formal collective negotiations, but its sister associations in other states, such as Oregon, became negotiating organizations after passage of legislation authorizing bargaining.

LACK OF LEGAL GUIDELINES

Despite extensive organization and collective relations in many sectors of the public service in Illinois, there is uncertainty as to the legality of negotiating practices in the absence of comprehensive legislation.

In six specific instances, however, the State Legislature has endorsed the principles of employee organization and collective negotiation either directly or indirectly.

1. In 1945 the Chicago Transit Authority was authorized to continue the collective bargaining procedures used when the transit system was in private ownership, including binding arbitration of a dispute over the terms of new contracts. The statute includes the following provision:

The Board may deal with and enter into written contracts with the employees of the Authority through accredited representatives of such employees or representatives of any labor organization to act for such employees, concerning wages, salaries, hours, working conditions and pension or retirement provisions; provided, nothing herein shall be construed to permit hours of labor in excess of those provided by law or to permit working conditions prohibited by law. In case of dispute over wages, salaries, hours, working conditions, or pension or retirement provisions the Board may arbitrate any question or questions and may agree with such accredited representatives or labor organization that the decision of a majority of any arbitration board shall be final, provided each party shall agree in advance to pay half of the expense of such arbitration. Ill. Rev. Stat., Ch. 111 2/3, Sec. 301-344 (1965).

2. In 1951 the University Civil Service System was authorized to enter into negotiations on wages and other conditions of employment with employee organizations representing nonacademic employees. On this point the statute (section 36-d) reads:

... Each employer covered by the University System shall be authorized to negotiate with representatives of employees to determine appropriate ranges or rates of compensation or other conditions of employment and may recommend to the Merit Board for establishment the rates or ranges or other conditions of employment which the employer and employee representatives have agreed upon as fair and equitable. Ill. Rev. Stat., Ch. 24 1/2, Sec. 3861-38m (1965).

3. In 1951 municipalities and their fire fighters were authorized to resort to advisory arbitration when impasses were reached in wage disputes. This statute reads as follows:

Whenever a dispute exists concerning wages, hours or labor, or conditions of employment of members of the fire department of any municipality with a population of 5,000 or more, a Firemen's Arbitration Board shall be appointed as provided in this article.

The Board shall conduct hearings with dispatch with the purpose of hearing evidence relevant to the subject of the dispute and shall, as soon as practicable, report its findings and recommendations to the corporate authorities and to any organization of the firemen of the municipality. The Board's recommendation shall be advisory only and shall not be binding upon the municipality or upon the members of the fire department. Ill. Rev. Stat., Ch. 24, Sec. 10-3-8-10-3-11 (1965).

4. In 1955 when the State Personnel Code was adopted, the State Director of Personnel was authorized to conduct negotiations affecting pay, hours of work, or other working conditions of employees subject to the Code. The Code contains the following language:

In addition to the duties imposed upon him elsewhere in this law, it shall be his duty:

... (7) To conduct negotiations affecting pay, hours of work, or other working conditions of employees subject to this Act. Sec. 9 (7). Ill. Rev. Stat., Ch. 127, Sec. 636101-636118 (1965).

5. In 1961 the Legislature passed a statute providing that any employee of the State "may authorize the withholding of a portion of his salary, wages or annuities for any one or more of the following purposes:"

... (3) For payment to any labor organization designated by the employee. Ill. Rev. Stat., Ch. 127, Sec. 351-360 (1965).

6. In 1963 the Legislature passed a law providing that:

Any local governmental agency . . . may by ordinance or resolution of its corporate authority authorize the withholding from the compensation of an employee the union dues of such employee payable to any labor organization and membership dues of such employee payable to professional organizations upon the written request of the employee which the employee may revoke in writing at any time. Ill. Rev. Stat., Ch. 85, Sec. 471-476 (1966).

All of these actions deal with aspects of employee organization and collective negotiations; they fail, however, to provide general policy or machinery to resolve issues of representation and recognition.

The Legislature has been silent with respect to strikes by public employees. The Conciliation and Mediation Service of the Illinois Department of Labor has been available to assist parties in reaching agreements, but its services have been used in only fourteen cases since July, 1964. These involved city workers of Carmi, Pana, Macomb, Freeport, and La Salle, employees of the Caseyview T.B. sanitarium, sanitary district employees in Champaign-Urbana, the police department of East Peoria, the Moline Public Hospital, teachers of the Chicago Junior Colleges, janitors of the University of Illinois at Urbana, the Brookfield Zoo, park employees in Joliet, and the Logan County Road and Bridge Committee. In seven cases, the main issue was union recognition; in five of the seven, the mediators were unable to resolve the recognition issue. In the seven other cases, economic issues were in dispute; all were finally resolved. Strikes ranging from one to three days were involved in four of the fourteen cases.

The courts have likewise played a minor role in establishing guidelines for public employee relations. In 1965 the State Supreme Court, in *Board of Education v. Redding*,[2] ruled that school janitors (and by implication all public employees) did not have the right to strike, but it avoided the issue of collective bargaining. In 1917 the Court decided, in *People ex rel Fursman v. City of Chicago*,[3] that a rule by the Board of Education prohibiting union membership by school teachers was valid and employees who violated the rule could be discharged. However, in 1966, in *Broman v. Board of Education of the City of Chicago and Fewkes*,[4] two lower courts upheld the right of the Chicago Board of Education to enter into an exclusive collective bargaining relationship with a union after the holding of an election. The *Broman* case has been appealed to the State Supreme Court for a final decision. Early in 1967 the State, County, and Municipal Employees Union filed

[2]62 Ill. 2d 567, 207 N.E. 2d 427 (1965).
[3]278 Ill. 318 116 N.E. 158 (1917).
[4]Ill. App. Co. First District, No. 51378 (Nov. 9, 1966).

suit with the Circuit Court in Chicago against the State Director of Personnel and the State Director of Labor, asking for an order requiring them to meet and respond with respect to wages, hours, and working conditions under the terms of the Personnel Code. The Circuit Court Judge issued an order to this effect. The order is being appealed.

CONFLICT AND CRISES

The lack of a clear public policy on collective negotiating rights and responsibilities and the absence of any systematic procedure for the orderly resolution of disputes has created "problem situations" in many sectors of public service. The following situations which were brought to the Commission's attention are illustrative. Only some highlights of these situations are given, but they are indicative of how legislative policy might have promoted public harmony and efficiency.

Cook County Public Aid Commission

On January 6, 1966, the Independent Union of Public Aid Employees petitioned for sole bargaining rights. The request was rejected by the Director of the agency, partly on the ground that another union had been recognized. A one-hour work shutdown occurred on May 11, allegedly over wage inequities. A number of the participants were given fifteen-day suspensions. A twelve-day strike for full organizing privileges, a collective bargaining election, and no reprisal against strikers followed. The State's Attorney for Cook County expressed the view on May 23, 1966, that the County Board did not possess the legal authority to execute any collective bargaining agreement or enter into any collective arrangements with any group or union. The strike was resolved after meetings with the Board of Commissioners and the Mayor of Chicago led to an agreement to establish a fact-finding board to determine whether a representation election should be held. The Board, on October 12, 1966, recommended the holding of a secret ballot election. The election was conducted on December 14 by the American Arbitration Association under the direction of Professor Arnold Weber. It was won by the Independent Union, and the latter was subsequently recognized as negotiating agent. The manner in which this whole situation was resolved raised problems concerning the authority and efficiency of such *ad hoc* machinery.

Chicago Board of Education

Strike threats, but no strikes, have been a common feature of the Chicago Teachers Union's relations with the Board of Education at each step in the process of achieving collective negotiations: in February, 1964, to obtain recognition as a negotiating agent for its members; in April, 1964, to obtain a formal grievance procedure; in May, 1965, to protest a plan to freeze teachers in existing positions and to obtain higher salaries; in September, 1965, to obtain higher salaries and an election to determine sole collective negotiating rights; and in November, 1966, to complete negotiations on a new contract. At each step the Board raised questions of whether it had legal authority to meet the union's demand. The decision to hold a representation election has been challenged in the courts through a taxpayer's suit. As of this date two lower courts have approved the Board's agreement to hold an election and to recognize the union as exclusive negotiating agent. The issue is currently before the State Supreme Court.

Chicago Junior College Board

In April, 1966, the Cook County College Teachers Union (an affiliate of the American Federation of Teachers) picketed the Amundsen-Mayfair branch of the Junior College, seeking a representation election and collective negotiations. In October the union won an election and was recognized by the Junior College Board as negotiating agent. Negotiations started in late October, but difficulties arose over the issue of a no-strike provision and alternative means of resolving disputes. On November 30, the union began a three-day strike over the Board's no-strike statement and for a collective agreement on salaries, teaching loads, class sizes, and other terms of employment. The Board sought and received a court injunction to halt the strike. Negotiations were resumed, and a stipulation was reached in which the union disclaimed any strike intentions and the Board negotiating committee stated that it would recommend that the ultimate results of the negotiations be incorporated in a signed agreement. In addition the Board negotiating committee was to recommend that the Board's 1967 budget include provisions for several insurance plans as well as salary increases. On January 5, 1967, however, discussions again broke down and a one-day strike occurred. This was terminated after intervention by the Mayor, and a memorandum of understanding for a two-year period was reached regarding salary increases, teaching loads, and class size. Negotiations for a comprehensive, signed agreement were still incomplete at the time of the writing of this Report.

Cook County Hospital

On September 2, 1966, nurses at the Hospital threatened mass resignations unless they received wage increases. The increases were given. On September 7, nurses at Oak Forest Hospital, under the jurisdiction of the Cook County Board, successfully picketed the Board for pay increases. On October 19, nurses at the Cook County School of Nursing (a private non-profit organization) ended a two-day "sick call" after receiving pay increases. In November Du Page County Health Department nurses threatened resignations unless their salaries were aligned with those in Cook County. In none of these situations had there been any formal recognition or negotiations prior to the use of resignation threats. . . .

LABOR-MANAGEMENT RELATIONS LAWS
IN PUBLIC SERVICE

Joseph P. Goldberg

The spread of work stoppages involving public employees, particularly in local government, has stirred a renewed interest in approaches to dealing with these situations. The prevailing legal view that public employees do not and should not have the right to strike has not changed over the years. But the approaches to the problem of handling such strikes when they occur have changed—from demanding punitive measures to advocating rightful opportunities for government employees to form labor organizations and obtain their recognition, while providing alternative approaches to strike-inducing impasses.

The change in attitude is the product of slow but steady development at federal, state, and local levels. The pressing need has been to provide government employees with avenues, comparable to those available to workers in the private sector, for expressing their views on the conditions under which they work and for safeguarding their common interests. A recent editorial in *Business Week*[1] provides a perspective on the matter:

> The outbreaks of conflict too often obscure certain constructive approaches that have been made in government-employee relations over the past few years. Rights of public workers to organize and bargain collectively have been written into many State laws. State mediation and factfinding measures have been provided in comprehensive laws in 7 States, and on a more limited basis in others. There is much evidence that, in States following such procedures, factfinding has resulted in many settlements without strikes.

EMPLOYMENT AND ORGANIZATION

Public employment has grown faster over the past two decades than in other major industry sectors. It has more than doubled since 1947, increasing from 5.5

Joseph Goldberg is Special Assistant to the Commissioner of Labor Statistics, U.S. Department of Labor. Reprinted from the *Monthly Labor Review,* June 1968 (revised by the author to cover developments in 1968-69).

[1]February 17, 1968, p. 172.

million to 12.2 million.[2] A distinctive feature is the prominent representation of professional, administrative, and technical personnel, comprising about 50 percent of state and local employment, with teachers accounting for 1.8 million of the 3.9 million in these occupations.

Organizing among public employees, particularly by professional organizations of teachers and by civil service associations, has been widespread for many years. In recent years there has been a rapid growth in public employee membership in national and international unions, bringing the total in 1968 to 2.15 million—well over twice the number of a decade earlier. Among state and local public employees, it increased from 1962 by about two hundred fifty thousand to eight hundred four thousand, with substantial gains for the State, County and Municipal Workers and the American Federation of Teachers. Increased militancy among professional and unaffiliated civil service organizations to gain recognition and to negotiate for advances for their members makes their membership an integral part of the picture. With the more than 1 million classroom teachers in the ranks of the National Education Association and with the substantial membership in civil service associations, the total of organized public employees is a potent and growing factor in the pluralistic structure of American society.

SOURCES OF EXPERIENCE

The sources of experience in dealing with the problems of organization, representation, and collective bargaining for public employees have been limited, and largely of recent origin. The traditional view in law and judicial decisions has been that government could not negotiate with its employees, for this would involve a diminution of its sovereignty. Strikes of public employees have almost universally been considered illegal, and this view remains largely unaltered even as avenues for negotiation have been provided by law or administrative action.

Public employees were specifically excluded from the coverage of the National Labor Relations Act and its amendments. The Taft-Hartley Act banned strikes by federal employees, with the penalty of automatic discharge and a three-year ban on reemployment for the violators.[3] Several state laws in the early post-World War II years also provided for automatic discharge of strikers with opportunity for reemployment only after one to three years' suspension, and then only at the salary at which discharge had occurred. The most prominent example was the New York

---

[2]About 90 percent of this 6.7 million increase was in state and local employment, which totaled about 9.5 million in 1968; federal employment increased substantially (to 2.7 million), but at a slower pace. Projected gains in state and local employment will be substantial, though made at a slower pace, with an expected total of about 11.5 million in 1975. ("State and Local Government Manpower in 1975," *Monthly Labor Review,* April 1967, p. 14.)

[3]Public Law 330, 84th Congress, 1955, repealed section 305 of the Taft-Hartley Act, making it a felony (punishable by up to $1,000 in fines and a year and a day in jail) for federal employees to strike or assert the right to strike or knowingly belong to an organization that does. In a recent decision, the U.S. District Court for the District of Columbia held that the statutory provisions and implementing oaths banning assertion of, or membership in an organization asserting, the right to strike violated the First Amendment of the Constitution. The ban on striking was not in question. *National Association of Letter Carriers* v. *Blount,* Civil Action No. 1843-69, October 30, 1969.

State's Condon-Wadlin Act, of which Governor Rockefeller said in signing its successor, "The necessity of this [new] law has unquestionably been demonstrated over the years by utter inadequacy of the Condon-Wadlin Law to resolve paralyzing strikes and threats of strikes by public employees."[4]

The other avenue to experience has been that available to employees in private enterprise who, where subject to federal jurisdiction, enjoy the right to organize and bargain collectively as provided by the Labor Management Relations Act. Further, one-third of the states have enacted labor relations acts to provide like opportunities and procedures for employees of private enterprises subject only to state jurisdiction. As the problems of labor relations in public employment grew, several cities, notably New York and Philadelphia, developed machinery to deal with their employees. The states increasingly accorded, by statute, administrative action, and judicial decision, their employees the right to organize and to confer with public employers. The means for regularizing such arrangements through representation elections, bargaining procedures, and impasse-breaking measures remained to be developed.

A landmark was set by the enactment of the Wisconsin Municipal Employee Relations Act in 1959, which conferred on municipal employees the right to organize and negotiate with their employers. Even greater impetus to employee organization and state action was generated by the federal government's Executive Order 10988, issued by President Kennedy in 1962, which directed government agencies to recognize employee organizations except those maintaining the right to strike.[5] Exclusive representation would be accorded organizations representing a majority in the unit, with informal or formal recognition when fewer were in the organization. The specified areas of negotiation were outlined, with wages and fringe benefits excluded since these are subject to congressional action.

APPROACHES TO LEGISLATION

The altered climate for public employee relations in recent years has been evidenced by the establishment of federal, state, and local commissions to examine trends and experience, with recommendations for new or amended legislation. Most notable, of course, was the 1961 report of the President's Task Force on Employee-Management Relations in the Federal Service, whose recommendations formed the basis for Executive Order 10988.[6]

Similar use of study committees by a number of state and local governments has provided extensive background and considered recommendations which have

[4]State of New York, *Governor's Memorandum on New Public Employees' Fair Employment Act*, April 21, 1967.

[5]Excluded also were organizations advocating the overthrow of constitutional government, or discriminating on the basis of race, creed, color, or national origin. The Order has stimulated federal employee organization. Over 1.4 million federal employees were covered by exclusive recognition agreements at the end of 1968, including approximately four hundred thousand white-collar workers. "Union Recognition in the Federal Government, November 1967 and November 1968" (U.S. Civil Service Commission, release of May 15, 1969).

[6]Following the review of experience under Executive Order 10988, President Nixon issued Executive Order 11491 on October 29, 1969.

been incorporated in statutes (Connecticut, Minnesota, New Jersey, New York State, New York City, Rhode Island) or provided bases for ongoing discussions on legislation (Illinois, Michigan, and Pennsylvania).[7] The makeup of the committees has varied. The Michigan and New York State groups consisted of public members. State legislators, along with public, labor, and public management representatives, composed the Connecticut, Illinois, Minnesota, New Jersey, and Pennsylvania groups. The Rhode Island commission consisted of state legislators and public representatives. The New York City study group was tripartite. Extensive consultation was generally had with officials of public agencies and public employee unions and associations, and often with spokesmen for business, civic groups, and practicing attorneys. The reports have included comprehensive examination of the situation in the respective jurisdictions in relation to national and outside state developments in labor law and administration, public employee organization, strike trends, and developments in public collective negotiations.

All of the reports have stressed the need for regularization of the means whereby organizations of public employees may be given an opportunity to obtain representation, to represent the employees of the appropriate unit in the determination of their working conditions and in effectuating the agreement, and to provide the devices for avoiding impasse situations that impede agreement. They have viewed such arrangements as enhancing the merit system, not as conflicting with it.

Cited prominently was the importance of adequate training in techniques of negotiation and contract administration for both public management and public employee representatives, so as to ensure good faith bargaining and observance of agreements as integral to the regular operations of the agencies covered. In making statutory recommendations, the reports stressed openmindedness and flexibility in this new field, with continuing assessment of initial experience, so that the law and its administration could be improved.

STATE VARIATIONS

The study committees' recommendations have varied with differences in existing statutory and constitutional arrnagements in the states, the judgment of the commission members, the strength and influence of employee organizations, the role of compromise within the study group, and varying assessments of the limited experience in the public employee field. These variations are reflected in such

[7] Overall analysis of developments are available in the *Report of the Task Force on State and Local Government Labor Relations,* National Governors' Conference, 1967, and the 1968 Supplement (published by Public Personnel Association). Leading commission reports include: Connecticut, *Report of the Interim Commission to Study Collective Bargaining by Municipalities, 1965;* Minnesota, *Report by Governor's Committee on Public Employee Relations Laws, 1965;* New York, *Governor's Committee on Public Employee Relations, 1966, Interim report, 1968,* and *Recommendations January 1969;* Rhode Island, Commission to Study Mediation and Arbitration, 1966; City of New York, *Report of Tripartite Panel to Improve Municipal Collective Bargaining Procedures, 1966;* Michigan, *Report of Governor's Advisory Committee on Public Employee Relations, February 1967;* Illinois, Advisory Commission on Labor-Management Policy for Public Employees, 1967; New Jersey, Public and School Employees' Grievance Study Commission, 1968; Pennsylvania, Governor's Commission to Revise the Public Employee Law, 1968.

matters as concern about what agencies should be responsible for dealing with representation and impasse situations, the approach to unit recognition and special employee groups, the nature of recognition, the procedures for negotiating and impasse handling, and sanctions to be applied in the event of work stoppages.

The use of existing state agencies was recommended in the Connecticut, Minnesota, Michigan, and Pennsylvania reports, while new agencies were proposed for New York and Illinois. In Connecticut, the separate boards for representation and mediation would handle these matters, but not for teachers; in Minnesota, the Division of Labor Conciliation would handle the entire process, but not for teachers. In Michigan, the existing mediation board would handle all matters, but would establish a separate panel to handle factfinding procedures. The New York and Illinois reports proposed all-inclusive coverage of both state and local employees, and new agencies to handle labor relations—in the former, an autonomous unit in the State Civil Service Agency; for the latter, an independent agency. For New Jersey, separate agencies were proposed in the Department of Labor and Industries, one to administer public employee laws and regulations, and another to handle both public and private employee dispute settlements.

There were variations in the several sets of recommendations on the scope of the proposed legislation and on treatment of supervisors, teachers, policemen, and firemen. The Connecticut committee, acting within its legislative mandate, restricted its proposals to municipal employees other than teachers. It left to the parties the determination of supervisory levels to be excluded, but suggested guides. While including school boards among municipal employers for the purpose of dealing with custodial employees, it concurred with the legislature's separate treatment of teachers "in view of the special nature and role of education in municipal government." Policemen and firemen, "because of the special nature of the public safety function," were each required to be in separate units.

The Illinois report recommended the coverage of both state and local employees, with no special legislation for any particular occupational or professional group. Separate laws (for example, for police or teachers) with different administrative arrangements were viewed as "neither equitable nor efficient in the Illinois context," and would lead to additional special laws for other professions or occupations. Policemen's organizations, however, were to be limited to representing only policemen, "to avoid possible conflict between police reponsibilities and occupational loyalties." They were not to be affiliated with organizations having members other than policemen, so that "their legitimate interests would be protected without jeopardizing their legal responsibilities." Firemen and prison guards were viewed differently since "such police functions as these groups may have, do not involve possible conflicts with other employee groups."

The Michigan report, reviewing the experience under the 1965 Public Employment Relations Act, commented on the public employers and employees who are exempt from the act. This apparently is in reference to the state employees under the jurisdiction of the Michigan Civil Service Commission established by the state's constitutional provisions. The report found that the arguments against exclusive representation and collective bargaining for these employees "have no greater validity than corresponding arguments at one time made with respect to other public employees." No circumstances "sharply distinguishing" this group from the majority of public employees to whom these rights are available could be found.

The committee recommended, therefore, that the Michigan Civil Service Commission should adopt policies "granting 'rights of unionization,' including the principles of exclusive recognition and collective bargaining, comparable to those required of employers who are subject to the Public Employment Relations Act." It also recommended continued "rights of unionization" for supervisors, but restricted such organization to supervisor membership.

The New York State report proposed coverage of all state and local employees under a single statute. On the question of whether supervisors and professional employees should be separated from employee units, the report held that there were "important reasons for going slow" on this matter.[8] New Jersey and Pennsylvania reports also proposed unitary coverage of all public employees.

UNIT DETERMINATION

A prominent feature in the reports was the question of the appropriate unit for representation and negotiation. The clash between the employees' efforts to advance the interests of particular occupational groups and the customary civil service approach to statewide and communitywide determination of basic working terms was analyzed in the New York State report. In terms of organization, this represented a divergence of the overall unit approach of the Civil Service Employee Association and the multiunit structure—with the resultant fragmentation—sought by organizations representing occupational and craft groups. The report concluded that "occupational representation should not be denied and can be provided without undermining the civil service system." Suggested as the basis for determining appropriate units were the employees' community of interest, traditional patterns, and the employees' own determination (particularly on the inclusion of supervisors and professionals). It was also proposed that in determining the terms of employment and the extent of the unit, consideration should be given to the discretionary authority of the public employer and the joint duty of administrators and employees to the public. Generally, the other reports also recommended like standards for the determination of units, derived largely from the experience under the Federal Labor Management Relations Act.

All of the reports called for procedures for the determination of appropriate bargaining units by the covered jurisdiction, whether state or local. Except for Minnesota and New York, statutory authorization for exclusive recognition of the majority organization was recommended. The Minnesota report recommended formal recognition for the majority organization and informal recognition in other situations. The New York committee recommended that, for the time being, government agencies be merely authorized, rather than required, to agree to exclusive recognition in view of the many employee groups of diverse negotiating jurisdictions.

---

[8]The report stated: "The effectiveness of the employees' collective influence in the terms of their employment in some areas of public employment may be related more to the community than to the conflict of interest between employees and their supervisors. In other areas this may not be the case. The application of an arbitrary 'no-supervisory-membership-in-the-organization' criterion fails to differentiate between the two situations."

NEGOTIATIONS AND IMPASSES

Generally, the reports required the public authorities to establish procedures for negotiating with employee organizations, with the results of the negotiations to be executed in written agreements. Attention was called to the need for scheduling negotiations so as to conclude an agreement before the date on which budget proposals were to be considered by the given authority.

Settlement of disputes over contract terms was an overshadowing concern of all the study groups. Only the Pennsylvania report recommended a limited right to strike only when all collective bargaining avenues had been exhausted, and following a determination that the "public health, safety or welfare are not endangered." The others all stated in their recommendations that public employees had no right to strike, and stressed the need for arranging procedures that would obviate any disputes leading to strike action. All recommended factfinding procedures and opposed compulsory arbitration. However, the Michigan report proposed experimentally the adoption of a third-party binding dispute resolution in the case of policemen and firefighters. The approaches differed in detail but were uniform in intent. At a set date in advance of budget determination, at the request of either or both parties or on the initiative of the state labor agency, a factfinding panel would be established to mediate and, if necessary, to issue recommendations. Some committees proposed an intermediate stage of private and tentative recommendations. In all instances, panel recommendations would finally be made public.

Different reports had somewhat different proposals on how to proceed if panel recommendations produced no agreement. The Michigan report proposed giving the factfinding function to a standing Public Employment Relations Panel, which, upon certification by the State Labor Mediation Board, would hold hearings, attempt mediation, make private and tentative recommendations to the parties, and finally make formal public recommendations on which the parties would comment. The panel would then hold a "show cause" public hearing and in the absence of agreement would report all the relevant facts, with an evaluation of the reasons for failure to reach a settlement. The New York report included designation of factfinding boards among the functions of the new Public Employment Relations Board. Show-cause hearings in impasse situations, at which the parties would comment on the factfinding recommendations, were to be held by the appropriate legislative body or committee prior to final legislative action on the budget or other pertinent matter.

The Illinois report proposed that the Public Employee Relations Board, following investigation on the need for factfinding, should appoint a factfinding panel that would hold public or private hearings and issue a report and recommendations within thirty days. Within fifteen days of the issuance of the report, the parties would report on the state of the dispute and their views on the recommendations, following which the board would make their report public. Commenting on this procedure, the study committee's report stated, "Such publicity may be especially effective in the public sector since the availability of funds will usually depend on legislative action with respect to budgets and taxation."

STRIKE SANCTIONS

The matter of sanctions in the event of strike has been a particularly sensitive subject with public employee unions, in view of the history of such statutes as New York's Condon-Wadlin Act. The reports dealing with this subject evidenced a keen awareness of the history and of the unions' attitudes. The effort to balance these against the ban on striking was of paramount concern which resulted, as in other areas, in different approaches. All the reports recommended elimination of any existing automatic penalties against individual employees, while recommending that strike definitions include action by employee organizations. The divergence of approaches is reflected particularly in the New York and Michigan reports.

The New York committee recommended explicitly the use of three strike deterrents: the obligation of public authorities to seek injunctions against employee organizations in the event of an imminent strike, with criminal contempt proceedings to follow the violation of the injunction; penalties against employees for misconduct under the procedures of the state civil service law; and, as in the case of federal employees, a requirement that the organizations seeking certification agree not to assert the right to strike against the government. The discretion would be left with public authorities for determination of whether the employee organization was responsible for the strike, had tried to prevent it, and was making bona fide efforts to terminate it, and whether the employing agency had engaged in acts of extreme provocation. The penalties would include, under criminal contempt proceedings, fines and imprisonment of the union officers and decertification of the union following a show-cause hearing by the Public Employment Relations Board. The report stated, "We think it wise expressly to discourage public employer agencies from waiving or negotiating away their rights to have such strikes enjoined by the courts or their right to have the court command respect for and compliance with its order or decree through the contempt proceedings."

The Michigan group also proposed explicit utilization of injunctive procedures. However, it distinguished between strikes occurring before full utilization of the impasse-handling machinery, in which case injunctions would be mandatory, and strikes in other contexts, when court orders would be "available in accordance with traditional 'equity' principles." The courts would be authorized to consider complaints by the defendants that the public employer violated some statutory provision, and could order the employer to comply with the law.

The Illinois report proposed explicit affirmation of the power of the courts to enjoin public employee strikes, asserting the duty of employing agencies to seek injunctions in the event of a strike. The Connecticut report did not go beyond an express prohibition on any strikes against a public authority.

STATE LAW TRENDS

Since the enactment of the 1959 Wisconsin Municipal Employee Relations Act, legislation in some dozen states has included comprehensive statutes authorizing or requiring public employers to recognize and negotiate with organizations chosen by their employees, and generally provided for factfinding in the event of impasses. In most other states, employees are accorded—by statute, executive order, or administrative action—the right to organize, and in many instances their organizations have the right to present proposals and grievances. In a number of states where comprehensive legislation with broad public employee covering is lacking, statutes have been enacted authorizing union recognition or establishing factfinding procedures or both, for such special occupational groups viewed as intimately concerned with the public interest as firefighters, policemen, transit system employees, and nurses. Only Texas and Virginia statutes specifically forbid bargaining with public employee unions, and only North Carolina and Alabama statutes specifically forbid state employees from joining unions.[9]

Laws authorizing bargaining with organizations of public employees have been enacted in at least twenty-one states since 1959. Classification of the statutes into broad categories is necessarily subject to limitations in view of the diversity of terms and the absence of analysis of experience. In general, the statutes of fourteen states require mandatory bargaining for all or some public employee groups: Connecticut (local and teachers), Delaware (state and county, teachers; municipalities make decision), Maine (local), Massachusetts (state and local), Michigan (local), New Hampshire (state), New Jersey (state and local), New York (state and local), North Dakota (teachers), Oregon (state and local), Rhode Island (state and local), Vermont (state and local), Washington (local), Wisconsin (state and local). Nevada requires bargaining, but sets forth such broad authority for public authorities as to raise questions regarding the scope for effective bargaining. Other state statutes merely set "meet and confer" provisions, although these are sometimes coupled with the requirement of "in good faith," as in the case of California, Minnesota, and Missouri. Some broad statutes (South Dakota and Nebraska) appear to have little more effect than mere authorization statutes (Alaska, New Hampshire local). Other states during this period have enacted statutes granting the right to organize to all public employees, as in Iowa and Florida, or only to special groups, as to firefighters in Wyoming, nurses in Montana, or firemen and transit workers in Illinois.

The table presents some leading features of the more comprehensive statutes. The complexity and variety of the approaches permits only a brief treatment of major aspects here.

Scope

The statutes vary in their scope. Some include all local and state employees, others cover municipal employees, often excluding or separating teachers and covering them by other laws. Special provisions for policemen and firemen may be made in a more inclusive law, or may be included in separate statutes.

[9]The Texas statute permits unions, which do not claim the right to strike on behalf of public employee members, to present grievances. In a North Carolina case, the U.S. district court held unconstitutional the ban on membership in nationally affiliated organizations, and invalidated the penalties for joining, while upholding the provisions forbidding state or local bodies from negotiating agreements (*Atkins* v. *City of Charlotte,* 70 LRRM 2732). The Alabama statute excludes city, county, and the State Docks Board from the ban, as well as teachers employed by cities or counties. A 1967 Alabama statute specifically grants firefighters employed by state and municipal authorities the right to organize and present proposals on salaries.

Administrative Machinery

Generally, the existing machinery for mediation and for determining employee representation for collective bargaining relationships in private enterprise has been used. Some statutes leave administrative machinery to local authorities, particularly for teachers. Maine, New Jersey, Nevada, New Hampshire, Oregon, and Vermont (state employees) have set up new agencies to deal with public employee matters. In New York the Public Employment Relations Board has been established as an autonomous unit within the State Civil Service Commission, dealing with both representation and impasse situations. However, under this statute, local authorities are authorized to establish their own representation procedures if they meet the state's requirements.

Bargaining

Most statutes require mandatory bargaining by the public employer with public employee organizations and execution of written agreements. Bargaining is mandatory for state and county employees, but only permissive for municipal employees, under the Delaware statute, and the Vermont statute's coverage of city employees is permissive. The mandatory right "to meet and confer" is accorded all covered employees in Minnesota and California. In Washington and Oregon, mandatory bargaining is required for state and local employees, while the mandatory right to "meet and confer" is accorded to teachers.

Where machinery is established for representation, mediation, and factfinding, existing state agencies are usually utilized. Existing labor relations boards are utilized for both representation and mediation situations in Michigan and Wisconsin. Where separate labor relations boards and mediation agencies are established, the functions of representation determination and mediation are separated, as in Connecticut, Massachusetts, and Rhode Island. The state department of labor is utilized in Delaware, Minnesota, and Vermont, the mediation board in Missouri, and civil service commissions in Oregon and Washington. In Wisconsin, however, the state director of personnel has the function of representing the state as employer.

The special statutes for teachers generally leave to local school boards the determination of representation and mediation procedures. Mediation services under these laws are generally provided by the state department of education. Under the Rhode Island teacher statute, representation certifications are made by the labor relations board.

Representation Status

Almost all of the recent statutes requiring bargaining provide machinery for the election and certification of employee organizations, with exclusive representation rights. Minnesota grants a formal status to organizations with a majority status, and informal status to other groups, with the right to "meet and confer." The teachers' statutes, as in the case of Connecticut and Washington, require local boards to

State Public Employee Laws—Selected States, Including Aspects of Recent Enactments

State	Coverage	Administrative machinery	Bargaining	Representation	Dispute provisions	Strikes
Calif.	State and local (1968) amendments do not apply to state employees)	Governmental subdivisions	Required "to meet and confer in good faith" (1968 amendments authorized nonbinding memoranda of agreement with "determination" by governing body	Subdivisions may adopt procedures after consultation with employee organizations; guides suggested for recognizing employee organizations	Authorized agreement on third party in local negotiations	—
	Teachers	School district, county board of education, etc.	Required to "meet and confer"	Negotiating councils with proportionalq representation	None specified	—
Conn.	Local	State Labor Relations Board (SLRB) Board of Mediation and Arbitration (BMA)	Duty to negotiate, including written agreement	SLRB determines representative; exclusive representation	BMA mediates, and fact finding	Prohibited
	Teachers	Local Boards of Education; State Board of Education (SBE)	Duty to negotiate, including written agreement	Procedures set forth; exclusive representation	SBE mediates	Prohibited
Del.	State and local	State Department of Labor and Industrial Relations (SDLIR); State Mediation Service (SMS)	State and county— duty to negotiate Municipalities— independent decision; includes written agreement.	SDLIR determines; exclusive representation	SMS mediates	Prohibited

State Public Employee Laws—Selected States, Including Aspects of Recent Enactments (Continued)

State	Coverage	Administrative machinery	Bargaining	Representative	Dispute provisions	Strikes
Del. (cont.)	Teachers	Local boards of education; State Board of Education (SBE)	Duty to negotiate authorizes agreement	Procedural guides for exclusive representation but administered by local boards; appeal to SBE	Authorizes local mediation and fact finding but bans arbitration	Prohibited; exclusive representative loss of representation rights for two years; loss of check off for one year
Maine	Local, including teachers	Commissioner, Department of Labor and Industry (CDLI); Public Employees Labor Relations Appeals Board (PELRAB); Board of Arbitration and Conciliation (BAC)	Duty to negotiate, including written agreement	Subdivisions may representation; elections, if required, conducted by CDLI; appeal to PELRAB	May call on BAC for fact finding; permits binding arbitration, but advisory only on wages	Prohibited and may be enjoined; strikes are unfair labor practice
Md.	Teachers	Local boards of Education; State Board of Education (SBE)	Negotiation includes the duty to "confer in good faith" and "reduce to writing" agreed upon matters	Procedures established; local board may designate majority organization as exclusive representative; SBE establishes rules for elections and supervises	SBE assistance; report and recommendations	Prohibited; penalties, revocation of exclusive bargaining representation for two years and loss of dues checkoff for one year

State Public Employee Laws—Selected States, Including Aspects of Recent Enactments (Continued)

State	Coverage	Administrative machinery	Bargaining	Representative	Dispute provisions	Strikes
Mass.	All local, including teachers	State Labor Relations Commission (SLRC); State Board of Conciliation and Arbitration (SBCA)	Duty to negotiate, including written agreement	SLRC determines; exclusive representation	SBCA fact finding	Prohibited
	State	State Director of Personnel (SDP)	Duty to negotiate, including written agreement	Rules for determination by SDP; exclusive representation	—	Prohibited; strikes are unfair labor practice
Mich.	All local, including teachers	State Labor Mediation Board (SLMB) (separate administration of the labor relations and mediation function)	Duty to negotiate, including written agreement	SLMB determines; exclusive representation	SLMB mediates grievance	Prohibited; sanctions against strikes subject to appeal and court review
Minn.	State and local	Division of Labor Conciliation (DLC)	Requested to "meet and confer"	DLC determines; formal recognition to majority organization, informal to others	DLC mediates; then adjustment panel for findings	Prohibited continues earlier penalties against individuals, with right to review
	Teachers	School boards	Requested to "meet and confer"	Recognition to single organization; where more than one, proportional representation on teachers' council	Adjustment panel for findings	—

State Public Employee Laws—Selected States, Including Aspects of Recent Enactments (Continued)

State	Coverage	Administrative machinery	Bargaining	Representation	Dispute provisions	Strikes
Mo.	State and local, except teachers, police, state police	State Board of Mediation (SBM)	Required to "meet, confer and discuss," results "reduced to writing"	SBM resolves issues; exclusive represen-	—	Prohibited
Nebr.	State and local	Local jurisdictions; State Court of Industrial Relations (SCIR)	Authorized, recognition, negotiation, and written agreement by public employers	Jurisdictions may grant exclusive recognition or conduct elections; SCIR certifies	SCIR jurisdiction may be invoked to determine terms	Prohibited; Continues earlier penalties against individuals
	Teachers	School boards; State Court of Industrial Relations (SCIR)	"To meet and confer" is authorized on vote of majority of school board	Authorizes exclusive representation	Authorised parties to establish procedures for fact finding; decision-making authority of SCIR may be invoked	Prohibited
Nev.	Local, including teachers	Local jurisdictions; State Local Government Employee Management Relations Board (SLGB)	Duty to negotiate	No strike pledge as condition for recognition; exclusive representation accorded by local jurisdiction; appeals available to SLGB	SLG notified, and and may appoint mediator; fact finding if impasse persists	Prohibited; public employers may seek enjoinment; penalties for violation of enjointment set out; by court, against employee organization (maximum fine), individual of officers (maximum fine or

State Public Employee Laws—Selected States, Including Aspects of Recent Enactments (Continued)

State	Coverage	Administrative machinery	Bargaining	Representation	Dispute provisions	Strikes
Nev. (cont.)						imprisonment); individual employees (dismissal or suspension); by public employers against individual dismissal, demotion or suspension; with hold salaries, cancel contracts
N.H.	State	State commission established	Obligation to negotiate for purpose of reaching agreement	State commission conducts election and certifies results; exclusive representation	—	Prohibited; every agreement to contain no strike clause; employees subject to disciplinary penalties provided by law and personnel regulations for serious misconduct

40

State Public Employee Laws—Selected States, Including Aspects of Recent Enactments (Continued)

State	Coverage	Administrative machinery	Bargaining	Representation	Dispute provisions	Strikes
N.J.	State and local, including teachers	Division of Public Employment Relations (PERC) autonomous tripartite unit in Department of Labor and Industry. Public Employment Relations Commission (PERC) in PERD for policy and rule making	Required to bargains including written agreement	Majority organization is exclusive representative; determined by employee designation or by election; elections conducted by and rules determined by PERC	PERC to aid in mediation; may recommend or invoke fact finding	States that the Act of 1968 is not to be construed to "diminish in any way the right of private employees to strike"
New York	All state and local	Public Employment Relations Board (PERB) (autonomous in State Department of Civil Service)	Required to bargain, including written agreement	Procedures for recognition by local authorities, subject to "affirmation by such organization that it does not assert the right to strike against any government…." To PERB for resolution if no local procedures, and for state employees	a) Parties establish own procedures; b) or recourse to mediation and fact finding through PERB c) Recommendations not accepted, legislative body or committee conducts hearing and takes action	Prohibited; organizations may be fined and chief executive of government involved required to notify PERB For violation, PERB to order forfeiture of representation rights and dues check off for such period as PERB determines. Chief executive required to deduct 2 days' pay for each day employee on strike, and employee

State Public Employee Laws—Selected States, Including Aspects of Recent Enactments (Continued)

State	Coverage	Administrative machinery	Bargaining	Representation	Dispute provisions	Strikes
New York (cont.)						on probation without tenure for a year Right to review
N. Dak.	Teacher	Education Fact Finding Commission (EFFC)	Required to negotiate, and written agreement	Local board accepts majority organization, or conducts election; if disagreement, EFFC rules govern election	Determined by parties; or call on EFFC for fact finding	Prohibited; individual teacher may be denied full salary during period of violation
Ore.	State and local	Public Employee Relations Board (PERB);	Required to negotiate and enter agreement	Local jurisdictions may determine or call on PERB	Local jurisdictions may determine or call on PERB for mediation and fact finding	Prohibited
	Teachers	School boards	Required to "confer, consult and discuss in good faith"	Local election to determine whether an employee organization or a committee representing teachers is to be exclusive representative	Mediation	—

State Public Employee Laws—Selected States, Including Aspects of Recent Enactments (Continued)

State	Coverage	Administrative machinery	Bargaining	Representation	Dispute provisions	Strikes
R.I.	Local	State Labor Relations Board (SLRB)	Required to bargain	SLRB determines; exclusive representation	Mediation by SDL with arbitration on request of either party (but decisions involving expenditures are advisory)	Prohibited
	State	State agencies	Required to bargain	Represents members		Prohibited
	Teachers	School boards; State Labor Relations Board (SLRB); State Department of Education (SDE)	Required to bargain	SLRB determines; exclusive representation	SDE mediation; either party may request arbitration by decisions involving expenditures are advisory	Prohibited
S. Dak	State, local, including teachers	Individual jurisdictions	"Tentative settlements" to be implemented by ordinance, resolution, or memorandum of understanding as may be appropriate	Recognition only for members; informal recognition to any organization	—	Prohibited: state and local governments required to apply to courts for immediate relief. Penalties against organization by courts set at maximum of $100,000 and or imprisonment of officials for 1 year. Employees, right to court review,

43

State Public Employee Laws—Selected States, Including Aspects of Recent Enactments (Continued)

State	Coverage	Administrative machinery	Bargaining	Representation	Dispute provisions	Strikes
S. Dak. (cont.)						fine of $1,000 and/or 1 year imprisonment
Vt.	Local employees, excludes "professional employees"	State Labor Relations Board (SLRB); Department of Industrial Relations (DIR)	Authorized to bargain	SLRB determines; exclusive representation	Mediation by DIR and governor; effort to have parties agree to arbitration; otherwise, fact finding by labor emergency board	Prohibited; states right of public employer to petition for injunction
	State	State Employee Labor Relations Board (SELRB)	Required to bargain; written agreement	SELRB certifies, exclusive representation	SELRB may authorize fact finding	Prohibited; strikes are unfair labor practice
	Teachers	Local boards of education	Required to negotiate, and written agreement	School board may waive elections for exclusive representation	Parties may use mediation or fact finding	Injunctions by court only after due hearing that action "poses clear and present danger to sound program of school education. . . is in best public interest to prevent"

State Public Employee Laws—Selected States, Including Aspects of Recent Enactments (Continued)

State	Coverage	Administrative machinery	Bargaining	Representation	Dispute provisions	Strikes
Wash.	Local	Department of Labor and Industries (DLI)	Required to bargain, and written agreement	Exclusive representation. Parties may decide; or invite DLI to decide and conduct election, if necessary	Mediation	Prohibited
	Teachers	School districts; State Superintendent of Public Instruction (SSPI)	Required to "meet and confer"	Procedures adopted locally; exclusive representation	Assistance of committees of educators and school directors appointed by SSPI	—
Wisc.	Local	Wisconsin Employment Relations Board (WERB)	Required to bargain	WERB determines, exclusive representation	WERB fact finding; unless local authorities have established comparable procedures	Prohibited
	State	WERB	Required to bargain	WERB determines, exclusive representation	WERB fact finding	Prohibited

45

establish procedures for determining the majority status for representation purposes. In California and Minnesota, where more than one organization represents
the teachers, provision is made for employee organization councils based on proportionate representation.

Negotiations, Impasses, and Strikes

The statutes of all the states with recent legislation on government employees
contain varying provisions on negotiations and disputes. Characteristically, some of
these measures outline guides on negotiations, with due consideration to timing as
regards budgetary determinations. On inability to conclude agreements, a provision
is made for mediation and factfinding by state boards and for nonbinding recommendations, notably in the case of Connecticut, Massachusetts, Michigan, Minnesota, and Wisconsin. Recourse to state mediation services is provided in the
Delaware and Rhode Island statutes. The Rhode Island and Vermont statutes provide for efforts to obtain agreement on voluntary arbitration.[10] Strikes are
specifically prohibited in most of the statutes.

Generally, sanctions are not set forth specifically, leaving actions deemed
necessary by the public authorities to be taken through the courts. Notable exceptions are the recent amendments to the New York State statute, and the sanctions set forth in the recent enactments in Delaware (teachers), Maryland
(teachers), Nevada (local), North Dakota (teachers), and South Dakota (state and
local). By contrast, the Vermont teachers' statute requires a finding of "clear and
present danger" on the facts in the immediate situation before an injunction is
issued.

STATE AND LOCAL PUBLIC EMPLOYEE COLLECTIVE
BARGAINING IN THE ABSENCE OF EXPLICIT
LEGISLATIVE AUTHORIZATION

Richard F. Dole, Jr.

The new phenomenon of public sector collective bargaining involve numerous
problems which are not present in the private sector. How can public sector collective bargaining be reconciled with the separation of powers between the legisla-

Richard Dole is Associate Professor, University of Iowa College of Law. The author gratefully
acknowledges the contributions to this article of Henry P. Vander Kam and Eli J. Wirtz, third-
year students at the University of Iowa College of Law. Reprinted from *Iowa Law Review* LIV,
1969, 539, 540-51, 558-59. Footnote references have been deleted from edited version.

[10]The Rhode Island statute states that arbitration on money matters is not binding. In
Vermont the governor may appoint a "labor emergency board" in a dispute substantially
affecting the state's economy if other efforts fail.

tive, executive and judicial branches of government? Can public sector collective bargaining take place without intolerable disruption of public services by strikes? What impact will public sector collective bargaining have on the civil service systems which exist in most states? The definitive answers to these questions must be derived from experience with public sector collective bargaining. However, it already seems clear that the mere existence of these questions is not an insuperable obstacle to collective bargaining in the public sector.

The pressure to do something about public employee labor relations has induced a growing number of states to enact new legislation. However, relatively few states have laws comparable to the comprehensive statutes in Massachusetts, Michigan, New York and Wisconsin. These statutes guarantee public employees the right to bargain collectively, establish procedures for selecting employee representatives and remedying unfair labor practices, and provide dispute-resolution mechanisms as alternatives to the strike.

Iowa is typical of those states with little or no legislation dealing with public employer collective bargaining. The most recent enactment on the subject is inconsequential. The new statute specifies that the prohibition on political contributions by municipal civil service employees does not preclude those employees from commenting on their conditions of employment. Needless to say, this statute does not invalidate the three opinions by former attorneys general which conclude that Iowa state and local units of government do not have the power to engage in collective bargaining.

However, these attorney general opinions have been repudiated by an Iowa District Judge. In *State Board of Regents v. Local 1258, United Packing House Food and Allied Workers* the court declared:

> [T]he opinion of the Attorney General of August 16, 1961 [the most recent attorney general's opinion on point] incorrectly interpreted Iowa law with respect to the right of a public employer to undertake collective bargaining and enter into collective bargaining agreements.

The *Board of Regents* decision, which is presently on appeal to the Iowa Supreme Court, raises the question whether, as a matter of principle, a public employer should have implied power to engage in collective bargaining, and, if so, whether this is a proper conclusion under Iowa law. The answer to this question transcends the fate of the *Board of Regents* case in the Iowa Supreme Court. Implication of a governmental power to engage in collective bargaining is an important issue wherever a legislative response to the increasing militancy of public employees is blocked, or is slow in coming.

PROPRIETY OF IMPLYING GOVERNMENTAL POWER TO ENGAGE IN COLLECTIVE BARGAINING

The gist of collective bargaining is negotiation of the terms and conditions of employment by management and employee representatives. Public employer collective bargaining thus invariably involves consultation between a public employer and a representative of its employees. As long as a public employer is willing to consult with every organization which represents its employees, legislation authorizing consultation is patently unnecessary. A public employer's general power to carry out its assigned functions is sufficiently inclusive to permit consultation with all persons affected by those functions. The constitutional right of the people to petition government for a redress of grievances also provides analogical support for an affirmative governmental effort to ascertain the wishes of public employees and other persons interested in the terms and conditions of public employment. This consultation serves the public interest by permitting informed governmental action without abridging governmental freedom of action.

On the other hand, recognition of an exclusive employee representative for purposes of collective bargaining, and contracting concerning the terms and conditions of employment does impose limitations on a public employer's future freedom of action. Exclusive recognition constitutes a pledge that the public employer will not negotiate with another representative of the same employees, while a collective bargaining agreement commits a public employer to establish certain terms and conditions of employment. It is dispute concerning the desirability of these limitations which lies at the core of the controversy concerning public employer collective bargaining.

This article accordingly focuses on the legality of negotiating and contracting with an exclusive employee representative, and that is the sense in which collective bargaining is hereafter used. As a practical matter, execution of a collective bargaining contract almost never occurs without some form of exclusive recognition. Because other employee representatives are not bound by the contract, a public employer usually accomplishes little by contracting with a non-exclusive employee representative.

There are three levels of objection to public employer collective bargaining. The process has been considered totally impermissible; permissible only if specifically authorized by the legislature; and permissible only if executed in a certain manner. The blanket objection to public employer collective bargaining is that it involves an improper delegation to private persons of governmental authority over the terms and conditions of public employment. This objection is specious. Because a public employer does not have to agree to an employee representative's proposals, a public employer delegates no authority to a representative by attempting to negotiate a collective bargaining contract. Furthermore, any agreement that results is an exercise of discretion rather than a delegation of authority by the public employer.

The view that public employer collective bargaining is only permissible where explicitly sanctioned by the legislature derives from several sources. Many of the cases dealing with public sector collective bargaining have involved local governmental units. In the absence of home rule, the power of local governments has traditionally been interpreted strictly. A leading nineteenth century treatise on municipal corporations, for example, states that "[a] ny fair, reasonable, substantial doubt concerning the existence of power is resolved by the courts against the corporation, and the power is denied." Notwithstanding the marked changes that have occurred in public attitudes toward the need for governmental services, strict construction of local governmental power persists in the law of a number of states and is often applied to counties and school boards as well as to cities and town.

The separation of powers between the executive and legislative branches of government is another source of the view that specific legislation is a prerequisite to public employer collective bargaining. Allocation of the power to fix the terms and conditions of public employment has been considered a legislative function.

However, neither of these rationales is pertinent where a legislature has granted a public employer general power to contract in the course of its operations. Power to confer exclusive recognition and execute collective bargaining contracts can be fairly implied from a general power to contract. Indeed, where there is strong employee support for collective bargaining, a power to engage in collective bargaining can be necessary to the utilization of the various governmental powers which would otherwise be impaired by work stoppages. This analysis applies a fortiori to units of state government whose power is not construed as narrowly as that of local governments.

If a public employer has the authority to execute individual employment contracts and is interested in efficiency and administrative simplicity, those individual contracts will contain standardized terms. Once one realizes that contracts negotiated for the same kind of work—office clerical, for example—are subject to standardization, it becomes apparent that a general power to contract can fairly encompass powers to confer exclusive recognition and execute collective bargaining contracts. A collective bargaining contract is essentially a master contract which sets the terms and conditions of employment for individual employees without requiring formal negotiation of these matters with each employee. If a public employer can standardize individual contracts of employment, it should also be able to utilize the more efficient master contract negotiated with an employee representative to achieve the same result. To say that standardized individual contracts are permissible, but a master contract is not, is to exalt form over substance.

Power to confer exclusive recognition is a corollary of power to execute a master contract. Where there are actual or potential rival employee representatives, it is difficult for a public employer to obtain a master contract without resort to exclusive recognition. Competitive pressures make each representative reluctant to reach agreement until every representative is willing to accept the same terms. Exclusive recognition also simplifies the administration of a master contract. In the absence of exclusive recognition, employees claiming infringement of their rights under a master contract can shop around for a representative who is willing to press their claims. This, of course, introduces competitive considerations into contract administration and can require a public employer to deal with an inordinately large number of employee representatives. Exclusive recognition both relaxes competitive pressure on the recognized representative and permits a public employer to channel all employee claims through a single representative.

The position that a civil service or merit employment system preempts the field is another variant of the view that specific legislation is necessary to authorize collective bargaining. There is no doubt that a civil service system affects what can be agreed upon by a public employer in a collective bargaining contract. To the extent that a civil service system creates statutory rights, those rights cannot be varied by agreement. For example, a collective bargaining contract would not negate a statutory requirement that initial personnel appointments must be governed by performance on a written examination. On the other hand, in the absence of an express statutory prohibition, a civil service system does not preclude the negotiation of collective bargaining contracts which are consistent with the system. The content of civil service examinations and the definition of satisfactory performance would therefore be proper subjects of collective bargaining agreements. Of course, if as is most often the case, a civil service system is administered by an independent commission or board, any agreement between a public employer and an employee representative concerning the administration of a competitive examination would merely constitute a joint recommendation to the Commission. Yet, this would not prevent reduction of the agreement to writing or vitiate the practical value of the agreement which relates to matters covered by a civil service system, it is advisable to utilize a standard clause which declares that the contract "is to be construed so as not to impair employee rights under applicable civil services laws and regulations."

Some courts seem to have been as perturbed by exclusive recognition as by the negotiation of collective bargaining contracts. There are several older decisions indicating that it is an abuse of discretion for a public employer to grant exclusive recognition to an employee representative if all employees concerned are not already supporters of the exclusive representative. However, the more recent cases conclude that exclusive representation of both members and nonmembers is permissible where there is satisfactory evidence of at least majority employee support for the exclusive representative, the exclusive representative is required to represent all employees regardless of union membership, and employees are given assurances that exclusive representation will not preclude individual presentation of complaints to the public employer.

Still another objection relates only to the negotiation of certain collective bargaining contracts. Basic democratic principles are reflected in the precept that public officials should not ordinarily enter into contracts which bind their successors. If the voters have turned the rascals out, they should not continue to be bound by the actions of the ousted administration. However this precept poses no insuperable burden to execution of collective bargaining contracts by officials with substantial unexpired terms. Furthermore, where public officials were near the end of their terms, practical necessity has led some courts to conclude that it was proper for them to execute a collective bargaining contract which extended into the terms of their successors.

The inconclusiveness of the justifications for refusal to imply a governmental power to bargain collectively suggests that courts have not been candid in dealing with the issue. Two important underlying considerations seem to be judicial failure to perceive how an implied power to engage in collective bargaining would be exercised and deepseated judicial failure to perceive how an implied power to engage in collective bargaining would be exercised and deep-seated judicial fear of encouraging public employee strikes. Both attitudes have been occasionally stimulated by union lawyers in the course of litigation.

It is clear beyond peradventure that a public employer with an implied power to engage in collective bargaining would not have to exercise that power unless it chose to do so, and, even if collective bargaining were initiated, would not have to agree to unacceptable contract terms. It would also be proper for the public employer to insist that any collective bargaining contract be terminable at will. Nevertheless, there are a number of state decisions which take the position that the power to engage in collective bargaining would necessarily lead to an intolerable abrogation of governmental discretion. In view of the permissive nature of an implied power to engage in collective bargaining, these decisions ironically and unnecessarily deny a public employer discretion in the name of preservation of discretion. The most that can be said for these decisions is that they are matched by the equally indefensible position of some union lawyers that the existence of power to engage in collective bargaining means that collective bargaining must take place. A mandatory duty to engage in collective bargaining should never be implied.

The most significant factor inhibiting implication of a power to bargain collectively is the unfounded fear that the legitimization of public employer collective bargaining will increase the incidence of public employee strikes. Collective bargaining and strikes do not necessarily go hand in hand. Public employee strikes have occurred where collective bargaining was considered illegal. Indeed, a number of public employee strikes have taken place because collective bargaining was considered illegal. A major cause of public employee strikes is the refusal of public employers to recognize employee representatives for the purposes of collective bargaining. Furthermore, legitimization of collective bargaining by public employers does not require legitimization of strikes in support of bargaining demands. The legality of public employer collective bargaining and the legality of public employee strikes are separable issues. In the *Board of Regents* case the court held that the Regents could engage in collective bargaining, but that their employees could not lawfully strike.

This is a realistic distinction. If good faith collective bargaining takes place, public employees may not need to strike to achieve reasonable settlements. Moreover, even where public sector collective negotiations have broken down there has been encouraging experience with the use of mediation, factfinding, and arbitration by third parties, in lieu of economic weapons, as devices to bring the parties together. These dispute-resolution techniques are provided for by statute in a number of states. Yet, even in the absence of legislation, at least nonbinding mediation and factfinding can be invoked through mutual agreement of the parties to a public sector labor dispute. Because traditional arbitration leads to conclusive resolution of a dispute, legislation is necessary to empower a public employer to arbitrate disputes which involve matters of policy. On the other hand, advisory arbitration, which is akin to factfinding, should be permissible without statutory confirmation.

On balance, there is a compelling case for implication of a power to engage in collective bargaining from a general governmental power to contract. Implication of this power enhances governmental discretion in dealing with public employee labor problems and lessens the likelihood of public employee strikes for recognition. Where employees insistently demand collective bargaining, the implied power to engage in collective bargaining permits a public employer to commence negotiations without having to undergo strikes for recognition until enabling legislation is obtained.

A series of strikes for recognition may be a high price to pay for legislative authorization to engage in collective bargaining. A strike for recognition is injurious in its own right and can also poison future employer-employee relationships. A collective bargaining relationship that is initiated after a strike for recognition is more likely to be difficult and involve subsequent strikes than a relationship that is initiated without a strike for recognition. . . .

CONCLUSION

It is fashionable to maintain that legislative guidelines are needed to put public employer collective bargaining on a sound footing. There is a good deal to be said for legislative guidelines, but their advantages should not be allowed to overshadow the significance of an implied governmental power to engage in collective bargaining. Where government officials call for legislative guidelines, they sometimes are asking for little more than legislative moral support for an opportunity to bargain collectively. This is made evident by the recently-enacted California "meet and confer" public employer collective bargaining law.

The new California statute authorizes California public employers, the state excepted, to grant nonexclusive recognition to employee representatives, meet and confer with recognized employee representatives, utilize mediation where agreement is not reached, and establish procedures for recognition of employee representatives and for dispute-resolution techniques in addition to mediation. Virtually all of these features of the California statute are inherent in an implied power to bargain collectively. Why should a legislature have to allocate its limited time and resources to confirming a power which already exists? If legislative effort is to be invested in providing guidelines for public employer collective bargaining, the effort would be better directed to developing comprehensive statutes like those in force in Massachusetts and Wisconsin. As long as the courts exercise proper judicial restraint, the implied power to bargain collectively will permit a public employer to respond adequately to employee unrest.

CHAPTER 2

THE PARTIES
TO PUBLIC SECTOR BARGAINING

It is impossible to understand public sector bargaining without understanding the participants in the bargaining process. These participants include management and their representatives; employees and their organizations; and other individuals and groups, usually government agencies, who assist the other two parties.

Greater variety exists within each of the three groups of participants in the public sector than in any other sector of our economy. Management in the public sector can mean an elective legislative body, a single elected official, a single appointed official such as a city manager or an agency head, or an elected or appointed board such as a board of education or a welfare board. Employee organizations in the public sector include both professional associations and unions. Some unions enroll only public employees; others enroll both public and private employees. Some unions include only white- or blue-collar workers; others combine both white- and blue-collar employees in the same union. Finally, neutral administrative agencies run the gamut from agencies that confine their activities to the public sector to agencies that regulate both public and private employees to a voluntary tripartite agency.

The first group of articles includes three case studies of employee organizations in the public sector. All three of the articles, which were written specifically for this volume, describe organizations attempting to adjust to the rapidly changing field of public sector bargaining. Griner describes the American Federation of Government Employees (AFGE), the largest union of federal government employees. Wurf and Hennessy analyze developments in the American Federation of State, County and Municipal Employees (AFSCME), the largest union of state and municipal workers. Moskow compares the National Education Association and the American Federation of Teachers—the two rival organizations of public school teachers.

In the next group of articles Crouch uses the results of an extensive survey to analyze public sector management's attitude toward unions. Stanley examines the effects of unions on merit systems and public sector management in general. Mustafa describes the ways in which management has adapted to negotiations and bilateral decision making.

The final group of articles focuses on neutral agencies that administer public sector bargaining. These agencies lay the ground rules, interpret statutes, and take other steps to insure that the parties are adhering to their obligation to bargain. All three articles were written expressly for this volume by three outstanding neutrals in the field. Slavney, chairman of the Wisconsin Employment Relations Board (WERB), describes the activities of the WERB which regulates labor relations for both private and public sector employees. Helsby, chairman of the New York State Public Employment Relations Board (PERB), focuses on PERB's activities in administering the Taylor Law which applies only to public employees. Finally, Anderson, chairman of the Office of Collective Bargaining (OCB) in New York City, describes the operations of the OCB which is a tripartite board.

THE AMERICAN FEDERATION OF GOVERNMENT EMPLOYEES: FASTEST GROWING UNION IN THE UNITED STATES

John F. Griner

Which is the fastest growing union in the United States? The American Federation of Government Employees (AFGE). This is not merely a catchy introduction or a propaganda device; the claim is supported by solid evidence.

MEMBERSHIP AND ORGANIZING

In November 1969, the Bureau of Labor Statistics released a comparative study of union growth patterns for 1966-68. The study reveals that AFGE's 47.4 percent growth during those two years was nearly twice the average 24.7 percent rise for other public sector unions, and nine times the average 5.4 percent growth for all unions. Our closest competitor in this growth race was the American Federation of Teachers, and they were a distant second, recording a 32 percent rise.

AFGE's growth in absolute membership numbers has been equally impressive. In 1962, when I was first elected national president, AFGE had 83,767 members. Less than eight years later our dues-paying membership had quadrupled to three hundred twenty-five thousand. And even these figures understate our growth in relation to other unions.

AFGE is the only growth union that operates in a "right-to-work" context for its entire jurisdiction. None of the other contenders for the growth title—whether in private industry or the public sector—has that calamity to suffer, every day, everywhere.

A truer picture of relative numerical strengths can be gained by looking at employee representation rights. In November 1969, according to a U.S. Civil Service Commission survey, AFGE represented some four hundred eighty-two thousand federal employees for collective bargaining purposes.

AFGE has successfully recruited members in every job category. Carpenters, astrophysicists, janitors, secretaries, welders, nurses, electronic technicians, accountants, plumbers, economists, truck drivers, customs inspectors, laundry workers, and engineers mingle easily in AFGE. Likewise doctors, lawyers, and hopper dredgers! While we do not have a detailed occupational breakdown of AFGE's membership, our organizing efforts have met with some success across the board in all job categories.

John Griner is President, American Federation of Government Employees. Article prepared specifically for this volume.

White-collar employees are traditionally more difficult to organize than blue-collar workers, yet 55 percent of the employees represented by AFGE are in the General Schedule (GS) category, the federal pay system for white-collar workers.

Furthermore, AFGE has organized white-collar workers successfully both in mixed units with blue-collar workers and in separate, all-GS units. For instance, Tinker Air Force Base, Oklahoma City, Oklahoma, Local 916, represents eleven thousand Wage Grade and ten thousand GS employees in one unit. They have negotiated one contract covering all twenty-one thousand employees. On the other hand, the Social Security Administration, Baltimore, Maryland, Local 1923, represents some fourteen thousand GS employees in an all white-collar unit. Both methods have proven successful.

While AFGE has been successful in white-collar organizing, we realize there is a long road to travel before the federal white-collar worker is *really* organized. The Civil Service Commission study revealed that only 27 percent of all GS employees are covered by union exclusive recognition. AFGE aims to intensify its efforts; our staff and literature will be oriented more toward white-collar recruitment. And although stereotypes of unions are as fierce among the federal sector white-collar employees as they are in private industry, we have already proven that a union can shear through these prejudices. We are confident that AFGE will continue and in fact increase its successful GS organizing pace.

BARGAINING FRAMEWORK

AFGE's growth rate is all the more remarkable considering our unique collective bargaining problems. Congressional legislation directly sets wages, hours, and fringe benefits for the 1.3 million GS employees. It also directly determines the fringe benefits for the eight hundred thousand WG employees. Since we cannot sit down at the negotiating table, we must use a more indirect lobbying approach to achieve employee benefits. The results of our union effort are not as easy to see as a one-to-one relationship of bargaining and benefits; hence the union has often not been given credit where credit was due.

Until 1970 bargaining over working conditions was severely hampered. Management had unilateral veto rights. Thus an agency review team could reject an agreement mutually arrived at and mutually satisfactory to local management and union, and they could do it even if the agreement was within agency regulations and legal statute. AFGE suffered this barb many times during the 1960s. Each time the members' perseverance was strained to the limit.

Consider the following example. At Warner Robins Air Force Base, Macon, Georgia, Local 987 negotiated a contract in 1967 covering some fifteen thousand employees. The negotiations spanned six months, since in this first contract the language needed careful drafting and negotiating. Finally an agreement was reached, mutually acceptable to the base management and local union. It fell within the confines of agency regulation. It did not violate any legal statute. But the agreement had to be approved at the agency level. It wasn't. Some official disagreed with language in a minor clause; his individual veto kicked the whole agreement back down to Warner Robins. Everybody had to return to the negotiating table, to get language that would be agreeable to someone who would never have to work by these rules. A total of eighteen months elapsed before the fifteen thousand employees could gain the benefits of a collective bargaining agreement from the union they had voted to represent them.

Nor is Warner Robins a unique case. Other AFGE locals waited even longer—as long as three years in one case—before getting their contracts approved.

On top of this, during the last decade we could not appeal to outside sources—to binding arbitration—if there was an impasse or differing interpretations of contract language.

REASONS FOR MEMBERSHIP GROWTH

Why, then, did hundreds of thousands of employees voluntarily join a union? And why AFGE?

Until 1962 agency management set personnel policies unilaterally, building up a long history of favoritism and employee disgruntlement. When President John F. Kennedy issued Executive Order 10988, establishing union recognition and collective bargaining in the federal sector, the employees saw a means to lift themselves toward equality and justice. No matter that the collective bargaining rights were modified, truncated, almost emasculated. EO 10988 was the federal employees' Magna Charta. The workers saw their opportunity. They grasped it. They joined the union in droves.

Incidentally, a similar pattern had also occurred in the industrial sector, too. The first General Motors contract with the United Automobile Workers was one sentence, recognizing the UAW's mere existence. And the union grew a millionfold.

Perhaps equally important for federal workers was the strongly worded warning in EO 10988 to all management personnel that antiunion behavior and reprisal tactics were strictly taboo. It lifted slightly the tight curtain of fear that had long netted union organizing drives.

In addition, unions now had access to employees at the worksite—though only on off-duty hours. Union representatives could use bulletin boards, hand out leaflets, talk directly to employees. The union was accepted and acceptable, an especially important ingredient for success among federal employees.

But why was AFGE the overwhelming choice?

After all, numerous other unions had a toehold in the federal sector. The Metal Trades Department of the AFL–CIO had long organized the naval shipyards. The unaffiliated National Federation of Federal Employees (NFFE) had been around since 1912 and was as large as AFGE in 1962. AFGE was a relative baby, founded by the AFL in 1932, when NFFE disaffiliated from the organized labor movement.

However, five hundred members in twelve NFFE locals would not buy disaffiliation from the AFL. They constituted the initial ranks of AFGE. For the next twenty years growth was consistent—steady but slow. Membership rose to 25,356 in 1938, 35,276 in 1946, 51,606 in 1954, and 83,767 in 1962.

Without collective bargaining rights or real local union recognition, AFGE's recruiting strength rested heavily on its legislative skills. By 1961 the union had developed an effective legislative program. It was known on Capitol Hill, but in the field the "union" image was lowkeyed and muted.

Then President Kennedy issued Executive Order 10988. In short order AFGE outstripped all the others. By 1966 AFGE had more members, represented more employees, and negotiated more contracts than all the other competitors put together. By 1970 AFGE was the largest union in the entire federal sector, including the postal unions.

NFFE had two strikes against it. First, it was heavily dominated by management personnel and initially took court action in an effort to nullify EO 10988. Second, there was the matter of AFL–CIO affiliation. AFGE argued that AFL–CIO strength and bargaining skills could greatly help federal employees. The arguments were telling. NFFE dropped out of serious contention, and in 1970 represented only fifty-eight thousand employees compared to the four hundred eighty-two thousand represented by AFGE.

The Metal Trades Department, AFL–CIO, did not suffer the same disadvantages. But it was concentrated in the naval shipyards, while the federal workforce sprawled into hundreds and thousands of other categories.

In 1962 AFGE's immature development was an asset. Our 917 locals were scattered throughout the service; they were really skeleton organizations.

UNION ORGANIZATION AND OPERATIONS

In fact the whole union was a skeleton. The field staff—fifteen national representatives, each assigned multistate territories—hardly had enough time to visit locals, let alone give detailed assistance to them. The National Office had only eleven professional employees (including the national president and secretary-treasurer!) and seven secretaries. Not a very large staff for seventy-five thousand members. And certainly inadequate to organize the hundreds of thousands who were clammering for union recognition.

But AFGE did have dedicated leadership. Its fifteen national vice presidents were full-time government employees, who met quarterly to set federation policy and returned the next day to their federal jobs. Evenings, weekends, and every annual leave day was spent pursuing union matters, representing employees' problems, organizing. In those hectic days none of us could afford to spend even a spare minute with our families. The staff spent many an evening at the National Office, pitching in to get out a mailing—and I am including the national president, too!

Likewise AFGE local union leaders. Their "spare" time—that is, every minute off the job—went to the union. It is no exaggeration. We had no other recourse. We were busy building our union.

By 1970 AFGE staff numbered 269. AFGE's field staff had increased to 153. Specialists in handling employee problems, negotiating contracts, organizing locals, and performing all the other tasks that go into servicing union members. All national vice presidents are now full-time union officials, who serve as the administrative officers of their respective districts. The National Office is now staffed with 116 full-time employees, available to assist locals and members whose problems require agency-level attention, available to perform a myriad of other services of national import.

We have education, research, public relations, staff counsel, insurance and organizing departments which generally follow traditional union patterns of operation. But in addition we have created special departments—contract negotiations, wage systems, labor-management relations, fair practices—that deal with some of the specialized federal sector problems.

In fact, the special personnel structure in the federal sector increased the normal union servicing load found at the national level. In the dawn of federal collective bargaining, during the 1960s, regulations and agency channels still set the course of much union representation. So our Labor-Management Relations Department was comprised of sixteen specialists. Their task: to process more than two thousand cases monthly, including grievance appeals, discharge cases, reduction in force appeals, and compensation claims. All were proscribed by rigid and complicated systems set into the federal personnel code.

But now, as we move further into the era of collective bargaining, undoubtedly this process will be modified. Union representation will be governed more and more by union contract language.

In any case AFGE is a union that has come of age.

The effect of union recognition and collective bargaining is especially evident at the local level. One of the keys to a strong local union is the development of a strong steward system. Most AFGE negotiated agreements spell out an allotment of stewards, as well as their rights to handle union business on government time. Thereby the steward's status is enhanced at the shop level. The local structure, in turn, is strengthened.

After a contract was negotiated, it was delivered to all employees. Each time the AFGE local showed a spurt forward in membership, increased participation, a strengthening of the entire union structure.

Nothing is simple in the federal government. So it would be an oversimplification to give sole credit to collective bargaining for the molding of AFGE's structure and its staff recruitment and training.

Of necessity legislation played an important role in our union's development. Mobilizing rallies, letter-writing campaigns, and the like have motivated many of our local leaders and have set a course for much of our National Office work.

Then, as another example, we can cite the pay-fixing process for some eight hundred thousand blue-collar workers. In 1968 the Civil Service Commission introduced a new coordinated wage grade system, allowing for union participation in the wage-fixing process. As the largest union of federal employees, AFGE was chosen to serve on 86 of 147 area wage survey committees, on all agencywide committees, and on the National Wage Policy Committee.

As usual, the system was weighted in favor of management—they always have one more vote than the union—but it was the first time the employees had a say in determining their wage rates. We decided to make an effort to make the system work, to gain equity for the wage-grade employees.

However, the wage grade system revolves around the determination of equal pay for like jobs in private industry in a specified local geographical area. It is an extremely complicated system that requires extensive training of union staff and committeemen. So another process helped strengthen the AFGE structure. One could also interpret this system as another peculiar modification of the collective bargaining process.

UNION PROBLEMS

Interestingly enough, all this activity—the growth and pattern of AFGE's development—took place in the absence of any strikes or strike movements. In fact, AFGE has always had set into its national constitution a no-strike clause. That constitutional bar was challenged at the 1968 National Convention, and a motion to delete it was beaten back soundly by a 2-1 margin.

Nevertheless, discontent among federal employees is increasing. It has resulted already in the postal strike and the crisis is far from over. In fact, massive discontent is bound to occur within the union as well as the workplace, unless some means of gaining a full measure of justice is opened to federal employees.

If this justice is to be achieved, collective bargaining by law must be high on the list of priorities, and the bargaining must be over wages as well as working conditions. Full legal guarantees are a precondition for the next step forward if that step is to be peaceful and orderly.

The membership of AFGE comes from a workforce with little previous union exposure or organizational experience. We are therefore constantly faced with an incipient local leadership crisis. Expertise can be gained, as it usually is, on the firing line, but we are trying to augment this traumatic learning process with a great emphasis on our educational programs.

AFGE holds weeklong Leadership Training Institutes, weekend training courses, one-day programs, and evening seminars. Everywhere and at every opportunity we try to provide our people with the tools they need to build their union strong. Subjects include union administration, grievance handling, collective bargaining techniques, wage system analysis, and communications, as well as broader social issues. Our education program instills and refurbishes an organizing spirit among the student/leader delegates, a spirit they carry back to the worksite.

Dedication and solid training will carry forth our AFGE motto: "To do all that which none can do for himself." We aim AFGE to be a union that will be heard from for long years to come.

AMERICAN FEDERATION OF STATE, COUNTY AND MUNICIPAL EMPLOYEES

Jerry Wurf

Mary L. Hennessy

The American Federation of State, County and Municipal Employees (AFSCME) was founded in the depths of the depression by some thirty independent local unions of state and city employees scattered around the country.

Jerry Wurf and Mary L. Hennessy are President and Assistant Director of Research, respectively, American Federation of State, County and Municipal Employees. Article prepared specifically for this volume.

These government workers organized primarily for job security—and in the thirties civil service was an all-important issue to them. In 1935 the locals merged briefly with the American Federation of Government Employees, but because their problems differed from those of federal employees a split occurred the following year. AFSCME was chartered as an international union by the AFL on October 8, 1936. Arnold S. Zander, founder of the union, served as president until 1964.

THE FORMATIVE YEARS

In its formative years, AFSCME saw itself as part of the movement to reform government and to work for enactment of civil service laws. The spoils system was the order of the day. In 1936 there were genuine merit systems in only eleven states. The union saw civil service as the sole means of ending political kickbacks and protecting members who might be fired because of political turnover.

This stress on civil service rather than on collective bargaining was logical according to the standards of the time. Unionism in America was just beginning to come of age, and implementation of workers' rights through labor legislation was still struggling for acceptance.

Labor leaders, let alone the general public, did not then recognize any rights of public employees beyond the citizen's right to petition government. The conventional wisdom rejected collective bargaining for the public sector.

During this period AFSCME viewed civil service protection and lobbying as the most viable methods of improving wages and working conditions. Outlined in its early constitution were these primary objectives: the promotion of employee welfare, efficiency in government, and the extension of merit systems. But as the years passed there began a development—parallel with the emphasis on civil service—which aimed at establishing a system of collective bargaining. A significant early step in this direction was made when an AFSCME local negotiated a labor agreement with the city of Philadelphia in 1939. The Philadelphia contract, unfortunately, was almost unique.

AFSCME had 9,737 members when it was chartered in 1936. By 1940 the average annual membership had risen to 29,087. As the union grew, councils were formed to represent groups of locals in the same city, county, or state. The councils provided services which individual locals could not perform.

Despite the war and employer opposition, AFSCME made gains in membership during the forties. It began to recognize that civil service alone was inadequate to achieve the union's objectives. However, the union had not yet resolved its policy on the relationship between bargaining and civil service.

DECADE OF FERMENT

In 1950 membership stood at 83,697, but AFSCME's activities still differed little from previous years. The union concentrated on expansion of membership. In the early fifties, although the international assigned some emphasis to recognition, signed agreements, grievance procedures, and checkoff, its orientation was still civil service. Some locals and councils, however, sought de facto bargaining through informal arrangements because they had small hope of securing enabling legislation.

Two events of importance to the organization took place in the mid-1950s. After the AFL and CIO merger, AFSCME became the first union to join with another under the AFL—CIO banner. A merger between the Government and Civic Employees Organizing Committee, CIO, and AFSCME took place in 1956. The next year AFSCME headquarters were transferred from Madison, Wisconsin, to Washington, D.C.

In the late 1950s, the thinking of a number of AFSCME leaders moved toward endorsement of labor relations practices similar to those in industry. These men were encouraged by promulgation in 1958 of Mayor Robert E. Wagner's Executive Order 49 granting recognition to organizations of New York City employees. EO 49 was obtained largely through the efforts of AFSCME District Council 37, with little assistance from the organized labor movement. The Wagner order, together with a strengthened program in Philadelphia, meant that two major U.S. cities backed the collective bargaining principle for their employees.

During this same period the issue of internal democracy gave rise to a struggle within the international. The insurgents called for new procedures to elect the International Executive Board and for voting strength of convention delegates based on number of members represented. Jerry Wurf led the insurgent group which included Joseph Ames, Victor Gotbaum, Robert Hastings, Thomas Morgan, and Normal Schut. This group felt the time had come to push militantly for collective bargaining. It criticized the international for not preparing the locals and their staffs for this course of action. Wurf and the others regarded civil service as a management-dominated personnel system which could not substitute for bilateral negotiations.

THE 1960s—PERIOD OF CHANGE

The internal struggle on union democracy boiled over at the 1960 convention. AFSCME had 182,504 members by then. The convention floor fights revolved around a per capita tax increase, proportionate representation of members at conventions, and the method of selecting international vice presidents. However, the underlying issue was the relationship between the international and its locals and councils. Without debate, the words "collective bargaining" were inserted in the constitution for the first time. Attainment of union objectives was to be sought through several methods, including "collective bargaining resulting in working agreements and contracts."

The struggle continued through the 1962 and 1964 conventions. At the 1964 convention Jerry Wurf was elected president and his slate won a large majority on the Executive Board.

At a subsequent constitutional convention in 1965, the 1960 phrase on attainment of objectives through bargaining was deleted and the following objective substituted: "To promote the welfare of the membership and to provide a voice in the determination of the terms and conditions of employment. *We are committed* to the process of collective bargaining as the most desirable, democratic and effective method to achieve this. Both as union members and as citizens, we shall also employ available legislative and political action."

CHANGES IN PUBLIC OPINION

The 1960s were years of change in philosophy for many academicians, law-makers and public managers. They began to see the pressure of public employee unions for bargaining as both desirable and socially constructive. The general public, which for many years considered government employment as a secure, desirable sinecure, now began to realize that salaries and fringe benefits lagged behind those in the industrial sector. The public began to entertain the notion that public employees had the right to organize and bargain. The change in thinking and philosophy was greatly influenced by President John F. Kennedy's Executive Order 10988. While the order was limited to bargaining by federal employees, it neverthe-less had a tremendous impact on state and local government bargaining relation-ships. The Kennedy order, incidentally, was largely drawn from Mayor Wagner's order.

In the response to the thrust for collective bargaining, some state legislatures and city councils enacted laws authorizing or mandating bargaining for government workers. AFSCME sought legislation as a basic step, but it also urged and was successful in getting collective bargaining in the absence of legislation.

Organized government workers demanded recognition for bargaining on mean-ingful issues and rejected the old pattern of "collective begging." As in the private sector, they wanted to participate in the determination of their wages, hours, and other conditions of employment. AFSCME locals were in the forefront of this crusade for dignity and recognition. In some cases, if recognition was not granted, they struck.

The most publicized strike was that of the Memphis garbage collectors in 1968. The entire American labor movement supported the thirteen hundred predomi-nantly black workers in their nine-week strike. Not until the assassination of Dr. Martin Luther King, Jr., did Mayor Henry Loeb capitulate to nationwide pressure and accord recognition to AFSCME Local 1733.

NEW AFSCME POLICY STATEMENTS

A no-strike provision has never appeared in the AFSCME constitution. The only exception is the absolute prohibition on use of the strike weapon by police and other law enforcement officers. AFSCME leadership recognizes the gravity of government strikes, but it has always fully supported locals that strike. The majority of strikes in recent years have been to win recognition and bargaining.

In 1966 the union's Executive Board issued a policy statement affirming the right of public employees (except law enforcement officers) to strike. The board added that AFSCME locals are completely autonomous in making a decision to strike or to end a strike. This policy statement was later endorsed by the member-ship at the 1968 convention.

In addition to affirming its members' right to·bargain collectively and to strike, AFSCME has made other important policy decisions since 1964. Its Executive Board called for enactment of bargaining laws covering public employees where none exist, strengthening of existing statutes as to coverage and scope of bargaining, and establishment of truly impartial tripartite boards for administering the law and for resolving impasses. The board urged that federal standards for collective bargaining, as then provided by federal Executive Order 10988, be included in grants-in-aid programs to states and municipalities. The board also rejected the concept of compulsory arbitration to resolve bargaining disputes.

CASE FOR FEDERAL LEGISLATION

In 1969 AFSCME made the decision to seek federal legislation providing collective bargaining for public employees. This decision came only because of complete frustration at the state level. For years the union avoided seeking federal laws in the hope that the state and local governments would fulfill their duty toward their own employees. Unfortunately, decent collective bargaining laws for public employees are infrequent in the U.S. Moreover, there has been a rash of repressive state statutes such as the New York Taylor Act and South Dakota legislation.

The proposed federal legislation would provide minimum standards. Any state would be permitted to adopt legislation at least substantially equivalent to the federal law, in which case the state law would apply. This proposal was a drastic step for AFSCME to take, and the union took it only because it no longer expected many state and local governments to set up reasonable and responsible labor relations programs.

COMPOSITION OF MEMBERSHIP

In 1964 AFSCME had 234,840 members. By early 1970 it had almost doubled in size, and it now nears the half-million mark. One of the fastest growing unions in the AFL–CIO, its membership continues to expand at a constantly accelerating rate.

As of the beginning of the seventies, AFSCME has 1,900 locals in almost every state in the union, the District of Columbia, Puerto Rico, and Panama.

Its heaviest membership lies in New York, Michigan, Wisconsin, Ohio, and Massachusetts.

The table on page 65 illustrates jurisdiction and occupational composition of the organization.

Although AFSCME has professional, clerical, and technical employees, the blue-collar workers predominate by two to one. Most locals are organized on the vertical or industrial union concept although some craft locals exist. The use of district councils as bargaining representatives has also encouraged the industrial union approach.

INTERNAL STRUCTURE

The union's internal structure resembles that of other internationals. Its supreme governing body is the biennial international convention. The convention consists of delegates from affiliated local unions, with each local represented in direct proportion to its dues-paying membership.

Type of Employer	Percent
State	28
County	10
Municipal	47
School District	6
University and College	4
Special Authority	2
Private and Nonprofit	3

By Job Category	Percent
Medical Institution Attendants	15
Domestic and Custodial	10
Food Service	7
Trades and Labor	15
Public Works	10
Police, Correctional, Detention, Park, Recreation, Conservation	8
Clerical and Allied	16
Supervisory and Inspection	5
Professional	8
Other	6

The International Executive Board is the legislative and policymaking body of the union. Subject to constitutional limitations, it has full power to act for the union during the period between conventions. The board enacts policy and acts in a watchdog capacity. The board is comprised of the president, the secretary-treasurer, and seventeen vice presidents. One vice president is elected from each of the seventeen legislative districts. The legislative districts are established geographically on the basis of membership.

Administration of AFSCME affairs and policy is entrusted to the president. The president, with the approval of the board, appoints the salaried staff of the union and directs its work. The secretary-treasurer is the other elected officer of the international; he handles financial, recording, and other administrative duties.

The departments of the international are built around the needs of members. At its headquarters are the following departments: Legal, Organization, Education, Research, Legislation and Community Affairs, Career Development, and Publications and Public Relations.

Spreading out from headquarters is the field organization. There are fifteen regional areas, each headed by an area director. Working under the area directors are field representatives who organize new locals and assist existing locals. The international is readying plans to staff its area offices with education, legislation, and publications personnel to help locals and councils.

STAFF TRAINING

The professional staffs of the international, the district councils, and the larger local unions now number over five hundred. This number continues to grow as AFSCME membership expands.

Working for any union requires an assortment of skills. But working for a public sector union requires even more. The staffs must be familiar with a bewildering variety of laws, ordinances, rules, and prohibitions regulating government relations. These legal requirements vary not only from state to state, but from jurisdiction to jurisdiction within a state. In addition, the structures of public agencies themselves vary. Since bargaining is relatively new in the public sector, the staffs must frequently cope with inexpert antagonists representing management. Its own members must be educated in labor relations concepts and techniques.

Like other unions, AFSCME runs training programs for local union officers and stewards. But AFSCME has two additional programs. One is the Staff Education Program for professional staffs of the international and the councils. This intensive six-day program is conducted about eight times a year at the University of Maryland. Special emphasis is placed on collective bargaining, with other time devoted to organizing, the impact of laws and lack of laws on public employee unionism, problems of the inner city, and profiles of government employment and public sector unionism.

The international also conducts a Staff Intern Program to educate future leaders. The interns, all AFSCME members, come from many locations and from many types of public employment. A number hold local or council officer positions. After three weeks of intensive classwork, the trainees are sent into the field for two months where they learn specific techniques of organizing and service. The goal of the program—to train AFSCME members as staff organizers—appears to have been achieved.

THE FUTURE

State and local government employment has virtually tripled in the postwar period. Today one out of every seven American workers is employed by a state or local government. All expectations are that the growth will continue.

AFSCME will be part of this growth.

THE AMERICAN FEDERATION OF TEACHERS AND THE NATIONAL EDUCATION ASSOCIATION

Michael H. Moskow

Two national organizations represent teachers in the United States: the National Education Association (NEA) and the American Federation of Teachers (AFT).

Michael Moskow is Associate Professor of Economics, Temple University. Parts of this article are reprinted from *Collective Bargaining in Public Employment,* Random House, 1970.

NATIONAL EDUCATION ASSOCIATION

The structure of the National Education Association and its affiliates is quite different from labor unions in the United States. The NEA is a national organization which enrolls members directly from school districts and other educational agencies. State and local education associations enroll their members and collect dues separately, and these associations affiliate with NEA by paying an annual $5 fee. The national organization does not actively charter locals, as do most labor unions.

Only 67 percent of the members of state associations have joined NEA. The percentages vary widely among states: 100 percent of the state association members in nine states and less than 30 percent in three states. Recently, NEA has encouraged unified membership by decreeing that a person cannot join only one of the local, state, or national organizations but must join all three. In 1968, nine states had unified membership.

The loose structure of NEA has important implications for its activities in collective bargaining. The NEA cannot exercise strong control over the activities of its state and local affiliates. It can only provide assistance when requested, and state and local affiliates can act independently, even contrary to the policy or advice, of the national organization.

The national organization has more than one million members consisting of "classroom teachers, school administrators, and specialists in schools, colleges, and educational agencies which are both public and private." Classroom teachers in public schools constitute over 85 percent of the total membership. One of the major beliefs of NEA, however, is that since education is a profession unique unto itself, membership in associations should not be limited to classroom teachers. Most state and local affiliates therefore accept both teachers and administrators as members. In fact, several state associations will not accept local affiliates unless they are open to both classroom teachers and administrators. According to the NEA *Handbook:*

> The NEA is an independent, voluntary nongovernmental organization available to all professional teachers. It believes that all educators, regardless of position, rank, or authority, are workers in a common cause. It cooperates with all groups in American life who seek to improve education. It works for better schools and, to further that end, for the improvement of the professional status of teachers. Under such policies, the National Education Association has become the largest professional organization in the world and the only overall professional association for teachers in the United States.

The NEA has thirty-four departments, twenty-five commissions and committees, eighteen headquarters divisions, and a staff of over nine hundred. Its research division is staffed by twenty professional and administrative personnel and about thirty-five skilled clerical, secretarial, and statistical workers. It has a state-level affiliate in each of the fifty states and a local affiliate in over 8,000 school districts.

The thirty-four departments reflect the diversity of the activities of NEA. The largest department is that of classroom teachers, which includes approximately 800,000 teachers in elementary and secondary schools. Until 1969 school administrators were members of departments such as the American Association of School Administrators (AASA), the National Association of Secondary School Principals (NASSP), and the Department of Elementary School Principals (DESP).

In June 1969, the superintendent group and the secondary-school-principal group severed their ties as departments and became "Associate Organizations" within the NEA framework. In this category they operate as highly autonomous organizations, and neither their officers nor their members are required to become members of NEA.

The state education associations with almost 1.6 million members, representing 89 percent of the instructional staff, have had a substantial impact on education in the United States. Dayton D. McKean documented the power of the New Jersey teachers' lobby in the 1930s; Virgil Blanke found that chief state school officers perceived education interest groups (the state NEAS were prominent in these groups) as having about average influence with legislators. According to Campbell:

> Each legislative session in each state finds state association lobbyists working feverishly for passage of teacher welfare bills. Elaborate mechanisms for enlisting grass roots support for all kinds of educational legislation have been perfected. Local associations and individual members are kept well informed on activities of legislatures and legislators. Score cards and progress charts are maintained and success is measured in terms of bills passed or defeated.

On the other hand, until recently local education associations were usually weak organizations. Although the number of full-time staff members working for local associations has increased rapidly in recent years, less than one hundred local associations have paid staff. In 1960, Myron Lieberman described the local associations as typically engaging "in futile efforts to improve their conditions of employment. Other than this, they give teas for new teachers in the Spring, and perhaps listen to a few travelogues in between."

AMERICAN FEDERATION OF TEACHERS

The American Federation of Teachers, affiliated with AFL–CIO, was formed in 1919. The stated objectives of AFT are:

1. To bring associations of teachers into relations of mutual assistance and cooperation.
2. To obtain for them all the rights to which they are entitled.
3. To raise the standards of the teaching profession by securing the conditions essential to the best professional service.
4. To promote such a democratization of the schools as will enable them better to equip their pupils to take places in the industrial, social, and political life of the community.
5. To promote the welfare of the children of the nation by providing progressively better educational opportunity for all.

With approximately 450 local affiliates, AFT has approximately 140,000 members, most of whom are concentrated in large cities. The AFT permits each local to decide whether it will accept principals as members; its constitution excludes school superintendents from membership. Separate locals for administrators are now prohibited; prior to 1966 they were permitted only if the local AFT affiliate approved. The AFT constantly emphasizes that it is the only organization specifically devoted to the interests of the classroom teacher.

Although NEA and AFT have been in competition since 1919, the struggle gained new impetus in December 1961, when the United Federation of Teachers, a local affiliate of AFT, was elected bargaining agent for 44,000 New York City public school teachers. The UFT received nearly three times as many votes as NEA's hastily formed contender, the Teachers Bargaining Organization. More important though was the fact that for the first time the labor movement gave active support, in the form of personnel and financial resources, to a local of AFT. If AFT could run a successful nationwide membership drive, the image of unions in the eyes of other white-collar and professional workers would be greatly improved. For this reason UFT received more aid than any other union local had so far received in a collective bargaining election. Shortly after the victory, AFT joined the Industrial Union Department of AFL–CIO, which had been the major contributor to UFT.

After its overwhelming victory, UFT immediately began negotiating with the school board. When negotiations broke down in April 1962, UFT called a strike and over 20,000 teachers refused to work. The work stoppage lasted only one day, however, and after the mayor of the city and the governor of the state became involved, a salary agreement was reached. By the end of August, the parties had negotiated a forty-page written agreement, which was surpassed in its detailed provisions only by later agreements reached between the same parties.

CHANGES IN NEA POLICY

While UFT was negotiating its written agreement in the summer of 1962, NEA was holding its annual convention in Denver. Dr. William Carr, executive secretary of NEA, entitled his address "The Turning Point," which aptly describes the dramatic changes that took place in NEA's policy toward collective negotiations at this convention.

In earlier years, NEA had occasionally discussed the necessity for group action by teachers, but it had no organized program and issued no guidelines or directives for implementation. At the 1962 convention NEA official policy on negotiations was formulated. NEA passed a resolution emphasizing the need for "professional negotiation," thus ending its search for a suitable substitute for the term "collective bargaining." In earlier years, other terms suggested included "cooperative determination," "collective determination," and even "democratic persuasion."

Another 1962 convention resolution of particular significance is resolution 19 entitled "Professional Sanctions":

> The National Education Association believes that, as a means of preventing unethical or arbitrary policies or practices that have a deleterious effect on the welfare of the schools, professional sanctions

should be invoked. These sanctions would provide for appropriate disciplinary action by the organized profession.

The National Education Association calls upon its affiliated state associations to cooperate in developing guidelines which would define, organize, and definitely specify procedural steps for invoking sanctions by the teaching profession.

This resolution, which was introduced from the floor of the convention instead of by the resolution committee, marks the beginning of the official adoption of a pressure tactic by NEA.

The main significance of Carr's speech to the 1962 convention was that it set the stage for the battle between AFT and NEA. Carr identified unionization as a major crisis in education, and he outlined the policy NEA would follow to meet the challenge from the labor movement. "This . . . is the first time in which forces of significant scope and power are considering measures which could destroy the Association."

At the February 18, 1962, meeting of the NEA board of directors, less than two months after the UFT victory in New York City, a motion was passed urging each state affiliate to hold regional conferences to ". . . explain *why* professional organizations should exist on an independent basis, with professional responsibility and autonomy." More extensive conferences dealing with the same topic were urged in cities with populations over 100,000. State affiliates were also urged to secure passage of state legislation implementing NEA policy on professional negotiations.

At the convention itself, Carr explained that the urban project would be formed to meet the needs of large city teachers and to direct the NEA fight against unionization of teachers. The urban project budget was set at $203,900 for fiscal year 1962-1963. In fiscal year 1964-1965 the urban project cost $884,663, including $437,990 which had been ". . . spent from the Reserve for Future Emergencies as authorized by the Board of Directors." By 1968, the urban project had been elevated to the divisional level in NEA, with a budget of over $1 million out of a total NEA budget of almost $10 million.

Initially, "professional negotiation" was a generic term used by NEA for a wide variety of different relationships between school boards and local teacher associations. For example, a local affiliate is considered to have a level=I professional negotiation agreement if the school board has made a written statement (which may be included in the minutes of the board meeting) that it recognizes the association as the representative of all teachers in the district or even merely as the representative of its own members. Level-II agreements consist of recognition and establishment of a negotiations procedure. If a means for settling impasses is added, the agreement is considered level-III. When an impasse arises, it provides for various forms of third-party intervention, most of which consist of modified forms of mediation and fact-finding. Level-III agreements rarely provide for the utilization of state labor relations agencies or state mediation agencies, because, NEA believes disputes should always be settled through "educational channels." In extreme cases or when agreement cannot be reached, NEA will resort to sanctions, ranging from publicizing unfavorable teaching conditions in a particular school district to a mass refusal to sign contracts by all teachers employed in the district. At its 1967 convention, NEA took an even more militant stand by voting to support local affiliates who had gone on strike. Level-IV agreements include terms and conditions of employment.

Since 1962, NEA policy on professional negotiations has gradually become firmly established. The association favors exclusive recognition whereby one organization represents all staff members in the district and negotiating units which include both teachers and administrators, although decisions on negotiating units are a matter for local option. The NEA now favors written agreements that include terms and conditions of employment, a grievance procedure with binding arbitration as the terminal point, and a termination date to the agreement.

Clearly, NEA and its affiliates have changed drastically. Statewide and local sanctions and strikes have been used on numerous occasions. Local associations have called strikes or "professional holidays" when agreement on employment conditions has not been reached. At other times they have refused to lead extra curricular activities or have publicized "unprofessional" conditions in a district as a means of enforcing their demands. In brief, NEA and most of its state and local affiliates are now militant and determined organizations.

AFT POLICY ON COLLECTIVE BARGAINING

The AFT makes no effort to distinguish its approach to teacher-board relations from the collective bargaining carried on in private industry. Delegates to the 1963 national convention passed a resolution which recognized the right of locals to strike under certain circumstances and urged ". . . the AFL–CIO and affiliated international unions to support such strikes when they occur." This resolution constituted a change in AFT policy; in prior years, it had no official strike policy, even though it had supported locals when they had gone on strike.

Since 1935, AFT has advocated collective bargaining for teachers; before that time the union had encouraged teachers' councils and more teacher participation in policy-making. Evidence indicates that only after the UFT victory in 1961 did AFT actively begin to encourage its locals to strive for collective bargaining rights. For example, a survey conducted in 1947 showed that none of the forty-one AFT locals, whose members constituted the majority of teachers in their district, had ever engaged in collective bargaining. In answer to the question in the same survey "What further part does the local feel it should play in administration and policy formation?" only seven of 141 respondents answered "bargaining agents."

Until recently, AFT displayed no clear understanding of exactly what collective bargaining for teachers entails. In fact, the confusion over the AFT definition of collective bargaining was similar to that exhibited by NEA on professional negotiations. For example, although AFT claimed to have approximately twelve written agreements between school boards and teachers' unions in 1964, only four of them included terms and conditions of employment; the others were merely recognition agreements. Moreover, several agreements did not provide for exclusive recognition, and in two cases the school boards signed written agreements with both the NEA local and the AFT local.

The agreement negotiated by the United Federation of Teachers in New York City rapidly became the model for agreements negotiated later in other cities. By 1969, AFT locals had won representation rights for teachers in many of the large city school systems in the United States—Baltimore, Boston, Chicago, Cleveland, Philadelphia, Washington, D.C., and Wilmington. They had negotiated collective bargaining agreements covering approximately 10 percent of the classroom teachers in the United States. . . .

THE AFT AND NEA COMPARED

By early 1970 both the AFT and NEA had dramatically changed their policies and actions. In fact, the two organizations are now strikingly similar. Both are structured and function to benefit primarily the classroom teacher. The important leadership role and membership recruitment role of administrators in the NEA and its affiliates has in great part disappeared. There are still a few exceptions, but the trend to a "classroom teacher" orientation is unmistakably clear. Five state associations (Colorado, Florida, Michigan, Minnesota, Ohio) have already severed ties with state teacher organizations. In 1969 the American Association of School Administrators and the Department of Secondary School Principals severed ties as departments and became "associate organizations" within the NEA framework. As associate organizations they have a very loose affiliation with the NEA; in fact, their officers and members do not have to join the NEA. These developments have occurred both as a result of pressure from teachers and from school boards, who want superintendents to be "their" man in negotiations.

Another important similarity is that both organizations now have almost identical policies on collective negotiations—for example, exclusive recognition, scope of negotiations, and grievance procedures with arbitration as the terminal point. They both favor inclusion of the same types of clauses in collective agreements and they use the same tactics in negotiations. Since the NEA has dropped its opposition to teacher strikes, both now support local affiliates on strike and favor granting the legal right to strike to teachers. Some form of organizational security has also become a necessary part of negotiation because of the economic pressure on the organization designated as exclusive representative of all teachers in the negotiations unit. Local and state affiliates of the two organizations now favor the "agency shop" under which teachers would not have to join the organization but would be required to pay a service fee equal to dues and initiation fee if they do not join.

In terms of comparative strength, the NEA has clearly lost ground. In 1960 the NEA enrolled 49 percent of the classroom teachers in the United States; in 1969 they enrolled 47 percent. NEA state affiliates dropped from 93 percent to 81 percent during the same period while the AFT increased from 3.8 percent to 7.5 percent. The NEA was 12 times larger than the AFT in 1960, but it was only 6 times larger in 1969. Its state affiliates were 23 times larger in 1960, and only 10 times larger in 1969.

Finally, talk of merger is at an all-time high. Even more important than the rhetoric are the recent actions that have taken place. Local affiliates have already merged in Los Angeles, California, and Flint, Michigan, and the state organizations in Massachusetts are conducting exploratory discussions. Clearly, the national organizations are closer to merger today than ever before. Whether a national merger can be consummated, however, is still an open question.

THE AMERICAN CITY AND ITS ORGANIZED EMPLOYEES

Winston W. Crouch

Observers of the urban scene have frequently speculated whether a city's form of government affects policy outcomes in local political systems. This same speculation applies equally validly to the formation and conduct of such extraorganizational bodies as public employee associations and unions. The data presented in this study indicate there is a relationship between the form of government and the existence of representational bodies in the city work forces. How much this relationship may be influenced by other factors—such as the size of the city (or work force), geographic location, and political attitudes in individual local communities—cannot be determined entirely from these data.

When sources such as Table 1 are examined, other factors must be weighed as well. For example, a greater portion of the large, metropolitan central cities operate under a mayor-council form of government than under the council-manager or commission types. Furthermore, a majority of suburban and non-metropolitan cities have elected the council-manager system of government. In addition, the bulk of the localities in the 10,000-to-25,000 population category are council-manager cities that operate with relatively small work forces.

Two final observations must also be kept in mind. The western states—particularly those on the Pacific Coast—have adopted the council-manager plan extensively. Those states demonstrate a preference for nonaffiliated local associations. At the same time, 2 southern areas (West South-Central and South Atlantic) are also sections in which the council-manager plan has been widely accepted. But these are areas in which employee organizations exist in comparatively slight numbers.

Table 1 indicates that an aggregate category of "other" cities, commission, and town meeting types ranks highest in employee organizations, with the mayor-council and council-manager groups ranking well below. Mayor-directed cities appear to prefer national organizations (including unions), whereas the council-manager ones show some preference for local nonaffiliated groups.

Comparing the council-manager and mayor-council cities by use of the figures on membership affiliation held by various occupational groups, one notes an oft-repeated pattern. Employees of the largest portion of council-manager cities select local associations to represent them, whereas the employees of mayor-council

Winston Crouch is Professor of Political Science, University of California at Los Angeles. Reprinted from International City Managers' Association, *Urban Data Service,* I, No. 3, March 1969.

table 1 Extent of Municipal Employee Organizations

Distribution	Number of Cities Reporting (A)	Cities Without Organizations No.	% of (A)	Cities with Organizations No. (B)	% of (A)	Both Nationals and Locals No.	% of (B)	Nationals Only No.	% of (B)	Locals Only No.	% of (B)
Total, all cities	1.105	276	25	829	75	309	37	402	49	118	14
Population group											
Over 500,000	19	0	0	19	100	15	79	4	21	0	0
250,000-500,000	21	1	5	20	95	13	65	7	35	0	0
100,000-250,000	66	2	3	64	97	25	39	34	53	5	8
50,000-100,000	139	14	10	125	90	66	53	42	34	17	13
25,000- 50,000	256	48	19	208	81	84	40	95	46	29	14
10,000- 25,000	604	211	35	393	65	106	27	220	56	67	17
Geographic division											
New England	82	4	5	78	95	52	67	23	29	3	4
Mid-Atlantic	149	28	19	121	81	33	27	61	50	27	23
East North-Central	245	28	11	217	89	73	34	138	63	6	3
West North-Central	116	36	31	80	69	25	31	54	68	1	1
South Atlantic	129	68	53	61	47	16	26	40	66	5	8
East South-Central	26	6	23	20	77	8	40	12	60	0	0
West South-Central	99	51	52	48	48	13	27	32	67	3	6
Mountain	54	19	35	35	65	14	40	17	49	4	11
Pacific Coast	205	36	18	169	82	75	44	25	15	69	41
City type											
Central	182	15	8	167	92	88	53	77	46	2	1
Suburban	549	125	23	424	77	145	34	189	45	90	21
Independent	374	136	36	238	64	76	32	136	57	26	11
Form of government											
Mayor-council	324	64	20	260	80	95	37	143	55	22	8
Council-manager	736	206	28	530	72	196	37	241	45	93	18
Other*	45	6	13	39	87	18	46	18	46	3	8

*Includes 30 cities with commission government, 11 with town meeting, and 4 with representative town meeting.

municipalities choose either national associations (such as FOP) or nationally affiliated unions (IAFF or AFSCME).

Yet when the percentages of mayor-council communities that report employee organizations are compared with those for council-manager cities, the data show the 2 groups to be similar. The 1 important divergence, from this pattern is in the representation of police protection employees; 62% of the mayor-council cities report their police have joined organizations, whereas only 51% of the council-manager cities so report. Furthermore 27% of the council-manager cities having organizations deal with local associations of police, whereas the mayor-council communities report only 15% of their number doing so.

The most impressive figures comparing cities by their form of government . . . indicate that 74% of all employees in mayor-council municipalities are represented by unions or associations. On the other hand, council-manager cities rank lowest, with 42% of their employees being represented, a figure considerably below the average for all cities, 64%.

When the trend data are examined, however, it appears that the council-manager group is experiencing the greater rate of growth in number of members who are being organized by unions. Approximately 45% more council-manager cities report the presence of unions in 1969 than did so in 1967. During the same period, this group (council-manager cities) was the only one experiencing an increase in number of all-city employee associations. The third set of trend data indicates that council-manager municipalities are experiencing more work disruptions than are those operating with different forms of government.

REASONS FOR DIFFERENCES

Several factors besides population suggest tentative explanations for differences between cities having an elected mayor and those employing an appointed manager as chief executive or administrator. The mayor-council form of city government offers competition between 2 institutions, each of which may respond to constituents and group pressures in a number of ways. Moreover, political parties play active roles in the governmental life of a large portion of mayor-council communities. These bodies offer an additional access route by which groups may gain entry to the city's policy formulators. Finally, the tone of the governmental process in the mayor-council cities is definitely political, in the true sense of that term.

In constrast to this style of mayor-council government stands a different style associated with the council-manager form, although individual cities in both groups show many deviations from the basic pattern. The relationship between the council and the manager is characterized less by rivalry than by coordination. Since the council can dismiss a manager, the administrator's actions reflect council attitudes. Despite the fact that several council-manager cities elect councilmen on party tickets, the great majority of these councilmen are nonpartisan, and therefore the style of the political process is distinctive. Finally, the tone of governmental life in council-manager cities tends to emphasize analytical methods, problem-solving, and advance planning. It tends to be less political, in the broad sense.

Table 2 Local Laws and Policies Regarding Municipal Employee Organizations and Negotiations

Local Laws / Response	Cities Reporting No. (A)	% of (A)	Organized Cities No. (B)	% of (B)	Cities without Organizations No. (C)	% of (C)	Cities with Locals Only No. (D)	% of (D)	Cities with Nationals Only No. (E)	% of (E)	Cities with Mixture of Nationals, Locals No. (F)	% of (F)
Total	1,105	—	829	—	276	—	118	—	402	—	309	—
Permit general employees to join nationally affilated organizations												
No answer	12	1	8	1	4	1	1	1	5	1	2	1
Yes	363	33	331	40	32	12	33	28	138	34	160	52
No	20	2	11	1	9	3	2	2	7	2	2	1
No policy	710	64	479	58	231	84	82	69	252	63	145	47
Permit general employees to join local associates												
No answer	19	2	13	2	6	2	1	1	9	2	3	1
Yes	344	31	318	38	26	9	44	37	121	30	153	50
No	19	2	9	1	10	4	1	1	6	1	2	1
No policy	723	65	489	59	234	85	72	61	266	66	151	49
Forbid public safety personnel to join nationals												
No answer	27	2	19	2	8	3	3	3	9	2	7	2
Yes	49	4	35	4	14	5	8	7	12	3	15	5
No	343	31	317	38	26	9	27	23	147	37	143	46
No policy	686	62	458	55	228	83	80	68	234	58	144	47
Forbid public safety personnel to join locals												
No answer	26	2	18	2	8	3	4	3	12	3	2	1
Yes	335	30	315	38	20	7	45	38	119	30	151	49
No	25	2	11	1	14	5	2	2	6	1	3	1
No policy	719	65	485	59	234	85	67	57	265	66	153	50

Category	Response													
Authorize management to punish general employees for organization activity	No answer	24	2	18	2	6	2	2	1	1	12	3	5	1
	Yes	23	2	18	2	5	2	2	2	2	7	2	9	3
	No	380	34	339	41	41	15	33	28	28	139	35	167	54
	No policy	678	61	454	55	224	81	82	69	69	244	61	128	41
Authorize management to punish public safety employees for organization activity	No answer	35	3	26	3	9	3	5	4	4	14	3	7	2
	Yes	26	2	20	2	6	2	1	1	1	5	1	14	5
	No	380	34	341	41	39	14	35	30	30	148	37	158	5
	No policy	664	60	442	53	222	80	77	65	65	235	58	130	51
Permit recognizing unit representing majority of general employees	No answer	38	3	21	3	17	6	3	3	3	14	3	4	1
	Yes	220	20	205	25	15	5	28	24	21	84	21	93	30
	No	143	13	108	13	35	13	12	10	11	44	11	52	17
	No policy	704	64	495	60	209	76	75	64	65	260	65	160	52
Permit recognizing unit representing majority of public safety employees	No answer	65	6	41	5	24	9	6	5	5	20	5	15	5
	Yes	160	14	150	18	10	4	20	17	15	62	15	68	22
	No	159	14	128	15	31	11	11	9	14	55	14	62	20
	No policy	721	65	510	62	211	76	81	69	66	265	66	164	53
Authorize signing negotiated agreements	No answer	33	3	20	2	13	5	3	3	2	10	2	7	2
	Yes	242	22	229	28	13	5	21	18	25	99	25	109	35
	No	127	11	103	12	14	5	11	9	12	49	12	43	14
	No policy	703	64	477	58	—	—	83	70	61	244	61	150	49
Authorize arbitration of disputes—general employees	No answer	43	4	28	3	15	5	3	3	4	15	4	10	3
	Yes	212	19	194	23	18	6	19	16	19	76	19	99	32
	No	155	14	135	16	20	7	22	19	14	58	14	55	18
	No policy	695	63	472	57	223	81	74	63	63	253	63	145	47
Authorize arbitration of disputes—public safety employees	No answer	44	4	28	3	16	6	4	3	3	13	3	11	4
	Yes	207	19	188	23	19	7	19	16	19	78	19	91	29
	No	158	14	136	16	22	8	21	18	14	56	14	59	19
	No policy	696	63	477	58	219	79	74	63	63	255	63	148	48

MANAGEMENT POLICIES AND PRACTICES

Municipal policies for dealing with organized employees and their representatives vary considerably. Table 2 reveals that a substantial majority of municipalities have no specific policy on most issues of management-employee relations. While it may be contended that cities that have not been confronted by employee associations prefer to meet specific events as they arise, it appears somewhat surprising that cities already organized have no stated policies on these subjects.

Frequently it is in cities whose workers have formed only local associations that no policies have been adopted on memberships, recognition of representational units, and related matters. Yet substantial percentages of cities having national organizations, or mixtures of local and national bodies, also report that they have no stated policy on these subjects.

In Table 3 the "no specific procedures" response, given by nearly half of the cities responding to the question about recognition procedure, continues the same theme. Barely 11% of the municipalities surveyed make recognition of employee organizations by management depend upon procedural specifications designed to inject a degree of formality into employer-employee relationships. The chief approach to these relationships, in the governmental sphere, appears to be informal, with the city's chief administrative officer the focal point on the management side.

Despite the prominent role apparently given the administrative officer in the preliminary stages of the recognition process, other items in Table 3 show that many other officials become involved in negotiations. The council, or a committee of that

table 3   Management Practices: Recognition and Negotiation Procedures

	Number of Organized Cities Responding* (A)	Organized Cities		Locals Only		Nationals Only		Locals and Nationals	
		No.	% of (A)	No.	% of (A)	No.	% of (A)	No.	% of (A)
Recognition procedure									
Submit bylaws and list of officers	82	82	100	16	20	30	37	36	44
Request appointment with chief adminstrative officer	279	277	99	31	11	118	42	128	46
Request to be heard by city council	92	90	98	8	9	51	55	31	34
No specific procedure	276	270	98	52	19	132	48	86	31
City representative in negotiations									
City manager	374	368	98	64	17	155	41	149	40
Council committee	86	86	100	11	13	54	63	21	24
Entire city council	57	57	100	7	12	30	53	20	35
Personnel director	48	47	98	2	4	15	31	30	63
Civil service commission	10	10	100	2	20	4	40	4	40
Mayor	72	71	99	7	10	40	56	24	33
Chief appointed administrative officer	40	39	98	6	15	16	40	17	43
City employed arbitrator	20	20	100	0	0	5	25	15	75
Department heads	29	28	97	3	10	19	66	6	21
No negotiations	67	65	97	7	10	42	63	16	24
Conduct of negotiations									
Council hearings	36	35	97	4	11	14	39	17	47
Committee negotiation sessions	123	122	99	12	10	76	62	34	28
Chief administrative officer: negotiation sessions	236	234	99	27	11	96	41	111	47
Chief administrative officer: informal	220	215	98	46	21	99	45	70	32
Personnel board hearings	30	30	100	7	23	7	23	16	53
Mayor: negotiation sessions	54	54	100	3	6	30	56	21	39
Other	53	53	100	5	9	24	45	24	45

*Organized cities column does not always equal total column since not all responding cities answered all questions.

body, evidently plays a direct role in negotiations in a large number of cities. The conclusion is that most cities involved in employer-employee relationships have not yet sorted out the proper roles for chief administrators, department heads, mayors, councils, and personnel boards. Consequently, in most municipal administrations, no clearly defined procedures have yet emerged.

Table 4, on the other hand, presents some interesting procedural developments related to the settlement of management-employee disputes. The table shows that 63% of the cities have developed some type of grievance procedure, either offered unilaterally or negotiated. Interestingly enough, the large central cities rank high in the use of this procedure. Council-manager cities also rate at the top in its use.

To many observers, data on the use of binding agreements reveal an unexpectedly high percentage of cities that employ the device. Moreover, the distribution among the 6 population groups of cities is surprisingly even. On the other hand, the high percentage of cities in New England that enter into agreements is fully consistent with the analysis given earlier in this report showing that area to be heavily organized. It is also consistent with the fact that most of the New England states have approved legislation clarifying municipal powers to enter into agreements with employees.

The figures for the number of cities that engage in arbitration of disputes are also somewhat higher than expected. At the same time, the distribution among the geographic areas of cities participating in this activity parallels the former analysis of distribution of employee organizations affiliated with the labor movement.

Relationships between these policy outcomes (binding agreements, arbitration, and grievance procedures) and forms of city government fall into reasonably clear

table 4   Binding Agreements, Arbitration, and Grievance Procedures

Distribution	Number of Organized Cities Responding (A)	Binding Agreement		Arbitration		Grievance Procedure	
		Yes	% of (A)	Yes	% of (A)	Yes	% of (A)
Total, all cities	829	324	39	109	13	523	63
Population group							
Over 500,000	19	6	32	6	32	16	84
250,000–500,000	20	8	40	3	15	15	75
100,000–250,000	64	25	39	12	19	48	75
50,000–100,000	125	45	36	19	15	94	75
25,000– 50,000	208	86	41	23	11	129	62
10,000– 25,000	393	154	39	46	12	221	56
Geographic division							
New England	78	66	85	20	26	67	86
Mid-Atlantic	121	71	59	25	21	62	51
East North-Central	217	118	54	38	18	137	63
West North-Central	80	20	25	15	19	51	64
South Atlantic	61	7	11	2	3	35	57
East South-Central	20	6	30	1	5	5	25
West South-Central	48	2	4	2	4	28	58
Mountain	35	7	20	4	11	22	63
Pacific Coast	169	27	16	2	1	116	69
City type							
Central	167	67	40	37	22	125	75
Suburban	424	161	38	48	11	256	60
Independent	238	96	40	24	10	142	60
Form of government							
Mayor-council	260	133	51	52	20	146	56
Council-manager	530	170	32	48	9	356	67
Other*	39	21	54	9	23	21	54

*Includes 25 cities with commission government, 11 with town meeting, and 4 with representative town meeting.

**table 5   Cities Affected by State Mandating, by Occupational Category
and Type of Requirement**

Occupational Category by Municipal Function	Total	Salaries & Wages	% of Total	Hours of Work	% of Total	Working Conditions & Fringe Benefits	% of Total	Employee Qualifications	% of Total	Information Not Available	% of Total
Highways	89	30	34	41	46	55	62	23	26	10	11
Police	365	182	50	167	46	186	51	164	45	4	1
Fire	336	146	44	211	63	177	53	100	30	5	2
Sewage	127	36	28	41	32	53	42	65	51	6	5
Sanitation	95	33	35	42	44	52	55	29	31	8	8
Parks & recreation	97	36	37	43	44	57	59	25	26	11	11
Libraries	89	31	35	34	38	48	54	25	28	10	11
Water supply	117	29	25	36	31	48	41	61	52	6	5
Other	49	17	35	16	33	27	55	21	43	2	4

patterns. Mayor-council municipalities and those with "other" forms are about equally high in the use of agreements and arbitration, whereas council-manager cities are notably low, in comparison. At the other extreme, council-manager cities have been more active in installing grievance procedures than have cities with other forms of government.

STATE MANDATED POLICIES

The legal status of cities as creatures of the state has come into view with increased interest as many cities, seeking to come to terms with their organized employees, find critical decisions being made at the state capitol rather than at the city hall.

The reasons for this situation are several. In some instances, rural and small-town legislators seek to keep central metropolitan localities operating under the state's leading strings. In many states, the cities seek greater fiscal assistance from state sources and find it necessary to accept some state mandating of policy in return. Again, some mandating has been developed after the cities have failed to respond to new problems pressed upon them. In several states, legislation that formulates policies directing the cities to recognize and negotiate with their employee organizations was produced in the belief that uniform state policies and administrative machinery are required to keep the peace in public employment.

Public employee organizations, as well as the management of cities, compare policies and practices among governments throughout a state or region and seek to gain a degree of uniformity. Therefore, public employee groups and their allies in the labor movement have often been active, lobbying state legislatures and governors to secure legislation assuring rights to organize. On other occasions they seek legislation to set minimum salaries, hours of work, public holidays, or fringe benefits.

Table 5 gives results of a preliminary inquiry into mandating legislation. The larger number of cities affected by state mandates is subject to state legislation covering police and fire salaries, hours of work, and fringe benefits. Other municipal functions most frequently affected are water supply and sanitation. In these instances, most cities indicate that the state is interested in setting standards for selection of employees.

The advent of municipal employee organizations has expanded the arena in which public employment policy is made. It has also brought into being new procedures for determining policies.

WHAT ARE UNIONS DOING TO MERIT SYSTEMS?

David T. Stanley

As unions of public employees grow in numbers and influence the question naturally arises, "What are unions doing to merit systems?" The question may have a tone of alarm for long-term practitioners, advocates, and beneficiaries of civil service systems. The gains of civil service, now nearing its century mark in this country, have been won and maintained with difficulty; alternatives are understandably dismaying. This question has been explored in the past by expert and interested persons in this journal and other publications.

We now have some preliminary results from a study of the impact of unions on public administration that throws further light on this question as it applies to local governments.[1] Our raw material comes from about ten days of interviewing and document-grabbing in each of fifteen cities and four urban counties. (Cities: Binghamton, New York; Boston, Massachusetts; Buffalo, New York; Cincinnati, Ohio; Dayton, Ohio; Detroit, Michigan; Hartford, Connecticut; Milwaukee, Wisconsin; New Orleans, Louisiana; New York, New York; Philadelphia, Pennsylvania; San Francisco, California; St. Louis, Missouri; Tacoma, Washington; and Wilmington, Delaware. Counties: Dade, Florida; Los Angeles, California; Multnomah, Oregon; and New Castle, Delaware.)

The localities studied all have merit systems, but differences in strength, competence, and age of these systems were very obvious. There is great variety also in the state laws governing the conditions under which public employees may unionize and bargain. All these variations make it hard to generalize from the experience of these nineteen governments, but we can present some of the patterns we found. We do not contend that these cities and counties are truly representative of all local governments, only that they show what is going on in a variety of places where unions have been active.

A mixed and moderate report results from the study. Civil service is not disappearing, nor is it fighting unions to a standstill, nor is there beautiful collaboration everywhere. In general, unions, bargaining, and contractual provisions are invading more and more precincts previously occupied only by civil service commissions or personnel offices. How good or how bad this is depends upon the value systems of the beholder.

David Stanley is Senior Research Fellow, the Brookings Institution. Reprinted by permission from the *Public Personnel Review*.

[1]This is one of five studies on unions, collective bargaining, and public employment, sponsored by the Brookings Institution with the aid of the Ford Foundation. . . .

What do we mean by merit systems? We should distinguish them from the merit principle under which public employees are recruited, selected, and advanced under conditions of political neutrality, equal opportunity, and competition on the basis of merit and competence. Public employee unions do not question this principle in general and have done little to weaken it, as yet. When we say merit systems, however, this has come to mean a broad program of personnel management activities. Some are essential to carrying out the merit principle: recruiting, selecting, policing of anti-politics and anti-discrimination rules, and administering related appeals provisions. Others are closely related and desirable: position classification, pay administration, employee benefits, and training. Unions are of course interested in both categories.

What unions are we talking about? We refer particularly to the American Federation of State, County, and Municipal Employees; the Service Employees International Union, the International Association of Firefighters, the various police associations, the nursing associations, the International Brotherhood of Teamsters, the unions of licensed practical nurses.

This article will speak rather generally of union attitudes and pressures. Some are expressed through the collective bargaining process, with the results embodied in a formal agreement; some are stated as representations to the boards of local government. Or the pressure may be more informally applied, as when a union delegation meets with a department head or a steward meets with the first-line or second-line supervisor.

THE IMPACT IN GENERAL

The major and most distinct effect of union activity is a weakening of what might be called management-by-itself. The era of unilateralism, of unquestioned sovereignty, is about over. The age of bilateralism—consultation, negotiation, and bargaining—is already here. The "independent" civil service commission, responsible over the years for rule-making, for protection of career employees from arbitrary personnel changes, for adjudication of appeals from employees, still exists but is losing functions. Civil service commissions may not go out of business, but more and more of their vital organs will be removed by the bargaining process until, whether officially in existence or not, they are husks of their former selves. This change is occurring not because employees are clearly dissatisfied with existing merit systems but because they feel that unions will get more for them—more pay, more benefits, more aggressive protection against possible arbitrary management actions.

At the same time management is becoming more careful, more responsible, and more responsive. The fact that management at all levels is prodded, observed, objected to, and reasoned with by union stewards and business agents means that management must watch its step. Another effect is that this change from unilateralism to bilateralism brings transitional difficulties. First-line and second-line supervisors in government are not used to dealing with unions, and the unions have many inexperienced stewards who are busy fumbling hot potatoes. The passage of time and the application of effort and good will should reduce these problems.

ORGANIZATION FOR LABOR RELATIONS

Each of the governments we studied has had to provide organizationally for dealing with unions. In Hartford and Philadelphia, for example, the function has been clearly lodged within the city personnel office. This contrasts with Detroit and New York where a separate labor relations office operates in cooperation (and some competition) with civil service commission. In other governments labor relations are handled by some different administrator: a fiscal executive in Buffalo; the assistant to the mayor in Binghamton; the chairman of the Board of County Commissioners in Multnomah County, and the county manager in Dade County.

These varied patterns of organization result from both tradition and personality. It is much too early to say that any one system works better than another, and indeed, our findings may reflect personalities rather than organization schemes. It seems natural to predict, however, that the longer labor relations functions are separated from personnel functions, the more trouble we are going to have in the future. The activities of "independent" civil service commissions intensify the diffusion of managerial authority and make union negotiations more difficult. Even more important, it is impossible for a personnel officer (or civil service executive secretary) to be both an impartial defender of employees' rights and an adversary of unions as a management negotiator. It is perfectly possible to foresee governments adopting the industrial pattern: a department of labor relations headed by a vice-mayor or assistant city manager for labor relations who will supervise not only bargaining and employee relations, but also selection and training activities.

HIRING

We have already noted that unions accept the merit principle, and our field research shows that they are inclined to accept most of the qualification requirements and examining methods that are customarily part of the civil service system. Here and there we found some union resistance to the lowering of qualification standards, such as height requirements for policemen, high school graduation for custodians, or college degrees for caseworkers. There are various motives for such resistance; the wish to work with well-qualified associates (or with people like themselves) and the wish to argue that higher qualifications deserve higher pay.

On the whole unions have shown little interest in examining methods except where they have taken up the cause of citizens whose educational experiences do not prepare them to excel on pencil-and-paper tests. In those cases unions would naturally prefer performance tests to examinations which involve verbal aptitude. The civil service office discussing this should be in a position to show that the tests used are valid for their intended purposes. Unions have also affected selection by pushing management to shorten probation periods. Such a change clearly limits management's freedom to discharge unsatisfactory employees.

When the government runs special recruitment and training programs for disadvantaged citizens of the cities, the unions are put in a somewhat difficult position.

Union leaders support such programs both because of altruism and because they see the new recruits to city service as potential union members. On the other hand, union members do not want to see these less privileged citizens occupying a preferred position in selection and training in comparison to themselves. ("I had to take a civil service examination to get that job. Why doesn't he?" "We had to have high school diplomas before we could have such a job. Why don't they?") So acceptance depends on whether those recruited under the "new careers" and other comparable programs are regarded as allies or as threats to employees who are the real backbone of the union membership.

More important than all of these factors is the increased adoption of the union shop. Four of our localities (Hartford, Philadelphia, New Castle County, and Wilmington) provided this form of union security. The effect is that employment is limited to citizens willing to join unions—who may or may not be the best-qualified candidates. The effect is slightly less for the agency shop (Dayton, Detroit, and Boston) under which employees, if not willing to be union members, must pay fees in lieu of union dues because they presumably benefit from union services.

PROMOTIONS

The unions' naturally strong interest in promotions is expressed in support of measures that favor inside candidates for jobs and limit management's freedom of selection. When a job above the usual entrance level is to be filled, they strongly prefer that promotion lists be used ahead of open competitive lists and departmental promotion lists ahead of service-wide promotion lists. These policies are reflected anyway in many civil service laws and procedures, perhaps to excess, so the union influence reinforces some preexisting rigidities. In some cities promotion lists are limited to the union bargaining unit. This provision may be another wave of the future.

Another point of emphasis, clearly consistent with the others, is insistence on "rule-of-one" certification. Even in some places where "rule-of-three" prevails, union pressures are directed toward selecting the top person certified unless there is some extremely compelling reason for not doing so. In effect, management has to show cause why the top eligible on the list should not be appointed.

In rating candidates for promotion, unions have rather consistently opposed the use of oral examinations and performance ratings, at least arguing for a reduced weighting to be given such factors, and for increased weight to be given to seniority. They would prefer promotion by strict seniority among those basically qualified for the higher job. Thus far, however, this last provision has been negotiated in only a few contracts. Where we did find it, the promotions were not to supervisory positions but to higher-rated nonsupervisory jobs (laborer to truck driver, truck driver to bulldozer operator) within the bargaining unit. In these respects unions are still supporting the merit principle but maintaining that senior employees have more merit.

TRANSFERS

There is little union interest in interdepartmental transfers except in cases where the union helps an employee move to another department because he is facing disciplinary action or is involved in a personality conflict in his present department.

The situation is different, however, with respect to transfers to new locations or to other shifts within a department. Unions would like to have assignments to preferred places or times made on a basis of seniority among those who request such assignments. We found this policy in a few contracts, but in general management has full freedom to assign employees where they are needed.

TRAINING

Unions have had two kinds of impact on employee training programs. First, they urge or even arrange training to help their members gain promotions, such as on-the-job training in operation of more complex equipment or group training to prepare for promotion examinations. In Detroit, for example, the Teamsters Union in cooperation with the civil service commission has arranged for drivers to learn heavy equipment operation. The Service Employees International Union in California is pressing for training of psychiatric technicians to meet new state licensure requirements. Second, management has had to train its supervisors in labor relations, sometimes with the aid of university professors. In general, however, training continues to occupy an unfortunately low position in the unions' scale of values, as in that of management.

GRIEVANCES AND DISCIPLINARY APPEALS

One of the clearest patterns to emerge from our field research is the trend in grievance procedures. Most of the governments studied use negotiated procedures, usually going through four or five steps and ending in third-party arbitration, which is more often binding than advisory. This pattern replaces the usual grievance procedure which advances from lower to higher levels of management, ending with the civil service commission as the final "court of appeal." The arbitration provided in the new pattern may take various forms. A single arbitrator may be chosen from a list supplied by an impartial source. Or there may be a panel of arbitrators of whom the aggrieved employee (or his organization) appoints one member, management appoints a second, and the two agree upon a third, sometimes using nominations, again from an impartial source.

When we speak of grievances covered by these procedures, we are referring to grievances on supervisory relationships or working conditions. Work assignments and eligibility for premium pay are frequent subjects for such appeals. We are not referring to appeals of adverse personnel actions such as suspensions, demotions, or discharges. In most of the governments studied such adverse actions are still handled through civil service channels. A trend is beginning, however, to administer them like other grievances, and it is only a matter of time before adverse actions will be subject to arbitration in unionized urban governments. Without this change unions will continue to maintain that civil service decisions are made by pro-management bodies.

CLASSIFICATION

The position classification process—sorting jobs by occupation and level—is still a management activity but it is under several kinds of pressure from employee groups. Unions may claim that some jobs are undervalued in relation to others and urge, sometimes successfully, that they be upgraded. Unions also press for new job levels (e.g., supervising building custodian, senior caseworker) which will provide promotion opportunities for their members. Such claims and pressures may be expressed in the bargaining process. In Detroit and New York, for example, union and management bargainers have agreed on joint recommendations to civil service authorities.

A related problem arises from the insistence by unions that employees be paid at the proper rate for out-of-classification work. Sometimes there are difficult management determinations as to whether the employee really did work out of the classification, and for how long. Unions contend that differences over such matters should be resolved through the grievance procedure. In one of the cities we studied, however, the civil service authorities went to court to insist that such cases be settled under management's classification authority, not through the grievance procedure. Civil service lost this one.

PAY

In all but a few of the localities studied, pay changes are made as a result of collective bargaining. In one of the remaining cities (New Orleans) only part of the local government is covered by collective bargaining procedures. In still others (San Francisco and St. Louis) the urges of employees to have fatter paychecks are expressed through group pressures on the civil service commission and more intensively on the legislative body. This form of pressure may be just as effective as bargaining. In all these bargaining-for-pay situations the end result is resolution of a complex group of factors: surveys of prevailing pay levels; the skill and influence of the chief executive; the political and economic power of the unions; the responsiveness of the city council to all sorts of pressures; the attitude of the state government, and many others.

It is terribly hard to say whether unions are getting more for employees through bargaining or other pressures than less organized employees might have obtained for themselves. Another study will undertake to demonstrate statistically the extent to which effective unionization correlates with salary increases. Our own data are not conclusive on this point. We know, of course, that both union and non-union pay have risen impressively. Looking at our nineteen governments as a whole (and it is very hard to generalize) pay rose seven to ten per cent on the average in each of the last two years, when the consumer price index was going up only four or five per cent a year. In a couple of these local governments where employees had not been given a raise for quite a time they "caught up" with something like a 20 per cent increase. There are also the special cases of underpaid groups like some laundry, food service, and custodial workers who have been compensated so poorly for so long that union pressure results in a significant jump in their incomes.

FRINGE BENEFITS

Fringe benefits too show great variation in local governments, depending upon charter provisions, management attitudes, and priorities of union objectives. The clearest trends are those toward increased leave allowances and more generous financing of health benefits.

LOOKING TO THE FUTURE

It is clear that unions are here to stay, to grow, to become involved in more and more public personnel activities. Their influence is exerted now in many different ways but will increasingly be felt through formalized collective bargaining ending in written agreements.

In general unions do not quarrel with the merit principle although their definition of merit may be a little different from that of management. They are inclined to question the ability of management to determine who is the best of a number of employees or candidates, particularly if there are rating differences of only a point or two. Unions will resist such fine distinctions and will favor seniority as a basis for assignment and promotion.

It is clear also that pressure from unions brings increases in pay and fringe benefits which will at least keep up with and may outrun the advances in the cost of living and perhaps in prevailing wages. The time will come, however, when unions will have won the major gains that are possible in this area, and at that point one can expect them to turn their attention more aggressively to the make-up of work crews, the conditions of assignment to shifts, and other aspects of work assignment and supervision.

Public personnel jurisdictions will have to give a great deal of thought to the way in which they are organized to meet the evergrowing strength of employee organizations. It is clear that the "independent" civil service commission is waning in power and influence and that personnel departments (whether or not subservient to a civil service commission) will also decline in influence unless they can take on the labor relations functions, as they have done very satisfactorily in some places.

I am inclined to predict that ultimately governments will establish strong labor relations departments, part of whose work will be the personnel function as we have known it in the past. With or without such a change in organization, public personnel systems need strong and experienced hands to conduct collective bargaining, to deal with grievances, and to be management's voice in matters which go to arbitration.

In general, the relationship between unions and merit systems is dynamic and immature. We are only beginning to learn the lessons that private commerce and industry learned more than a generation ago. Urban administrators would be well advised to ponder some of these lessons, notably those which concern management's freedom to organize the work and to select employees for promotion to supervisory positions. Finally, management people at all levels should somehow take the time and summon the energy to consult systematically with and listen sympathetically to union representatives.

AGENCY ADAPTATION
TO LABOR-MANAGEMENT COOPERATION

Husain Mustafa

An examination of what has occurred in the area of federal labor-management relations would reveal that various agencies encountered a monumental task in their efforts to implement programs of cooperation. For more than seven years agencies have been laboring to mold the concepts of unionism into a pattern compatible with the special requirements of public administration. The search for philosophy, direction and technique continues. At the same time, exposure to bargaining sessions and union demands remains a new experience to many officials who accept it only halfheartedly.

This situation is perhaps most evident in the Post Office Department, where major progress toward accepting worker participation in personnel policy determination has been achieved; yet, substantial disagreement over both degree and content persists.

Admittedly the postal program is unique in a number of respects. It is differentiated by great size, a built-in decentralization, and an extremely high extent of unionization. Over 92 per cent of the 700,000 postal employees belong to unions. In federal terms this is comparable to about 30 per cent of union membership for the government generally. . . .

Husain Mustafa is Associate Professor and Chairman of Graduate Studies in Public Administration of Kent State University. Reprinted from *Labor Law Journal*, July 1969.

The ... paper will describe the arrangements which have helped to make this procedure operational. In any complex task, the numerous opportunities for difference of opinion, as to the precise objective sought and the best method for accomplishing it, could frustrate even the most efficient procedure. For instance, the emphasis on local negotiations may lead to exaggerated notions of independence, self-determination, and eventually substantial fragmentation. In such circumstance, there is a real need for a standard which would help in defining correct action and forcing conformity to national policies, and for a well-understood method of umpiring disputes and resolving conflicts.

The most effective standardizing influence is the National Agreement which leaves limited room for further local agreements.[1] Clearly, the local agreements are extensions or refinements of the National Agreement. The latter would set down general rules covering, for example, seniority rules; questions relative to seniority on which it is silent, however, could be further negotiated locally. Often, this would result in local differentiation within the overall national policy; items negotiated contrary to the National Agreement are invalidated at the Regional Office level, which, thereby, exerts a standardizing influence. In addition, the Bureau of Personnel, the Labor Relations Division, and the Board of Appeals and Review, each serves a significant integrating and purifying function.

The postal agreement is significant not only because of its extent of worker coverage, but also for its scope and detail of provisions. The administration of the policy it has established under Executive Order 10988 has entailed added responsibilities for the Bureau of Personnel, creation of a Labor Relations Division, a Board of Appeals and Review, and strengthening the regional staff. What follows is a commentary on some aspects of the adjustment.

BUREAU OF PERSONNEL

The Bureau of Personnel has had to play a central role in putting into effect the new labor relations concept, a new appeals system, and a new emphasis on equal employment opportunity. It is required to consult with organizations accorded formal recognition nationally and to negotiate and conclude an agreement with seven national exclusive organizations. The current agreement became effective March 8, 1968; it covers over 600,000 employees and runs for two years. The signing concluded more than three months of collective bargaining and signaled the pioneering use in the federal service of mediation in an attempt to resolve negotiating impasses.[2]

The Bureau must also oversee contract negotiations and administration in over 24,250 separate craft units. Further, it is responsible for planning and providing training for management officials through the Department in order to prepare them for acting effectively in the labor relations area. Finally, it must coordinate the basic reserach needed to develop comprehensive plans and policies for future formal dealings with employee representatives.

---

[1]Chester A. Newland, "Collective Bargaining Concepts: Applications in Government," *Public Administration Review,* Vol. XXVIII, No. 2, 1968, p. 121.

[2]House, Post Office Department Appropriations Hearings, 1969, p. 164.

In accordance with the provisions of the National Agreement, the Department, through appropriate officials mostly in the Bureau of Personnel, meets with employee representatives in regularly scheduled, monthly one-day consultation sessions. In addition, meetings are held whenever it is necessary to confer with respect to nationwide personnel policies, matters affecting working conditions, matters affecting the National Agreement, or interpretations and disputes arising out of the administration of local agreements. Similarly, quarterly meetings are required also at the regional and local levels to confer on the status of current projects, programs and other activities of interest to employees. Since the Department also consults with unions prior to issuing new policy pronouncements, meetings are held practically daily. The number of officials involved in these meeting vary from three to twenty, depending on the subject matter discussed and whether the meeting is a session with one union or a general session.[3]

These activities have had, and will continue to have, the effect of increasing the workload for the departmental personnel staff. Changing functions are clearly reflected in the creation of the Labor Relations Division and the Board of Appeals and Review.

LABOR RELATIONS DIVISION

The two principal headquarters officials who represent management in dealing with unions are the Assistant Postmaster General for Personnel and his Deputy. The latter has an immediate staff organized as the Labor Relations Division and engaged in research, coordinating negotiated items with the postal manual, getting them out in the form of regulations available to all post offices. It also studies the labor relations programs of other governmental agencies and major corporations in order to benefit from their experiences. Recently, it has been attempting to relate automatic data processing to the labor negotiation function.

The stated responsibilities of the Division are:

"(1) Developing and issuing instructions and guidelines on the conduct of labor-management activities, including recognition, negotiation and review of contracts.

"(2) Analyzing and evaluating labor-management staff activities on regional and local levels; reviewing local negotiating procedures, agreements, application of national agreements, and preparing format for written agreements.

"(3) Controlling and editing all regulations affecting personnel to ensure proper technical review, interbureau clearance, and coordination with employee organizations.

"(4) Supervising the conduct of national and local employee organization representation elections, auditing returns and preparing for approval the certifications for the organizations selected for representation.

[3]The employees who represent the unions in negotiations are paid by the unions themselves; they are off-the-clock in negotiating sessions. In terms of consultations, when the department calls a representative of the union in, it would pay for his time on a no gain or loss basis, except when he is a full-time national officer. Therefore, such payments are rarely made at the headquarters level. On the other hand, at the regional level, employee leaders called in for consultations are compensated if they are not full-time officers.

"(5) Providing staff representation to assist on national negotiation and consultation teams and in interbureau discussions of labor-management problems."[4]

REGIONAL STAFF

Each of the 15 regional directors is involved in the labor-relations program, at least to the extent of making decisions at the first appellate level. Continually increasing personnel issues that require intelligent and speedy consideration, as well as the complexities of implementing Executive Order 10988, have dictated the addition of a specialist in labor-management relations in each region who is primarily concerned with labor questions. In each region the responsibilities of the Special Assistant for Employee Relations are as follows:

(1) Serves as focal point for contact with employee organizations, participates in management meetings whenever policy or procedural changes are considered, and arranges for all joint management-employee organization meetings.
(2) Discusses with postmasters and supervisors the techniques for sound employee relations and meets with employees, local representatives of employee organizations, and supervisors as necessary to maintain sound employee-management relations.
(3) Obtains facts on discrimination complaints made at the regional or local levels, and recommends appropriate corrective action; reviews employment program procedures to ensure the full application of the President's directives on equal employment opportunity.
(4) Undertakes inquiries into the background of industrial labor problems as they affect postal operations; keeps the Regional Director informed of such matters.
(5) Prepares recommendations for the resolution of grievances, analyzes and studies the frequency and type of grievances for similar nature or location to determine whether their incidence can be reduced by a change of directive or policy.[5]

At least in the larger regions, such as New York, Chicago, Boston, Philadelphia and San Francisco, the regional specialist and his relatively small staff have not been able to operate effectively. In many cases he is compelled to cover a wide geographical area and is not available for prompt consideration of personnel matters. Moreover, specially from the point of view of employee organizations, his subordination to the Regional Director and his staff deprives him of the independence essential to his job.

BOARD OF APPEALS AND REVIEW

Procedures oriented toward conflict management become essential whenever many decisions and actions become continuing centers of controversy, thereby

[4]Report of the Comptroller General, GAO, cited at footnote 5.

[5]Report of the Comptroller General, "Review of Selected Aspects of Labor-Management Program, Post Office Department," to Chairman, House Appropriations Subcommittee, Treasury and Post Office Departments, General Accounting Office, February 23, 1967.

precluding a settlement acceptable to the contestants. For this reason an independent Board of Appeals and Review was created in 1962 in order to establish the responsibility of correcting management if it made an incorrect decision. In this way, an old postal tradition of rarely overriding management was upset. The Board has from time to time overridden postmasters. Generally, however, the Board has sustained management in approximately 85 per cent of all adverse action and grievance cases adjudicated and has recommended upholding postmasters in 84 per cent of their recommendations on equal employment complaints.[6]

The Board has the following responsibilities:

(1) To serve as a final appellate level within the Department for decisions on adverse action appeals and equal employment opportunity appeals.

(2) To review and recommend management actions on employee grievances appealed to the Department.

(3) To determine the need for investigation on adverse action or equal employment opportunity appeals when additional information is required to reach an equitable decision.

(4) To represent the Department in hearings and in discussions with the Civil Service Commission and other federal agencies on matters pertaining to employee appeals.

There are two basic procedures involved in the appeal category.[7] An adverse action procedure relates to management decisions, such as reduction in rank or compensation, that entail demotion, suspension or termination of employment. On the other hand, the formal grievance procedure is usually filed by an employee, or a union acting on his behalf, or a group of employees, whenever they are dissatisfied with a particular situation. Most grievances are initiated and settled at the local level. A few that cannot be settled at the supervisory level may be brought through channels to the postmaster, the regional director, and ultimately to the Board of Appeals and Review in Washington for a final ruling.

Employees have increasingly used the Department's appeal procedure as confidence in the impartiality of the board has grown. It should be noted that members of the Board, now four, are appointed by the Postmaster General and report to the Assistant Postmaster General, Bureau of Personnel, for administrative purposes. However, in terms of arriving at their decisions, they are in an "independent" board. It is significant also that both the Postmaster General and his Assistant for personnel, have the authority to finally override board decisions, although they have never exercised it.

COST IMPLICATIONS

The annual man-hours being devoted to the labor-management program department-wide is indicative of its dimensions. Although the Department's

---

[6]House, POD Appropriations Hearings, 1968, p. 129.

[7]E. O. 10987, dated January 17, 1962, relates to adverse action and employee appeals. It sets up minimum procedural standards that govern the appeal system and the grievance procedure and extends to nonveterans the same right to appeal to the Civil Service Commission as traditionally granted to veterans.

accounting system does not identify the costs incurred in carrying out this program, departmental estimates are available.[8]

Departmental personnel costs	$ 376,000
Regional personnel costs	738,000
Post Office personnel costs	
Negotiations	384,000
Consultants	126,000
Adverse action and	
grievance appeals	119,000
Total	$1,743,000

The General Accounting Office, after reviewing these estimates, has taken the position that they substantially understate the cost involved at the post office level.[9]

> To this figure should be added an estimated $2,000,000 in costs of training supervisors, orienting officials at all levels, and preparing them to deal with unions effectively. This includes also training a number of clerks, carriers, and supervisors in conducting appeals hearing to prepare them for service on equal opportunity, grievances, and adverse action cases.[10]

In the dues check-off program, more than 300,000 employees are taking advantage of the program. It is completely paid for by the unions themselves. The department charges a standard two cents per monthly deduction for each employee. The check-off is made regionally and the fees collected from the National organizations to which funds collected are then remitted on a monthly basis. In turn, the National organizations remit to the regional and local unions. The reimbursement made to the department goes into the postal fund. In other words, the Department pays the cost of doing the check-off out of the regular appropriations, but the reimbursement made by the unions is not available to it to cover the man-hours involved. In this sense, this is an additional cost to the department, but not to the government as a whole.[11]

CONCLUSION

This attempt to gauge the impact of the labor-management program on postal management and organizational structure has revealed that a considerable change has occurred. There is, first, an increased sensitivity to employee problems and demands. One consequence of this unprecedented attention accorded personnel

[8] Report of the Comptroller General, cited at footnote 5.

[9] Report of the Comptroller General, cited at footnote 5.

[10] House, POD Appropriations Hearings, 1967, p. 375.

[11] House, POD Appropriations Hearings, 1965, p. 172.

matters is a new pattern of bilateral decision-making which permits considerable employee participation according to an agreed-upon and binding procedure. The attendant gains in employee morale and involvement are substantial. Similarly, management has benefitted greatly from employees' ideas obtained prior to program implementation. It is able now to test employee reactions before final decisions are made. Very often, proposed issuances are modified after consultation. Consequently, there has been a sharp decline in critical attitudes toward policies. Moreover, National organization's officials, in particular, now have a keen appreciation of management problems and are exhibiting a great sense of responsibility in seeking cooperative action. Generally, consultations with employee groups and the give and take of negotiations have brought a new maturity and orderliness to relations between the two parties.

Finally, basic structural adaptations have had to be made in order to fix responsibility for implementation, coordination and control in specified organizational units. The adaptation permeates the postal system from headquarters, through the regional offices, all the way to the individual post offices. At the local level, the change may entail no more than ensuring the availability of the necessary skills. Yet, even locally, the reallocation of management's time among various functions indicates a growing share for labor relations.

A COMMON AGENCY
FOR ADMINISTERING COLLECTIVE BARGAINING
BY PUBLIC AND PRIVATE EMPLOYEES

Morris Slavney
Howard S. Bellman

The Wisconsin Employment Relations Commission (WERC) regulates labor relations with regard to virtually every employer in the state of Wisconsin except federal employees and employees of railroads. Its authority in this regard is vested by three separate statutes, all of which contain basic procedures necessary and desirable to promote peaceful employment relations in private employment and in local and state government employment.

Morris Slavney and Howard Bellman are Chairman and ;staff member, respectively, of Wisconsin Employment Relations Commission. Article prepared specifically for this volume.

The Wisconsin Employment Peace Act (WEPA), adopted in 1939, created the Wisconsin Employment Relations Board, now known as the Wisconsin Employment Relations Commission, to administer this law which governs labor relations in private employment. Since its coverage in some areas is broader than the federal labor law, certain of its provisions apply to employers also subject to the jurisdiction of the federal act. In 1961 the commission commenced the administration of the municipal employment labor relations act, and in 1967 it began to administer the provisions of the state employment labor relations act.

Procedures with respect to the determination of bargaining representatives, the adjudication of unfair labor, and prohibited practices, and the mediation and arbitration of labor disputes are common to all three statutes. In addition, the WEPA contains provisions with respect to the authorization of union security provisions and the municipal and state employment labor relations laws contain procedures for fact finding as a means of resolving disputes.

While the procedures with respect to the establishing of collective bargaining representatives in all three statutes are somewhat similar to the procedures established under the federal act, the same cannot be said with regard to the adjudication of unfair labor or prohibited practice cases. Unlike the National Labor Relations Board, the commission does not issue complaints in unfair labor or prohibited practice cases nor does it prosecute same. Such proceedings are initiated by complaints filed with the commission. The commission or its staff, in this area of involvement, acts as a tribunal to determine whether a violation of the statute has occurred. In the area of mediation, the commission operates similarly to the Federal Mediation and Conciliation Service (FMCS) by providing mediation either by the individual commissioners or members of its staff. Commissioners and the professional staff also act as arbitrators at the request of the parties and issue final and binding awards. While the commission and its staff participate in procedures perliminary to fact finding, the actual fact finding and recommendations emanating therefrom are performed by individuals appointed on an ad hoc basis by the commission from outside the commission and its staff.

The Wisconsin Employment Relations Commission is the only agency in the country headed by a full-time commission, which administers separate and distinct labor relations statutes in private and public employment. The three commissioners are full-time employees and are prohibited from engaging in other employment.

There are no obvious criteria for judging the effectiveness of the administration of laws and of mediation and arbitration in a given situation. Nevertheless, the writers are convinced by their own statistics and intuitions that the commission's effectiveness in all its functions has been at least as impressive as that of any other governmental labor relations agency, no matter how specialized. In one way or another the WERC competes for cases with the FMCS (re mediation and arbitration services) which has four offices in or immediately adjacent to Wisconsin, the state and federal courts which share jurisdiction in cases involving violation of collective bargaining agreements, and the American Arbitration Association which also offers mediation and arbitration services. Our experience indicates no material diminution in the use of these services, even in view of much more aggressive approaches sometimes adopted by the other bodies. In fact, our less aggressive attitude toward the utilization of our services—for example, proposing "preventive mediation"—may enhance our general reputation as service-oriented rather than bureaucratic. With regard to public employment disputes, although there has been little or no activity in Wisconsin by other agencies, we believe the continual request for our services in this area indicates satisfaction with such functions. We are impressed by the growing and voluntary use of our arbitration service by public sector parties who must have developed some of their attitudes toward us during experiences wherein our presence was due to our exclusive jurisdiction.

The likelihood of such an impact by existing agencies is discussed by Jean T. McKelvey in her article "The Role of State Agencies in Public Employee Labor Relations" (*Industrial and Labor Relations Review,* XX, No. 2 [Jan. 1967], 179-97). Examined there are various types of administrative bodies which have been entrusted with state and local employment policies including the labor relations and mediation agencies already operating; the "new" public agencies; the "professional agencies," such as civil service commissions; and the "private agencies," such as the American Arbitration Association. Professor McKelvey concludes that

> the advantages of using existing labor agencies can be enumerated as follows:
> (1) The experience and expertise which the states have developed in the private sector in such matters as unit determination, mediation, arbitration, and fact finding are easily transferrable to the public sector. (2) It is more economical and efficient in terms of overhead, administration, personnel, etc. to use the same agency or agencies in both the private and public sectors. (3) The familiarity of unions in the state with existing agencies and their procedures and services should facilitate recourse to these agencies, unless the familiarity has bred contempt! (4) The extension of their activities to the public sector should not only provide a new lease on life for those agencies which may be stranded in the no-man's land between federal and state jurisdiction in the private sector; it should also stimulate new energy and interest on the part of boards and staffs in exploring a new and challenging frontier.

Expertise, the first advantage, is not only transferrable but relevant and appropriate. There is an ever-running debate concerning the relative importance of the various distinctions one may draw between the public and private sectors. The issues are by no means resolved in favor of the distinctions and against the analogies. Legislatures and executives, whether or not they have created new agencies, have patterned their statutes, ordinances, and orders more or less to match the Labor Management Relations Act, thereby emphasizing the similarities.

Economy, the second advantage, is not merely a value to be listed. Political realities may make arguments well grounded upon economy persuasive when all other bases are unimpressive and ineffective. The savings inherent in a particular structure as opposed to the costs of another proposal may determine not only which is enacted but whether any enactment will occur.

The third advantage listed is the familiarity of unions with the established agency and its procedures. That public employers were never regulated before does not mean that they are unfamiliar with the agencies that have operated in the private sector. Not only do such agencies have a reputation known to people generally interested in government, but many public employers—for example, school boards—are comprised of individuals who are also involved with private employers or with unions. They may have direct experience with all or some of the private sector state and federal agencies. (Furthermore, in some instances the employee organizations operating in the public sector have had no association with the private sector agencies.)

The final advantage noted is based on the belief that the private sector agencies need "a new lease on life." Neither our private sector case load nor case law indicates any reduction of the commission's activities in the private sector. Perhaps where private sector agencies are so unstimulated or unacceptable as to indicate such needs, cynicism as to their being rejuvenated is appropriate.

McKelvey summarizes arguments against conferring jurisdiction on the existing agencies as follows:

> (1) Problems of unit determination and the resolution of impasses in the public sector are sufficiently different from those encountered in the private sector as to warrant the creation of new agencies which will not be bound by past practice and labor precedent. (2) Public employers and most professional organizations are suspicious of collective bargaining. Whatever negotiations they may be prepared to undertake will be aided if they have confidence in neutrals who are familiar with the unique problems of public employment. (3) Existing state agencies have little experience with delegating jurisdiction to local agencies. In the interests of flexibility, autonomy, and experimentation, it would be advisable to create a new agency empowered to delegate authority. (4) Existing agencies are underbudgeted and understaffed and therefore unable to provide adequate service in a rapidly expanding field.

Once again the differences may be emphasized in Professor McKelvey's analysis without due regard for the analogies which may be more significant. Certainly where differences between the public and private sectors are real and material they should be recognized, but who is better equipped to recognize them and be resourceful about them than those who have been regulating labor relations with incisiveness and imagination. That officials with such qualities may not be easily come by is as true for new agencies as for existing ones. The WERC has struggled to adjust traditional concepts of labor relations to fit the realities of public employment. In the adoption of unit determination guidelines, criteria for supervisory status and rules for timeliness in the initiation of representation proceedings, for example, factors peculiar to public employment must be recognized. That our mediation techniques are sensitive to the peculiar pressure of public administration is indicated to the extent they have been successful.

The suspicions of public employers may be alleviated by many devices, including real examples of integrity and neutrality and efforts to show interest in their problems outside of actual case processing. This includes commission participation in any educational program to which it is invited and informal discussions of problems on a person-to-person basis.

For some suspicious neophytes, the only persons whose familiarity with their "unique problems" (that assumption again) will be satisfactory are fellow public administrators whose neutrality may be questionable by the unions. There is a tendency among these officials to overemphasize their peculiarities; some of them, and their employees as well, would require a special agency for single professional groupings. But good employment relations techniques are applicable with appropriate modifications to an enormous variety of settings. Employment relations experts, rather than experts in the various governmental line functions, must be located within such employers as well as within the regulatory agencies.

The Wisconsin statute governing local employees allows local governments to create their own agencies for fact finding. To our knowledge, none have done so to date although some legally inadequate efforts have been made.[1] Futher, a fact-finding commission chaired by Professor Nathan P. Feinsinger recommended the creation of a Milwaukee Labor Peace Agency, but this suggestion has not been implemented.

No one is proposing that existing agencies should be disbanded or depleted. McKelvey's point is that they are already "underbudgeted and understaffed," which may be the case in some jurisdictions, although usually not in Wisconsin. Nonetheless, it is continually suggested that new agencies manned by experts not drawn from existing agencies be set up on every level and in every jurisdiction. Where in the world such neutral experts are going to come from is apparently too specific a problem for such proposals to address, however. In this regard we also note simultaneous complaints about the general lack of trained neutrals and the advancing age of many of our most respected neutrals.

We have used McKelvey's excellent article as a focusing device here and intend no general criticism of her analysis. She left "the task of striking a balance" to her readers among whom we number. Our comments are intended to indicate what our experience in Wisconsin teaches about the issues she faced and about the items she would place on the scales. We recognize that there are extreme variations in political climates, labor-management communities, industrialization, urbanization, union militancy and resistance thereto, and many other relevant variables which should dictate what is appropriate to a given jurisdiction.

The commission consists of three commissioners, one of whom is designated as the chairman, appointed by the governor at two-year intervals for six-year terms, a professional staff, and supporting personnel. Over the years commissioners have been appointed from industry, labor, and law practice, and from various areas of the state. There have been reappointments despite initial appointments by governors of the other party. It seems fair to conclude that the commissioners have deemphasized their political identities, if any, and accordingly have not been vulnerable to criticism grounded on allegations of political motivation. On the other hand, they have taken an active, conspicuous role on "the firing line" as skilled professionals.

The professional staff, which presently consists of ten individuals officially titled "mediators," has been hired according to the state's general Civil Service procedures. Six are lawyers and six have earned advanced degrees in some employment relations-related area. Their previous employers include government, labor, and management. Their median age is 30.5 years, and they are relatively highly paid.[2] Only five are Wisconsin natives. The commissioners and professional staff

---

[1] See *Shawano County*, Dec. No. 6388; *Pierce County*, Dec. No. 6573; *Barron County*, Dec. No. 6574; *City of Wauwatosa*, Dec. No. 7106; *Village of Whitefish Bay*, Dec. No. 7494, aff'd, 34 Wis. (2d) 432.

[2] A very thorough study of state mediators by Berkowitz, Goldstein, and Indik ("The State Mediator: Background, Self-Image, and Attitudes," *Industrial and Labor Relations Review*, XVII, No. 2 [January 1964], 257-275) indicates *inter alia,* that "the typical state mediator" is

members may and do act as mediators, arbitrators, hearing officers in representation cases and trial examiners in unfair labor and prohibited practice cases. Each acts in all of these capacities in all three sectors of employment. The commissioners share the same workload carried by their staff. In terms of responsibilities they are distinguishable mainly by their review function in unfair labor practice cases; their decision-making function in representation cases; and their administrative duties and responsibilities associated with being in charge of the agency. The only limiting factors to assignment of a particular staff member or commissioner are caseload, scheduling realities, and a general policy against assigning a man who has participated as a mediator in a particular situation to be an arbitrator or trial examiner in the same situation, and only lawyers act as Hearing Examiners in unfair labor and prohibited practice complaint cases.

The commission, upon request, will provide a panel of ad hoc arbitrators outside of its staff, in the manner of the American Arbitration Association or the Federal Mediation and Conciliation Service. It also appoints ad hoc fact finders from outside its staff in public employment disputes. Ad hoc arbitrators and the fact finders are paid jointly by the parties, but no fee is paid for mediation or arbitration performed by those in the employ of the agency.

It is our contention that the commission's arrangement works because its neutrality has proved acceptable and its representatives are trained and experienced. Each commission representative speaks with some knowledge of private and public employment relations, and of both the legal and the nonlegal aspects of such affairs. May not the NLRB's construction of bargaining in good faith suffer from their isolation from bargaining? Is it not possible that some mediators could be more helpful if they were aware of the legal framework that is the exoskeleton of bargaining, or if they arbitrated? Does not the public sector legal structure, rightly or wrongly, resemble that of private labor relations? Wisconsin experience seems to demonstrate that engaging in a multiplicity of related roles contributes to one's effectiveness in each role; in a sense, the resultant whole is materially greater than the sum of its parts. (Apparently, many members of the arbitration profession share these conclusions as they, who are most commonly trained in the law and experienced in the private sector, offer their services in the public sector.)

The absolutely necessary impression of neutrality may also be the result of prior operations in the private sector. It has already been established that the commissioners are not political in any manner that might put off public officials, and they do not represent any particular "interest." Likewise, the staff is impartially chosen from diverse backgrounds under conditions which allow the commission to compete for and keep qualified personnel. The Wisconsin labor relations

---

forty-five to fifty-four years old and has "some college education." Thirty-six percent had been paid union officials and half had been management officials and a few had been both. The 1969 salary survey of the Association of Labor Mediation Agencies indicates that among city, state, and provincial agencies, Wisconsin salaries are very close to the highest and very much higher than most with a maximum of $19,692 per year available to all staff members. This does not compare quite as favorably with FMCS salaries. Unfortunately, similar data regarding state and federal regulatory labor agencies with which the WERC must also be compared is not available. However, we judge from informal conversations that the state and local level comparisons would be approximately the same, whereas few NLRB staff members would reach the salary levels available at the WERC. Of course, part of our competitive appeal also lies in a diversity of work unavailable anywhere else.

community has known for some years about the quality of the commissioners and their staff.

The typical age of the staff members may be indicative of their adaptability to new circumstances. The need to teach "old dogs" is minimized. The likelihood of their being acceptable to certain of the "professional" types who get so much attention in the public sector is maximized. The impression that some mediation agencies give of being an alternative to retirement for former union and company officials is avoided.

The Wisconsin community includes many small employers and their employees located in the least industrial areas. Now that these areas, where public employers might otherwise be "suspicious," are reached by our public sector activities, we are known as administrators who have found unions as well as employers guilty and who never assume an advocate's role.

Perhaps, most importantly, the Wisconsin labor relations community has achieved a relatively high level of maturity and sophistication. The unions here have been enjoying success in organizing and in bargaining for a substantial number of years and are generally believed free of unwholesome elements. Employer acceptance of this is the norm, although hardly to be characterized as surrender. Some local public employers in Wisconsin have been bargaining with their employees' representatives since long before any statute supported doing so. The American Federation of State, County and Municipal Employees, which was born here, has been an important representative of the state's employees for decades. We believe that mutual respect has developed within this community and that over the years of this development the Wisconsin Employment Relations Commission also has achieved respect and skills which would have been squandered had another agency been created for public employee relations.

A SEPARATE AGENCY
FOR ADMINISTERING COLLECTIVE BARGAINING
BY PUBLIC EMPLOYEES

Robert D. Helsby
Thomas E. Joyner

In establishing his Committee on Public Employee Relations on January 15, 1966, Governor Rockefeller requested it "to make legislative proposals for protecting the public against the disruption of vital public services by illegal strikes,

Robert Helsby and Thomas Joyner are Chairman, and Director of Research and Analysis, respectively, New York State Public Employment Relations Board. Article prepared specifically for this volume.

while at the same time protecting the rights of public employees." The committee consisted of E. Wight Bakke, David L. Cole, John T. Dunlop, Frederick H. Harbison, and George W. Taylor.

The problem faced by the committee was to develop a system for public sector labor relations applicable to nearly one million state and local employees. Its task was complicated by the fact that nearly three hundred thousand municipal employees in New York City had been engaged in one form of collective bargaining or another for a number of years, while about seven hundred thousand had no bargaining history. The Taylor Committee summarized its assessment of the problem as follows:

> Despite many complexities, we believe it is both feasible and desirable to develop a system of collective negotiation in the public service. This can be achieved in a manner which is consonant with the orderly functioning of a democratic government. It cannot be achieved by transferring collective bargaining as practiced in the private enterprise sector into the governmental sector. New procedures have to be created.[1]

In accordance with this conclusion, the Taylor Committee recommended that a state Public Employment Relations Board be created which would be empowered to:

1. Resolve disputes arising with respect to the representation status of an employee organization.
2. Resolve impasses arising out of collective negotiations through the institution of mediation procedures and, if necessary, the appointment of fact-finding boards.
3. Determine, in the event of a strike, whether or not the dues checkoff privilege of the employee organization should be suspended.[2]
4. Compile data with respect to wages, salaries, and other conditions of employment and conduct research with respect to issues requiring additional legislation.

In 1967 the legislature enacted the Public Employees' Fair Employment Law, popularly known as the Taylor Law, which basically followed the recommendations of the Taylor Committee. The law, in addition to the functions of the Public Employment Relations Board (PERB) outlined above, continues the prohibition against public employee strikes, provides for judicially imposed penalties on striking employee organizations, and imposes a duty upon public employers to negotiate with recognized or certified employee organizations with respect to wages and salaries and other conditions of employment and the administration of grievances.

In 1969 two major amendments were enacted. A section prohibiting improper practices by public employers and employee organizations was added. The penalty

---

[1]Governor's Committee on Public Employee Relations, Final Report (Taylor Committee), p. 19.

[2]The Taylor Committee recommended in addition that the board should be empowered to suspend the representation rights of the employee organization, but this recommendation was not incorporated into subsequent legislation.

section was amended, and penalties applicable to employees who strike were added. Other, mostly clarifying, amendments were also adopted. The functions of the Public Employment Relations Board were increased in that it was charged with administering the improper practice provisions. In this connection the legislature reasserted the differences between the public and private sector by saying:

> In applying this section [improper practices] fundamental distinctions between private and public employment shall be recognized, and no body of federal or state law applicable wholly or in part to private employment, shall be regarded as binding or controlling precedent.[3]

As a result of legislative enactment of the Taylor Committee recommendations, the New York State Public Employment Relations Board is charged with responsibilities which, in the private sector, are sometimes distributed over as many as three separate agencies. Representation and unfair labor practice determinations are sometimes handled by one agency—for example, the National Labor Relations Board, the New York State Labor Relations Board, and so on. Negotiation deadlocks are sometimes handled by a separate agency—for example, the Federal Mediation and Conciliation Service, the New York State Mediation Board, and so on. Research functions are also usually separate—for example, U.S. Bureau of Labor Statistics, New York State Department of Labor, and so on. In some states a single agency has been made responsible for representation, unfair labor practices, and conciliation matters. In Wisconsin and Michigan, for example, such agencies have been given both public and private sector responsibilities.

The Taylor Committee and the legislature gave no public consideration to the approach followed by some states—special legislation for occupational categories such as teachers, police, and so on. The Taylor law places all state and local public employees essentially under the jurisdiction of one agency.

The Taylor Law also provides for the creation of local public employment relations agencies. The most notable of these is the Office of Collective Bargaining (OCB) in New York City. Somewhat more than two hundred thousand public employees are subject to OCB jurisdiction. As of September 1969 there were twenty-three local boards in existence which had jurisdiction over fifty-five thousand employees. With the exception of OCB, local legislation and procedures of the local boards are subject to the approval of the state board. Essentially, local boards exercise the same functions as the state board with the major exception that local boards have no jurisdiction over improper practices. The law assigns this responsibility to the state board only.

The viability of the concept of a separate agency to administer public sector labor relations depends on the validity of several assumptions. The two most important are:

1. There is a basic difference between public and private sector labor relations.
2. Aside from other differences, a public sector strike prohibition is so pervasive that it influences all aspects of public sector labor relations.

[3]Civil Service Law, Sec. 209a(3).

While space prevents a full exposition of the differences between public and private sector labor relations, the following examples are illustrative. Unit determination questions in the public sector present a different range of issues than in the private sector. The common applicability of civil service laws and regulations to employees in diverse occupations may give them a community of interest not shared by such employees in the private sector. Also, public sector management is not the same as private sector management. The exclusion of first-line supervision from rank-and-file units may make little sense in the public sector as such supervisors, in many instances, have a community of interest with those they supervise. Exclusivity in the private sector precludes management from discussing issues with rival or minority groups. This type of prohibition is not appropriate in the public sector where all types of organizations, both inside and outside government, may have a constitutional right to discuss issues with government.

With respect to unfair labor practices, it is clear that an unfair labor practice determination against a public employer whose officials must face reelection is a substantially different proposition from an unfair labor practice determination against a private corporation.

Public sector negotiations are also very different from those in the private sector where, under normal conditions, the authority of management to negotiate is not in dispute. In the public sector the authority of management to negotiate is complicated by the existence of civil service laws, finance laws, determinations of attorneys general and comptrollers, and a wide range of other constitutional and legislative provisions which place restraints on what public management can negotiate about or what agreements require changes in law before they can become effective.

The approach to resolving impasses is necessarily different. Because of the strike prohibition, alternative techniques have to be devised to resolve disputes. Public sector efforts normally include mediation, which for practical purposes is compulsory, and fact finding—with or without public recommendations. In the private sector a mediator normally goes into a situation only with the consent of the parties and if mediation fails a strike is a normal expectation. The emphasis in the public sector on compulsory impasse procedures differentiates conciliation techniques from those used in the private sector.

The debates about how much the constitutional, legislative, and political setting influences comparability between governmental and nongovernmental activity are not confined to labor relations. These elements pervade almost all the procedures and processes of government and result in marked differences in both substance and administration from the private sector. In part, the debate as to whether or not public sector labor relations is significantly different from private sector labor relations is similar to that found in public administration literature as to whether or not the constitutional and legal framework which surrounds public administration makes a significant difference.

The public sector strike prohibition pervades all aspects of public sector labor relations. It affects organizing efforts, unit determination questions, negotiating techniques of both parties, and impasse procedures. The fundamental fact about labor relations in the public sector is that, for the most part, neither public employers nor employee organizations expect a strike to take place, and neither has developed a strike strategy. For example, in their approach to unit determination questions, most public employers have not insisted that first-line supervisors be excluded from rank-and-file units. Many public employers have, initially at least, not even recognized the necessity for providing themselves with adequate staff support for negotiating purposes by excluding such personnel from units.

On the employee side, it may not be possible to mount effective strikes in diversified general units. Even a cursory review of public sector strikes has been mounted by organizations with a clear occupational orientation—for example, teachers, sanitation workers, and so on. At the same time many employee organizations are so small that there is serious question as to whether removal of the strike prohibition would not actually weaken their present position. The average employee organization (local) in New York State has less than seventy-five members. Such organizations are largely dependent on compulsory impasse procedures. Thus the expectation in the public sector is not that of negotiations supported by mediation, if required, followed by a strike in case of deadlock. The public sector norm is negotiations supplemented by various types of third-party assistance—mediation, fact finding, voluntary arbitration—or various variations and combinations thereof. Public sector impasse procedures are still in the experimental stage. No final prescription or panacea is in sight.

Since September 1, 1967, when the Taylor Law became effective, about nine hundred thousand of the nearly one million state and local employees in New York State have exercised their rights under the law, some six hundred thousand of them for the first time. It is estimated that some eleven hundred public employers have negotiated collectively with their employees in some twenty-five hundred negotiating units. Those employees who have not exercised their rights under the law are for the most part employed by small municipalities with five employees or less. There are several thousand such employers.

With respect to representation issues, most public employers and their employees have been able to resolve both unit and organizational questions without resort to third-party assistance. From September 1, 1967, through October 1969, some 420 petitions have been processed by PERB. These were concerned with a range of unit and organizational questions ranging from a few school bus drivers to more than one hundred thirty-five thousand state employees. After an initial surge of representation petitions, the number received appears to be stabilizing at about seventy-five annually. In this initial period there were only three strikes over representation issues. The one major representation strike involved attendants at state mental hygiene institutions in November 1968.

Since the law became effective, third-party assistance has been provided in more than one thousand impasses through October 1969. About half were settled through mediation. The other half went to fact finding. However, about 25 percent of the cases which went to fact finding were settled without the issuance of a report—the fact finder was able to bring about a resolution of the dispute through mediation. In about half of the cases in which fact finding was required, the fact finder's recommendations were accepted by both parties. In the remaining 25 per cent, additional negotiations took place subsequent to the issuance of the fact-finding report. The range of such negotiations varied from minor rearrangements of the package to full-scale negotiations with additional third-party assistance. In most instances staff mediators provided such assistance.

Some 80 percent of the conciliation workload involves school districts. This situation arises not only because of teacher militancy but also because of a larger number of school districts with significant numbers of employees than other types of jurisdictions. School budget dates are in the spring and early summer and most other local government budget dates come in the fall. In order to handle peak workloads, the Board maintains a small conciliation staff and per diem panels of mediators and fact finders. An attempt is made to process all requests for assistance within twenty-four hours. Fact finders normally submit their reports and recommendations within one month after assignment.[4] Since the impasse procedures are designed as a substitute for the right to strike, speed is essential. It should also be noted that the costs of mediation and fact finding constitute a charge against the state.

Impasse procedures and strike prohibitions do not, of course, prevent all strikes. The objective is to minimize the number of work stoppages. In 1968 there were 26 work stoppages in New York State involving 73,399 employees. In 1969, through November, there have been 10 stoppages involving 1,343 employees. The New York City school strike in the fall of 1968 accounts for most of the difference between 1968 and 1969. This strike involved fifty-three thousand employees and resulted in the loss of 1,860,000 man-days lost, 93 percent of the time lost in the state due to public employee stoppages.

As previously indicated, penalties—particularly prior to April 1, 1969—were largely applicable to employee organizations. Such penalties were either imposed judicially—for example, fines for contempt of court—or by PERB or a mini-PERB, with regard to the suspension of dues checkoff. Unlike the situation which prevailed under Condon-Wadlin, the statutory penalties have been applied in almost every situation in which responsibility could be attributed to an employee organization. The difference can be attributed to the fact that under Condon-Wadlin penalties were administered by the employer and thus became negotiable, whether properly so or not, even though legislative acquiescence was required in several instances. Public employers have for the most part been reluctant to file charges. In twenty-one instances in which charges relative to the suspension of dues checkoff have been filed with the board, such charges have been brought by the public employer in six instances and by the board's counsel in fifteen.

Since both the Taylor Committee and the legislature visualized the Taylor Law as somewhat experimental, the law charges the board with certain research functions:

> To make studies and analyses of, and act as a clearing house of information relating to, conditions of employment of public employees throughout the state.
> . . .To request from any government, and such governments are authorized to provide, such assistance, services and data as will enable the board properly to carry out its functions and powers.
> . . .To conduct studies of problems involved in representation and nego-

---

[4]Fact-finding in New York State appears to be somewhat different than that found in other states. For example, a Wisconsin study indicates that an average of five months is required to get a fact-finding report to the parties. (Edward Krinsky, "An Analysis of Fact Finding as a Procedure of Labor Disputes Involving Public Employees," unpublished Ph.D. dissertation, University of Wisconsin.)

tiation, including but not limited to (i) whether employee organizations are to be recognized as representatives of their members only or are to have exclusive representation rights for all employees in the negotiating unit, (ii) the problems of unit determination, (iii) those subjects which are open to negotiation in whole or in part, (iv) those subjects which require administrative or legislative approval of modifications agreed upon by the parties, and (v) those subjects which are for determination solely by the legislative body.[5]

In discharging these responsibilities, policy studies have been conducted or are under way with respect to exclusivity, characteristics of bargaining units, the scope of bargaining, the exclusion of managerial and confidential personnel from basic units, and contractual grievance procedures. In addition, numerous salary and fringe benefit surveys have been undertaken or data compiled.

The case for a separate agency to administer public sector collective bargaining depends not only on the assumption that the public sector is different from the private sector, but also on the assumption that the mix of responsibilities assigned to the agency is compatible. This in turn depends on how successful the agency is in keeping the disparate functions from conflicting with one another.

For example, in a strike situation the conciliation section has the responsibility of assisting the parties in arriving at a settlement while the counsel's office must at some point undertake an investigation. Similarly, some near settlements have collapsed because of the release of research reports on wages and salaries indicating that the prospective settlement was out of line with prevailing rates.

Representation disputes resulting in petitions may have an unfortunate relationship to the negotiating of a new contract. Improper practice charges may facilitate or exacerbate negotiations by removing certain questions and issues from the table or by increasing the bitterness between the parties.

The problem in administering such an agency is to maintain an overall image of neutrality, impartiality, and fairness. At the same time, however, the exercise of prudent discretion in the timing of how certain issues are handled is essential if the disparate responsibilities of the board are to be prevented from interfering with one another. Of course, this cannot always be prevented, and in many instances should not be.

The experience of the past two years demonstrates that the particular mix assigned to the Public Employment Relations Board is workable in the New York State situation. The transferability of the New York approach is a fundamental question.

In a recent speech, Clyde W. Summers of the Yale University Law School, while taking issue with the viewpoint that public sector bargaining is significantly different from that in the private sector, suggested that in the public sector the principle of nontransferability should be accepted for a time so that private sector premises could be reexamined.[6] Experience in New York State and other states suggests, however, that if the public sector is different and if that difference is to be maintained, an agency with only public sector responsibilities should be assigned to the task. To a more limited extent, this appears to be true if those private sector

[5]Civil Service Law, Sec. 205.5(a), (f), and (g).
[6]GERR, October 13, 1969, p. B-6.

concepts which are utilized in whole or in part in the public sector are to be chosen with care.

One basic problem is that all, or almost all, of the practitioners are well grounded in the private sector and resist any more than minimal alteration. In some respects this is also true of analysis based in the halls of academe. Thus it would seem that chances for an independent look are better if the administering agency is independent and its responsibility is limited to the public sector.

In conclusion, a separate agency to administer public sector labor relations, based on the initial two and a half years of experience in New York State with the Taylor Law, appears warranted because:

1. There are significant and basic differences between public and private sector labor relations.
2. A separate agency provides greater assurance that private sector concepts will be reexamined before being adopted intact and without challenge in the public sector.
3. A single agency can successfully administer the various responsibilities without undue difficulty.

All approaches to public sector labor relations should at this point be considered somewhat experimental. If private sector methods and techniques have not been fully perfected in more than forty years, it cannot be expected that the final answer in the public sector will emerge in a few short years. However, the experimental concepts of the New York State Taylor Law show promise of pointing the way toward resolution of some of the pressing problems of public sector employee relations—indeed one of the most critical problem areas of our generation.

THE OFFICE OF COLLECTIVE BARGAINING IN NEW YORK CITY

Arvid Anderson

The Office of Collective Bargaining (OCB), a pioneering tripartite administrative experiment in public employee labor relations, began operations in New York City on January 2, 1968. The OCB was created by the New York City Council and was implemented by Mayor John V. Lindsay's Executive Order 52 as a result of the 1967 agreement between the city and most of the municipal unions with which it bargains.[1] The agreement was developed by a panel under the auspices of the Labor

Arvid Anderson is Chairman, Office of Collective Bargaining, New York City. Article prepared specifically for this volume.

[1] Local Law 53 (1967), New York City Charter, Chapter 54; Executive Order 52 (1967).

Management Institute of the American Arbitration Association, which had begun the task at the request of Mayor Robert F. Wagner in 1965 and completed its work at the request of Mayor Lindsay in 1966.

The panel endorsed the concept of public employee collective bargaining as "the most effective means in our society for matching employer requirements with employee needs" and concluded that an administrative procedure was essential to effectuate the collective bargaining process. The tripartite agreement emphasized the necessity of administrative procedures to determine bargaining units, to define the scope of bargaining, and to establish procedures for the resolution of impasses in bargaining.

BACKGROUND

Mayor Wagner in 1954 established a city Department of Labor and later that year, based in part on a report of that department, issued an interim order on the conduct of labor relations between the city of New York and its employees. The interim order enunciated the principles that city employees have the right to join labor organizations, that each city agency must establish a grievance procedure, and that each agency must also establish a joint labor management committee to "assist" in formulating policy and to "suggest" changes in wages, hours, and working conditions.

In 1958 Mayor Wagner issued Executive Order 49 which formally authorized collective bargaining between the city and its municipal employee organizations. As a result of Executive Order 49 and of the organizing efforts of prior years, a large number of city employees joined a variety of municipal unions. Organization took place along departmental lines and on the basis of job or occupational titles. Bargaining certifications were issued by the city Department of Labor for individual titles. Executive Order 49 was a building block approach designed to encourage employee organization and provided for informal, formal, and exclusive means of employer recognition. Unions which represented less than 10 percent of the employees of a proposed bargaining unit were granted informal recognition. Unions with more than 10 percent but less than 50 percent of representation in a bargaining unit were granted formal recognition. Exclusive recognition was granted to majority representatives in an appropriate bargaining unit. Thus collective bargaining units were established based on the extent of organization without any particular regard to the impact of such certification on subsequent collective bargaining policies. As the majority of city employees became organized, there were many examples of conflicting union jurisdictional claims and disputes over whether subjects were bargainable.

A dispute over the appropriate subject matter of bargaining was a cause of a strike by welfare case workers in May 1965, one of the first major strikes by public employees in the country. As a result, city and union officials sought to work out a better method of resolving public employee disputes, and Mayor Wagner authorized the tripartite study.

One of the problems was that representation questions and dispute settlement procedures were in the hands of the city labor department, an arm of the mayor, and thus regarded by the unions as a tool of management. To meet this complaint, the tripartite structure was created. For the first time anywhere public employee labor relations for unit determinations, dispute settlement machinery, scope of bargaining, and many other responsibilities were placed in the hands of an agency in which the three interested parties—the governmental employer, the employee, and the public—would be represented.

ORGANIZATION

The Office of Collective Bargaining consists of two boards: a seven-member Board of Collective Bargaining and a three-member Board of Certification. The Board of Collective Bargaining has two labor representatives, two city representatives, and three impartial members. The two labor representatives are designated by the Municipal Labor Committee (MLC), an organization of some 85 local unions with more than 130,000 members representing city employees.[2] The New York City Collective Bargaining Law provides that membership in the MLC shall be open to any employee organization to which some or all of the provisions of the statute are applicable.[3] The two city representatives are chosen by the mayor. The election of the three impartial members must be unanimous. The salary and expenses of the impartials are shared equally by the city and by the Municipal Labor Committee. The impartial members also constitute the Board of Certification which is authorized to determine questions of representation. The chairman, who is also the director of the Office of Collective Bargaining, is full time and salaried; the other two impartial members are paid on a per diem basis. The city and labor representatives serve without compensation.

In order to distinguish further the city's governmental role from its role as an employer, the mayor, by Executive Order 38 in 1967, created a separate management negotiating team, the Office of Labor Relations. The head of the OLR is directly responsible to the mayor and is in charge of all negotiations between the city and the various unions with which it negotiates. Formerly, negotiating responsibility had been shared by the budget director, the personnel director, and other officials representing the city. Such officers now serve in a consulting and advisory capacity, but the major responsibility for bargaining is now in the Office of Labor Relations.

The New York City Collective Bargaining Law operates under the general authority of the state Taylor Law which is administered by the Public Employment Relations Board.[4] The state statute authorizes New York City to set up its own collective bargaining and dispute settlement procedures so long as they are substantially equivalent to the state law. The OCB functions in two general areas: formal legal proceedings and disputes.

The Board of Certification determines representation questions: establishing

---

[2]While jurisdiction of the OCB does not depend upon membership in the MLC, nearly all have joined. A few unions representing city employees have not joined, although several of the large unions which did not initially join the MLC, such as the Social Service Employees Union and the Uniformed Firefighters Association, have joined during the past year.

[3]New York City Collective Bargaining Law, sec. 1173-9.0.

[4]Sec. 212, Public Employees' Fair Employment Law (Taylor Law).

appropriate bargaining units and certifying employee organizations on the basis of dues checkoff or by conducting elections. The Board of Collective Bargaining decides disputes over the scope of bargaining and disputes over the arbitrability of unresolved grievances. This board also makes advisory determinations on whether there has been full-faith compliance with the terms of the collective bargaining statute. The OCB administers dispute settlement machinery, designating mediators, impasse panelists, and grievance arbitrators.

The basic concept of the OCB is rooted in its tripartite structure, which relies heavily on consent procedures. Such procedures are considered by the interested parties to offer the greatest prospect for success in labor relations. Just as the impartial members of the OCB are chosen by consent, all impasse panel members, grievance arbitrators, and mediators employed by the OCB have been placed on the registers of the OCB only by mutual consent. The parties share the expenses of all neutrals. Even the procedural rules of the agency were established by tripartite agreement of the city, the MLC, the OCB, and members of both boards.

Such agreement was possible because there is one major employer, the city of New York, and because the major unions involved and the city wanted an agreed procedure for New York City. Agreement was not easily achieved because of the large number of unions with varying and competing interests and because the city of New York is a complex governmental structure with more than fifty departments and related agencies and authorities.

JURISDICTION

By the mayor's option under Executive Order 52, OCB jurisdiction includes all mayoral agencies such as Police, Fire, Sanitation, Parks, Hospitals—some fifty agencies in all. Other nonmayoral agencies were authorized by law to use OCB procedures and come under OCB jurisdiction upon approval of the mayor. Many such agencies agreed to the procedures, including the Judicial Conference covering the city court system, the Housing Authority, the Board of Higher Education for its nonteaching employees, and offices of the comptroller, the five borough presidents, the five district attorneys, and, most recently, the five public administrators and the Board of Elections. By the end of its second year the OCB had some two hundred thousand city employees under its jurisdiction. Public employers not participating were the Board of Education, the cultural and scientific institutions such as the libraries, museums, and zoos, and the Transit Authority.

THE TAYLOR LAW AND THE OCB

The 1969 session of the state legislature revised the Taylor Law and mandated New York City's mayor to recommend changes in the local law dealing with jurisdiction, the subject of budget submission dates in relation to negotiating procedures, and finality in impasse proceedings.[5] Thus Mayor Lindsay submitted a report

[5]Sec. 212, Taylor Law as amended, Chapter 24, Laws of 1969.

to the 1969 legislature recommending the expansion of OCB jurisdiction to include all agencies that provide municipal services to the people of New York City. Particularly, this would extend OCB jurisdiction over all nonmayoral agencies, including the Board of Education, the Board of Higher Education for teaching employees, cultural and scientific institutions, and even the Transit Authority which is part of the state-operated Metropolitan Transportation Authority. The state legislature declined to act on the question of jurisdiction in its 1970 session and is expected to take up the matter again in 1971. Also, in the 1971 session, the legislature is expected to review the matter of continuing OCB jurisdiction over improper practices. The mayor had requested that this jurisdiction, which OCB has had since its inception, be continued. The most significant of the proposals recommended by the Mayor would authorize the Board of Collective Bargaining to make final and binding decisions on impasse panel recommendations that had been rejected by either of the parties. The proposal was before the city council at the time of this writing.

The major substantive problems confronting the OCB since its inception have been the structure of bargaining, which is the concern of the Board of Certification; the scope of bargaining, which is the responsibility of the Board of Collective Bargaining; and the resolution of bargaining impasses, which is handled by the OCB's disputes division.

STRUCTURE OF BARGAINING

The complexity of the task facing the Board of Certification becomes apparent by examining the problems relating to the levels of bargaining. Departmental certificates convey only the right to process grievances, a right that exists only if there is no citywide certificate holder.[6] A citywide certification is issued to a union which represents a majority of employees in a particular job title or occupational group—such as clerks, usually involving a number of city departments. A citywide certification entitles the union to bargain on wages and other related matters. Still another level of bargaining applies to matters which must be uniform throughout the city for all employees in the Career and Salary Plan which encompasses virtually all city employees in the uniformed forces. District Council 37, AFSCME, in addition to the citywide certifications it holds for bargaining on wages and related matters, has been designated as the union which represents the majority of employees in the city Career and Salary Plan. Thus it is also authorized to bargain on matters which must be uniform—such as pensions, overtime, sick leave, vacations, holidays, shift premiums, and summer hours. A similar bargaining designation is authorized to be issued to holders of citywide certifications for bargaining on conditions of employment which must be uniform for all the employees in a particular department such as Hospitals and Social Services.

It has been a major goal of the Office of Collective Bargaining to consolidate bargaining units along broad occupational groups as one means of diminishing the rivalry in bargaining.

The building block approach of establishing bargaining units based on extent or organization eventually resulted in some eight hundred different job title certifica-

[6]Board of Certification Decision No. 45-69, Local 246, SEIU.

tions being combined in some two hundred different bargaining entities, combinations of bargaining certifications, with which the city's Office of Labor Relations now negotiates. That office negotiates approximately one hundred contracts a year with some ninety local unions which are affiliated with approximately fifty parent labor organizations.

Efforts to consolidate bargaining units are now limited by existing collective bargaining contracts and by the no-raiding agreement of the AFL–CIO. The no-raiding pact precludes efforts by AFL–CIO unions to seek to represent employees already represented by another AFL–CIO union. In a move to minimize the effect of the no-raiding policy, the Board of Certification has ceased issuing departmental certificates.

The structure of bargaining in New York City is also affected by Section 220 of the State Labor Law, a prevailing wage statute administered by the comptroller which provides for wage determinations primarily for skilled and maintenance employees. Employees covered by Section 200 of the labor law are authorized under the New York City Collective Bargaining Law and the Taylor Law to bargain on nonfiscal matters such as grievance procedures. Section 220 does not provide for exclusive representation.

Another problem area demanding much of the Board of Certification's time is the status of managerial and supervisory employees. During its first two years of operation the Board of Certification received 279 representation cases and closed 215.[7] As the board entered the year 1970, twenty of the sixty-four pending cases concerned disputes over managerial status. It has been the policy of the Board of Certification to exclude managerial and confidential employees from bargaining rights under the statutes. The rationale is that the employer is entitled to a representative in bargaining, in the high-level administration of the contract, and in the formulation and implementation of the major goals of the agency which should not be entitled to bargaining rights. The board states, "Employer-dominated unions are prohibited because collective bargaining is meaningless when the employer sits on both sides of the bargaining table. The same principle is applicable when employees occupy both seats."

While managerial, executive, and confidential employees are excluded from bargaining rights, supervisory and professional employees are expressly authorized by statute to establish their own bargaining units if they wish to do so.

SCOPE OF BARGAINING

Closely related to the structure-of-bargaining question is the problem of the scope and level of bargaining. What is bargainable and by whom? The Board of Collective Bargaining has the responsibility to determine whether a matter is within the scope of collective bargaining under the terms of the applicable executive order and also whether or not a particular grievance is arbitrable. Such determinations are of critical importance because disputes which have not been resolved in bargaining may be submitted to an impasse panel for recommendations. Under the proposed amendments to the New York City Collective Bargaining Law, the recommenda-

[7]Second annual report, OCB, 1969.

tions of impasse panels may become final and binding upon the parties. Under such circumstances it is important that disputes over the scope of bargaining be determined prior to their submission to ad hoc impasse panels. Section 5 of Executive Order 52 defines in considerable detail matters within the scope of bargaining. Section 5(c) of that order contains a broad management rights clause:

> c. It is the right of the City, acting through its agencies, to determine the standards of services to be offered by its agencies; determine the standards of selection for employment; direct its employees; take disciplinary action; relieve its employees from duty because of lack of work or for other legitimate reasons; maintain the efficiency of governmental operations; determine the methods, means and personnel by which government operations are to be conducted; determine the content of job classifications; take all necessary actions to carry out its mission in emergencies; and exercise complete control and discretion over its organization and the technology of performing its work. The City's decisions on those matters are not within the scope of collective bargaining, but notwithstanding the above, questions concerning the practical impact that decisions on the above matters have on employees, such as questions of workload or manning, are within the scope of collective bargaining.

Of particular significance is the last qualifying sentence of 5(c) which provides that the city's exercise of managerial discretion—for example, on workload and manning questions—may come within the scope of bargaining if such decisions have a practical impact on employees. In a major decision the Board of Collective Bargaining has held that it has the authority to determine if there is "practical impact" on employees and that if the employer's efforts did not correct the impact or the parties could not agree, the matter could be submitted to an impasse panel.[8] Practical impact was defined as an unduly excessive and unreasonable workload as a regular and continuing condition of employment.

In another major dispute the Board of Collective Bargaining considered the city's challenge to the bargainability of some 151 of 241 contract demands by the Social Service Employees Union. The board adopted the private sector guidelines of "mandatory," "prohibited," and "voluntary" subjects of bargaining in resolving challenges to the duty to bargain. The board held that voluntary subjects could be "discussed" by mutual consent and included in agreements without being considered mandatory in future negotiations.[9]

During the two-year period of its operations, the Board of Collective Bargaining determined 35 challenges to grievance arbitration, 7 scope-of-bargaining cases, and 7 full-faith compliance actions. The full-faith compliance disputes are analogous to unfair labor practice cases in the private sector.

For example, the Board of Collective Bargaining determined that the city had not refused to bargain in good faith on the subject of merit increases for employees.

---

[8]Board of Collective Bargaining Decision No. B-9-68, City of New York Fire Department and Uniformed Firefighters Association & Uniformed Fire Officers Association.

[9]Board of Collective Bargaining Decision No. B-11-68, City of New York and Social Services Employees' Union.

The board ruled that the city had the right to grant merit increases at its own discretion but that procedures and criteria for determining these increases were within the scope of collective bargaining.[10]

IMPASSE RESOLUTION

A critical test of labor relations procedures is whether they are effective in the resolution of bargaining impasses. The question is particularly significant in the public sector when a state law prohibits the right to strike.

The two-year OCB experience in the resolution of impasses indicates that it is possible to have effective collective bargaining without the right to strike. During this two-year period there were fifty-three requests for impasse panel procedures, but it was necessary to have formal impasse reports issued in only twenty-five cases. Other disputes were resolved short of the formal issuance of impasse reports. All impasse panel recommendations to date have been accepted, although in a few instances there were initial rejections of the reports. The OCB is persuaded that the method of joint selection of expert impasse panel members has been a major factor in the success of the procedure to date. The record indicates that the parties are determined to make the process work when they feel a continuing stake in the procedure for settlement as well as in the result of a particular impasse dispute.

During the two-year period there were forty-three mediation requests, of which twenty-two cases were settled through mediation. Fourteen mediation cases were subsequently referred to impasse procedures and the others were resolved by the parties.

There has been a growing acceptance of the use of arbitration as a means of resolving grievances of employees. In its first two years the board received 101 grievance arbitration requests; 71 were closed. Many cases were settled without issuing formal awards.[11]

The dispute settlement and grievance arbitration procedures have affected virtually every category of public employment including police officers, firemen, sanitation men, hospital workers, nurses, doctors, motor vehicle operators, Housing Authority employees, court officers, probation officers, lifeguards, fire alarm dispatchers, attorneys, and administrative employees.

Not all the OCB efforts to resolve disputes have been successful. OCB efforts to resolve the sanitation dispute in February of 1968 did not result in an agreement.

AN EVALUATION

After two years of operation the question remains whether or not a tripartite administrative procedure is a successful and permanent means of resolving municipal labor disputes. We do not know the final answer at this time, but the record to

---

[10]Board of Collective Bargaining Decision No. B-9-69, City of New York and Civil Service Bar Association.

[11]Second annual report, OCB, 1969.

date is encouraging. Having had experience with both a private and public sector statute—one tripartite in nature and one all public—the writer makes no special argument that one procedure is vastly superior to the other. He does feel that for the New York City situation, which in many ways is *sui generis,* the tripartite concept dealing largely with one major employer has been soundly conceived and is workable in administration.

But there are problems. Analysis of some of the problems has resulted in proposed changes in the New York City Collective Bargaining Law and the Taylor Law.

Certainly the law can be no better than the people who administer it. To date the parties have determined that the law shall be administered by a professional staff and an impartial panel selected without regard to partisan political considerations.

Ultimately, the parties will determine whether the procedure will endure. To date the city, through its Office of Labor Relations, and the mayor, the Municipal Labor Committee, and its representatives, and the state, through its administrative agency the Public Employment Relations Board, have demonstrated that they want the tripartite procedures in New York City to work.

The fact that the procedures have worked so far in New York does not mean that the tripartite concept will automatically work elsewhere. The parties have made it work in New York because they have participated in writing the law, established the administrative structure, participated in the selection of neutrals, shared in the cost of its administration, participated in naming the impasse panels, grievance arbitrators, and mediators, and, through board members, participated in the determinations of the Board of Collective Bargaining.

To date virtually all decisions of the Board of Collective Bargaining have been by unanimous decision. While the city and labor representatives have vigorously advocated the position of their respective constituencies, thus far they have not automatically voted a partisan position. This has been true in determining disputes over scope of bargaining, arbitrability of grievances, and full-faith compliance decisions. Whether a tripartite procedure would work effectively in the event that the city and labor representatives insisted in maintaining a partisan position regardless of the merits of the dispute is a matter of speculation.

Regardless of whether or not a tripartite procedure is enacted elsewhere, I respectfully suggest to administrators of other labor relations statutes that there is much to be learned from the New York City experience.

CHAPTER 3

THE PROCESS
OF COLLECTIVE BARGAINING
IN PUBLIC EMPLOYMENT

Industrial relations practitioners and academicians often criticize the news media for publicizing strikes and other failures of collective bargaining without giving "equal time" to its successes. By emphasizing only the strikes and not the settlements, it is claimed, the public receives a distorted view of the institution. In view of this criticism of the news media, it is ironic that most of the scholarly writing on public employee bargaining devotes so much attention to the problem of public employee strikes at the expense of other aspects of public sector bargaining.

This section focuses on the process of collective bargaining in the public sector. Relatively few articles have been written analyzing the problems of recognition, unit determination, scope, grievance processing, and grievance arbitration. These are the areas that need further research and analysis.

Some very basic questions regarding the process of public sector bargaining remain unanswered. For example, given the highly political environment of the public sector, in what ways do the parties behave differently in bargaining? Is there a tendency for larger or smaller bargaining units than are found in the private sector? Do public officials accept smaller bargaining units more readily because they are accustomed to dealing with many small and diverse groups of citizens? In what way, if at all, does the scope of bargaining or the topics discussed differ from the scope of clauses in the collective bargaining agreement? Are dual grievance procedures viable in practice? These questions are only a few of the many that need further research and analysis.

The articles in this section deal with some aspects of these general questions. Rock discusses the determination of bargaining units in the public sector, emphasizing the difficulties faced by public employers who must deal with many small bargaining units instead of a few large units. Rehmus focuses on the difficulties local governments face in collective bargaining because of the many constraints placed on them by state laws regulating their taxing power. Readers will be interested to compare the Rehmus article with the articles by Wellington and Winter in Section VI which emphasize the inability of local governments to resist demands by unions of its employees. Gerhart discusses the differences between the scope of bargaining in the public sector and in the private sector. Rock analyzes some of the characteristics of grievance procedures and arbitration in the public sector.

BARGAINING UNITS IN THE PUBLIC SERVICE:
THE PROBLEM OF PROLIFERATION

Eli Rock

It is becoming increasingly clear that of the numerous problems which complicate the practice of collective bargaining in the public sector, none is more important than the appropriate unit question. In the public sector as well as in private industry, determination of the size and composition of the bargaining unit at the initial stages of organization and recognition can be decisive of the question of which employee organization will achieve majority recognition, or whether any organization will win recognition. Save for the employee organization which limits its jurisdiction along narrow lines such as the craft practiced by its members, the normal tendency may be to request initially a unit whose boundaries coincide with the spread of the organization's membership or estimated strength. The public employer, on the other hand, may seek to recognize a unit in which the no-union votes will be in the majority, or a favored employee organization will have predominant strength; or the employer may simply seek to avoid undue proliferation of bargaining units.

The problem in the public sector, however, is of far greater depth than the initial victory-or-defeat aspect of recognition. In the private sector, it is clear that the scope and nature of the unit found to be appropriate for bargaining has acted as an important determinant of the union's basic economic strength—that is, its bargaining over bread-and-butter economic issues. In the public sector, it seems clear that the scope and nature of the unit found to be appropriate will also affect the range of subjects which can be negotiated meaningfully, the role played in the process by the separate branches of government, the likelihood of peaceful resolution of disputes, order versus chaos in bargaining, and ultimately, perhaps, the success of the whole idea of collective bargaining for public employees.

Although the appropriate unit question has received much attention in the private sector during the past thirty years,[1] it has not received the same attention

Eli Rock is a professional arbitrator and was Labor Relations Advisor, city of Philadelphia, 1952-62. Reprinted from *Michigan Law Review*, LXVII (March 1969), 1001-11016.

[1] *See, e.g.*, Grooms, *The NLRB and Determination of the Appropriate Unit: Need for a Workable Standard*, 6 Wm. & Mary L. Rev. 13 (1965); Hall, *The Appropriate Bargaining Unit: Striking a Balance Between Stable Labor Relations and Employee Free Choice*, 18 W. Res. L. Rev. 479 (1967); Maddux, *Bargaining Unit Appropriateness in National Labor Relations Board Representation Proceedings*, 38 L.A. BAR. BULL. 298 (1963); Note, *The Board and Section 9(c)(5); Multilocation and Single-Location Bargaining Units in the Insurance and Retail Industries*, 79 Harv. L. Rev. 811 (1966).

for public sector employees until recently. The purpose of this Article is to focus on certain distinguishing aspects of both the problem and the experience in the public sector, and to discuss a possible approach or philosophy for the future. The primary concern here is undue proliferation of units among the large pool of blue-collar and white-collar employees in the public service. No attempt will be made to deal with special groups such as policemen and firemen, in which the unit question is less difficult. Nor will I discuss the unique problems of supervisors and professional employees, such as teachers, which are sufficiently important and complex to require separate treatment.

PAST TENDENCIES AND PATTERNS

Traditionally, the public employer and union have given little thought to the appropriateness of a unit that requested recognition. More often than not, in the years prior to the enactment of definitive rules for recognition of public employees, a union requesting and receiving some form of recognition was considered the spokesman for its members—in whatever job classifications, functional departments, or physical locations they happened to be. This lenient approach was facilitated by (and perhaps had its start in) the fact that "recognition" frequently carried no legal consequences beyond the ability to appear before legislative or executive bodies hearing budgetary requests or the power to lobby with key political figures.[2] Even when recognition was followed by a procedure similar to bargaining—including in some instances an embodiment of the bargain in a written agreement or memorandum—little if any consideration was given to the appropriateness of the unit being dealt with. Apart from the obvious problems stemming from the failure to grant "exclusive bargaining rights" to these early public employee units and from the inattention to the matter of excluding supervisors from the units representing those whom they supervise, a groundwork was laid for the creation of illogical unit lines. All too frequently the result was a proliferation of bargaining units. The task of changing this ill-conceived basis has often proved troublesome in the current period of rule-oriented bargaining.

Nor has the enactment of rules in the past ten years invariably led to a different pattern.[3] For example, under New York City's Executive Order 49, issued by Mayor Wagner in the late fifties, certificates of recognition were granted for over 200 separate units, some containing as few as two employees. The proportion of units to number of member-employees found in New York City is perhaps exceeded only in Detroit, where some seventy-eight separate units have come into existence. At the federal level, marked proliferation of units has also characterized

---

[2]*See* Norwalk Teacher's Assn. v. Board of Educ., 138 Conn. 269, 82 A, 2d 482 (1951). Miami Water Works, Local 654 v. City of Miami, 157 Fla. 445; 26 S.2d 194 (1964); Smith & Clark. *Reappraisal of the Role of the States in Shaping Labor Relations Law,* 1965 Wis. L. Rev. 411, 423.

[3]For an excellent discussion of the recent experience with the unit issue at all levels, *see* A. Thomson, Unit Determination in Public Employment, part of a series entitled "Public Employee Relations Reports," published by the New York State School of Industrial and Labor Relations at Cornell University.

the pattern of recognition under Executive Order No. 10,988;[4] a similar tendency seems inherent in a number of recently enacted state legislative standards for unit determination.[5] . . .

At the state and local levels, virtually all of the significant legislation passed since 1960 has spelled out standards of some type for unit determination. In many instances these state enactments made possible further proliferation by adding to the existing illogical patterns of recognition new units made possible through espousal of the federal "community of interest" standard and its converse, separate units for groups having "conflicting interests"; by providing for *Globe*-type elections or similar approaches designed to facilitate small unit separation; and, in the states of Delaware[6] and Minnesota,[7] by permitting the government agency to rely on the extent of employee organization. Notwithstanding the fact that some of the state laws embody specific standards used by the National Labor Relations Board for the private sector,[8] observers familiar with bargaining conditions in both sectors have contended that the degree of fragmentation in some of the states exceeds that of the private sector.[9]

Clearly, at both state and federal levels the standards place a high premium on the subjective judgment of the decision-making body or individual, and results are also shaped to a high degree by the happenstance of the petitioning organization's requested unit at the time of the petition. Particularly when there is no rival organizational claim for a larger unit—which is often the case—the over-all effect has been to encourage recognition of the smaller unit. Even if a union succeeds in winning recognition in a large unit, employees in that unit are generally not required to become members of the union. The relative lack of union security clauses in the collective bargaining agreements of the public service assures that, to a degree unparalleled in the private sector, dissident small-unit groups are able to maintain their separate identities and to prolong the battle for break-off from the larger group's exclusive bargaining agent.

THE CASE FOR AND AGAINST THE SMALL UNIT

It cannot be assumed automatically that the pattern of many small units is wrong. A single craft, classification, department, or installation which would other-

---

[4]3 C.F.R. 521 (1959-1963 Comp.). *See* Barr, *Executive Order 10,988: An Experiment in Employee-Management Cooperation in the Federal Service,* 52 Geo. L.J. 420 (1964).

[5]*See, e.g.,* CONN. GEN. STAT. ANN. §§7-471, 10-153(b) (Supp. 1969); DEL. CODE ANN. tit. 19, 1304 (Supp. 1966); MICH. COMP. LAWS ANN. §423. 213 (1967); MO. REV. STAT. §105. 500(3) (Supp. 1968); ORE. REV. STAT. §662. 705(1) (1967); R.I. GEN. LAWS ANN. §28-9.4-4 (1969); Sullivan, *Appropriate Unit Determinations in Public Employee Collective Bargaining,* 19 MERCER L. REV. 402, 410-16 (1968).

[6]DEL. CODE ANN. tit. 19, §1304 (Supp. 1967).

[7]MINN. STAT. ANN. §179.52 (1966).

[8]*See generally* Smith, *State and Local Advisory Reports on Public Employment Labor Legislation: A Comparative Analysis,* 67 MICH. L. REV. 891, 897-8, 903 (1969).

[9]*See* A. Thomson, *supra* note 3, at 10.

wise constitute a small minority if included in a larger unit can argue with some justification that its specialized interests and needs may be subordinated to the wishes of the larger unit's majority. Moreover, the smaller unit which performs a particularly essential function may also be capable of striking a better bargain for itself when left to do its own negotiating.

"Community of interest" is more than a catch phrase. It not only points up that like-situated employees will better understand their own problems and press their unique needs, but it also recognizes the instinct of exclusiveness which causes employees to *want* to form their own organization rather than become part of a larger organization in which they may feel themselves strangers. The desire to possess such "freedom of choice" or "self-determination" should, it can be argued, receive greater weight for public employees, because they are "public," than for those in the private sector.

There is nothing inherently wrong in permitting an employee organization to gain a foothold in a smaller unit, if the employees in that unit select it; and, if the union is effective in the small unit, it may grow and achieve recognition in other separate units or in a single large unit. This consideration may be particularly significant in the early period after the promulgation of legislation or executive orders emcompassing a vast group of employees whose right to representation had not previously been formally legitimized. It is frequently easier for unions to secure employees' allegiance in smaller, distinctive groups than in larger, heterogeneous ones.

At the same time, there are important considerations which, it seems, point toward a unique, long-range need for larger units in the public sector. The special problems of unit determination in the public sector were most clearly recognized legislatively in 1967 in New York's Taylor Law, which included, in addition to the common standards of community of interest and necessity to promote the public welfare, the further requirement that in defining an appropriate unit the following standard should be taken into consideration: "the officials of government at the level of the unit shall have the power to agree, or to make effective recommendations to other administrative authority or the legislative body with respect to, the terms and conditions of employment upon which the employees desire to negotiate . . . ."[10] The latter clause clearly reflects awareness of the fact that the employer-negotiator in the public service frequently has only limited authority, and that this condition will affect the scope of bargaining. As pointed out by the New York Governor's Committee on Public Employee Relations,[11] the picture in the public sector is fundamentally different from that in the private sector. In private business, the authority to bargain on all of the normally bargainable matters is present or can be delegated, no matter what the size or make-up of the bargaining unit. By contrast, in the public service the necessary authority may not be delegable to lower-level functional units; legal requirements and tradition often call for uniformity of certain working conditions for like categories of employees throughout the governmental entity, regardless of bargaining unit categorization; and, even at the top of the particular level of government involved, authority is normally divided

[10]N.Y. CIV. SERV. LAW § 207(1)(b) (McKinney Supp. 1968).

[11]Governor's Committee on Public Employee Relations, State of New York, Final Report 15-18 (March 31, 1966).

at least three ways—among the executive branch, the legislative branch, and a civil service commission.

Inherent in the previously quoted section of the Taylor Law,[12] therefore, is the necessity that some consideration be given to the nature of the subject matter sought to be bargained upon in seeking to arrive at the appropriateness of a unit.[13] This provision of the Taylor Law also recognizes that the subject matter of bargaining must normally be limited by the scope of the "employer's" authority to make agreements or effective recommendations, and a likely consequence is that the smaller the unit decided upon, the more restricted the scope of the bargaining by that unit will be.

Apart from this inhibiting effect on the bargaining experience, an approach which permits or favors small units makes it very difficult to resolve other institutional complications which arise in bargaining in the public service. The New York Governor's Committee, in both its 1966 Report[14] and its 1968 Report,[15] pointed out the unique importance of completing a negotiation with public employees in time to incorporate the agreement's financial essence in the budget of the governmental unit—which, by law, generally must be submitted to the legislature by a specified date.[16] However, many of the annual bargaining sessions in the public sector today are extraordinarily prolonged, starting with direct negotiation, followed by resort to mediation and the frequently used machinery of fact-finding or impasse panels. After all of this there may be further extensive dealings with upper-echelon individuals or groups in the executive and legislative branches. Thus, the sheer weight of the process[17] may lead to its breakdown if the trend toward proliferation of bargaining units in numerous jurisdictions continues unabated. It is noteworthy that in the City of Philadelphia[18] —which is frequently cited as an example of well-established, peaceful, and effective bargaining at the municipal level—all employees except policemen and firemen have been represented by a single unit for most of the last two decades. Even with only a single unit and without use of impasse resolution machinery, however, the experience in Philadelphia has been marked by many instances of abnormally prolonged annual negotiations. The Philadelphia experience also demonstrates the need to establish detailed liaison between the executive branch, the legislative branch, and the civil service

[12]*See* text accompanying note 15 *supra.*

[13]Governor's Committee, *supra* note 16, at 25-27.

[14]*Id.* at 33-34, 39.

[15]Governor's Committee on Public Employee Relations, State of New York, Interim Report (June 17, 1968).

[16]*See generally* Rehmus, *Restraints on Local Governments in Public Employee Bargaining,* 67 MICH. L. REV. 919, 924-25 (1969).

[17]For example, a February 27, 1968, report by an impasse panel for the unit of Detroit police officers recommended a procedure for future bargaining. The essential steps which the panel proposed were to extend over a period of nine months in a particular year. *Excerpts from Detroit Police Panel Report.* GOVT. EMPLOYEE REL. REP. [*hereinafter* GERR] No. 235, at D-1, D-10 (March 11, 1968).

[18]The author was the labor relations adviser to the City of Philadelphia between 1952 and 1962.

commission during the course of an annual bargaining program in order to minimize the chaotic effects of overlapping authority on the government side.

While it is possible that a city the size of Philadelphia might also have had a history of successful labor relations in the public sector under a pattern which broke down the public employee bargaining group into a small number of separate units, there is little question that the success could not have been achieved under the patterns of excessive fragmentation found elsewhere. In any event, the existence of the single large unit clearly contributed significantly to that city's ability to surmount effectively the institutional obstacles complicating public sector bargaining. Moreover, proliferation can and does breed excessive competition among rival organizations. One consequence of this may be a high incidence of breakdowns in peaceful bargaining. To be sure, competition in bargaining is to some extent unavoidable; this condition is not necessarily undesirable socially, and will continue to characterize the experience in private and public sector alike, regardless of the size of units involved. Nevertheless, there is hardly a permanent justification for permitting what appears to be a great proliferation of bargaining units in the public sector than that now prevailing in the private sector. The institutional factors discussed above add a unique dimension to the task of achieving peaceful and successful bargaining in the public sector. Because of this, and because of the likelihood that proliferation will result in an increased number of breakdowns in the bargaining process, larger units must become the accepted norm in the public sector.

SOME SIGNIFICANT RECENT EXPERIENCES

A number of specific case histories furnish valuable insight into both the unit determination problems posed in the public service and the steps which may be taken to resolve those problems. For example, the Post Office Department, whose employees had long been members of various employee organizations, was faced with problems of unprecedented magnitude and complexity in formalizing its bargaining structure under Executive Order 10,988. The approach decided upon was to establish one set of appropriate bargaining units at the national level for national issues, another set at the regional level for regional issues, and a third set of 24,000 units at the local level for local issues.[19] Separate representational procedures were instituted to select majority bargaining agents at each level, and subsequently bargaining agreements were entered into at each level encompassing the issues pertinent and bargainable at that level. At the national level, it should be added, a single joint agreement was reached with seven separately designated exclusive bargaining agents.[20]

Under the above format, an employee who has one bargaining agent at the local level may be represented by rival organizations at the higher levels; there are,

[19]Postmasters have recently voiced some dissatisfaction with this solution, since a union which is unsuccessful in obtaining a desired provision at the local level may try again at the regional and national levels. GERR No. 265, at A-3, A-4 (1968).

[20]The seven unions are the Natl. Assn. of Letter Carriers, the Natl. Assn. of Post Office & Gen. Service Maintainance Employees, the Natl. Assn. of Post Office Mail Handlers, Watchmen, Messengers & Group Leaders, the Natl. Assn. of Spec. Delivery Messengers, the Natl. Fed. of Post Office Motor Vehicle-Employees, the Natl. Rural Letter Carriers Assn., and the United Federation of Postal Clerks. GERR No. 212 at A-5 (Oct. 2, 1967).

in fact, at least eleven examples of "triple representation" for a particular craft or grouping in the Post Office Department.[21] However, the disadvantages of this condition appear to be outweighed by the practical value of this highly innovative technique designed to permit maximum bargaining under extremely difficult circumstances. On the one hand, the solution affords a high degree of local "self-determination"; at the same time it recognizes the significant principle that, in establishing bargaining units in the public sector, attention must be given to the relationship between the subjects sought to be included in the bargaining and the degree of meaningful "employer" authority to bargain with the proposed unit. Moreover, when issues arise that affect the Post Office Department on a national scale, the ability of the seven designated national bargaining agents to enter into a joint agreement greatly minimizes the normal institutional difficulties indigenous to public sector bargaining. . . .

Another interesting development is taking place in New York City. With the creation of the Office of Collective Bargaining,[22] New York City began to consolidate its bargaining units through techniques such as recognition by citywide job classifications.[23] This transition was followed, in the spring of 1968, by the truly basic step of recognizing one exclusive bargaining agent for *all* the employees of the mayoral agencies[24] for purposes of those citywide working conditions which are required to be uniform for such employees.[25] Separate representation in smaller units continues for purposes of other issues, and this condition is no doubt prolonging the same problems that are found elsewhere; but the basic trend appears to be a salutary one.

A third experience of interest involves the employees of the State of New York. Prior to the enactment of the Taylor Law, which defined the first set of rules for bargaining by both state and local government personnel, the majority of the state's 124,000 employees[26] had belonged to the statewide Civil Service Employees Association (CSEA)—an organization which, at least in its earlier years, had shunned the concept of formalized collective bargaining.[27] Following enactment of the Taylor Law, the state, as employer, recognized the CSEA as the bargaining agent for a "general unit" of all the employees.[28] After nearly a year of bargaining by this unit, the Public Employment Relations Board (PERB), the state agency charged with administering the Taylor Law,[29] received petitions challenging the

[21]PRESIDENT'S COMMISSION ON POSTAL ORGANIZATION, TOWARDS POSTAL EXCELLENCE 118 (1968).

[22]The office was established by Local Law of the City of New York No. 53, GERR, No. 205, at E-1 to E-10 (Aug. 14, 1967).

[23]*See, e.g.,* the decisions on certification reported in GERR No. 253, at B-2, B-3 (July 15, 1968).

[24]N.Y. Times, Feb. 27, 1968, at 1, col. 1.

[25]*Id. See also* Editorial, *Milestone in Municipal Labor,* N.Y. Times, Feb. 29, 1968, at 36, col. 1.

[26]The figure does not include approximately 3,500 state police and approximately 10,000 employees of state universities. GERR No. 219, at B-7 (Nov. 20, 1967).

[27] *See* Governor's Committee, *supra* note 16, at 11-12.

[28]GERR No. 219, at B-7 (1967).

[29]N.Y. CIV. SERV. LAW § 205 (McKinney Supp. 1968).

appropriateness of the general unit.[30] In opposition to the CSEA, twelve separate employee organizations requested recognition in twenty-five different bargaining units.[31] The proposed units were drawn along highly diverse occupational, departmental, or installation lines.[32]

Shunning the extremes of either one general unit or twenty-five separate units, the PERB ruled in favor of five separate statewide negotiating units and directed elections to determine the majority agent in each of those units.[33] The units were constituted along lines cutting across departments; instead, the employees were grouped into families of occupations primarily on the basis of function and training. In denying the requested continuance of the general unit, the PERB adopted an earlier finding of its Director of Representation [34] regarding the unit's inconsistency with the "community of interst" standard of the law[35] and, noting that the employees were divided among ninety occupational groupings, encompassing more than 3,700 separate job classifications, held: "The enormity of this diversity of occupations and the great range in the qualifications requisite for employment in these occupations would preclude effective and meaningful representation in collective negotiations if all such employees were included in a single unit."[36] On the other hand, the PERB concluded that accepting the opposite extreme of twenty-five separate units would foster a proliferation of small groups and would cause "unwarranted and unnecessary administrative difficulties" which "might well lead to the disintegration of the State's current labor relations structure."[37] In addition to these policy considerations, the PERB relied upon the provision of the Taylor Law requiring that the bargaining unit be "compatible with the joint responsibilities of the public employer and public employees to serve the public."[38] This standard, the PERB determined, "requires the designation of as small a number of units as possible consistent with the overriding requirement that the employees be permitted to form organizations of their own choosing" in order to achieve meaningful representation.[39]

---

[30]Immediately after the Governor recognized the CSEA as exclusive bargaining agent, the Public Employment Relations Board issued an order withholding recognition of the CSEA pending the Board's disposition of petitions by other employee organizations. GERR No. 221, at B-1 (Dec. 4, 1967). The CSEA petitioned to vacate that order and, although the petition was dismissed by the Supreme Court, CSEA v. Helsby, 55 Misc. 2d 507, 285 N.Y.S.2d 806 (1967), it was upheld, and the order vacated, on appeal, CSEA v. Helsby, 29 App. Div. 2d 196, 286 N.Y.S.2d 956 *affd.*, 21 N.Y.2d 541, 236 N.E.2d 481, 289 N.Y.S.2d 203 (1968).

[31]*See In re* State, GERR (PERB 1968) No. 279, at G-1, G-1 to G-3 (Jan. 13, 1969), *petition to set aside dismissed,* CSEA v. Helsby, 58 Misc. 2d 745, 296 N.Y.S.2d 246 (Sup. Ct. 1969).

[32]*Id.*

[33]*Id.*

[34]*In re* State, GERR (PERB 1968) No. 262, at E-1 (Sept. 16, 1968).

[35]*Id.* at E-8.

[36]*In re* State, GERR (PERB 1968) No. 279, at G-1, G-3.

[37]*Id.*

[38]N.Y. CIV. SERV. LAW § 207(1)(c) (McKinney Supp. 1968).

[39]GERR No. 179, at G-1, G-4.

The PERB did not make specific reference to the statutory standard requiring consideration of a requested unit in terms of the employer-agency's existing authority to deal effectively with possible bargaining subject matter within such a unit.[40] There seems to be little question, however, that the size and nature of the five designated statewide units insure adequate authority, on the side of the state's negotiating representatives, to make meaningful agreements or recommendations with respect to a large portion of the substantial issues normally deserving of consideration in an effective collective bargaining relationship. Moreover, since the employees were geographically dispersed and because the general unit presented serious problems of providing direct representation, the PERB's breakdown of the employees into five large families of jobs probably maximizes the possibilities for self-determination and adequate union responsiveness in representing the various segments within each family.

The New York experience is also noteworthy because the direct confrontation between the two opposite extremes presented by the requested patterns at the inception of newly formalized public sector collective bargaining afforded an opportunity to weigh the basic implications of excessive fragmentation. In contrast to policy makers in cities like New York and Detroit and in some of the departments at the federal level, the New York State PERB was able to adopt a coherent policy at a time when the damage had not yet been done. At the same time, the Board's decision rejected a monolithic bargaining unit which would have been neither proper nor realistic for public employees at this stage of history.

CONCLUSION

From the foregoing examination of some of the problems and practical experience associated with the appropriate unit issue in the public service, it seems relatively clear that the answer, at least for the present, cannot lie in "instant" creation of large single bargaining units, however desirable that solution might be from the standpoint of administrative convenience. . . .

Nevertheless, there is sufficient experience to warrant the twin conclusions that there has been too much fragmentation of public employee bargaining units thus far, and that this condition will inhibit the evolution of orderly collective bargaining arrangements for the future. Apart from the details in individual cases, I believe that a basic philosophy is required which will generally favor larger units rather than smaller units. The special problems of the public service call for such an approach, to a significantly greater extent than in the private sector. The available evidence also reveals that this basic philosophy is not being implemented, except in isolated instances such as the above-described decision by the Public Employment Relations Board in New York. Unfortunately, the general tendency has been in the opposite direction, particularly when the freedom-of-choice argument has been given special weight in light of the "public" nature of the employment.

The problem might also be viewed as a two-stage phenomenon, however. Given the fact that basic bargaining authorization was often granted almost overnight to a

[40]N.Y. CIV. SERV. LAW § 207(1)(b) (McKinney Supp. 1968).

large mass of employees who were essentially naive and inexperienced regarding collective bargaining, and given the further fact that these *were* public employees, the marked initial tendency toward small units was perhaps understandable. It was reasonable to expect that employee organizations which were suddenly permitted to engage in bargaining over a large number of problems for the first time would seek to establish their powers in small units; perhaps it was also reasonable that, from a public policy viewpoint, the employees who were encountering a new experience in labor relations were afforded an initial period of familiarization through comfortable association with their counterparts in small groups.

Nevertheless, because we have long since entered and in some instances passed through such a stage, the question arises as to what the second stage should be. Fragmentation into too many small units can severely limit the scope of bargaining subject matter, and that in turn might defeat the basic bargaining right. . . .

THE SCOPE OF BARGAINING
IN LOCAL GOVERNMENT LABOR NEGOTIATIONS

Paul F. Gerhart

The "scope of bargaining" usually refers to the range of issues included in negotiations between the parties to a labor agreement. Significant variations in scope occur among labor agreements in both the private and public sectors. The principal aim of this paper is to examine the impact several selected factors may have on the scope of bargaining. The study is limited to the public sector at the local level.

The paper is divided into two parts. The first part is an effort to clarify some conceptual aspects and problems encountered in the analysis; the second part is an analysis of the impact the selected factors have on the scope.

Paul Gerhart is Assistant Professor of Labor and Industrial Relations, University of Illinois. Reprinted from the *Labor Law Journal,* August 1969.

This paper is based on research sponsored by the Brookings Institution under a grant from the Ford Foundation. The author wishes to express his gratitude to his associates, particularly John Burton and Charles Krider, of The University of Chicago, for their comments. The two sources of information were intensive field interviewing and extensive contract analysis, both conducted in connection with the Brookings Labor Project. To date, some 30 cities have been visited and over 265 collective bargaining agreements between local governmental units and employee organizations have been examined.

DEFINITIONS

"Real" v. "Formal" Scope of Bargaining

Those familiar with collective bargaining in either the public or private sector are aware that the set of issues covered by a formal contract or agreement need not coincide completely with the set of issues upon which there has been joint decision-making by representatives of the parties. Any analysis of the scope of bargaining must take account of this distinction between the "formal" scope, the issues covered by agreement, and the "real" scope, those issues upon which there is joint decision-making.

The following four quadrant table represents the four possible categories into which all issues of a particular collective bargaining relationship may be placed. Each issue may be placed in one, and only one, of the categories. Quadrants (1) and (2) represent those issues in the real scope; quadrants (1) and (3) represent the issues in the formal scope; quadrant (4) represents the issues which are outside both the real and formal scopes, for example, management prerogatives.

table 1   Real Versus Formal Scope

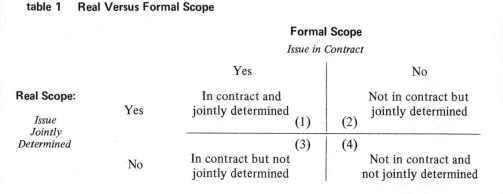

		Formal Scope *Issue in Contract*	
		Yes	No
Real Scope: *Issue* *Jointly* *Determined*	Yes	In contract and jointly determined (1)	Not in contract but jointly determined (2)
	No	(3) In contract but not jointly determined	(4) Not in contract and not jointly determined

Examples of Issues Which Fall into Quadrants (2) and (3) The case in which jointly determined issues do not appear in a formal agreement (quadrant (2)) is common. As an example from the public sector, civil service regulations in Philadelphia permit variations in the eligibility requirements for individuals desiring to take examinations for vacant positions. These variations are made at the discretion of the personnel department in accordance with guidelines established by the Civil Service Commission, While negotiations regarding civil service regulations are not reflected in the formal contract, the union has been able, in some cases, to gain significant influence over eligibility requirements for particular exams. Union officials reported that many exams which were formerly "open competitive" exams (current employment status is not a factor in determining eligibility) are now limited to employees of the city or to employees of the particular department in which the vacancy occurs. This assures promotion from within, which is currently acceptable to the union in lieu of promotion on the basis of seniority. The union officials reported that this shift in eligibility is the result of their increased influence. Yet, nothing in the contract suggests joint decision-making on the eligibility issue.

On the other hand, the formal scope of many public (as well as private) agreements actually exceeds the real scope (quadrant (3)). That is, some issues mentioned in the agreement are not actually jointly determined by the parties. For example, local, state or federal laws and ordinances regarding such topics as vacations, holidays, pensions or exclusive recognition are frequently repeated in local agreements even though the union may actually possess no joint decision-making role in the issue. An example of a frequently found clause appears in the agreement between the City of Milwaukee and District Council 48, AFSCME. Federal law requires that an employee returning from compulsory military service must, under certain circumstances, be re-employed by his former employer. The Milwaukee agreement simply restates the statute:

> Upon completion and release from active duty under honorable conditions, such employees shall be reinstated into the positions they held at the time of taking such leave of absence or to a position of like seniority, status, pay, and salary advancement . . . . [1]

The Two Dimensions of Scope

In considering the scope of bargaining, the question is not merely one of discovering the areas in which the union has achieved some influence but also of measuring the amount of influence actually wielded by the union within each of these areas.[2] In any collective bargaining situation there appears to be a trade-off by the parties between breadth (number of issues covered) and depth (degree of influence on particular issues held by the union).

At the present state of development in public sector labor relations, management's concern has not been with breadth, but depth. That is, management appears willing to place no limit on the number of "negotiable issues" so long as the actual power of the union over the issues is severely limited. Management negotiators indicate a willingness to "discuss" *any* issue with union representatives. Except in the few instances where bargaining is well developed, however, management officials are unwilling to admit that any issues are "jointly determined" on an equal basis with the union representatives. In their opinion joint determination would be equivalent to a delegation of their authority which they feel is not permitted by law.

It is predictable that management in the public sector will begin to shift its focus toward limiting breadth. This process has already begun in some jurisdictions. The prediction is based upon three factors. (1) Unions are becoming stronger vis-à-vis management, thereby achieving greater depth of penetration. (2) More formal

---

[1] *Agreement between City of Milwaukee and Milwaukee District Council 48, AFSCME, AFL–CIO and its Appropriate Affiliated Locals, January 1, 1966,* p. 33 (now expired).

[2] Professor Chamberlain has indicated that "union penetration of managerial areas" may be measured ". . . by seeking to establish the number of areas where unions now share . . . decision-making power and by attempting to estimate the importance of their share . . . ." *The Union Challenge to Management Control,* Harper, New York, New York, 1948, pp. 74 *et seq.*

(written) agreements are appearing. (A written agreement increases management's commitment to the terms of the agreement and thereby reduces management's flexibility.) (3) Public policy in some jurisdictions mandates joint decision-making on some issues.

FACTORS RELATED TO THE SCOPE OF BARGAINING

The first section, below, considers some factors expected to have some impact on the *formal* scope of bargaining; the second section considers the impact that public policy may have on the *real* scope of bargaining; and finally, the third section considers the interrelationships among several factors and their impact on both the real and formal scopes of bargaining.[3]

Impact of Alternate (Informal) Channels of Influence

This section explores the proposition that the availability of informal channels of communication and influence between union and public officials is associated with a smaller formal scope of bargaining.

Size of Bargaining Unit Informal channels are more likely to be available when the unit is small. Grievances, promotions, and similar matters may be adequately controlled through the informal channels. As the size of the bargaining unit increases so should the formal scope of bargaining, other things being equal.

The following tables present data on the relationship between the size of the unit and the formal scope of bargaining. Since public policy appears to create important differences among bargaining units, the following procedure was used to standardize for it. First, in order to assure rough comparability among the states as regards industrialization and general attitude toward unionism, only non-Southern states were used in the analysis. Then the remaining states were divided into three categories: (1) six states with well-developed (favorable) public policy regarding unionization among public employees, (2) 19 states with no explicit legislation with regard to the right of public employees to unionize, (3) 11 states with intermediate development such as those with "meet and confer" statutes.[4] The third group was omitted from the analysis because it lacked both intragroup uniformity on the public policy variable and sufficient agreements for meaningful analysis. The two remaining groups were analyzed independently.

In Table 2 the columns represent the number of *key* issues covered by the agreement. "Key" issues are a selected list of 11 issues usually covered in private sector agreements: (1) exclusive recognition, (2) union security (membership main-

---

[3]It is tempting to postulate causal relationships flowing from the factors to the scope of bargaining. In some instances it is safe to attribute a causal impact to the factors, but in most there is likely to be a feed-back effect. For a discussion of the relationships among union power, membership support and the scope of bargaining see Chamberlain, cited at footnote 3, at pp. 100-104.

[4]See Richard S. Rubin, *A Summary of State Collective Bargaining Law in Public Employment*, NYSSILR (Ithaca, New York, 1968), Mr. Rubin's survey coincided temporally with the Brookings Project contract analysis.

table 2   **Formal Scope of Bargaining by Size of Unit and Public Policy**

Per Cent of Contracts Covering

Size of Unit (employees)	6 or less Issues	7 or 8 Issues	9 to 11 Issues	Total Number of Contracts
States with well-developed public policy:				
Under 25	15	30	55	20
25-50	0	29	70	17
51-100	5	24	71	21
Over 100	12	24	64	25
Non-Southern states with no explicit public policy:				
Under 25	38	31	31	13
25-50	15	38	46	13
51-100	33	17	50	12
Over 100	9	9	82	11

tenance), (3) checkoff, (4) wages, (5) hours, (6) overtime (7) paid time off (holidays, vacations or sick leave), (8) welfare benefits (pensions, medical or life insurance), (9) grievance procedure, (10) arbitration, and (11) promotion procedures.

Following the proposition stated above with regard to alternate informal channels of communication and influence, we should expect that smaller units would show a relatively larger propostion of agreements with "6 or less issues" covered while larger units would show a larger proportion of agreements with "9 to 11 issues" covered.

Table 2, section a, based on contracts in states with well-developed public policy, does not conform to the proposition at all. There is only the slightest tendency for smaller units in Table 2, section a, to cover fewer issues. On the other hand, Table 2, section b, covering agreements in states without explicit public policy, does yield the expected results.

It is not readily apparent why the hypothesis with regard to size of unit tends to be relevant in states without explicit public policy while it is clearly not relevant in states with well-developed policy. One possible consideration is the difference between these groups in the "area of coercive comparison." The geographic density of contracts in the well-developed states is much greater than in the states without explicit public policy. This might lead to a greater uniformity of contracts within the former group regardless of unit size.

Political Power   Informal methods of resolving issues are more likely to be available if the union has access to political channels. Collective bargaining agreements negotiated at the local leval are frequently subject to ratification or approval by the local legislative body. This is particularly true with regard to wage rates or other economic issues requiring financing. When union officials seek to alter the terms of employment, then, an alternative to the formal collective bargaining agreement is simply direct political action to revise the relevant ordinances or resolutions.

Unions frequently prefer this "political" approach, particularly in states lacking explicit public policy with regard to collective bargaining in the public sector. The political approach is also popular in "machine" style cities regardless of public policy. In some cities, such as Chicago, the political approach completely replaces formal collective bargaining.

In addition to direct action at the local level, political action is possible at the state level. This process is known as "leap-frogging," or "double decking." The process is likely to be used where some or all locals lack the power to negotiate the desired terms locally, so they seek to establish state policy on the issue. The issue is thereby removed from both the formal and real scope of bargaining at the local level.

An example of the use of informal influence at higher levels occurred recently in Illinois. The state fire and police organizations lobbied successfully for a state minimum wage for uniformed personnel. The minimums had their greatest impact in smaller communities where the employee organizations had the least strength. Employee organizations in larger cities supported the measure, though, because the wage rates of smaller communities are always used for comparative purposes in their wage negotiations.

Impact of Public Policy on the "Real" Scope of Bargaining

Variations in public policy (specifically, the legislation pertaining to unionization in the public sector) have their primary impact on the *real* scope of bargaining.[5] Policy variation may affect the real scope of bargaining in two ways. Frequently, legislation pertaining to unionization has a *direct* impact through coverage of specific issues, thereby removing them from the real scope of bargaining. The automatic granting of exclusive recognition to unions which enjoy majority status, legalization of check-off and the prohibition of any union membership requirements are cases in point.

The second way in which public policy may influence the real scope of bargaining is through its *indirect* impact on union strength. Any change in public policy which is favorable to union aims with regard to specific issues, particularly union security, will "free" the unions' resources to be employed in seeking other goals. Automatic exclusive recognition provides a measure of union security for unions with majority status in Hartford, Connecticut, which unions in St. Louis do not enjoy. While the latter strive to maintain their membership in the face of management pressure and particularly rival unions, the AFSCME local in Hartford is free to confront management with wage or fringe demands.[6]

The following table shows the relationship between the scope of bargaining and public policy. In the table the formal scope has been used as a proxy for real scope.

---

[5]It is likely that the impact on the real scope will also be reflected in the formal scope.

[6]This case is analogous to the argument with regard to Section 14(b) of Taft-Hartley in the private sector. There, the argument is that "right-to-work" laws cause a drain on union resources a the union strives to maintain its membership in right-to-work states, thereby weakening itself vis-a-vis the employer.

The issues considered and the two groups of states used for the analysis are the same as those developed in Table 2 above.

It appears that a well-developed (favorable) public ·policy is related to a larger scope of bargaining. Conclusions from the above table must be tempered, however, for two reasons. First, the data reflect the formal scope of bargaining, not the real scope. Second, the table merely counts the issues and does not take into account the depth of penetration achieved by the unions. Assuming the trade-off hypothesis set forth in the first section of the paper has some validity, it is possible that unions in states without explicit policy have a greater tendency to trade depth for breadth. Such a propensity would bias the results of the table. In my opinion, neither of these problems is sufficient to cause us to disregard Table 3 because of the substantial differences reflected in that table.

table 3   Formal Scope of Bargaining and Public Policy

| | Per Cent of Agreements Covering | | | |
	6 or less Issues	7 or 8 Issues	9 to 11 Issues	Total Number of Contracts
Non-Southern states with no explicit public policy (19 states)	32	24	44	71
Non-Southern states with well-developed public policy (6 states)	8	25	67	122

Organized Labor, Union Strength and the Scope of Bargaining

It is obvious that union strength relative to the employer is an important factor in determining the real scope of bargaining. Several problems are associated with the use of strength as a variable in the analysis, however.[7]

Instead of measuring union strength directly, we shall consider factors which might (1) contribute to union strength or (2) inhibit the development of union strength.

General Strength of Organized Labor General union strength in a community should provide a clue to the "acceptance" of unionism by the general public. In addition, it may be hypothesized that public sector unions which are affiliated with local central labor bodies or with international unions which have organized substantial portions of the private sector could derive some strength from those sources. In fact, however, the field work of the Brookings Labor Project did not reveal the simple relationship hypothesized above. The fact that private sector unionism is strong in an area does not reveal anything about the strength of the public sector unions nor, consequently, anything about the scope of bargaining, formal or real. What the field research suggested was that any impact of private

[7]It is difficult to measure empirically, and the direction of causality between union strength and scope is less clear than with the other factors considered above.

sector labor on the public sector was modified by a complicated set of relationships involving public officials, private sector union officials, public sector union officials, and the "style" of politics in the city.

Style of City Politics   In machine-type cities it is likely that successful union organizations will be part of the party machine. If such an organization does gain any strength independent of the machine, either through the private sector unions or through its own efforts, "alternate informal channels of influence," discussed above, are likely to be available. Therefore, regardless of the real scope of bargaining achieved, the formal scope of bargaining will be limited.

In "reform" style cities, the employer-employee relationship resembles the private sector. City business tends to be conducted on a formal basis. Under these conditions an increase in the formal scope of bargaining is likely as a public sector union gains strength through the assistance of organized labor or through its own efforts.

Private-Public Sector Relations   Those familiar with public sector unionism are aware that private sector union officials do not always look upon the developing public sector unions with the kindest regard. In New York City, for instance, the central labor council, for years, enjoyed the favored role as the spokesman for all of organized labor including the city employees. The AFSCME District Council, in the past five years, has achieved a strong position vis-a-vis the city administration, independent of the central labor body. The latter views this as a challenge since some of its power has been eroded. There are examples of other cities in which the reason for the poor relationship would differ. The point is that when the relationship between public and private sector unions is strained, one might expect no assistance at all from the private sector for public employees. In fact, if the relationship is very poor, there may even be an inverse correlation between private sector strength and public sector strength.

Synthesis   A pattern of the impact of organized labor on union strength and the scope of bargaining emerges in a comparison of Chicago and Cleveland, on the one hand, with Dayton and Milwaukee, on the other. In Chicago, the employees represented by the various craft unions do have considerable depth of real scope in bargaining with Mayor Daley. The Teamsters, for instance, have been able to maintain a prevailing rate for garbage truck drivers in the city. In Cleveland, the building trades have significant strength and have played a major role in "maintaining standards" for their members. By contrast, this influence over the terms of employment is not shared by unions which represent noncraft employees of the cities. AFSCME, which enjoys very little stature in the Cleveland central labor council, has had virtually no impact on wages and working conditions in recent years. Finally, the formal scope of bargaining in these patronage style cities is limited or nonexistent. Until last year neither Chicago nor Cleveland had any written agreements with its employees. The conclusion is that in patronage style cities where private sector unions enjoy a measure of influence, and where such unions take an interest, at least in particular groups of employees, the real scope of bargaining will be significant for those unions while the formal scope will be limited. Any increase in private sector union strength would be reflected in the real scope but not the formal.

Milwaukee and Dayton are reform style cities. Although organized labor is strong, its role in city politics has been limited. In Milwaukee the relationship between private sector union leaders and the AFSCME District Council has been strained. Historically, Dayton experienced similar difficulties although presently relations are neutral or friendly. Alternate informal channels have not been available both because of the style of politics and the public-private sector union relationships. Therefore, the real scope of bargaining is reflected by the formal scope. As union strength increased in both cities, overtime, and real scope increased with it, the formal scope also increased.

CONCLUSION

Most of the factors influencing the scope of bargaining, both formal and real, are familiar in the private sector. Public policy, informal channels of influence, and the strength of the union vis-à-vis management all have an impact in the private sector as well as the public. The application and relative importance of these concepts in the public sector are at variance from the private sector, however. The most interesting difference is the important role the informal channels play in cities without public policy guidelines. The development of public policy in the public sector at either the state or local levels probably leads to greater similarity between the sectors in that the formal scope more accurately reflects the real scope.

It is part of the nature of the public sector, however, that unions will always have access to politicians sympathetic to their views. These may be at either the local or higher levels. These conditions will lead to the tendency for unions to rely more on informal "politics" or higher level legislation when formal negotiation at the lower level appears less fruitful. This dependence on legislation will prevent the scope of bargaining at the local level from achieving the breadth or depth of the private sector.

CONSTRAINTS ON LOCAL GOVERNMENTS
IN PUBLIC EMPLOYEE BARGAINING

Charles M. Rehmus

It is to the basic financial and administrative constraints upon the powers of local governing units that this Article is primarily directed. The examples used are taken largely from Michigan experience and Michigan law. The same limitations upon the financial and administrative powers of local government, however, exist in

Charles Rehmus is Professor of Political Science, University of Michigan, and Co-Director, Institute of Labor and Industrial Relations. Reprinted from *Michigan Law Review*, LXVII (March 1969), 919-30.

almost all other states. The Michigan experience with public administration and public employee bargaining should provide both a warning and a guide to other states as they cope with the so-called public employee revolution.

FINANCIAL LIMITATIONS ON LOCAL GOVERNMENTAL UNITS

Three major sources of revenue are available for financing government: taxes on sales, on income, and on property. Of these, the property tax is the workhorse of local government; it accounts for ninety per cent of local tax revenues in the United States.[1] Local governments in Michigan—municipalities, counties, and school districts—have no authority to levy sales taxes,[2] and the development of city income taxes is just beginning.[3] Thus, Michiganders have traditionally relied heavily on the property tax not only to finance city and village governments, but also to support townships, counties, and school districts. In many areas, three or four local governing units, not to mention special district authorities, all depend upon the same overburdened property tax base. Nevertheless, the state legislature, jealous of its own tax sources and protective of its citizens, has not permitted much change in local taxing structure. The new Michigan Constitution adopted in 1963 theoretically delegated broad taxing powers to home rule charter cities.[4] Despite this, the state legislature has reserved most nonproperty taxes to itself and has prohibited municipalities from levying such taxes without specific legislative authorization.[5] Moreover, Michigan, like most states, limits the total amount of millage that can be levied upon property without specific authorization from the voters.[6] The specific limit in Michigan upon a city council's unrestricted taxing power is twenty mills, and another fifteen mills must be divided among township boards, county supervisors, and school boards.[7]

Even those cities that desire to tax themselves more heavily often find that the legislature forces them to beg for the privilege. States that permit cities to levy income taxes frequently place limitations upon the amounts that can be obtained through this resource. It is common to find statutes which restrict municipalities to a flat rate rather than a progressive income tax, limit the percentage of residents' income which they can tax, and place even more severe limitations upon the percentage of commuters' incomes which they can reach. Michigan, for example, limits city income taxes to a flat rate of one per cent (except Detroit which is now permitted two per cent) and the tax on commuters' incomes to half that amount.[8]

[1]COMMITTEE FOR ECONOMIC DEVELOPMENT, A FISCAL PROGRAM FOR A BALANCED FEDERALISM 21 (1967).

[2]MICH. COMP. LAWS ANN. § 205.51 (1967).

[3]At the present time, fewer than 200 cities in the United States levy an income tax, but growth of this form of taxation will undoubtedly expand rapidly.

[4]See MICH. CONST. art. 7, § 22.

[5]MICH. COMP. LAWS ANN. § 141.91 (1967).

[6]MICH. CONST. art. 9, § 6. Pennsylvania is an important exception. It is alone among the states whose public employees are strongly organized and which permit local governing bodies to levy unlimited property taxes without specific voter authorization.

[7]MICH. CONST. art. 9, § 6.

[8]MICH. COMP. LAWS ANN. § 141.611 (1967).

Moreover, state legislatures commonly allow voters a veto over new city income taxes, a privilege seldom if ever accorded for similar state levies. Under the uniform Michigan city income tax law, the imposition of city income taxes is subject to a protest referendum.[9] In order for city councils to obtain an affirmative vote in these referendum elections, they must often promise the voters major property tax reductions. Thus, the amount of new money generated is limited, and much of the purpose of the new taxes is defeated. Related to this, the Michigan Constitution prohibits cities from issuing general obligation bonds without an affirmative vote of property owners.[10] Consequently, many cities, rather than attempting to get the voters to approve capital bonds, squeeze capital improvements out of their operating millage and further limit the resources available for short-run operational flexibility.

These constitutional and legislative constraints upon the taxing powers of home rule charter cities are sometimes aggravated by the cities themselves. Some cities have in their original charters limited the total operating millage which they can levy administratively to an amount lower than the state-imposed twenty-mill maximum.[11] This handicaps them further in generating the funds necessary to meet employee demands.

In summary, a state-imposed obligation upon local governments to negotiate wages and fringe benefits inevitably entails increased budget expenditures for employee compensation. If the state simultaneously maintains existing limitations upon the unilateral taxing power of local governments, the situation often becomes intolerable. Local government administrators are helplessly caught between employee compensation demands, public unwillingness to vote for increased operating millage levied on property, and the state legislature's reluctance to allow local governments the freedom to impose income, sales, or excise taxes.

An example which highlights the problem recently occurred in Detroit. Following both a "ticket-writing strike" and a "blue flu" epidemic among police officers, the disputants finally referred the issue of police salaries to a neutral three-member panel for recommendations. The panel found that police officers' salaries should be substantially increased. Money to pay the recommended increases could be found on an emergency basis within Detroit's current operating budget, but beyond the first year, the panel concluded:

> the City of Detroit urgently needs new taxing authority which can be granted only by the State Legislature. . . Detroit is in serious financial trouble, and we join others who have suggested that the State Legislature raise the authorized level of the municipal income tax, to restore the authority to levy local excise taxes, and to revise the 2 percent restriction on property tax levies.[12]

The problem of financial straight-jacketing in the face of collective bargaining pressure is equally serious for school districts. Collective bargaining for Michigan

[9]MICH. COMP. LAWS ANN. § 141.503 (1967).

[10]MICH. CONST. art. 2, §6.

[11]Only six of the sixteen largest cities in Michigan are presently levying the twenty-mill maximum.

[12]Detroit Police Dispute Panel, Findings and Recommendations on Unresolved "Economic" and Other Issues 32-33 (Feb. 27, 1968, unpublished mimeo).

public school teachers appears to have produced annual pay increases averaging ten to twenty per cent higher than those which the teachers would otherwise have received.[13] Over all, the salaries of Michigan teachers have increased by about one third in the last three years. Most, if not all, of these increases were long overdue, but they resulted in severe pressure on school district budgets. In the 1966-1967 academic year, the first full year of teacher bargaining under the 1965 Act, these increases in teacher compensation were paid for largely from minor economies and from new revenues. Among the new revenue sources were increases in state aid, imposition of previously authorized millage, and growth in assessed valuation. In the second full year of collective bargaining, however, school districts began to use less desirable sources of funds to pay the wage increases demanded by organized teachers. Administrators generated new sources of funds through liquidation of operating reserves and contingency funds, transfer of millage from building and site reserves to operating accounts, and substantial program cutbacks. Most important— and despite the fact that Michigan law is generally construed to forbid school districts from deficit financing[14]—a quarter of the school districts studied in one survey showed a deficit by the end of fiscal 1968.

The financial constraints on local governments constitute the most serious problem they face in coping with public employee collective bargaining. However, public officials must contend with at least three other problems which, although related to financing, are not as severe as the shortage of funds per se. The first problem is that of coordinating the budget-making process with collective bargaining. An acute aspect of this problem is the difficulty which local governmental units face in meeting budget deadlines, particularly when the state legislature itself imposes the deadlines. The collective bargaining process often entails months of negotiations, mediation, and fact-finding or arbitration; it does not respect time limits. Yet budgets must be filed under the law, and this requires local officials to make preliminary estimates. As a result, municipalities may often feel constrained to take rigid positions based upon estimates which were submitted to the legislature before bargaining is completed. A second aspect of the coordination problem arises after budget submission deadlines have been passed: the issue then is whether negotiated pay increases should apply prospectively from the date of the agreement or retroactively from the beginning of the budget period. Finally, it may be difficult to synchronize legislative decisions concerning the amount of funds to be allocated to local governmental units with local governmental responsibilities in the bargaining process. For instance, teacher bargaining for the 1967-1968 school year in Michigan proved exceptionally difficult because the state legislature failed to act on the school aid formula until August 1967. Consequently, spring and summer bargaining in many school districts dragged on beyond budget submission deadlines because school administrators were unable to predict how much state funding would be available to help them meet teacher demands. The state legislature avoided this problem the following year by acting on the school aid formula in April, well before budget deadlines. Perhaps as a result, a smaller number of bargaining impasses occurred during teacher negotiations for the 1968-1969 school year. This problem of coordinating the budget-making process with collective bar-

[13]The statements in this paragraph are based upon C. REHMUS & E. WILNER, THE ECONOMIC RESULTS OF TEACHER BARGAINING (1968).

[14]1959-1960 BIENNIAL REP. ATT'Y GEN. 147 (Mich. 1959).

gaining is more an irritating than an insurmountable obstacle. The difficulties can be minimized by using open-ended budgets, resorting to short-term internal and external borrowing, allowing more time for bargaining before budget deadlines, and negotiating collective bargaining contracts for longer terms than are currently settled upon.

A second complication of collective bargaining in the public sector results from the tradition that public budgets and accounts are not secret documents. In the private sector the employer may under most circumstances refuse to disclose his profit and loss figures, but the public employer is forced to open his books to all interested persons. As a result, any operating reserves or contingency funds that may be available simply become targets for the employees to shoot at. Prudent management—whether in business or in public administration—ordinarily requires the retention of some operating reserves. It is not reprehensible for a public administrator to maintain a reserve account to pay operating costs in periods before tax money becomes available or to provide for unforeseen contingencies. In practice, however, even if cities and school districts have not had to resort to deficit financing in order to meet collective bargaining demands, the retention of operating reserves has proved almost impossible. Many cities and most school districts in Michigan, their reserves depleted to satisfy the bargaining demands of employees, are now operating on little better than a year-to-year cash basis. In jurisdictions where reserves remain, this result has often been accomplished by padding various budget items—a recurrent practice but hardly one to be encouraged.

A third anomaly of collective bargaining in the public sector is that the union can often invade the management decision-making structure. Particularly in public school and junior college districts, organized teacher groups have succeeded in electing their members, relatives, or sympathizers to school and governing boards. Under these circumstances it is often impossible for the management decision-making group to hide its bargaining strategy and tactics from employees. Democratic government does allow almost anyone to run for office, but this tactic may make collective bargaining a farce.

OTHER STATE-IMPOSED CONSTRAINTS ON COLLECTIVE BARGAINING

State legislatures have imposed many limitations upon the authority of local governmental units to manage their own personnel systems. One of the most common limitations is the statutory or de facto requirement that home rule cities establish a civil service and merit system for recruitment and promotion of personnel.[15] This requirement, although beneficial in its thrust and general impact upon city government, operates to reduce substantially the flexibility of local governmental units at the collective bargaining table. State legislatures have seldom given enough thought to the problems that may be encountered when they impose a collective bargaining requirement covering "terms and conditions of employment"[16] upon an existing merit structure.

[15] 1967 Executive Committee of the National Governors' Conference, Preliminary Report of Task Force on State and Local Government Labor Relations 36-37.

[16] *See, e.g.,* MICH. COMP. LAWS ANN. § 423.215 (1967).

The civil service concept ordinarily contemplates the establishment of a non-partisan board or commission at the local or state level with rulemaking authority to assure adherence to the merit principle. In practice, merit systems have over the years grown to encompass many aspects of employee relations and personnel management other than recruitment, classification, and promotion. These new areas of concern include the handling of grievances, employee training, salary administration, safety, morale, and attendance control programs—the very subjects that most employee organizations regard as appropriate for bargaining. If an independent civil service commission has authority over bargainable matters, then perhaps bargaining responsibilities should lie with the commission. But as it is, authority to bargain is usually vested in the chief executive officer of the local government unit. If he has the duty to bargain over the terms and conditions of employment while authority over many personnel matters remains with an independent commission, the scope of negotiations will be unduly restricted.

This problem is not insoluble. If the principal of collective bargaining by local governments is to be effectuated, all nonmerit functions should be transferred from the civil service commission to a personnel department under the chief executive officer of each local unit. In practice, however, such a transfer of authority has seldom been made. In Massachusetts, for example, the state collective bargaining law for public employees specifically states that it shall not "diminish the authority and power of the civil service commission, or any retirement or personnel board established by law . . . ."[17] The Wisconsin public employment relations statute[18] excludes from the mandatory scope of bargaining a large range of matters established by law or governed by civil service. In practice, in localities where public employee collective bargaining is fully developed, informal bargaining arrangements to deal with these problems are already appearing.[19] At the very least, any state considering collective bargaining legislation for public employees should carefully analyze its personnel system in order to minimize the potential conflict between bargaining relationships, existing merit systems, and the rules promulgated by civil service boards and commissions.

State legislatures contemplating collective bargaining in the public sector should also ensure that they have not imposed undue restrictions upon the permissible scope of bargaining. Some years ago the Michigan legislature imposed upon its municipalities a fifty-six-hour maximum duty week for firemen.[20] This law not only raised municipal fire protection costs substantially, but also eliminated from the scope of bargaining one of the major subjects which should have been left there. In Pennsylvania, the state legislature prohibited combined police-fire departments,[21] another potentially bargainable subject. Laws of this kind place many

[17]MASS. ANN. LAWS ch. 149, §178N (Supp. 1967).

[18]WIS. STAT. §111.91 (Supp. 1967).

[19]For example, Michigan's Wayne County has created special labor boards with the power to negotiate collective agreements with employees. The labor board for a negotiation is composed of a representative of the county Civil Service Board, a representative of the county Board of Supervisors, and a representative from the particular administrative unit involved (such as the county Highway Department).

[20]MICH. COMP. LAWS ANN. §123.841 (1967).

[21]PA. STAT. ANN. tit. 43, §217.1 (Supp. 1969) (by implication).

local governments, particularly smaller communities, in a Procrustean bed. These municipalities are obligated to bargain over wages and hours, yet uniform state laws fundamentally weaken their negotiating position by creating mandatory high-cost requirements without the freedom to trade cost reductions in one area for new expenditures in another.

State legislatures have also limited the negotiating flexibility of school boards. For example, the Attorney General of Michigan has recently ruled that under existing law boards of education lack statutory authority to award severance pay, to pay for any unused portion of sick leave at the end of a school year or upon termination of employment, or to reimburse teachers' tuition for college credit courses beyond the baccalaureate degree.[22] Under the Michigan collective bargaining statute, school boards had assumed prior to the Attorney General's ruling that they were obligated to bargain on all of these subjects, and concessions had in fact been made on many. Probably a majority of existing teacher collective bargaining agreements in Michigan call for one or more of these payments that have now been declared to be unlawful. The attempt of school boards to negotiate such benefits back out of existing contracts is likely to engender bitter conflict. A new grant of authority to make the disputed payments would seem to be a preferable alternative.

Another important source of conflict is the discrepancy between union security arrangements in collective bargaining agreements and the provisions of state teacher tenure laws. The Michigan Labor Mediation Board has ruled that union security—specifically, an employee demand for an agency shop—is a mandatory subject of bargaining, at least so far as home rule counties are concerned.[23] A number of Michigan school boards, assuming that this ruling applied to them as well, have agreed to agency shop clauses in their master contracts. These provisions ordinarily call for terminating the employment of bargaining unit members who refuse to pay either union dues or an equivalent agency fee. Yet a basic condition of the Michigan Teacher Tenure Act is that a school board must show a "reasonable and just cause" relating to job performance for terminating a tenured teacher's employment.[24] This conflict between Michigan's Public Employment Relations Act and its Teacher Tenure Act must ultimately be resolved by the state supreme court. In the meantime, the conflict illustrates graphically the kinds of problems that can arise when a legislature mandates collective bargaining and simultaneously continues to legislate terms or conditions of employment for the employees of local governmental units.

CONCLUSION

A classic dilemma faces the management negotiator who has been instructed, "Don't give them anything, but don't let them strike." Increasingly, administrators of local units of government find themselves trying to carry out such impossible

[22]Mich. Att'y Gen. Op. No. 4583 (Oct. 11, 1968), No. 4667 (Feb. 24, 1969) (clarifying no. 4583).

[23]Oakland County Sheriff's Dept. & Metro. Council No. 23, Case No. C66 F-63 (Michigan Labor Mediation Bd. Jan. 10, 1968).

[24]MICH. COMP. LAWS ANN., § 38.101 (1967).

orders. The constraints that state constitutions and state legislatures place on local governing units have existed for many years. Most of them find their origins in jealousy over taxing power and the fear that locally elected and appointed officials might prove unresponsive to the state legislature's standards of "good government." Many limitations have been retained in an attempt to remove certain subjects from local collective bargaining altogether. In an environment where local administrators must negotiate their employees' wages and working conditions with employee representatives, these limitations on local authority are real obstacles to effective collective bargaining.

Freedom to trade one proposal for another and to balance cost reductions in one area against new expenditures in another is essential to bargaining flexibility. Freedom to raise new money to meet employee demands, or to withstand the consequences of refusal, is an equally essential part of the collective bargaining process. Much of this freedom and flexibility is presently denied local administrators. As a result, local public employee bargaining has resulted in impasses and employee pressure tactics more often than should have been necessary. Many of these problems would not be so serious if public employee bargaining were merely a transitory phenomenon. But Pandora's box has been opened. Employees who have gained a real voice in setting their compensation levels and their working conditions will not readily give up the collective bargaining process which has so often brought them real benefits. It is essential, therefore, that the administrators of local governmental units be given greater freedom than they now have to negotiate and to raise funds. Continued failure to grant them authority commensurate with their bargaining responsibilities is hardly likely to be in the public interest.

THE ROLE OF THE NEUTRAL
IN GRIEVANCE ARBITRATION
IN PUBLIC EMPLOYMENT

Eli Rock

Enormous overall changes have taken place in public sector bargaining in recent years. . . . It is clearly too early —and the information is inadequate—to permit any accurate conclusions regarding the extent to which grievance arbitration, binding or advisory, will come to represent the same basic part of the industrial relations behavior pattern which it has come to occupy in private industry.

Eli Rock is a professional arbitrator and was Labor Relations Advisor, City of Philadelphia, 1952-62. Reprinted by permission from *The Arbitrator*, the NLRB, and the Courts, copyright 1967 by The Bureau of National Affairs, Inc., Washington, D.C. 20037.

On one side, the relatively narrow scope of bargaining in many instances and the frequent exclusion from bargaining of such basic issues as discipline and job classification problems, plus the continued effort to limit arbitrability rather narrowly in the arbitration clauses themselves, suggest that wider unionization of public employees may not automatically carry with it proportionately widespread resort to grievance arbitration. Against this consideration is that, notwithstanding the limitation of subject matter, the contracts in public service, as have their counterparts in private industry, show signs, like union and management representatives and even a few arbitrators, of getting fatter with age. Moreover, some of the public contracts, particularly in the professional field, appear to be opening new areas of bargaining subject matter which have been unknown in the private field. There are also a few clear signs that earlier contractual restrictions on arbitrability are being broadened somewhat, although it is to be anticipated that some of the initially broader clauses may, in time and with some experience, move somewhat in the opposite direction.

Still another factor which must be weighed is the uncertain extent to which public employees, as a group, will make use of their grievance procedures. There is some scattered evidence that the grievance caseload is surprisingly small in some instances, but whether this is due to the newness of the experience (small use of at least written grievances has also characterized some of the older relationships) or to the limited nature of some of the contract subject matter or to some unique differences on this score arising from the separate nature of public employment or because the high number of professional unionists may view grievances differently is a matter which it is too early to judge.

It may be safely predicted, I believe, that the private industry experience of overall rise in the rate of arbitration over some period of years will be duplicated in the public service. Whether the sharp and dramatic recent rise in collective bargaining in the public service will be accompanied by a sustained sharp rise of the grievance arbitration curve in the early stages remains to be seen.

Recognizing that the rapid increase in the number of contract clauses providing for arbitration does not automatically presage use of those clauses, it should also be pointed out that in the private industry sector, where grievances were once a major source of work stoppages, this type of interruption has now virtually disappeared under the widespread acceptance of grievance arbitration. With the current preoccupation over the issue of strikes by public employees on contract matters, and with the difficulties of the search for a substitute on that score, it is not unreasonable to expect that for the relatively easier area of *grievance* resolution, where an established *peaceful* method is already at hand and where the legal and institutional obstacles to transference are clearly not as great, the trend toward increased acceptance and usage will continue.

To conclude otherwise would, in my opinion, be unrealistic, considering the dramatic growth in collective bargaining as such, the basic pattern of seeking to adapt public employee bargaining to the private industry framework wherever possible, and the other factors, which I have mentioned above. The only question at this state would appear to be *rate* of growth; and the evidence currently available is obviously too limited to permit more accurate projection on that score.

On the qualitative side, a whole host of actual and possible questions suggest themselves. On one major aspect the returns are, I think, already in. The basic and bitter battle over the sovereignty issue, which so long barred the way to acceptance of unionism per se in the public service, has by no means been terminated with the now-widespread pattern of recognition and written agreements. At least at this stage, it has been transferred, with basically similar concerns on both sides, to the issue of scope of bargaining; and even where some controverted subjects are accepted as falling within the scope of bargaining, the battle then often moves to the arena of the arbitrator and *his* scope of authority under the contract arbitration clause.

These issues may not be as serious when the arbitration is advisory; but at the local level, at least, that type of arrangement may already be relegated to the minority category. There is also evidence that even when the arbitrability of certain types of problems is accepted, the sovereignty issue may also be raised over the question of the arbitrator's authority to direct a remedy.

Dr. George Taylor has pointed out to me that the earlier stages of private industry grievance arbitration in this country were marked by many heated controversies, which were not dissimilar to some of those now arising in the public field—as, for example, the earlier battles over the authority of supervisors and the retained management rights question—but he has also recognized current differences and he has pointed out, too, that many years were required in the evolution of some of these early problems in the private sector.

Numerous other qualitative aspects of the problem range from matters like the impact of the political environment on a grievance in local government to such matters as the publication of awards and confidentiality of the arbitrator's relationship to the parties—and whether matters like these require a different approach because the parties in public service bargaining are public—to such questions as the basic method or style of arbitration in this field, and whether that should be different. It is at least possible that questions like enforceability and the trilogy, or procedural due process, which have been analyzed to death in the private sector, may now have to be analyzed all over again in the separate framework of the public sector. The relative newness to collective bargaining and arbitration by most of the parties in this field may create, when the varyingly unique characteristics of the field itself are also considered, a rather unfamiliar framework for many arbitrators. There is the danger that the procedures followed in hearings may be unrealistically oversimplified or, because of the nature of some of the problems, that they may become too formal, slow, or technical, defeating the goal of relatively expeditious resolutions. . . .

Considerable controversy is now taking place on the question of whether the state agencies and personnel assigned to administering some of the new state acts and programs in the public employee labor relations field should reflect the experience and background of the private industry sector or whether, as urged by some who regard the public sector as different, they should not. The same type of controversy may in time also arise in connection with the choice of grievance arbitrators for at least some parts of the public employee sector—although to date most of the arbitrators used in this field have apparently been men with the private industry background. Apart from the latter possible controversy as such, it may become necessary that arbitrators develop a particular expertise in this field, as so many already have for a number of the subheadings within the private industry arbitration field. . . .

The parties in the public field will often, on such questions as the basic sovereignty issue, be much better informed than the arbitrator, having fought over the issue at some length; it is easy enough to say that the arbitrator should therefore limit himself in the usual fashion to interpreting the language which they have written, but it must be recognized that because of the inherent difficulty of the problem, the language may often be less than clear or sufficient. When the latter *is* the case, and in coneection with other areas too, the unique difficulty of the problems may perhaps call for further arrangements of the Welfare Department type in New York, where the private industry experiences of the arbitrator are joined with the public service experiences of the parties in an informal program of mutual reasoning and assistance designed to adapt workable solutions for this field. In effect, private mediation, possible in some new forms, may become a process peculiarly fitted to the needs here.

Lawyers and staff men with experience in the private industry sector may conceivably also be required to lend assistance in the mutual adjustment process; and some of them have already become involved in that function. Some of the difficulties which have hitherto developed, I would feel, were unnecessary ones, stemming from the use of nonlabor relations experts, although as I have indicated, simple transference of that expertise alone may not be enough.

A whole host of persons already have been or are currently involved in the process of attempting to hammer out some basic solutions to the troublesome basic issues in this field, or in serving under some of the impasse procedures; and the experience of grievance arbitration, which may offer a window for viewing the practical aspects of some of the problems with which they are faced, might enhance their usefulness for those more basic tasks.

Ultimately, it would be my judgment that the arbitrator in this field will, with the help of the parties, be evolving his particular role and function in a rather gradual fashion—as the field itself changes and evolves. It is clearly too early to define accurately the precise outlines of that ultimate role. He may often find himself facing this question in the basic task of determining the style, nature, and content which should go into a particular decision. Some of those who have had experience in this fascinating new field will agree with me, I believe, that some of the cases thus far presented have involved extremely difficult and painful, as well as highly unique, problems.

The arbitrator's approach could, on the one hand, conceivably reflect the view that private industry decision writing today suffers from a hardening of the arbitral arteries, and that what is required particularly in this field today is the more forthright and free style of decision making which marked the earlier era of private industry arbitration, where the arbitrator perceived and sought to meet a need for basic guidance on the part of the parties themselves. Another school will, however, be influenced by another view—perhaps illustrated . . . by my own much-too-free indulgence in broad comments and projections in this particular paper. That view might be reflected in a recent quote by James MacGregor Burns from Cardinal Richelieu:

> Give me six lines written by the most honest man, I will find something there to hang him.

On this aspect, too, I can only say once again that it is too early to know.

CHAPTER 4

CASE STUDIES
ON PUBLIC SECTOR BARGAINING

Researchers and authors frequently must make a difficult choice between breadth and depth in their work. Those who attempt to give the "broad view" often lose the insights that can be obtained by studying one situation in great detail. This section includes four case studies in order to provide an in-depth view of the dynamics of public sector bargaining.

Of all strikes thus far by public employees, perhaps the most dramatic and certainly the most tragic in national terms was the 1968 organizational strike of Memphis sanitation workers during which Dr. Martin Luther King was assassinated. Marshall and Adams describe thoroughly the events leading up to the strike, including the racial issues that were so closely intertwined with the collective bargaining negotiations.

Weber describes the prelude to bargaining, the negotiations, the political pressures, and the strike in the Cook County (Illinois) Department of Public Aid. To provide some historical perspective to this section, the editors have included Spero's classic study of the 1919 Boston police strike. Another strike which will be analyzed and reanalyzed in future years is the 1970 postal strike. This was the first major strike of federal workers and it was immediately interpreted as opening a new era of collective bargaining with federal employees. It is too early to know what the full impact of this strike will be, but the editors believe it essential to include a description of the strike and a discussion of issues it raises.

RACIAL NEGOTIATIONS—THE MEMPHIS CASE

Ray Marshall
Arvil Van Adams

The Memphis strike of public works employees began and ended as a labor dispute between Local 1733 of the American Federation of State, County, and Municipal Employees, AFL–CIO (AFSCME) and the city of Memphis. Local 1733 numbered thirteen hundred members, predominantly Negro and a majority of whom were sanitation workers. Surrounding the economic issues in the dispute was the underlying issue of race. The racial composition of Memphis was approximately 50 percent white and 40 percent Negro. Although Memphis, unlike other southern cities of its size in the sixties, basked in relative racial tranquility, the surface changes in its public institutions obscured the perpetuation of economic and educational inequities. The support given Local 1733 by the Negro community during the dispute was a sign of racial dissatisfaction whose roots were far deeper than the basic economic issues of the strike itself. By drawing the Negro community together and providing articular spokesmen, the strike revealed the nature of the black workers' problems to upper-class Negroes as well as whites.

Hearings conducted in Memphis in 1966 by the Tennessee State Advisory Committee to the U.S. Commission on Civil Rights presented the record of Negro employment in private industry and government agencies. These Hearings concluded:

> In the area of employment, the need for training opportunities for Negro youth and adults is paramount . . . Old patterns of discrimination and exclusion on the part of employers have not disappeared totally. The problem seems most acute in the area of upgrading and promotion, and in the use of Negroes in supervisory positions.

The record for employment of Negroes was somewhat better at the county and federal government levels than at the city level. In the 1966 Hearings, the city

Ray Marshall and Arvid Van Adams are Professor of Economics, University of Texas, and Instructor in Economics, University of Kentucky, respectively. Reprinted from W. Ellison Chalmers and Gerald W. Cormick (eds.), *Racial Conflict and Negotiations: Perspectives and First Case Studies,* Ann Arbor: Institute of Labor and Industrial Relations, the University of Michigan–Wayne State University, 1970. This is one of a number of studies within a research project supported by the Ford Foundation exploring the potentials and limitations of the negotiating process in racial conflicts.

personnel director testified that there was no municipal regulation covering discrimination by hiring departments. He admitted that such discrimination could take place.

The desegregation of the Memphis city schools began in October 1961. In 1968, 53 percent of the one hundred twenty-five thousand children in the city school system were Negro, over 80 percent of whom were still attending predominantly all-Negro schools.

Dissatisfactions of Negroes also extended to housing and police treatment. The Negro community was particularly incensed by such injustices by the Memphis police force as were reported by the 1966 Civil Rights Commission Hearings:[1]

> Relations between the police and the Negro community are in a sad state of disrepair. Only prompt, bold and decisive leadership on the part of the highest officials of the city and county can avert the disaster which may coincide with the next incident.

Prior to the strike, therefore, there existed a general dissatisfaction within the Negro community with the white power structure. Progress in resolving their dissatisfactions had come too slowly and frequently was nonexistent. The strike and its issues served as a rallying point for the airing of the deeper dissatisfactions of the Negro community. The black community in Memphis could readily identify with the sanitation workers because the city's refusal to recognize their union was similar to the white power structure's unwillingness to recognize Negroes as equals and as persons with rights to decide their own destinies.

COMMUNITY ORGANIZATION

"Prior to the strike there never had been a more divided community than the Memphis Negro community," said Baxton Bryant, executive director of the Tennessee Council of Human Relations.[2] There was a natural rivalry provided by the churches, which competed fiercely for members and sometimes forgot ethics. Each minister dominated his own fiefdom, and agreement and coordination between ministers was an infrequent event.

There was also a spirited political rivalry within the Negro community. Dan Powell, Southeastern Regional Director of the AFL–CIO Committee on Political Education (COPE), noted that the Negro vote had been split in the governor's election of 1966, and again in the mayor and councilmen's election of 1967. Since no candidate received a majority of the votes in the mayoralty election, a runoff election was held between the two top candidates, William Ingram and Henry Loeb. NAACP sources estimate that the winner, Henry Loeb, received less than 2 percent of the Negro vote. The council races pitted Negro candidates against each other in two districts in the runoff election.

The strike had a unifying influence on the Negro community and the union served as a common denominator for various factions which had been split by

---

[1]U.S. Civil Rights Commission, *Hearings in Memphis* (mimeographed), p. 44.

[2]All quotes used in this paper were taken from interviews with the persons indicated, unless otherwise noted.

religious and political differences. Since its members belonged to the various churches and supported the separate Negro candidates, the union's determination to seek economic justice for its members caused the Negro community to close ranks in support of the strikers.

UNION ORGANIZATION

Local 1733 of the AFSCME was chartered by the international union October 13, 1964, but operated informally because the city refused to recognize any union as sole bargaining agent for a group of employees. Commissioner T. E. Sisson, elected Commissioner of Public Works in 1963, allegedly promised the union recognition in exchange for its political support. Sisson later denied this, contending that the city was prevented by law from negotiating with a union. (The "law" was actually a decision handed down by the Tennessee Supreme Court which held that strikes against the public were illegal. Neither the legal right to form a public employees union nor recognition and negotiation with such a union by a public body was ruled upon by the court.)

Local 1733 attempted to strike for recognition in 1965. Word leaked to the city administration about the union's plans and before the walkout could start an injunction against the strike was obtained by city attorneys in chancery court. The judge based his ruling on the earlier Tennessee Supreme Court decision, but went beyond it by ruling that picketing was also illegal.

Added to the lack of organization to the strike was the presence of a political leader whose popularity made it difficult to gather support for the strike from members of Local 1733 and the Negro community. Because of his relatively fair treatment of Negroes when he was city judge, William Ingram, elected mayor in 1963, won the support and respect of the Negro community. It was suggested, however, by Ingram's adversaries that he really didn't like Negroes, he just hated the police more. Nevertheless, Ingram's popularity in the Negro community helped him win election as mayor. "This popularity," Bill Ross, executive secretary of the Memphis AFL–CIO Labor Council, pointed out, "definitely had an impact in blunting support in the Negro community for the strike in 1965." Many members of the Negro community and the local were hesitant to cross the political path of the man judged to be their friend. Because of this attitude, the injunction, and the lack of organization, the strike never got off the ground.

The commission form of government also had been a nemesis to the union because the commissioners hid behind one another in refusing to establish a policy of recognition for public employee unions. On January 1, 1968, however, a new form of government replaced the commission form. The mayor-council system enabled the mayor alone to establish the policy of recognition. "This was fine," noted Don Powell, "except the wrong man was elected Mayor."

Mayor Henry Loeb, unlike his predecessor, did not enjoy the support of the Negro community. He was considered anti-civil rights and antiunion because of earlier actions while in city government. Upon taking office, he continued his opposition to recognition of the union.

The mayor did not stand alone on the issue of recognition of public employee unions. As Baxton Bryant pointed out, "Public employee unions and strikers against the government are bad words to the American public." Before and during the strike, the mayor enjoyed the widespread support of the white community in Memphis.[3] The issue of race need not have been present to have attracted the white community's support for the mayor, but it undoubtedly made white support stronger than it otherwise would have been.

Thus the intensification of dissatisfaction with the responsiveness of the white power structure to the needs of the Negro community, the fragmentation of the Negro community with the presence of the union as a unifying force, effective Negro leadership, and an untried political structure, coupled with an unacceptable political personality, provided the setting and the constraints for the confrontation. The negotiation process that was to follow was heavily influenced by this combination of constraints.

THE STRIKE

The strike, which started on February 12, 1968, and was settled about two months later, resulted in riots and disorder, a Negro boycott of downtown white businesses, and the tragic assassination of Dr. Martin Luther King. Although working conditions were the immediate cause of the dispute, these cannot be separated from the larger racial issues which were raised by this strike and the events leading up to it. Indeed, the walkout itself was not carefully planned, but was almost a spontaneous reaction by Negro workers to what they considered unfair treatment by the Department of Public Works.

The incident which sparked the strike occurred on January 31, 1968, when twenty-two Negro employees of the Sewer and Drain Maintenance Division of the Department of Public Works[4] were sent home because of rain, while white employees in identical work classifications were allowed to work and receive a full day's pay. The city responded to the Negro workers' complaints by unilaterally paying them two hours callup pay, but this was not satisfactory to the workers. A meeting was therefore called of Local 1733 and on February 12, after considerable discussion, the union's president, T. O. Jones, led his men out on a strike. The international was reluctant to support the strike at first, primarily because proper preparation had not been made for a strike and because garbage strikes are more effective if they occur in the summer than in the winter. However, the determination of Local 1733's membership caused the international to give the strikers full support.

Parties to the Dispute

There was no precedent in Memphis to deal with a striking public employees union. The mayor, the city council, and the mayor-council form of government

[3] J. Edwin Stanfield, *In Memphis: Mirror to America,* Report for the Southern Regional Council (Atlanta, 1968), p. 23.

[4] The Department of Public Works is divided into three divisions: Sewer and Drain Maintenance (with 170 Negro and 52 white employees), Street Maintenance, and Sanitation. A NAACP survey six months before the strike revealed 2,175 employees in the department, 1,597 of whom were black.

itself were new. Thus the negotiation procedure came about through a series of haphazard events.

Both formal and informal negotiations were aided by "neutral" third parties during the strike. The formal negotiations joined the mayor's representatives and the union's representatives with a mediator who had been appointed by a city council resolution. The informal negotiations consisted of interested third parties who sought to bring the union and the city together by creating a dialogue on the issues.

The mayor, Henry Loeb, was the dominant figure representing the city in both formal and informal negotiations. The city council interpreted the settlement of the dispute as an executive function and therefore would not intervene directly.

The mayor was described by friends and foes alike as a hard-driving, self-initiative, shirtsleeves type politician. He was also a man of deep pride and arrogance. Born in Memphis of an old-line Jewish family, he was educated in the East at Phillips Academy in Andover, Massachusetts, and Brown University. During World War II he commanded a PT boat in the Mediterranean. He was elected public works commissioner for the city in 1956 and mayor in 1960. He resigned from office in 1964 at the death of his father to take over the family laundry business, which he helped operate until 1966, when he sold his interest to his brother William.

Initially, Mayor Loeb considered the strike illegal. Therefore, throughout the strike he refused to recognize the AFSCME as sole bargaining agent for the public works employees and to approve a dues checkoff. In a mass meeting with union members February 13, he said, "This is not New York. [Reference to the ongoing New York sanitation strike.] Nobody can break the law. You are putting my back against the wall and I am not going to budge."[5]

Mayor Loeb was described by Baxton Bryant as a man who wanted to be fair, but whose definition of fairness came out of a white middle class society. The mayor's position publicly was taken not so much on the race issue as against the union. He was quoted by one source as saying that he would not be the first mayor in the South to recognize a public employees union.

Thus early in the strike the central figure for the city became committed to a stand that was difficult to back away from. He sought compromise on all issues except recognition and dues checkoff. He continued to talk informally throughout the strike, but his listeners from the union and the Negro community became fewer and fewer in number. At one point in the strike Baxton Bryant was reported to be the sole contact the union had with the mayor.

The union had unwittingly chosen to make its stand on organizing public employees in the South here in Memphis. "We didn't think the strike would escalate as it did," said Jesse Epps, special assistant to the international president of AFSCME, "but by the second week, we saw the city's position harden and the strike as coming to have a potential impact on our southern organization effort." Memphis became very crucial to the AFSCME and as a result the international became deeply committed to the local dispute.

The union sought economic equality for its members and establishment of a foothold in the door of southern organization. This was, as *The New York Times*

---

[5]*New York Times*, February 14, p. 31.

reported May 6, 1968, the coalition of labor and the civil rights movement so eagerly encouraged by Dr. Martin Luther King in 1961.

There were many "third parties" involved in informal negotiations throughout the strike. A local business leader, Frank Miles, former mediator with the Federal Mediation and Conciliation Service, who served as mediator in the formal negotiations, reported that the most substantive effort to bring the parties together for dialogue was made early in the strike by a few members of the Ministerial Alliance. The mayor, representing the city, and Jerry Wurf, international president of the AFSCME, representing the union, were brought together over a period of five days with the ministers serving as moderators. Their confrontation was described by observers as a three-way dialogue with each side directing its comments to the other side via the moderator. No direct negotiations between the parties occurred from the time these sessions ended on February 23 till formal negotiations were begun by Frank Miles on March 23.

The ministers moderating these sessions between the mayor and Jerry Wurf were white. However, "the white churches and churchmen were not notably involved throughout the strike,"[6] and our information confirms this conclusion. Indeed, the all-white Second Baptist Church in East Memphis split over its minister's participation in the strike on behalf of the union.

Many individuals in the community were deeply concerned at the outset. "It seemed," said Frank Miles, "as though every Saturday somebody had a new idea they wanted to try out to resolve this thing. All these attempts were sincere, but I'd have to say they were not realistic in attempting to deal with collective bargaining problems."

Frank Miles said of himself, "My concern at the beginning of this dispute, which was purely and simply a labor dispute, was that if it was not controlled to the point that it could be settled as a labor dispute, then it was liable to spill over into racial conflict." A former mayor, Edmund Orgill, was also actively interested in this strike. As a member of the Memphis Committee on Human Relations, he had long been involved with efforts in Memphis to provide interracial harmony. Therefore he worked with others to seek a peaceful resolution of the dispute. Baxton Bryant, in his capacity as director of the Tennessee Council of Human Relations, became an important intermediary throughout the conflict.

An ad hoc group of Negro ministers, entitled Committee on the Move for Equality (COME), was formed to support the strike. Indeed, the Negro community became organized as never before under the leadership of such men as Dr. Ralph Jackson, Reverend S. B. Kyles, and Reverend James Lawson. They communicated effectively the spirit and fiber of the Negro community's solidarity for the strikers and were able to mount nonviolent coercive pressures on the city and the white business community to support the strikers' demands. They also broke a local news freeze on the strike, got national support for the strikers, and embarrassed the local power structure by involving well-known national civil rights leaders in the strike on behalf of the union. The best expression of their ability to control is represented by the limited amount of violence that took place in the explosive environment surrounding the marches and Dr. King's assassination and the size of the crowds they were able to rally in support of the strikers.

[6]J. Edwin Stanfield, *In Memphis: More than a Garbage Strike*, p. 41.

THE ISSUES IN NEGOTIATION

The substantive economic issues of the strike reflected the Negro community's desire to change the process and product of the white-dominated power structure. This was a demand for a change in the institutional structure as well as a demand for a change in the output of the institutions. The racial issues—symbolized by recognition of Negroes' right to participate in economic and political decisions affecting their lives,—leading to the dispute and surrounding the bargaining process played a large role in determining the content and form of the negotiation process.

The major collective bargaining issues of the strike were recognition and dues checkoff. The city had already recognized several unions informally. However, it had never recognized as sole bargaining agent, signed a collective bargaining agreement with, or granted a dues checkoff to any union. These AFSCME demands were therefore the major hurdles that had to be overcome at the bargaining table.

Recognition, the main issue between the city and the union since Local 1733's inception in 1964, was the single most important issue of the strike. The remaining issues (dues checkoff, a grievance procedure, merit promotion, and wages) could have been resolved only after recognition of the Public Works Department employees' right to choose their own bargaining representative. The recognition issue was important not only because the local could not compromise it, but also because the city took the position that it would be illegal for it to recognize any union as sole bargaining agent. Since he considered the strike illegal, Mayor Loeb's initial position was that the workers would have to return to work before their grievances could be discussed. Although legality undoubtedly concerned the mayor, he obviously also thought collective bargaining was unnecessary in view of his "open door" policy to city employees.

Mayor Loeb undoubtedly understood that recognition of the AFSCME would have changed the city's decision-making process. As generally defined, recognition would have represented an obligation for the city and the union to meet and discuss wages, hours, and conditions of employment. In this instance recognition would have meant the entrance of the union and the Negro into the white decision-making process. It was this change that the mayor seemed to resist so vehemently.

The attitude of many Negroes toward the recognition issue was symbolized by a picket sign that appeared in the daily marches on city hall which read "I *Am* a Man." Its implication, discussed at length in the black community, was that no longer were Negroes in Memphis willing to let one white man—or a group of white men—control their destiny. The issue to these men was one of black identity. The recognition of themselves as men with certain rights was the first step in the process of change that was to follow. The second step was the exercise of these rights by gaining a role for the union in decision-making.

The recognition sought by the AFSCME was the right of the employee to determine freely who would represent him in any bilateral policymaking process. Thus the issue of black identity caused the recognition question to become a race issue. Collective bargaining meant replacing the unilateralism of Old South politics with the bilateralism of the New South.

The mayor also refused to compromise on the dues checkoff system which was a crucial security issue for the AFSCME because Tennessee is a "right to work" state. No provisions for membership maintenance therefore were available to the union except through a checkoff of dues. Thus the checkoff was a key issue in any hope the mayor had for diluting the union's strength.

The dominance of the recognition issue highlighted the initial confrontation and resulting negotiations. In this instance the change in process overshadowed the change in output of the existing institutions. There was tremendous resistance by the white-dominated power structure to the union's inclusion in the decision-making process, especially when that union was predominantly black and had black leadership. The mayor's strong antiunion position was supported by many elements in the white community, though apparently some white attitudes shifted as the strike went on.

The union, however, was only the vehicle of change. The real force of change came from the Negro community itself through the concept of black identity, the strength of which apparently was underestimated by white leaders. In his effort to defeat the union, it is questionable whether the mayor understood the significance of this force.

The Negotiation Process

Shortly after the walkout on February 12, the mayor challenged the extent to which the union actually spoke for the employees; the union answered his challenge with a march on City Hall by over a thousand union members. The mayor met with these men in Ellis Auditorium, next to City Hall, on February 13. He received such a rude reception after outlining his stand against the strike and the union that he ultimately walked out of the meeting.

Nevertheless, Mayor Loeb continued to take the position that the union leaders and the ministers really did not represent the employees. He therefore refused to deal with representatives of the strikers and made a unilateral offer directly to the strikers through an open letter, published in a local newspaper February 29, consisting of a wage increase of eight cents an hour, a grievance procedure, and certain insurance and overtime benefits. The wage increase was to be written into the city's budget and to begin with the new fiscal year, July 1. The mayor remained adamant, however, in refusing to recognize the union or grant the checkoff.

The remaining portion of the first five weeks of the dispute was marked by one more meeting between the mayor and union representatives and a series of informal negotiations. These informal sessions included efforts by individual citizens and the ministers from the Ministerial Alliance, all of whom sought unsuccessfully to establish a dialogue between the parties.

In the meantime coercive pressures were being applied by both sides. The union, with the support of the Negro community, reinforced its demands by daily marches; picketing of City Hall; and boycotts of downtown stores, the two daily newspapers, and firms doing business under the name of Loeb. In addition, reports of a growing militant mood among younger Negroes, though more a figment of journalistic sensationalism and white fears than a real force in the black community, placed further pressure on the city.

The city responded with legal tactics designed to halt the strike, the hiring of strikebreakers, continued garbage collection on a limited scale, and a show of large numbers of policemen at council meetings and marches downtown. The show of police force was especially significant in view of the deterioration of Negro-police relations.

Representatives of the union and the city searched for a means to settle the dispute. The mayor stated his willingness to compromise all issues except recognition and dues checkoff, and the AFSCME reportedly was willing to accept an informal exchange of letters between the mayor and the union in lieu of formal recognition. The informal exchange of letters would have provided the mayor a face-saving device for his adamant stand against recognition. The union also was willing to work out a checkoff of dues with the independent employees' credit union rather than directly from the city's payroll. However, the negative position taken by the mayor on these issues thwarted any hope of compromise.

Attempting to soften the mayor's stand, Baxton Bryant, in many informal conferences with the mayor, tried to explain the growth of black identity as an issue and what it meant to Negro union members. "At the close of each of these meetings," Bryant said, "the Mayor would seem to understand this concept as a reason for the strength of the Negro commitment to the strike, but by the next meeting, conservative elements seemed to get hold of him and he would remain unrelenting."

"The Mayor continued to refer to his term as Public Works Commissioner and how he understood 'his' men. He never could accept the idea that the men wanted the union," said Bryant. "He seemed to feel that the union organizers were 'outsiders' who weren't speaking for the men. He ignored the large numbers of workers appearing at the union meetings and instead pointed to the smaller numbers appearing for the daily marches as a sign of diminishing support for the strike."

By resolution of the city council, Frank Miles was asked to serve as mediator between the union and the mayor in the dispute. This was the first direct effort by the council to resolve the conflict, and it came after Mayor Loeb's opposition to third-party intervention was overcome. The mayor confused the neutral assistance of the mediator with the binding decision of an arbitrator, and agreed to mediation only after this distinction was explained to him. Up to this point the city council had maintained that the settlement of this matter was an executive and not a legislative function. The first meeting between the union and the mayor's representatives with Miles as mediator was set for 10:00 A.M., March 23. One city official said of the mayor's representatives, "It was a poor choice, they were from the don't-give-'em-an-inch school." The mayor's representatives were also unfamiliar with negotiation procedures and tactics and seemed to lack coordination in their initial approaches to the negotiations. The first meeting on March 23 therefore broke down when one of the mayor's representatives questioned the legality of the strike. A behind-the-scenes agreement had been reached with the mayor that this question would not be raised during negotiations, so this move by his representative apparently caught the mayor by surprise. The question was finally resolved by Miles and other intermediaries on the following day with the city agreeing not to press the legality issue.

When the meetings resumed March 25, discussion turned to what form the agreement, if any, would take. Frank Miles suggested the use of a "memorandum of understanding." This, Miles said, was a technique he had often used as a mediator—

that is, to get the parties to set out a memorandum of understanding of the issues as the mediator understood them. He agreed that if an agreement was reached at the meeting, he would present the memorandum to the city council and ask them to adopt it by resolution. This procedure, which was acceptable to both parties, would have given the union a written agreement approved by the legislative arm of the city.

Negotiations then moved to the issue of recognition. Miles commented: "We were on recognition Monday and Tuesday. Wednesday, March 27, we were still on recognition. Some progress had been made though. I find that when a word presents a particular problem, I can often get around it by defining it and using the definition in its place. Recognition means that the parties agree to meet periodically to discuss wages, hours, and conditions of employment. The City was willing to agree to this language, but [Dr. Jackson] a member of the union team, who had been appointed as a representative of the Negro community, objected to it. He felt very strongly that the word 'recognition' should be used because of its racial connotations in this case." After subsequent discussion, Dr. Jackson agreed to the compromise of spelling out the meaning of recognition. Dr. Jackson was particularly concerned about recognition of the union's right to represent the workers and the black man's right to speak for himself.

At this point Miles was prepared to reduce to writing the verbal agreement reached by the parties on recognition. The city's negotiators, however, objected to putting the agreement in writing because this would compromise their original position, thereby violating the common law prohibition on strikes. For them to agree, they said, would be a violation of the law.

The union then accused the city's negotiating team of failing to negotiate in good faith. Added to this charge was a statement by the union accusing the city of "leaking" to the press information about what had been going on in the negotiating sessions. "We knew that we couldn't negotiate in a fish bowl, i.e., the public media," said Epps. "This had been what the Mayor wanted from the beginning. It was for this reason and the failure to reduce the agreement on recognition to writing that we accused the city of a failure to negotiate in good faith."

Some members of the union team were restless because they were supposed to be at a meeting planning for the march to be led by Dr. Martin Luther King, Jr., the following day, March 28, so the meeting was adjourned with the understanding that they would meet again when called together by Miles. The union attached the condition that whenever the city was ready to sit down and negotiate in good faith they would be ready to meet. That evening, over local television, the union again charged the city with a failure to bargain in good faith.

The atmosphere for negotiations was exacerbated when the march the following day was broken up by windowbreaking and looting. Dr. King was taken to the Holiday Inn Rivermont for safety by his aides. Memphis city police, Shelby County sheriff's deputies, and Tennessee highway patrolmen reacted quickly and violently as they had in an earlier march on February 23. Charges of "police brutality" by marchers and observers were later investigated by a closed-door session of the U.S. Civil Rights Commission. The commission concluded that beyond doubt there was police misconduct.

Miles said that his first reaction was to let things cool down a bit before calling the parties together again. On the following Monday, April 1, he called the city and union representatives and set up a meeting for the following Friday, April 5. The meeting never took place as Dr. King was assassinated Thursday evening, April 4. Although the violence in Memphis following Dr. King's death was relatively minor, other cities, especially in the Northeast, experienced widespread disorder.

Following the assassination, President Johnson sent Undersecretary of Labor James Reynolds to Memphis. Reynolds reported that he was in his office April 5 when President Johnson called him.

> He asked me why I wasn't down in Memphis trying to settle that strike. I explained to him that the Department of Labor doesn't normally get involved with a strike unless both parties request this, and then it is the Federal Mediation and Conciliation Service that would be involved. The only other cause for the Federal Government to get involved would be a national emergency. He then told me, "I regard this as a matter of great danger having implications far beyond the strike itself. The urban problems facing our nation could be enlarged by the events of Dr. King's death. I want you to get down there and help settle that thing.

Before leaving for Memphis, Reynolds called Governor Buford Ellington of Tennessee and explained to him the President's directive. Governor Ellington welcomed Reynolds' entrance into the dispute and promised his cooperation. After arriving on Friday evening, April 5, Reynolds contacted Mayor Loeb, who was too tired to see the undersecretary that evening and suggested a meeting the following morning. Reynolds told the mayor that he "wasn't here to impose a solution or to circumvent his position, but . . . was here to bring the parties to some form of agreement they could live with." In the evening of April 5, Reynolds met with Frank Miles and with union representatives. Reynolds and Miles discussed the plan of action they would use when the parties were asked to meet again. The next morning Mayor Loeb agreed to Reynolds' entry into the case after the undersecretary explained that "this thing *had* to be settled."

After the mayor agreed to his mediation efforts, Reynolds and Miles called a meeting of city and union representatives for 3:00 P.M., April 6. The two sides met with mediators till early Sunday morning, April 7, and adjourned till later in the day. The second meeting carried into early Monday morning at which time the mayor and Jerry Wurf were called in. "Enough progress had been made in the language of the agreement, including the issues of recognition and dues checkoff," said Miles, "so that the issues were narrowed down to one, wages."

The dues checkoff issue was resolved by establishing a collection procedure through the independent employees' credit union. "This took time to accomplish," said Miles. "We had to get approval from the executive board of the credit union and also from its Washington headquarters since it was federally chartered, but the time was well spent for this was a very critical issue. James Reynolds was extremely helpful in cutting red tape," noted Miles. "He knew the right people in Washington to call to get this thing through for us."

The wage issue remained to be solved. Miles reported that the city was in real financial trouble at the time. Loeb made a presentation of the city's fiscal position which indicated that the city was in no position to grant even a token wage increase. Both Reynolds and Miles were impressed by the mayor's grasp of the city's fiscal problems after three months in office.

The mayor wanted to wait till the beginning of the city's fiscal year in July to grant a wage increase. "We knew members of the union would never stand for this," said Miles, "they wanted an increase immediately." The mayor was offering an eight-cents-an-hour increase and the union was asking for considerably more. The union had support from some members of the city council who suggested a fifteen-cents-an-hour increase. "With this support," said Miles, "I knew it was going to be difficult to get the union to settle for anything less than fifteen cents." The wage issue was therefore twofold. A means of compromise had to be provided on the amount as well as the timing of any wage increase.

The sessions were adjourned Monday, April 8, for the King Memorial March and Tuesday, April 9, for Dr. King's funeral. The parties met again on April 10, and each day thereafter until agreement on the wage issue was reached April 16.

The settlement was reached with the union members receiving a ten-cents-an-hour wage increase effective May 1, and another increase of five cents an hour to become effective September 1. The key to the solution was finding a means for the city to pay for a wage increase till June 30, the end of the fiscal year. The city had already indicated that a wage increase could be written into the budget for the new fiscal year beginning July 1. The compromise finally reached on this issue was the result of behind-the-scenes work of Frank Miles and other interested third parties. "An anonymous benefactor and long-time friend of this city provided our solution," said Miles. This individual contacted Miles, offering to supply $60,000 of his own money to finance the wage increase for the remaining months of May and June in the old fiscal year. The city agreed to accept the offer. "The solution to the wage issue would have been extremely difficult without this gesture," commented miles.

A merit promotion plan, a no-strike clause, a no-discrimination clause, and a grievance procedure were added to the agreement. The grievance procedure provided for nonbinding arbitration by an arbitration panel made up of three persons. The city and the union would each select one member of the panel and the third member, who would be chairman, would be jointly selected by the appointees of the union and the city. The final power to resolve a grievance remained with the mayor. "It would be unlikely," said Miles, "that the mayor could justify rejecting any decision reached by an impartial arbitrator."

The final Memorandum of Understanding was presented to the city council and passed by a twelve-to-one margin on April 16, 1968, sixty-four days after the walkout. It provided a working agreement between the union and the city through June 30, 1969. The one dissenting vote was cast by a councilman who also was a member of the city's negotiating team and who remained adamant against the union. The union voted unanimously to accept the agreement.

Elements Leading to a Solution

The "Memphis formula" can be reduced to a set of six variables, each with a number of supporting factors, that significantly affected the agreement reached by the AFSCME and the city of Memphis. These include unified Negro support of the strike, articulate Negro leaders, coercive pressures from the Negro community, support of organized labor and national civil rights leaders, communication through mediation and neutral third parties, and a factor which can be described as the "Memphis image."

At any given time one or more of these variables may have taken precedence over another. However, the continued unified support in the Negro community for the strikers was crucial to the success of the union in negotiations with the city. Earlier failure to mount strong support for the union during the Ingram administration underscores the importance of this factor. Mayor Loeb was convinced he could break the strike by the use of strikebreakers to provide limited garbage pickup, but he considerably underestimated the cohesiveness of the strikers and their supporters, a cohesiveness strengthened by the mayor's antiunion and anti-Negro image.

The presence of articulate Negro leaders was important in providing coordination for coercive pressures upon the city. Memphis Negro ministers generally had no record of being outspoken to the white establishment. Dr. Ralph Jackson, director of the Department of Minimum Salary of the African Methodist Episcopal Church, who became an active spokesman for the Negro community during the strike, was a case in point. Dr. Jackson was a friend of Mayor Loeb but, during a march of union members down Main Street February 23, he was maced by police along with other bystanders when a disturbance broke out between marchers and the police. After this incident he became an activist in support of the strikers. Following the macing incident, Dr. Jackson and others went to a meeting in the Mason Temple where they were given the details involved in the sanitation strike and "the inhumane conditions under which they were working at the time. . . . From that, a vast source of information was brought out about the over-all conditions in the city. . . . I had become . . . unaware of conditions in trying to make it under the system. We had really gotten away from the things that go on and the conditions under which people live and work, the types of wages and salaries they receive, the types of homes they lived in. All of these things were unfolded to us and we had to look at these and the sanitation strike in the light of the needs of the folk. The need for a commitment to change these things is what actually got me involved." At a mass meeting of strike supporters shortly thereafter, Dr. Jackson said, "I have a confession to make. For thirty years I have been training to hold myself in check. I couldn't understand what made some people lose control of themselves and fly off the handle. I never thought it would happen to me. But I lost thirty years of training in just five minutes last Friday [February 23] ."[7]

The macing incident involving Jackson followed a city council meeting at which council members refused to hear some black ministers and a Public Works Committee resolution (passed the day before) supporting the strikers. The Public Works Committee meeting held February 22 was the "turning point" for Rev. James Lawson, who had supported the strike, but had not been actively involved until that time. Lawson was infuriated because he thought the Public Works Committee hearing chairman, a black member of the city council, "was trying to coddle to Loeb and the white establishment."

COME was organized after the macing incident demonstrated that the police did not discriminate in their treatment of Negro marchers. The strength of black identity as an issue could be clearly seen at this point. COME, led by Rev. Lawson, directed the coercive pressures from the Negro community and the minister's congregations provided an important source of funds for the strikers. Ministers from COME also participated in discussions with the mayor.

[7]Stanfield, *In Memphis: More than a Garbage Strike,* p. 33.

The strength of these Negro leaders lay in their demonstrated ability to apply coercive pressures on the city. When the city council rebuffed the ministers on February 23 by refusing to hear the Public Works Committee resolution calling for a recognition of the union and some form of dues checkoff, the ministers took to their pulpits and called for the boycott of all downtown stores, the daily newspapers, and all Loeb businesses. It was successful. Business showed a marked decline downtown. Negroes did not shop there, white customers shopped out east in the shopping centers, and rural trade stayed away. The boycott's success caused businessmen to place pressure on the mayor to settle the dispute.

Included in the set of coercive pressures from the Negro community was the implicit threat of increasing militancy among younger Negroes. Groups like the Black Knights and Invaders, whether militant in their beginnings or not, were labeled such by the daily newspapers. Members of these groups had spoken at one or more of the meetings supporting the strikers. Edwin Stanfield reports one such incident when a young man spoke to a mass meeting.[8] The young man began:

> I'm a radical, I'll tell you just like that I'm a radical . . ..Before Henry Loeb will listen, the garbage has to be in the street . . . not in your back yard. As long as those trucks are allowed to roll, they can keep it picked up wherever they want it picked up . . ..
>
> Preaching and money raising are fine. Somebody has to do it. But there are some *men* out there, we've got to do some fighting. Not marching—fighting!
>
> And when you talk about fighting a city with as many cops as this city's got, you better have some guns! You're gonna need 'em before it's over!

Most Negro leaders subscribed to Dr. King's philosophy of nonviolence but, when met with white indifference to their pleas for justice for the strikers, they talked about "going fishing." This implied a threat of leaving things in the hands of the militants.

The white community through its police, newspapers, and other public media established a policy of alienation toward these young Negroes. It never sought to work with them but chose instead to work against them. Although the numbers of young people who might be labeled "militant" remained a very small minority, the city's policies of alienation, condemnation, and police force did not diminish their numbers. "The looting and breaking of windows during the march led by Dr. King, March 28, was what really awoke the community to what was happening," said Frank Miles. "It was at this point that the city realized this thing had to be settled before it got further out of hand." Although its importance was exaggerated in the press, the threat of violence produced movement behind the scenes to settle the dispute. There was, however, an apparent difference in the meaning of militant as used by Negroes and whites. Whites interpreted militant as meaning force and violence while blacks interpreted it as meaning unrelenting direct nonviolent action to achieve their ends.

Probably because they wanted to justify their own violent response to the demonstrations, the white community and the press exhibited a "radical paranoia" which caused them to exaggerate the significance of those in the black community

[8]Stanfield, *In Memphis: More than a Garbage Strike*, pp. 43-44.

who advocated violence. However, Negro leaders such as Dr. Jackson and Rev. Lawson minimize the importance of radicals. According to Lawson: "They never got past rhetoric. They bragged a lot about what they were going to do, but they never did it. We've got pictures of the disturbances and we *know* who was in on it. In fact, they discredited themselves in the black community by failing to go beyond their rhetoric. . . . I don't see that they really did bring in white support. It was really Martin's death that was the drawing point for whites." Dr. Jackson said: "Memphis has never really had a real violent effort here. Even the first march that was broken up, half a dozen windows were broken. When Martin was killed, less damage was done in Memphis than anywhere . . . largely because of the influence of leadership . . .which comes from the ministers." Dr. Jackson thought that the creation of radicals by whites "was the newspaper and the power structure method and effort of developing this thing. This was another way of solidifying the racism in the white community against what was being done. As long as they could show that Memphis had some of those folk you were reading about in those other towns, then this gave them the reason to use force to put it down."

The coalition of organized labor and the Negro community provided the civil rights movement with a new power base. The acceptance of the cause by local white unions was not immediate, however, "The insertion of race as an issue," said one union observer, "couldn't help but make it difficult to get widespread local white union support." Two locals, the Rubber Workers and the Retail Clerks, offered immediate support. Newsletters from the AFL–CIO Committee on Political Education (COPE) were sent to union locals outlining the economic issues of the dispute. In addition, resolutions from the AFL–CIO Labor Council in support of the strikers' demands were presented to the mayor. Absent at first, however, was the financial support of organized labor and the presence of its members in the daily marches on city hall.

The entrance of national personalities such as Bayard Rustin, Roy Wilkins, and Dr. Martin Luther King during the fourth week of the strike attracted national publicity and with this came financial support from several international unions. The entry of these well-known national leaders broke the local news "freeze" on the activities of the Negro-union coalition and focused national attention on the dispute. This attention attracted support for the strikers and criticism of Memphis and its leaders.

A significant force for settlement was the desire by local union leaders and the white power structure to emphasize the trade union rather than the race aspects of the conflict. These white attitudes strengthened the effectiveness of racial demonstrations especially after national publicity was focused on the dispute. The threat to "go fishing" by the Negro ministers and leave things in the hands of the militants strengthened efforts by local white union leaders to refocus on the trade union aspects of the strike in order to obtain local white unionist support. A march of nearly five hundred white union members on March 4 was organized by Tommy Powell, head of the Memphis AFL–CIO Labor Council. "Morale toward the middle of the strike," said Baxton Bryant, "became a real problem as did the lack of money." The presence of white support could not help but lift the morale of the strikers while it reinforced the position of those seeking to restructure existing white institutions over those wishing to destroy these institutions. It deemphasized racial aspects of the strike and underscored for the mayor the fact that he was dealing with trade union issues affecting both blacks and whites.

The AFSCME was an important vehicle for change. It provided the common ground around which the Negro community closed ranks. The presence of the international officers provided prestige and knowhow to the collective bargaining process while not usurping local control of the dispute. The coalition of the civil rights movement and organized labor was a significant element leading to settlement of the dispute.

The role of communication through "neutral" third parties and the mediation process also provided an important component in the eventual agreement. Memphis was perhaps unique in that it possessed a substantial number of white citizens capable of acting as third parties. This could have been a product of its early efforts at desegregation of public facilities and the subsequent creation of dialogue between the white and black communities. The failure of these individuals to bring the dispute to an early settlement was no reflection on their efforts. The continuation of dialogue between the city and the union was vital to any hope for settlement of the dispute at a minimum cost to all concerned.

Mediation took the dispute from the public media and placed it back at the bargaining table. It replaced the growing emphasis on racial issues with reemphasis of the economic issues. In view of the absence of a precedent for recognition of public employee unions and the newness of the city administration, the use of mediation took on special significance. It provided an arena for orderly discussion where the union could negotiate as an equal with city government. This level of participation was significant when viewed in the light of black identity as an issue.

Mediation relies on communication and the selection of a mediator who could effectively perform this function was important. In discussing Frank Miles, James Reynolds said, "He was respected by all concerned and had access to everyone. Having someone like this with a professional labor background is something for us to think about in other municipalities."

The Memphis case suggested that professional skills were more important than personal identification, though the latter cannot be totally disregarded. Frank Miles was without a doubt a member of the white establishment. He was a friend of the mayor and for a decade had been employed as a member of management. But he brought to the negotiation process a long record as a professional mediator and a highly refined understanding of labor-management problems.

James Reynolds brought to the negotiations the prestige of the President and federal interest. His role was important for this reason alone, but the real groundwork for the agreement was laid by Frank Miles. Miles' imaginative attacks upon the economic issues and the skill with which he handled the negotiations were important elements leading to agreement by the parties.

Another factor leading to the settlement was the "Memphis image," an undefined element that led to growing pressure on the mayor from members of the white community for resolution to the dispute. Memphis, which captions itself as the "place of good abode," suddenly found this epithet challenged by riots and the assassination of Dr. Martin Luther King. The national publicity given Memphis focused the attention of the nation and the world on it. "When *Time* magazine, following the assassination of Dr. King, described Memphis as a 'decadent river town,'" said John T. Fisher, a prominent local businessman, "some people really got their feathers ruffled and started doing things." Businessmen were the ones to benefit or lose most from the "image," not only because the boycott and rioting reduced sales immediately but also because the fear of social turmoil would impede the city's economic development. Businessmen consequently placed increased pressure on the city administration during the last three weeks of the strike. Just as the strike drew the attention of middle class Negroes to the problems confronting black workers, it also revealed those conditions for the first time to many whites whose understanding of race relations had previously been restricted to conversations with their servants.

Of course, Dr. King's assassination had a profound effect on the white, as well as the black, community. His assassination revealed to many whites the consequences of race hatred and stimulated fears that nonviolence would die with him. A number of white citizens who were deeply concerned about Memphis' race image therefore placed pressure on the mayor to settle with the union.

CONCLUSION

The confrontation in Memphis took the form of a labor dispute around which deeper racial issues settled. Negotiation brought a resolution to the dispute, but not before loss of human lives and destruction of property were sustained. The presence of a political structure whose leader remained insensitive to the racial issues surrounding the dispute contributed significantly to the conflict that followed.

The Memphis case demonstrates the value of negotiations in resolving racial conflict. The emergence of a power base provided by the coalition of organized labor and the Negro community gave new life to the old civil rights movement. The inclusion of organized labor provided a vehicle for the institutionalization of racial conflict. In addition, the contribution made by black identity as an issue to the nonviolent restructuring of the white-dominated institutions provides some evidence of its positive potential.

The confrontation between Negroes and the white power structure demonstrated the positive and negative aspects of many factors in the constellation of forces which led to the conflict. Racial discrimination, both overt and institutionalized, played an important role in creating the problems which led to this conflict. Racial prejudice and the fear of its consequences also caused many whites, especially white trade unionists and ministers, to be reluctant to openly support the black strikers. Racism also undoubtedly influenced the vigor of the white power structure's resistance to sharing decision-making power with the black sanitation workers through collective bargaining.

On the other hand, the obvious influence of racism and the forceful resistance to change by the white power structure, operating through the mayor and his police, tended to solidify the Negro community behind the strikers, giving them power they would not have had in a purely economic contest with the city, which, but for the support of the Negro community, could have crushed the strike in a matter of hours. The city's vulnerability on the race aspect of the dispute caused some leaders to attempt to minimize publicity given the strike and to emphasize legal and economic questions instead of the race and moral issues involved. However, the city's vulnerability on the racial matters was strategically very important to the ministers and civil rights leaders involved in the conflict. By a willingness to settle the collective bargaining issues, the city was able to prevent racial issues from resurfacing.

PARADISE LOST:
OR WHATEVER HAPPENED
TO THE CHICAGO SOCIAL WORKERS?

Arnold R. Weber

Collective bargaining in the public sector still has many of the attributes of a polar expedition. Each new exploration commands special attention or acclaim. In order to attain the distant objective, the parties must demonstrate endurance and the capacity to adapt to a harsh, changing environment. And once the goal is reached and the flag hoisted, the symbolic success must be assessed further in terms of its practical consequences.

The exploratory nature of collective bargaining in the public sector was exemplified by the special fact-finders' report (1966) concerning the Department of Public Aid in Cook County, Illinois.. . . In the report, the fact finders stated that there was no legal bar to collective bargaining in the Cook County Department of Public Aid (CCDPA), that a secret ballot election should be held to determine the exclusive bargaining agent, and that if a union won a majority of the votes cast, it should commence the negotiation of a bargaining agreement with the department. . . . It is the purpose of this article to complete the current record of developments in the CCDPA and to examine the broader implications of this experience.

PROLOGUE TO BARGAINING

Although collective bargaining may have taken root in other political jurisdictions, bona fide bargaining by city and county employees in the Chicago area has been as rare as a Republican alderman. Several efforts to enact comprehensive state legislation to promote collective bargaining by public employees in Illinois have been unsuccessful.[1] Consequently, state and local governments are under no legal

---

Arnold Weber is Associate Director, Office of Management and Budget. Reprinted from the *Industrial and Labor Relations Review,* XXII, No. 3, April 1969. Copyright©1969 by Cornell University. All rights reserved.

[1]For a history of state legislation dealing with collective bargaining in the public sector in Illinois see, Milton Derber, "Labor-Management Policy for Public Employees in Illinois: The Experience of the Governor's Commission, 1966-1967." *Industrial and Labor Relations Review,* Vol. 21, No. 4 (July 1968), pp. 541-558, especially pp. 541-543.

obligation to engage in negotiations with employee organizations. Indeed, the authority of public agencies to enter into bargaining agreements with unions is subject to considerable uncertainty.[2]

This void in public policy has not been filled by legislative action at the local level. Neither the Chicago City Council nor the Cook County Board of Commissioners has attempted to formulate any general ordinances or policies clarifying the status of collective bargaining by public employees. Chicago is, of course, a "union town" and several trade unions have substantial membership in the various city and county departments. However, they generally have not sought to obtain formal recognition or to engage in systematic collective bargaining. The conduct of labor relations in Chicago and Cook County is under the firm control of the administration and is closely intertwined with the operation of the patronage system. Most questions of wages, benefits, and even minor matters such as reclassification, have been subject to the ultimate control of Mayor Richard J. Daley, whose mastery of the governmental machinery in Chicago is now legendary. The craft unions, which occupy a key position in the metropolitan labor movement, have been placated by the generous application of the "prevailing wage" standard to wide categories of city and county workers. The American Federation of State, County and Municipal Employees (AFSCME), which has scored spectacular successes in other cities, claims only about 900 members in the Chicago area. Victor Gotbaum, who later led the highly successful AFSCME organizing campaign in New York City, was unable to pierce the administration's defenses despite several years of strenuous efforts.

Against this background, the special fact-finders' report was an auspicious departure from traditional practice. Briefly, between 1953 and 1966, representatives of Local 73 of the Building Service Employees International Union had met with officials of the Department of Public Aid to discuss various aspects of employee-employer relations in the agency. The relationship between the union and the department was similar to that which prevails in most municipal situations where a statutory framework for union-management relations in the public sector is lacking. No effort was made to determine the representative status of the union, recognition was informal in nature, "negotiations" took the form of persistent badgering by the union, and signed, written agreements were unknown. In 1965, various employees of the CCDPA established a separate organization known as the Independent Union of Public Aid Employees (IUPAE). This new union pressed for recognition and sole bargaining rights in the department. The refusal of the agency to accede to these demands precipitated a series of skirmishes, culminating in a full-scale strike by the IUPAE in May 1966. The strike was called off when, following the intervention of Mayor Daley, the Cook County Board of Commissioners established a tripartite fact-finding board to make recommendations concerning the feasibility of holding an election to determine "a sole collective bargaining representative" for the employees of the Department of Public Aid.

The fact-finders' report, supporting the development of collective bargaining in the CCDPA, was adopted without change by the Board of Commissioners in October 1966. Shortly thereafter, the parties moved to implement the fact-finders' recommendations. Initially, both Local 73 and the IUPAE vied for rights as exclusive bargaining agent. Local 73 withdrew from the election following the disposition of a dispute concerning the definition of the appropriate bargaining unit. As ultimately determined, the unit included almost all of the social workers and clerical employees and excluded supervisory and blue-collar workers.

The representation election was held on December 14, 1966, under the auspices of the American Arbitration Association. The union registered a substantial victory. The IUPAE polled 2,677 votes while 1,056 employees voted for "no union." The stage was now set for a new, constructive phase in public labor-management relations in Chicago. But as in the case of the polar explorer, the parties found that the closer they moved to the ultimate goal, the more difficult the trek became. In fact, the objectives spelled out by the fact finders have not yet been achieved, two years after the issuance of their report. In the absence of broader changes in public policy, it is unlikely that they will be attained in the foreseeable future.

BUREAUCRACY AND POLITICS

When representatives of the IUPAE and the Department of Public Aid came to the bargaining table, their actions were conditioned by a complex of administrative and political factors. First, it was not clear that the CCDPA had the authority to make decisions in many vital substantive areas of employee-employer relations. The CCDPA was created and is governed by statutes enacted by the state legislature. Rules and regulations concerning the expenditure of funds and the administration of the agency are prescribed by the Illinois Department of Public Aid. At the same time, the Cook County Board of Commissioners may adopt additional rules concerning the conduct and management of the CCDPA, provided they do not conflict with the rules promulgated by the state Department of Public Aid. Within these limitations, the director of the CCDPA can formulate policies and administrative procedures which are not inconsistent with the rules laid down by the state agency and the Cook County Board of Commissioners. Moreover, important elements of personnel administration are subject to the supervision and control of the Cook County Civil Service Commission. Still another layer of authority is provided by the U.S. Department of Health, Education and Welfare which imposes standards for the administration of federally supported assistance programs.

The CCDPA is financed from several sources within this labyrinth. Funds are forthcoming from a property tax levied in the city of Chicago, from the general revenues of Cook County and the state of Illinois, and from federal government appropriations—depending upon the particular welfare program involved. An estimated 65 percent of the CCDPA's budget is derived ultimately from federal support.

It is obvious that decision-making in this structure requires a combination of bureaucratic legerdemain and diplomatic cunning. In practice, the greatest administrative influence has been exerted by the Illinois Department of Public Aid, which controls the details of the major CCDPA programs and the salary levels of most of the personnel. The locus of decision making is so diffuse, however, that the authority relationships among the different agencies are often unclear. One of the first challenges to the union and the CCDPA was to relate collective bargaining to this structure to permit meaningful negotiations.

Second, collective bargaining in the CCDPA inevitably became enmeshed with broader political considerations in Cook County and the State of Illinois. The fact-finders' report had been adopted with the strong support of Seymour Simon, the President of the Cook County Board of Commissioners. Simon was a rising star in the Democratic party in Chicago and his election as President of the Cook County Board of Commissioners was viewed as an indication of greater things to come. But during his tenure of office, Simon apparently had a falling-out with high party officials and was not reslated by the Democrats to run for president of the board in the 1966 election. When the election was held in November, the office of president was won by a Republican, Richard Ogilvie, although the Democrats retained a fifteen to ten majority on the board. Ogilvie's victory was a significant setback for the Democratic machine and gave him great visibility as the potential Republican nominee for governor in 1968.[3] Ogilvie was associated with the conservative wing of the Republican party in Illinois. The ranking Democrat on the Board of Commissioners was George Dunne, who was chairman of its finance committee and one of Mayor Daley's top lieutenants in the Democratic party.

When Ogilvie took office in January 1966, the IUPAE had won the union representation election and was demanding the initiation of full-scale negotiations. While the situation in the CCDPA was a legacy of the preceding administration, Ogilvie had some room to maneuver. A few months before the end of Simon's tenure of office, Raymond Hilliard, the previous director of the CCDPA, died suddenly. Hilliard had held this position for twelve years and had built a reputation for efficiency and innovation that largely insulated him from political pressures.[4] Simon left the position vacant, giving Ogilvie the opportunity to make his own permanent appointment. Subsequently, he selected William Robinson as the new director of the CCDPA. The appointment of Robinson was an astute step which staisfied both political and professional requirements. Robinson was a Republican, a former representative in the state legislature, a professional social worker and a Negro.[5] The latter consideration was significant because it helped to build bridges between Ogilvie, the Republican party, and the Negro community, which had an important stake in the administration of welfare programs.

The implications of these political developments for collective bargaining in the CCDPA were ambiguous. As a conservative Republican, Ogilvie would not be expected to innovate in labor relations in the public sector. On the other hand, there were indications that Robinson would be sympathetic to the goals of the organized social workers. Robinson had made public statements supporting the IUPAE during the strike in May 1966. As a new appointee to the position of director, it was not clear how independent he could be in dealing with the union.

---

[3]Ogilvie was nominated for governor of Illinois by the Republicans and won the election in November 1968.

[4]Edward Banfield, *Political Influence* (New York: The Free Press of Glencoe, 1965), pp. 62-69.

[5]Ibid., pp. 72-73; 82-90. When Robinson was in the state legislature,he played a key role in the passage of legislation merging the Chicago Welfare Department with the Cook County Department of Public Aid, a move largely motivated by political considerations.

BARGAINING BEGINS

Bargaining between the union and the CCDPA began at a slow pace. Robinson asked the union to defer serious negotiations until he had time to familiarize himself with his job. Meanwhile, a management bargaining team was formed to carry out negotiations with the IUPAE. The team was comprised of various administrative officials of the CCDPA and was headed by the director of employee relations. The latter position had been created the previous year when problems of union-management relations assumed serious proportions in the agency. Robinson was not a member of the management bargaining team.

The union presented a full set of demands at the end of January 1967. The IUPAE was anxious to reach a quick agreement to satisfy the militant factions in the union and to avert a potential challenge from Local 73, which, from the sidelines, kept up a steady stream of criticism of the IUPAE. However, negotiations dragged on inconclusively through February and March. On several occasions the union complained that the management bargaining team did not have the authority to make decisions and insisted that Robinson enter the negotiations. Robinson refused and maintained that the director of employee relations was the duly authorized spokesman for the CCDPA.

Negotiations continued into the middle of April with little progress. Agreement was reached on some items such as the recognition clause, dues checkoff, and measures to improve the physical conditions of local offices, but an impasse developed on several key issues. The issues in dispute included the magnitude and distribution of salary increases, full payment by the employer of Blue Cross-Blue Shield premiums, union security, a grievance procedure terminating in advisory arbitration and conceding the right of temporary employees to utilize this procedure, automatic progression for certain clerical employees, a demand that the CCDPA distribute a handbook for welfare recipients prepared by the IUAPE, and a request to change agency rules to permit district offices to disburse emergency checks to recipients without prior approval from the central office.[6]

Each of these issues impinged upon some statutory, administrative, or political consideration. Management asserted that the authority to determine a new salary plan rested with the Illinois Department of Public Aid and the state legislature. Under these circumstances, the CCDPA and the Cook County Board of Commissioners could only make recommendations. The board did have the authority to assume the full cost of medical insurance, but if this concession were granted to the social workers it would have to be extended to all county employees, increasing substantially the total cost of the benefit.

The demands for some form of union security, the advisory arbitration of grievances, and automatic progression raised possible conflicts with existing civil service regulations. The demand to extend the right to use the grievance procedure

[6]*Chicago Tribune,* Apr. 27, 1968, p. 1; *Chicago Defender,* May 5, 1968 (Weekend Edition), p. 1; *Chicago Sun-Times,* Apr. 17, 1968. p. 3. The newspaper accounts were supplemented by interviews with management and union officials.

to temporary employees was an especially sensitive issue. Traditionally, temporary employees have been patronage employees who have been hired outside of normal civil service procedures. The retention—or dismissal—of such employees is governed essentially by political factors and a temporary employee may remain in temporary status indefinitely. To give temporary employees the right to resort to arbitration in matters of discharge or promotion could therefore inhibit the dispensation of rewards and punishments, vital elements of an effective patronage system.

The demands concerning the distribution of handbooks and the issuance of emergency checks posed problems extending beyond the employee-employer relationship. In common with most unions of social workers, the IUPAE viewed unions as more than a vehicle for the improvement of wages and working conditions. A vocal faction in the IUPAE ·sought to use the union to help reform the welfare system. The demands in question were a first, albeit limited, step in this direction. Thus, the distribution of the IUPAE handbook to the welfare recipients would afford the union a measure of prestige and professional status in the eyes of the recipients and the wider community. Similarly, the negotiation of a contract clause governing the disbursement of emergency checks would certify the IUPAE's interest in a more compassionate system of administration while also penetrating the area of management prerogatives. The CCDPA rejected these demands on the ground that they were outside the scope of bargaining. Probably of equal importance to the rejection was an unwillingness on the part of top officials to share with the union the political benefits that flowed from the administration of welfare programs in Chicago.

STRIKES AND SIT-INS

When continued negotiations failed to bring the parties close to agreement, the IUPAE called a strike, beginning on April 27, 1967. Estimates of the extent of the strike varied widely. The union claimed that as many as 2,000 employees remained away from work while the CCDPA stated that only 1,000 workers had joined the strike. Informed judgments indicated that the actual number of strikers was about 1,200 or 29 percent of the 4,200 employees in the bargaining unit.[7] Although the strike involved only a minority of all workers, it did enjoy the support of a majority of the professional social workers, who provided the leadership and most of the activists in the IUPAE.

Once the strike was under way, the immediate question concerned the response of the Cook County Board of Commissioners and the CCDPA. There were ample judicial precedents in Illinois to indicate that the stoppage was illegal, and undoubtedly county officials could have obtained an injunction to restrain the strikers.[8] This step was never taken, or even seriously threatened by the county.[9] Initially, there was some belief that the stirke would be short lived. When the strike

[7]*Chicago Defender*, May 5, 1968, p. 1.

[8]See Board of Education of Community Unit School, District No. 2 v. Doris Redding, *et al.* 32 Ill. 2nd 567, 207 N.E. 2nd 427 (1965).

[9]*Chicago Sun-Times*, Apr. 27, 1968, p. 3 and May 9, 1968, p. 12. According to reports, Robinson advised Ogilvie against seeking an injunction.

dragged on, the extent of employee support was not sufficient to shut down the operation of the agency. Almost all of the local offices remained open and provided some services. Under these circumstances, it would have been impolitic for Ogilvie to seek an injunction and run the risk of being branded a "strike-breaker," especially in view of his gubernatorial ambitions. At the same time, it was unlikely that the Democratic majority on the board would press for legal sanctions against a union, even one that had such a tenuous relationship to the local labor movement.

For the IUPAE, the main problem was to find effective means to exert pressure on the CCDPA or the board to bring about an acceptable agreement. This problem became more acute as the strike continued for seven weeks. First, the union sought to obtain impartial, third-party intervention in the dispute. By inviting the participation of a third party, the union hoped to "educate" management to the requirements of collective bargaining and, further, to establish a public presence in the negotiations. In the second week of the strike, the IUPAE proposed the use of a mediator. The CCDPA accepted this suggestion, and a mediator was selected for this task from the American Arbitration Association labor panel.[10] The acceptance of mediation by the agency helped to demonstrate good faith, and from management's point of view the mediator could serve as a restraining influence on the IUPAE's demands in the policy area.

Second, the IUPAE attempted to enlist the moral and financial support of other unions in Cook County. Some financial aid for the strike was elicited from industrial unions, such as the United Automobile Workers and the United Packinghouse Workers. Also, wider expressions of labor support were organized by the regional director of the Industrial Union Department of the AFL–CIO. This manifestation of labor solidarity proved ineffective in helping the IUPAE obtain a favorable settlement. Support from the local labor movement was significant only to the extent that it could exert pressure through the political structure in Chciago and Cook County. In this respect, Ogilvie, whose main political strength was in the white-collar suburbs, was not likely to be responsive to petitions from trade unions. If the unions were to exercise influence, the most effective channel was the Democratic party which still had a majority on the Cook County Board of Commissioners, From this point of view, the IUPAE was supported by the "wrong" unions. In Chicago, the craft unions enjoy the closest ties with the Democratic administration and they remained silent—along with the central labor body—during the course of the strike. While statements of sympathy from the industrial unions gave the strike greater public visibility, they did not induce the desired political intervention.

Third, the IUPAE made a concerted effort to become identified with the interests of the welfare clients, particularly those in the Negro community. This strategy had a dual purpose. By forming a coalition with the welfare clients, the union hoped to give emphasis to the professional character of the IUPAE and to demonstrate that its goals transcended those of a conventional trade union. In addition, if the union could gain the support of organized groups in the Negro community and, more broadly, civil rights organizations, it could exercise greater political leverage on the CCDPA.

The results of the IUPAE's campaign to involve the Negro community in the

---

[10]At various times during the course of the dispute, aid was also provided by the regional office of the Federal Mediation and Conciliation Service.

dispute were largely negative. Because the CCDPA continued to operate during the course of the strike, there was no denial of essential services to nor was there deprivation among the welfare recipients. From the clients' point of view, the critical "service" was the receipt of the monthly assistance check. The activities of the case workers, especially those which were investigatory in nature, were often viewed with displeasure. The CCDPA was able to disburse the checks without difficulty and the curtailment of the services of the case workers, by itself, was not the cause of any outcry from the agency's clients.

The most dramatic attempt by the IUPAE to enlist the support of the Negro community involved a debate at an open meeting at the West Side Organization, a major community organization in the ghetto. At the meeting, the positions of the parties in the strike were presented by Robinson for the CCDPA and the president of the IUPAE, who was then a white minister. By all accounts, Robinson, whose oratorical skills had been sharpened by his experience in the state legislature, scored heavily in the debate.[11] In any case, no formal support for the strike or the IUPAE was forthcoming from the West Side Organization, or from other important Negro groups in the Chicago area.

The civil rights groups also refused to take any action in response to appeals from the IUPAE. The reasons for this reluctance were not clear, but several considerations probably dictated a neutral position. The issues in the strike were relatively technical and did not involve questions with a direct appeal to the civil rights groups. Regardless of the union's protestations, it was true that the authority of the CCDPA to satsify the union's demands was ambiguous. In addition, Robinson had a reputation as a liberal, especially in the welfare area, and he had extensive connections with the leaders of the civil rights organizations. Despite considerable maneuvering behind the scene, the civil rights groups did not lend their influence or prestige to the IUPAE's cause.[12]

Finally, sit-ins and sporadic instances of violence took place during the strike without the sanction of the IUPAE. The incidents of violence were limited in nature and involved cases in which stink-bombs were reportedly thrown into local CCDPA offices and employees who continued to work were harassed or assaulted. Two sit-ins were also conducted by IUPAE members at the offices of top officials of the Cook County Board of Commissioners. The first demonstration took place in the third week of the strike in Ogilvie's office and another sit-in was held in the office of George Dunne, chairman of the finance committee. This show of force did little to strengthen the union's hand. In fact, the sit-ins probably had a deleterious effect on the union's position. In both cases, the demonstrators were arrested without arousing sympathy from the public. Ogilvie used the occasion to denounce the lawless behavior of the strikers and the unreasonable demands of the union.[13] Following the first sit-in, management introduced a highly punitive no-strike provision into the negotiations, further complicating the task of reaching agreement.

[11]*Chicago Daily News,* May 5, 1968, p. 50. Union officials confirmed that Robinson had been extremely effective at the meeting.

[12]It is interesting to note that the *Chicago Defender,* the largest newspaper serving the Negro community in the area, showed little enthusiasm for the strike. Several of the articles published by the paper gave primary attention to statements by Robinson that the IUPAE's demands were unreasonable. See editions for May 26, 1968, p. 1, and June 7, 1968, p. 1. The strike was supported by the Latin American Defense Organization, a small group comprised largely of Puerto Ricans.

[13]*Chicago Tribune,* May 14, 1968, p. 1.

PARADISE GAINED: THE STRIKE ENDS

While the various moves and countermoves were taking place outside the bargaining sessions, slow progress was made in negotiations. A tentative agreement finally took shape at the end of May, five months after the outset of bargaining, and five weeks after the strike began. The agreement embodied a series of compromises and trade-offs on the original issues in dispute. Instead of a conventional union security provision, the union accepted an arrangement whereby an IUPAE representative could meet with each new employee, as part of the normal orientation procedure, to discuss the benefits of the employee organization. A grievance procedure was established with advisory arbitration as the last step. However, advisory arbitration could not be used in disciplinary cases involving temporary or probationary employees. Automatic progression of the two lowest-rated clerical classifications was granted after twenty-four months. It was also agreed that the county would pay the full Blue Cross-Blue Shield premium for the individual employee but not for his family.[14]

Under the terms of the agreement, the salary issue was resolved by incorporation of a clause whereby the county would "endorse and support" a general salary increase of 21 percent across the board and would, "cooperatively and in good faith honor, support and seek to fulfill it through the appropriate fiscal authorities."[15] Behind this effusive pledge was the knowledge that the Illinois Department of Public Aid, which controlled the salary recommendations to the state legislature, was ready to propose an average increase of 12.5 percent distributed differentially among the various classifications.

The agreement was silent with respect to the IUPAE's demands in the policy area. Management refused to distribute the handbook prepared by the union. The question of giving district offices the right to issue emergency aid to welfare recipients was resolved by an understanding that the CCDPA was favorably disposed to the change and would give it further consideration outside the framework of collective bargaining.

In addition to the disputed issues, it should be noted that the agreement incorporated many provisions important to a constructive union-management relationship which had not been the focus of sharp controversy. These included clauses covering union recognition, management rights, dues checkoff, hours of work, vacations and holidays, sick leave, and various personnel policies. Overall, the proposed contract represented a long stride forward in developing a working accommodation between the parties.

PARADISE LOST: THE FAILURE TO RATIFY

Despite the progress that was made in reaching an agreement, the negotiating process had a tenuous, if not fanciful, quality. Because the administration of the CCDPA was subject to a complex system of control and finance by other govern-

[14]Agreement between the Cook County Department of Public Aid and the Independent Union of Public Aid Employees.

[15]*Ibid.*, Article XI.

mental units, there was persistent uncertainty whether the accord would be ratified. Undoubtedly, there was some prior clearance of contract provisions by management at higher levels. Nonetheless, the bargaining process never encompassed all the key functionaries at the county and state levels, nor was there any attempt to clarify authority relations with respect to collective bargaining. The negotiators recognized that they were swimming in murky waters and mutually agreed to the inclusion of a savings clause in the contract. This provision voided any part of the agreement that violated any rule or regulation of "the United States Department of Health, Education and Welfare; the Illinois Department of Public Aid; the Cook County Board of Commissioners; the Civil Service Commission of Cook County or any other agency having jurisdiction over the County, fiscal or otherwise."[16]

The savings clause related to individual provisions of the proposed contract but it was irrelevant to the more basic question of the acceptability of the very concept of a labor agreement for the CCDPA. Immediately after negotiations were concluded, the IUPAE asked that Robinson or the director of employee relations sign the agreement on behalf of the CCDPA. Management refused to sign without further action by the Cook County Board of Commissioners and was unmoved by the union's insistence that this step merely would be a token of good faith. The union then modified its stance and agreed to bring the agreement to the board in its present form. Although there had been few defections from the ranks of the strikers to that date, the union's position was weakening. The agreement—unsigned or otherwise—provided some tangible evidence for the members that the five-week stoppage had been fruitful. After some heated discussion, the rank and file voted to approve the contract in the hope of putting pressure on the board.[17]

When the crucial session of the board was convened on May 25, the IUPAE was optimistic that favorable consideration would be given to the agreement. With a large contingent of union members present, Robinson made a statement generally supporting the contract and asked the board to approve it. A similar presentation was made by the director of employee relations. The union's counsel added to the exhortations, pointing out that collective bargaining for the CCDPA had been endorsed by the board when it accepted the recommendations of the fact finders.

This show of unanimity was nullified by the board's action. In a move which confounded the union and surprised other observers, a motion was made to refer the contract to the public service committee of the board. The motion was passed without a dissenting vote by either the Democratic or Republican members. The public service committee was a rarely used committee-of-the-whole whose functions are obscure. The committee was directed to report back to the board at its next meeting on June 12. The stated reasons for deferring final consideration of the contract were twofold. First, several members asserted that the agreement included matters beyond the authority of the board. Second, it was feared that the medical insurance provision would impose a heavy financial burden on the county. If the county assumed the full cost of premiums for employees of the CCDPA it would have to extend the same benefit to all other county employees at a cost in excess of $2,000,000 per year.[18]

[16]*Ibid.*, Article XV.

[17]*Chicago Tribune*, May 24, 1968, p. 5.

[18]*Chicago Sun-Times*, June 2, 1968, p. 5.

The IUPAE responded to this setback by grasping at any available lever to pressure the county board before the next meeting. Mass picketing was conducted outside the county building. Representatives of twenty-six Chicago area unions urged the board to ratify the agreement without delay.[19] The union sought and received an audience with Mayor Daley, who endorsed the desirability of harmonious labor relations while cautioning the union to be realistic in its demands. And a second unauthorized sit-in was conducted, this time in the office of George Dunne, the leader of the Democratic majority on the board.[20]

None of these tactics was effective and the union's capacity to maintain the strike was sharply diminished. Further conversations were held between Dunne and the IUPAE leadership to seek a final settlement of the dispute. The last act took place at the June 12 meeting of the Cook County Board of Commissioners. A resolution was introduced and approved calling for the establishment of a grievance procedure by the CCDPA, a study to find ways of reducing excessive paperwork in the department, and a recommendation by the board to "the appropriate authorities" for a 21 percent salary increase for all employees. To soften the defeat for the union, the resolution specified that there would be no reprisals against the strikers, and that accrued vacation and compensatory time could be applied to the days lost as a result of the strike. Finally, in a hollow reaffirmation of support for collective bargaining, the resolution asserted

> ... that this Board will negotiate a contract with the Independent Union of Public Aid Employees on all reasonable matters found to be within the jurisdiction by constituted authority. Such determination will be made with dispatch, to the end that peace and tranquility will be restored to the Department.[21]

With the passage of the resolution, the IUPAE called off the strike, after forty-six days, and its members returned to work the next day. As a parliamentary footnote, the committee on public service never formally submitted a report on the agreement to the board.

EPILOGUE

Following the conclusion of the strike, the IUPAE, like a deposed monarch, sought to maintain its claim to legitimacy as the bargaining agent for employees of the CCDPA. Several additional attempts were made to obtain approval of the agreement. In particular, the IUPAE continued to petition Dunne and the Illinois Department of Public Aid, but without favorable response. The prospects for formal ratification of the agreement were further dimmed when the state legislature rejected a law authorizing collective bargaining for public employees.[22]

[19] *Chicago Tribune*, June 1, 1968, p. 16.

[20] *Chicago Tribune*, June 2, 1968, p. 11.

[21] Resolution of the Board of Commissioners of Cook County, June 12, 1968.

[22] The events surrounding the rejection of a state public employee relations law are described in Derber, *loc. cit.*

The provisions of the board's resolution that settled the strike were only partially realized. Notwithstanding the board's recommendation of a 21 percent pay raise, the new salary plan issued by the state provided for increases of 12 percent to 15 percent, depending on the job classification. A grievance procedure was established within the CCDPA, but the final step was the director of the agency rather than advisory arbitration as the union had demanded. In practice, the study of ways to reduce "excessive paper work" proved to be an empty gesture. The board's pledge to negotiate a contract with the IUPAE governing "all reasonable matters found to be within its jurisdiction" was overridden by an opinion of the state's attorney declaring that the board did not have the authority to enter into a bargaining agreement. This opinion was issued as a technical afterthought more than one year after the conclusion of the strike.[23]

The union attempted to compensate for these external setbacks by adopting an aggressive posture within the CCDPA. It vigorously represented its members in the processing of grievances, protested the administration of several aspects of the civil service examination system, and testified at budget hearings. When its requests were rebuffed by the director, the union brought its cases to Dunne, sometimes with success. Of particular importance to the union was the reversal by Dunne of a departmental decision denying employees the right to take a leave of absence to devote full time to union business.[24] The primary goal of the IUPAE was to maintain a viable organization until such time when, through either a process of erosion or legal enactment, it could redeem its status as bargaining agent, consistent with the recommendations of the fact-finding board.

CONCLUSIONS: BEYOND THE FRINGE

Although the primary purpose of this narrative has been to complete the record with respect to the Chicago social workers, certain limited inferences can be drawn from this case. Because of the special circumstances, these inferences can be little more than informed speculation. Nonetheless, informed speculation presumably enjoys some advantages over uninformed speculation and the inferences stated here may be related to events that have taken place in a broader context.

1. It is almost a truism, but at the current stage of development, the importance of a statute authorizing and protecting collective bargaining for public employees cannot be overemphasized. In the absence of such a statute, collective bargaining exists largely at the sufferance of management. A public agency may enter into good-faith bargaining on its own volition; however, considerations of self-interest inevitably assert themselves so that it is virtually impossible for management to divorce its role as an adversary from that of the arbiter of the bargaining process. Without statutory standards, public management will decide critical issues in its own interest without serious regard for the impact of these decisions on collective bargaining. In the Chicago case, for example, all actual or potential con-

---

[23]Legal Opinion No. 1281, State's Attorney of Cook County, Illinois, June 26, 1968.

[24]"Report to the Staff of the Cook County Department of Public Aid," by Douglas Cater, President, IUPAE, April 1968.

flicts between collective bargaining and the civil service system were resolved in favor of the latter. When questions arose concerning the authority of the Cook County Board of Commissioners to ratify the agreement with the IUPAE, the board extricated itself from the situation by repudiating a prior resolution endorsing the fact-finders' report. Without external constraints, public management has overwhelming incentives to maintain the status quo and the most unimaginative city solicitor or state's attorney can find some legal justification for inaction.

2. In order to develop effective collective bargaining in the public sector, explicit steps must be taken to rationalize the structure of management decision making. Even in the most simple situation, collective bargaining poses delicate questions involving the relationship between the executive and legislative branches of government. In many instances, collective bargaining in the public sector will embrace a variety of "management" units at different levels of government through a tangled network of statutes and fiscal arrangements. Without the clarification and/or modification of existing authority relations, the prevailing system of decision making will be so diffuse as to frustrate collective bargaining or will create a climate in which the union will be tempted to by-pass established procedures and go to alternative sources of authority.

Both reactions took place in the case of the CCDPA. The locus of management decision making embraced at least seven identifiable units of government at the county, state, and federal levels. This diffusion of authority reduced to an exercise in futility the attempt at arms-length bargaining with the county welfare agency. The union then sought favorable action from other sources of authority: the Illinois Department of Public Aid and the Cook County Board of Commissioners. These efforts failed because the IUPAE had no real leverage nor did these agencies see any advantage in accommodating the union. The outcome could have been reversed if the appropriate sanctions had been present. The basic lesson is that where collective bargaining is merely superimposed on the existing system of management decision making, bargaining in the conventional sense is not likely to take place.

3. Collective bargaining in the public sector is unavoidably political in nature. This observation is not surprising. Collective bargaining is also "political" in the private sector, but there management officials work out their destinies on a narrower stage. In private industry, management bargainers are sensitive to the consequences of labor negotiations for the firm, personal prestige, and individual power positions. The same considerations are present in the public sector; however, here the framework for decision making must be expanded to include overt political elements such as the political party and the electorate. The resolution of labor negotiations may affect a public official's chances for reelection or his relations with party leaders. Decisions on wages influence taxes, public resource allocation, and other issues which excite the interest of the electorate. The establishment of a grievance procedure may have profound repercussions for the efficacy of a patronage system. Only under extremely rare circumstances can the chief executive who is elected—or who is appointed by someone who is elected—insulate questions of bureaucratic administration from political factors in the classical sense.

The ubiquity of political considerations clearly complicates the task of rationalizing management decision making in collective bargaining, especially when dealing with local governmental units where the chief executive is close to his constituency. Despite the delegation of responsibility for labor relations to a bureaucratic official such as a city negotiator or agency head, the mayor or county commissioner is likely to come under intense pressure to intervene in the bargaining process. The decision to intervene and the nature of the intervention inevitably will reflect some political calculus. Many union tactics in public sector collective bargaining at the municipal level are specifically designed to impose costs on, or provide benefits to the chief executive *in his role as a political leader.* Therefore, the most challenging problem in the development of collective bargaining in the public sector is to rationalize the system of management decision making while accepting the continued presence of political considerations.

The relevance and importance of political factors can be seen at almost every point in the development and conduct of collective bargaining in the CCDPA. The original decision to permit collective bargaining was pressed by the lame duck president of the Cook County Board of Commissioners who had fallen out with the party leaders. When an impasse developed in negotiations, the IUPAE desperately sought to exert pressure on the Democratic leaders through a variety of means including expressions of solidarity by other unions and an abortive alliance with groups in the Negro community. The failure of the IUPAE to enlist important political support made it possible for the board to refuse to ratify the agreement, thereby nullifying the work of the management bargaining team.

4. A strike in the public sector is not necessarily the fearsome weapon that is implied by the blanket prohibitions of its use. While a primary justification for the ban on strikes by public employees is the assertion that the government cannot go out of business, it is equally true that government cannot be driven from the field of economic adversity. If a public service is curtailed because of a work stoppage, the government normally is not concerned that this opportunity will be seized by competitors. Even if substitutes are available, the fact that many services are prepaid by taxes affords the government a protected market position.[25] Thus public management will have little incentive to succumb to sanctions unless the service involved is "essential" in the sense that its curtailment will mobilize the consumer and impose political "losses" on the executive. In the CCDPA case, there were no competitors vying for the opportunity to provide funds and services to indigent persons.[26] The strike did not diminish revenue to the agency. And the IUPAE's efforts to arouse the consumers failed because the department was able to distribute the monthly welfare payments without interruption. When confronted by these defenses, the IUPAE attempted to create political pressure by exhorting the wlefare recipients to go to the local CCDPA offices to demand the full range of services. In the private sector, by contrast, the normal union tactic is to discourage the consumer from demanding the service. When the IUPAE's exhortations had no visible effect on the level of services demanded, the CCDPA could withstand the strike with relative impunity. The inability of social worker unions to impair a politically sensitive service helps to explain the consistent defeat of strikes by social workers all over the country.

[25] A strike may put economic pressure on the government if the service involved generates revenue. This is the case with transit, water works, and frequently with incinerator operators. It is also significant to note that "job action" by policemen's unions usually involve a refusal to write traffic tickets, which may cause the loss of considerable revenue for a municipality.

[26] There are, of course, private social welfare agencies. However, these private agencies usually complement rather than compete with public agencies.

5. There does not appear to be any unique or consistent relationship between the strength of public employee unionism at the local level and the strength of the local labor movement in general. At first glance, it may be contended that where unions are well-entrenched in the private sector in a particular metropolitan area, some of this strength will be transferred to the public employee unions. Although there probably is some truth to this piggyback theory of public employee unionism, the CCDPA case indicates that it grossly oversimplifies the relationships. For various reasons, the interests of the private sector unions may diverge from those of the public employee organizations. Unions whose primary interest lies in private industry may have reached an accommodation with the political structure of the city based on reciprocal favors and support. These unions may be reluctant to rock the boat where union officials hold positions in government agencies, where city contracts are let only to unionized firms, and the prevailing wage is extended to large categories of government employees. On the other hand, unions whose membership is largely or exclusively in the public sector tend to view government officials as "the boss" who should be treated accordingly. Because the onset of true collective bargaining in the public sector may strain the allegiances of the established private sector unions, this development will not always be greeted with enthusiasm.

In the situation described here the IUPAE was not able to organize any effective pressure from the local labor movement. The unions that supported the strike were generally those outside of the political alliance and had little to lose by an expression of solidarity. Significantly, the craft unions and the Chicago Federation of Labor remained silent throughout the entire course of events. In order to develop effective collective bargaining relationships with governmental units, the public employee unions will have to establish an independent power base. To the extent that they succeed in this objective, additional tensions are likely to arise in their relationships with the private sector unions.[27]

---

[27]In the period 1966-1968, strikes of social workers have taken place in Los Angeles and Sacramento, California; New York City; Lake County, Indiana; and Summit County, Ohio. In most cases, the unions of social workers have failed to achieve their stated objectives. Of particular interest was the eleven-month strike in Sacramento, California, which the union finally called off after 183 strikers had been discharged. U.S. Bureau of Labor Statistics, *Government Employee Relations Report* (Washington: G.P.O., Jan. 1, 1968), No. 225.

THE 1919 BOSTON POLICE STRIKE

Sterling D. Spero

In 1918 . . . the Boston policemen and firemen were waging a vigorous joint campaign for higher pay. At the height of the campaign, the firemen affiliated with the International Association of Fire Fighters and voted to strike if their demands were not met. The strike order was rescinded only after the city authorities had given definite promise of relief. Two months later, in November, the finance commission recommended a 100 dollar increase for both the firemen and the police. . . .

Yet throughout the previous summer, while the salary campaign was in progress, there was constant talk of unionizing the police even though the American Federation of Labor still barred them from membership. . . .

The pronounced unrest among the police was not quieted by the recommended 100 dollar increase. The sum, which would have brought the salary scale to range from 1,000 to 1,500 dollars, and was half of what the men had asked, just about covered the cost of official equipment. The police sent a committee of their organization, the Boston Social Club, to see the mayor and demand the full 200 dollars. They told him that unless adjustments were made, they would be compelled to leave the force to accept better paid jobs, and that the service would become demoralized because new men could not be attracted at the wages offered. But the mayor was not impressed. "In view of the serious financial condition of the city," he said, ". . . here is a limit beyond which we cannot go.". . .

. . . On December 30, 1918, . . . Edwin U. Curtis, the new [police] commissioner, began his official career with the announcement:

> Any member of the police department who is so dissatisfied that he cannot perform his work faithfully, honestly, and cheerfully, pending the decision regarding the requested salary increase, may resign.

The same day the Boston Social Club, the policemen's organization, unanimously decided not to accept less than a 200 dollar increase. Many of the 700 men who voted on the question said that they would resign from the force if the demand was not met.

Reprinted from Sterling D. Spero, *Government as Employer*, Remsen Press, 1948. Footnote references have been deleted from edited version.

A few days later a committee of the Social Club called upon the new commissioner to discuss the situation. Although Commissioner O'Meara [the previous commissioner] had recognized the Social Club as the mouthpiece of the force and had received its delegates and listened to their suggestions, Commissioner Curtis, despite the growing dissatisfaction of the men, refused to continue this practice. Instead he instituted a central grievance committee composed of delegates elected from the various stations. The first election of grievance officers, as the station delegates were called, took place in January 1919. The captains counted the ballots in their private offices and sent the names of men elected to headquarters. It was later reported to the Mayor's Committee to Consider the Police Situation that in one instance it was known that the name of a man was sent to headquarters as a delegate who was not elected by the men. The plan from the start proved most unsatisfactory.

A few weeks later Commissioner Curtis further aggravated the situation by forbidding the police to appear before the legislature in behalf of measures in which they were interested unless they first received his permission. This was a matter of real importance in the salary campaign, for under this order the police were forbidden to lobby for an increase in the city's tax rate in case such a step were necessary to insure them higher pay.

Meanwhile, soaring prices were making the minimum demand of a 200 dollar increase less and less adequate. The city council sent a committee to the mayor to see whether something could be done, but the mayor reiterated that he could not see how the city could possibly meet the men's demands. Then Police Commissioner Curtis entered the controversy, declaring that he thought the men's demands reasonable and urged that they be given the 200 dollar raise they asked. Two months later the mayor consented to a compromise. A sum of 88,400 dollars was to be added to the police and fire payrolls. The maximum salary was to be increased by 200 dollars to a level of 1,600 dollars, while the men in the lower grades were to receive advances of 100 dollars each.

This caused so much dissatisfaction that four days later the mayor granted the demands in full, admitting, however, that he had no idea where the city would get the money. Under the new scale entrance salaries became 1,100 dollars and maximum salaries 1,600 dollars.

However, by the time that these increases came, they were already inadequate. The sum of 200 dollars now just about paid for the patrolman's uniform whereas 100 dollars would have covered the cost a year before. In view of the difficulty which the men had had in obtaining this increase, it was apparent that far greater pressure would have to be brought to bring their pay abreast of prices once more.

A few weeks later, the American Federation of Labor met in convention and lifted the twenty-year-old barrier against the chartering of police unions. . . .

The response to the Federation's new policy was astonishing. Within nine weeks after the adjournment of the convention, 65 police organizations applied for charters. Thirty-three were granted to unions with a total membership of 2,265. By September, 37 locals had been chartered. The growth of these locals after admission to the Federation brought their membership to about 4,000. . . .

During the last days of July 1919, a petition for a union charter was circulated among the policemen of Boston. When this came to the attention of Commissioner Curtis, he declared: "I feel it my duty to say that I disapprove of the movement on foot.". . .

Accordingly, the Boston police went ahead with their plans. The Social Club voted to ask the American Federation of Labor for a union charter. On August 8, 1919, the men were informed that their charter had been granted. It was received the next day.

Two days later, on August 11, with the union an established fact, Police Commissioner Curtis issued the following order:

> No member of the force shall join or belong to any organization, club or body composed of present or present and past members of the force which is affiliated with or a part of any organization, club or body outside the department, except that a post of the Grand Army of the Republic, the United Spanish War Veterans, and the American Legion of World War Veterans may be formed within the department.

The next day the Boston papers reported the policemen "bitter" over the Curtis order. "It is safe to say," said the very conservative *Transcript,* "that not more than one-third of the entire force expected the commissioner to deny them the right to organize a union. This small minority comprises the older men who are against unionization." The paper also pointed out that the commissioner's order carried no penalty.

A number of the men who were interviewed pointed out that the order was so general and sweeping that it could actually be used to bar the police from any religious or fraternal organization. Although, strictly speaking, this broad and sweeping character of the order made its legal validity questionable, everyone knew that it was aimed at the policemen's union and that it would not be used for any other purpose than to destroy the union.

The union hired counsel who considered the possibility of enjoining the commissioner from interfering with their organization on the grounds that such action was in violation of the law of the state providing:

> No person shall himself or by his agents coerce or compel a person into written or oral agreement not to join or become a member of a labor organization as a condition of securing employment or continuing in employment of such a person.

The commissioner contended that policemen were not "employees' but officers of the state. He was willing, he told a committee of the city council, to have the validity of his rule tested in the courts. If the decision should be adverse to his contention that the police were public officers, he said, then his rule would be invalid and any man discharged for its violation would be reinstated. "But he made clear that he made no intimation," declared an interviewer, "'that any member of the police force who denying the rule's validity abandons his duty by a strike or walkout would not be reinstated if discharged for that reason even if he had power to reinstate.'"

This statement followed shortly upon the announcement that the commissioner had ordered the printing of 1,000 discharge blanks and 1,000 suspension blanks.

The union ignored this clear intimation that the commissioner meant to go the limit in his efforts to keep the force out of the organized labor movement. On the day following the announcement about the discharge blanks the union met, elected officers, and effected a permanent organization.

Three days later, the Central Labor Union of Boston met and welcomed the Policemen's Union to its ranks. "We urge them," it resolved, "to maintain their position and promise to them every atom of support that organized labor can bring to bear in their behalf in the event that they should need such support." The papers interpreted this as a threat of a general strike in case the police walked out, and the resolution undoubtedly encouraged the police to go on with their efforts. But when it came to the real test the organized labor movement of Boston forgot all about its solemn pledge. The patrolmen received not an atom of tangible support and were compelled to carry on their fight alone.

A week later, on August 26, the commissioner filed charges against 8 policemen who had been chosen officers of the union. Shortly afterwards, 11 others were added, 9 of whom were officers of the union and 2 whose names were included by mistake on information furnished by the commissioner's agents.

The day after these charges were filed against the first 8 of the 19, Mayor Peters issued a statement in which he said:

> The issue between the commissioner and the policemen is clear-cut. It is a question of whether the policemen have a right to form a union and become affiliated with the American Federation of Labor . . . .
>
> The American Federation of Labor deserves our cooperation and support in every proper way, but I do not think the policemen of any of our states or municipalities should become affiliated with it. This, as I understand it, is Commissioner Curtis' attitude and I think he is right.

The right to affiliate with the labor movement had by this time overshadowed all other issues between the authorities and the force. The economic and occupational grievances which had brought the union into being were now almost lost to sight. Yet low pay, long hours, unsanitary station houses, and unsatisfactory channels of communication between the department and the force were still the grievances which were causing discontent among the patrolmen and which they were depending upon the new union to correct.

The organization had not yet had time to draw up a new schedule of salaries to take the place of the existing one, which it will be remembered ranged from 1,100 to 1,600 dollars (and out of which the men were required to spend 200 dollars a year for uniforms). It did, however, repeatedly call attention to the inadequacy of this pay especially in view of the long hours which the men were obliged to work, i.e., seventy-three hours a week for day men, eighty-three for night men, and ninety-eight for wagon men. The station houses were crowded and some of the older ones were infested with vermin. Some of the Boston papers were disposed to treat this complaint as a joke. One of them wanted to know whether it took the American Federation of Labor to rid the police stations of mice. Commissioner Curtis, shortly after he took office, appointed a committee to investigate this matter and submitted a report to the mayor on April 10, 1919. Yet four months later when the situation became critical, no action had been taken. The condition could not be corrected without the expenditure of money and the patrolmen well knew that the city would make no outlay unless heavy pressure were brought to bear upon the authorities.

Under Boston's peculiar system of police administration, responsibility for the crisis up to this point could not be laid squarely at anybody's door. The police commissioner is appointed by the governor of Massachusetts rather than by the mayor of the city. At the same time, the cost of the upkeep of the department is borne by the city. Changes in wages and salaries are initiated by the mayor and city council and are subject to the approval of the police commissioner. On the question of pay and the condition of the station houses, the complaint of the men was against the authorities of the city of Boston whose duty it was to provide money for the maintenance of the department. For the displacement of the committee of the Boston Social Club with an official grievance committee, for the *ex post facto* order against the policemen's union, and for his general autocratic bearing, the complaint of the force was against the police commissioner.

The mayor, however, despite the fact that the ungenerous attitude of his administration in appropriation matters was the basic cause of the union movement, was clearheaded enough to see that if the commissioner went on with his plan to suppress the men's organization without providing some means of set- tling their grievances, a police strike would inevitably result. He was determined to prevent this if possible. Although the mayor had no authority over the police force, the commissioner being responsible to the governor of the state, he appointed a committee of 34 citizens to investigate the whole situation and, if possible, effect a settlement. This committee, headed by Mr. James J. Storrow of the banking house of Lee, Higginson and Company, was composed of representatives of the leading financial and business interests in the city. The mayor seemed to have gone out of his way to avoid the charge of having appointed a committee with a bias in favor of organized labor.

The citizens' committee was appointed the day after the police commissioner filed his charges against the officers of the union. . . . Before the committee was organized Mr. Storrow asked the commissioner whether he favored the appoint- ment of a citizens' committee and whether the chairman was agreeable to him. The commissioner's reply was that he would be glad to see the committee appointed and glad to have Mr. Storrow as chairman.

Later, on the same day, the chairman issued a statement declaring that police- men should not affiliate with the American Federation of Labor. This statement was submitted to the commissioner and approved by him before it was issued, and on the following day it was unanimously approved at a session of the entire com- mittee. The union through their counsel, James F. Vahey and John P. Feeney, issued a protest and asked for a conference with the committee. This was imme- diately arranged and for the next three days a subcommittee of the mayor's committee and the officials and counsel of the policemen's union were in constant consultation. On the fourth day, September 2, it was announced that the executive committee believed that an adjustment could be worked out whereby the men would give up their American Federation of Labor charter and at the same time obtain better working conditions. The committee stressed the point that no specific demands for higher pay or reduced hours had as yet been made by the men.

Up to this point the commissioner had been friendly and willing to cooperate. On the last day of the joint conference he came to Boston from his summer home and received the subcommittee "with utmost courtesy," although the only sug- gestion he made which seemed to bear in any way upon the discussions was that police officials should receive the same per cent increase as the men. No one objected to that.

Then almost suddenly the commissioner's attitude changed. Upon the advice of the Boston Chamber of Commerce that he engage special counsel, Commissioner Curtis appointed Herbert Parker, former attorney general of the Commonwealth, and one of the most prominent corporation lawyers in the state, to be his legal adviser. When the commissioner's choice became known, the Chamber of Commerce at once sent a committee to urge him to change his selection. According to Messrs. Vahey and Feeney, counsel to the policemen's union, several members of the mayor's committee, including Chairman Macomber of the Chamber of Commerce, were fearful of Mr. Parker's influence "not upon questions of law but upon the policy of the police commissioner."

These fears shortly proved to be justified. It was learned that the commissioner planned to hand down his decision regarding the men on trial for affiliating with the American Federation of Labor two days later, on September 4. The committee realized that finding the men guilty and imposing penalties on them at so early a date would end discussions with the union, would put a stop to further consideration of a voluntary withdrawal from the American Federation of Labor, "and at once precipitate a strike."

Determined to do everything in its power to prevent a strike, the mayor's committee dispatched a letter to Commissioner Curtis asking him to postpone his decision for a few days. This letter was considered of such importance that instead of entrusting it to an ordinary messenger, the committee had one of its members take it personally to the commissioner's office. Despite this, Mr. Curtis did not get the letter; his counsel, Mr. Parker, received and read it and refused to permit its delivery to the commissioner.

Immediately after this the commissioner notified counsel for the men on trial that he would hand down his decision the next morning. The citizens' committee then sought intervention of Governor Coolidge, the police commissioner's chief. Notwithstanding the plea that he ask the commissioner to postpone his decision and thus prevent an "avoidable strike," Governor Coolidge refused to intervene, stating that "he felt it was not his duty to communicate with the commissioner on the subject."

The next morning the mayor himself went to Curtis' office before the hour set for the announcement of his decision and asked the commissioner to postpone his findings until an agreement could be reached between the policemen's union and the Storrow committee. Curtis consented, announcing that his decision would be made four days later on Monday morning, September 8.

The Storrow committee took immediate advantage of this respite and set to work on a plan to avoid a strike. The counsel for the policemen's union were in touch with the committee at every step. Finally on September 6, a plan was drawn up which provided:

> (1) That the police surrender their American Federation of Labor charter but maintain their union as an independent organization.
>
> (2) That present wages, hours and working conditions require material adjustment and should be investigated by a committee of three citizens who shall forthwith be selected by the concurrent action of the mayor, the commissioner, and the Policemen's Union and their conclu-

sions communicated to the mayor and the police commissioner, and that hereafter all questions arising relating to hours and wages and physical conditions of work which the Policemen's Union desires to bring before the commissioner shall be taken up with the police commissioner by the duly accredited officers and committees of the Boston Policemen's Union and should any difference arise thereto which cannot be adjusted it shall be submitted to three citizens of Boston selected by agreement between the mayor, the police commissioner, and the Boston Policemen's Union. The conclusions of the three citizens thus selected shall be communicated to the mayor and the police commissioner and to the citizens of Boston by publication. The provisions of this section shall not apply to any question of discipline.

Subsequent clauses provided that there was to be no discrimination against any policeman who joined or failed to join the independent union and that no member of the force should be "discriminated against because of any previous affiliation with the American Federation of Labor."

The plan was submitted to the mayor and immediately won his approval. At the same time it was informally submitted to the commissioner for his "consideration, criticism and suggestion." When the commissioner failed to act on this informal request, the mayor submitted the plan formally by a letter delivered to Mr. Curtis at his home at nine o'clock in the morning, Sunday, September 7, just twenty-four hours prior to the expiration of the time limit which the commissioner had set for handing down his decision regarding the 19 officers of the union.

The mayor and his committee waited all day for Commissioner Curtis' reply but none came. Knowing that the announcement of the commissioner's decision the next morning would precipitate a strike the mayor gave the plan to the press in the hope that a favorable reception would hold the commissioner's hand. Seven of the city's 8 papers approved the suggested settlement. The *Transcript* alone seemed to think that a strike was preferable to the proposed "surrender."

While waiting for Curtis' reply on that feverish Sunday, the mayor and his committee tried a second time to induce Governor Coolidge to intervene in behalf of a reasonable settlement. But the governor was not to be found. . . .

The next morning the commissioner rejected the mayor's proposal and proceeded to find the 19 men guilty of violating his order. At roll call they were formally suspended from the service.

Thereafter the consequences generally predicted followed rapidly. A meeting of the Policemen's Union had been called for Monday afternoon to consider the committee's plan.

"It is true," said the mayor's committee, "that in the brief space of time between Saturday afternoon when this plan finally took shape, and nine-fifteen on Monday morning there had hardly been time for the members of the Police Union to reach a final determination as to whether they would surrender their charter and accede to the plan, yet the Executive Committee was clearly of the opinion that on Sunday the plan was on the point of being approved by their officials, and that it would also be approved at a general mass meeting of the men. The opinion of your committee in this regard was also confirmed by the fact that the counsel for the Police Union, Messrs. Vahey and Feeney, both unqualifiedly advised the officials to accept it, and also undertook to attend the general meeting of the Police Union and then unqualifiedly advise the men to accept it. Such a meeting could and would have been held probably on Monday afternoon, September 8, but instead of considering your committee's plan on Monday afternoon, the men as a result of the commissioner's finding of that morning (following his earlier declination to consider the plan) thereupon entered upon the business of taking a strike vote."

The members of the Policemen's Union, declaring that they were quite as guilty as the 19 men whom the commissioner had disciplined, voted by 1,134 to 2 to strike at five forty-five in the afternoon of the following day, September 9. Contrary to common belief, this step was not taken to force higher pay or better working conditions or to compel the recognition of the right to organize and affiliate with the American Federation of Labor. It was a demonstration of loyalty to the 19 men who had committed no greater wrong than their 1,100 fellows who belonged to the union but had not been tried for violating orders.

The city was hardly taken unawares. It had been predicted by the mayor, the citizens' committee, and the entire press that Commissioner Curtis' uncompromising course would force a strike. The counsel for the union had intimated that Mr. Parker, the special counsel to the commissioner, was the evil genius who dominated the situation. He was eager to force a strike, many believe, in order to discredit organized labor at the very moment that employers throughout the country were launching their open shop campaigns and antiunion drives. Parker's antiunion point of view was open and unconcealed. He represented some of the largest employers in the country. But whatever may have been the motives which actuated it, the commissioner's high-handed and autocratic attitude was the factor immediately responsible for the strike.

Even while the police were taking their strike vote, the mayor's committee continued its efforts to avert a walkout. After having tried in vain all morning to reach Governor Coolidge, the mayor sent the committee's plan to the State House with a letter which read in part:

> I have been and am still trying to get in touch with you on the telephone this afternoon as I should like to go over the matter with you personally; and I am now sending this information to you at the State House in order that it may be laid before you at the earliest possible moment . . . I am now presenting it with the opinion that it offers a basis of solution. I hope that you may feel that you can take steps to assist in the solution suggested and I am glad to cooperate in any way possible.

That night the leading members of the citizens' committee and the mayor met Governor Coolidge at the Union Club. He was urged either to accept the committee's plan or to take steps to insure the protection of the city when the police left their posts. In the words of the committee, they "expressed their strong conviction as to the necessity of troops to the number of not less than three or four thousand to be present in Boston on the following day at 5:45 P.M., either upon the streets or ready in the armories."

This third attempt to induce Governor Coolidge, the police commissioner's superior officer, to use his influence to prevent a strike was no more fruitful than previous efforts. Governor Coolidge would take no definite stand. Counsel for the union declared that they were told that the situation "was not hopeless, that something might come up as a result of the conference" even after the union's decision to strike had been announced on Tuesday morning. "It was not," they said, "until the governor sent his memorable letter to the mayor about Tuesday noon that the policemen or their attorneys, and, we believe, also the mayor's committee, knew where the governor stood."

This letter . . . ran as follows:

> Replying to your favor and to suggestions laid before me by your-) self and certain members of your committee, it seems to me that there has arisen a confusion which would be cleared up if each person undertakes to perform the duties imposed upon him by law.
>
> It seems plain that the duty of issuing orders and enforcing their observance lies with the commissioner of police and with that noone has any authority to interfere. We must all support the commissioner in the execution of the laws.
>
> Regarding the matter of improvements in the conditions of employment in the Police Department of Boston, the law requires that they be initiated by the mayor and city council, subject to the approval of the commissioner. If wages, hours, or station houses ought to be improved, such improvements can be initiated by the mayor and the city council without any consideration of the making or observance of rules, because over that the mayor and city council have no jurisdiction. If justice requires improvement in the conditions of employment, I believe such improvements will be made at the earliest possible time and without reference to any other existing conditions in the Police Department.
>
> There is no authority in the office of the governor for interference in making orders by the police commissioner or in the action of the mayor and city council. The foregoing suggestion is therefore made, as you will understand, in response to a request for suggestions on my part. I am unable to discover any action that I can take.
>
> Yours very truly,
> Calvin Coolidge

A defender of Governor Coolidge's part in the crisis has charged that the last sentence of this letter "has been lifted from its context, misconstrued, probably with intent, into the meaning that Coolidge was afraid to meet the situation." "Precisely the opposite," the writer continues, "is the case. *He would take no action to avoid the situation.* With the principle that public servants responsible for the safety of the city could not divide allegiance with an outside federation, everyone including Peters and the citizens' committee, had finally agreed. But Commissioner Curtis and Coolidge went further. They said any compromise by the loyal members of the force—that is to say, a promise to unionize locally if at all—could have no reference to the men already on trial. To this conclusion Coolidge clung, strike or no strike."

These words are taken from one of the ablest defenses in print of Governor Coolidge's part in the crisis. They give the impression that Governor Coolidge took a stand on the affiliation question prior to the outbreak of the strike. As a matter of fact, Governor Coolidge made no statement whatsoever on the subject of affiliation until after the strike was over. They also give the impression that he bravely endorsed Commissioner Curtis' stand when as a matter of fact he continually emphasized the point that he had nothing to do with conduct of the police department, that the commissioner and the commissioner alone was responsible for its administration, and that "we must all support the commissioner in the execution of the laws."

This attitude was further emphasized the afternoon before the strike when the Massachusetts State Federation of Labor meeting in Greenfield wired Coolidge to remove the police commissioner and reinstate the suspended men. His answer was: "The governor has no authority over the appointment, suspension, or removal of the police force of Boston."

By this time it was clear that the only persons aside from the police themselves who were in a position to prevent a strike had no intention of doing so. The mayor and his committee now turned their attention towards insuring the safety of the city. At one o'clock in the afternoon the mayor visited the police commissioner at his office and was assured by him that "he had the situation well in hand and had ample means at his disposal for the protection of the city."

"I asked him," said the mayor, "whether he did not think he ought to have the State Guard ready for emergencies, and he replied that he did not need it and did not want it."

. . . Commissioner Curtis greeted the announcement of the strike called by the union policemen with the statement, "I am ready for anything."

The *Post* announced that Mr. Curtis, when questioned as to whether he would adhere to a previous statement, "I am prepared for all eventualities," replied, "I am ready for anything."

The same afternoon the commissioner consented to see the governor in company with the mayor although he had told the mayor that such a visit was not necessary. At this conference, according to the mayor, the police commissioner reiterated his assurance that he had the situation in hand and had made ample provision for the city's protection, and again stated that he did not need or want the State Guard. Governor Coolidge said he was fully prepared to render support to the police commissioner in any measure which might be instituted by him. "I am relying on these promises," said the mayor.

Late that afternoon, at five forty-five, the union policemen struck; 1,117 of 1,544 patrolmen left their posts. That night there was disorder, rioting and robbery. While the situation was grave, the disorder consisted chiefly of boisterous rowdyism caused by smart-aleck boys, not a few of whom were sailors in uniform from United States vessels in the harbor. Shop windows were broken; some jewelry was stolen; shoes and hats were removed from show cases; cans were taken off the shelves in grocery stores. Men are reported to have come supplied with suitcases to carry off the loot. Yet there was no really serious plundering; there were no holdups, no banks were robbed, there was no exceptional major crime and the fundamental order of the state was not threatened. But this was just the beginning of the strike. Boston was hardly a safe or peaceful place and the police commissioner's repeated assurances that measures had been taken which would "afford ample protection to the people at large," had not been fulfilled.

The next morning the *Boston Herald*, a leading Republican paper and a firm supporter of Curtis and Coolidge, blurted out the truth in its leading editorial:

> Somebody blundered. Boston should not have been left defenceless last night in the face of the rioting of Liverpool and other cities.

After describing the disorder and declaring that "no hand appeared to stay it," the editorial went on to say:

> We must not have this again. The authorities should call the state militia to patrol the streets until we can maintain order by a newly organized police force.

"Blundered" was hardly the right word. The indications are that Commissioner Curtis in order to break the strike, turn public opinion against the policemen, and destroy the union, deliberately misled the mayor and left the city unprotected.

Some 500 volunteer police whom the department had been training for weeks amid great publicity, under the direction of retired Superintendent William H. Pierce, were not ordered to duty until fourteen hours after the walkout. Three hours before the time set for the strike, Superintendent Pierce said: "My instructions are to notify the volunteers under my charge to report for duty at 8 o'clock tomorrow morning. None of the volunteers will be called to duty tonight in any event. I am acting under orders from Commissioner Curtis."

It has also been charged that the 400 police who did not strike were kept off the streets. Newspaper reporters who looked into the City Hall Avenue station, which was close to a rioting center, claim that they saw policemen inside in spite of the nearby disorders. The Commissioner, however, claimed that the men who did not strike were on duty.

On the morning of September 10, after the night of disorder, the police commissioner wrote the mayor saying that he was of the opinion that the usual police provisions were inadequate to preserve order and suggested that it might be well for the mayor to call out the militia located within the city limits. This the mayor proceeded to do at once, and at the same time he assumed control of the police department under the authority of a statute which gave him the right to do so "in case of tumult, mob or violent disturbance of public order." The governor was then asked for additional troops which were quickly placed at the mayor's disposal.

With at least 500 special volunteers and 400 regular police as well as an overwhelming military force at his disposal, Mayor Peters quickly restored order. By the following morning the city was again going about its normal concerns. Then, for no apparent reason, Governor Coolidge, who heretofore either could not be found or persistently refused to have anything to do with the situation except to grant the mayor's request for troops in addition to those already on duty, issued a proclamation announcing the mobilization of the entire State Guard and calling upon all citizens to aid him "in the maintenance of law and order." All the Boston troops were already on duty so the effect of the governor's proclamation was merely to call out the military units in other parts of the state and to take control of the police department out of the mayor's hands and place it back under his own supervision.

The commissioner's course on the night of the walkout naturally led to questions which could not be ignored. Mr. Curtis attempted to meet these queries by distortion and misrepresentation. The patrolmen he claimed in his report, "carried on their purpose in secret." He did not know they were going to strike until they actually walked out and it was therefore impossible to have the special volunteers in the station houses. The uncertainty on the day of the strike was not greater than on the days immediately preceding it and the governor and mayor were therefore not warranted under the law, in calling out the State Guard on that day any more than on the preceding days.

Of course the commissioner did not mention the fact that the Boston papers carried the announcement of the men's decision to strike on their front page all day. The *Herald's* headline, in inch and a quarter type, read:

POLICE VOTE TO QUIT TODAY. TO STRIKE AT
5:45 P.M. ROLL CALL

Nor does the commissioner's report recall that troops were not called because he told the mayor that he "did not need them and did not want them," and that he was "ready for anything."

The commissioner's only extra precaution was to have 60 state police and 100 metropolitan park police placed at his disposal. He complained that the latter did not render the efficient service he had a right to expect. Since the park police have close contacts with the Boston police, one would expect to find a considerable proportion of their number in sympathy with their fellows on the city force. The commissioner did not take the trouble to secure a specially selected group of park police and therefore got a group with its due proportion of police sympathizers. Fifty-three were later suspended for refusal to do strike duty. Nineteen of these were tried for disobedience and dismissed. These men claimed that they would gladly have aided in suppressing riot if they had been so ordered, but their directions were to take up duty as strikebreakers. This, they admitted, they refused to do.

No one wanted to admit that the failure to provide for the protection of Boston on the night of the walkout was a deliberate attempt to use the inevitable disorder as a strike-breaking weapon. Every responsible party tried to dodge the blame for smashing police unionism at the expense of the lives and property of the people of Boston. Some officials of Governor Coolidge's administration went so far as to attempt to shift the burden of responsibility to the shoulders of Mayor Peters. The adjutant general of the Commonwealth in his report to the governor, according to the version published in the Boston papers, declared that "anticipating that the mayor would issue his precept during the course of the evening" certain military units which were holding drills that evening were directed to remain in their armories. But "no word having been received from the mayor up to 11 o'clock, and no serious disturbance having taken place up to that time," the troops were ordered home. The governor, however, refused to receive the report in this form because of its implied criticism of the mayor. "No one," he said, "had knowledge which would authorize him to call out military forces sooner than was done." The official report of the adjutant general accordingly made no mention of the mayor, but merely recited the fact that certain troops drilling in their armories on the night of the strike were relieved from duty when no call came for their services up to eleven o'clock.

The mayor in a statement explaining his course issued on the morning following the walkout disposes of these criticisms completely:

In view of the law which gives to the police commissioner the sole right to enforce the law, I had called out part of the state guard located in Boston when the commissioner stated that he did not wish their services. I would have had a body of men with no authority, and would have created tremendous confusion. . . .

Furthermore, in a recent communication from the governor, he states so plainly that no one has any authority to interfere with the police commissioner that I should have hesitated to take control of a situation which the police commissioner assured me was under control, even if I had the power.

AFTERMATH OF THE BOSTON STRIKE

The Boston strike was treated not as a labor dispute but as a revolt against public authority, an attempted political upheaval. The affair shows the advantages which the authorities have in a dispute with their employees, especially those engaged in the performance of vital public functions.

Prior to the walkout there had been a great deal of sentiment in favor of the police, but the disorder of the first night turned public opinion completely against them. Condemnation of the patrolmen was universal. The mayor's committee, and the newspapers which knew the facts and had printed them in their news columns, rallied to the support of the authorities and refused to utter a single word of criticism of anyone but the strikers. The *Boston Herald,* which alone was indiscreet enough to tell the truth on the first morning, never repeated its indiscretion. It became a matter of "my country right or wrong" and as usual in such circumstances, those who happened to be in authority succeeded in identifying themselves with "my country." The mayor's committee refused to publish its report telling the truth of the situation until long after erroneous impressions had become so widely and deeply instilled that belief in them could not be shaken. To report while the state was engaged in the immediate task of "asserting its sovereignty defeating the strike and reestablishing law and order," seemed "inopportune" to the committee.

It is usual for those in power to make political capital out of a situation like the Boston strike. If the favorable publicity had gone to Mayor Peters no one familiar with the situation would have been surprised. The mayor did his best to prevent the strike though, as he said in a public statement, he "received no cooperation from the police commissioner and no help or practical suggestions from the governor." He also restored public order after the commissioner failed to furnish the city the protection he had assured it. One could even understand if the acclaim had gone to the commissioner who was at least consistent in his attitude and prominent throughout the controversy. What is not only surprising but almost unbelievable is that the lion's share of the publicity should have gone to Governor Coolidge. The governor, it will be remembered, called out those units of the State Guard situated outside of Boston after the mayor had already restored order. The citizens' committee thus described the part he played:

By Thursday morning order had been generally restored in the city. On Thursday afternoon, September 11, the governor assumed control of the situation as indicated by his proclamation of that day.

This wholly unnecessary step was not taken until "the preponderance of opinion against the policemen joining the American Federation of Labor or exercising the right to strike was overwhelming." And even then, Governor Coolidge refused to take a definite stand on the fundamental issues involved. On the day after he issued his proclamation, he received the newspaper men at the State House.

"Governor," he was asked, "will you tell us why the state objects to the affiliation of police with the American Federation of Labor?"

"That," Coolidge answered, "is something the state has nothing to do with. Internal direction of the police department is wholly in the hands of the commissioner."

When asked later in the interview: "Would you permit the men to return with the understanding that they will form an association not affiliated with the American Federation of Labor?" he answered: "You are now coming to the question of whether the action of the police was as a matter of fact a strike, and whether the men who left their posts might under any circumstances be taken back. That is of course for the commissioner alone to determine."

On the following day, Commissioner Curtis, acting on the advice of the attorney general, declared the strikers' places vacant and announced that a new police force would be recruited at once. When this decision was made public, President Gompers wired Governor Coolidge to prevent such drastic punishment. This time, however, the governor departed from the position which he had consistently held, namely that control of the police was the commissioner's function and a matter with which he had nothing to do, and declared:

> The right of the police to affiliate has alwyas been questioned, never granted, is now prohibited. . . .
> Your assertion that the commissioner was wrong cannot justify the wrong of leaving the city unguarded. . . .
> There is no right to strike against the public safety by anybody, anywhere, at any time.

For this stand, taken after there was no longer any risk involved in it, Calvin Coolidge became a national hero. During his campaign for reelection as governor which immediately followed the strike, his role as savior of Boston and guardian of law and order was played up for all it was worth. The State Guard was kept on duty patrolling the streets constantly keeping the strike and Commander-in-Chief Coolidge, now in "control of the situation," before the public eye. This cost the taxpayers about a million dollars, not very much less than would have been the cost of an adequate increase in the policemen's salaries.

Governor Coolidge was reelected by 120,000 votes as against 17,000 when he ran the year before. President Wilson sent him a telegram hailing his victory as a vindication of law and order, thus contributing not a little to the making of the myth which later made it possible for Calvin Coolidge to enter the White House.

In addition to its political consequences, the Boston police strike had two important results for the policemen themselves. First, when Commissioner Curtis issued the announcement of his refusal to reinstate the strikers he inserted advertisements in all the Boston papers asking for recruits for a new police force. The new men were offered not the old minimum of 1,100 dollars, of which 200 dollars went for equipment, but the equivalent of the old maximum, i.e., 1,400 dollars plus a 200 dollar equipment allowance. The members of the union, while losing their places, won the strike for their successors.

Mayor Peters and the city council accepted these increases without a syllable of protest. No one grumbled about the necessity of increasing the tax rate. Nobody wondered how the city's finances could stand the strain.

At the same time steps were taken to consider the problem of hours of labor and to improve the condition of station houses.

The patrolmen's strike did more to correct the grievances of the police in half a week than all the polite agitation did in years. And the rush to improve the working conditions of police was by no means confined to Boston. City after city turned its attention to the matter and within a few months the number of communities in which police conditions were bettered could be counted by the score.

The second result of the strike was the complete destruction of the policemen's trade union movement. Those municipal officials who had accepted the unionization of their police forces without enthusiasm but with resignation, now became determined in their insistence that the police give up their charters. In other places where the authorities either favored or had no objection to a police union, the press succeeded in forcing the organizations out of existence. Promises of higher pay and more attractive conditions of employment frequently hastened the process of disbanding unions.

There is little doubt that but for the Boston episode, the police would have been as well organized within the labor movement as the firemen.

THE POST OFFICE STRIKE OF 1970

J. Joseph Loewenberg

Until the postal strike, the most sacrosanct, inviolate rule of federal employment relations was that employees could not strike against the federal government. The introduction and development of collective bargaining between the government and its employees in the 1960s in no way diminished the standing of this rule.[1]

The rash of strikes and strike threats that plagued public employee labor relations at the local level in the 1960s had no counterpart at the federal level. The

Joseph Loewenberg is Associate Professor of Management, Temple University. Article prepared specifically for this volume.

[1] See the development of federal employee bargaining in Section II.

federal government had experienced several work stoppages, but these involved relatively few people and brief time periods, and they were dealt with promptly. In one case, for example, eighty-five sheet-metal workers who struck the Tennessee Valley Authority in 1962 were fired.

The work stoppage by over two hundred thousand postal workers in March 1970 broke many traditions of the federal service and introduced new concepts into federal employee collective bargaining. The drama of the eight-day strike may be but a prelude to significant changes in the public employer-employee relationship.

BACKGROUND

The Post Office Department

The Post Office Department of the United States traces its history back to 1775. In 1970 it was, next to the Department of Defense, the largest department in the federal government, employing a total of approximately seven hundred fifty thousand workers who were located in almost every community of the United States.

The Post Office Department, as one of the executive departments of the federal government, received its funds from Congress. Any revenue collected by the department was turned over to the General Fund of the United States. By 1970 congressional appropriations to operate the department amounted to over $8 billion annually. The deficit between these appropriations and revenues was about $1¼ billion annually.

Congress also determined the wages, hours, and benefits of Post Office employees. Postal workers were on a separate wage classification system from other federal employees, but wage rates were traditionally linked among the various systems. Vacations, pensions, insurance, and other forms of supplementary compensation were identical for all federal employees.

When collective bargaining was introduced into the federal government on a large scale in 1962, only matters that were determined by the separate agencies or by lower levels within the agency were potential subjects of bargaining. Unions representing post office employees were quick to set up negotiations at the local level and at the national level of the post office. But they found it necessary to continue lobbying with Congress over economic matters, just as they had done long before the advent of collective bargaining.

The Unions

Postal employees had a long history of organization; many of the pronouncements of government officials on unions in the first decade of this century were specifically directed toward postal unions. By 1970 almost 90 percent of all postal workers were represented by unions that bargained in their behalf.

Seven major postal unions represented workers on a craft basis and were members of the AFL–CIO. The largest of these were the United Federation of

Postal Clerks (UFPC) and the National Association of Letter Carriers of the U.S.A. (NALC); together the two unions represented over five hundred thousand workers. The seven unions held exclusive recognition at the national level, which meant that they could bargain with the department for all workers in their craft. To facilitate bargaining, these unions dealt jointly on matters of common interest with the department.

Two other unions that represented nonsupervisory employees were organized on an industrial basis. The larger of these, the National Postal Union, had considerable strength in some major cities. Neither was recognized at the national level and therefore could not take part in bargaining with the agency at that level.

Despite the unions' bargaining activity and their continuing lobbying efforts with Congress, union members showed signs of unrest. In 1968 the United Federation of Postal Clerks and the National Postal Union eliminated the no-strike provisions from their constitutions. A similar move failed in the convention of the National Association of Letter Carriers, but the convention subsequently directed its officers to seek ways that would grant federal employees the right to strike. The union introduced legal suits to test the constitutionality of the federal statutes forbidding strikes by federal employees and the affidavit not to assert the right to strike required of every employee. The affidavit was declared unconstitutional by a federal court in December 1969; the government appealed the decision. Meanwhile, in the summer of 1969, eighty-eight clerks stayed away from work in a Bronx (N.Y.) post office; it was officially declared a two-week leave without pay rather than a strike.[2]

By early 1970 many postal workers were becoming increasingly restive with their working conditions, the government's proposals for reform of the Post Office Department, and the leaders of their unions. The pay scale for the vast majority of postal employees, including carriers and clerks, ranged from $6,176 to $8,442; the range was paid in twelve steps over twenty-one years. A pay raise contemplated for late 1969 was stalled in Congress and was tied to a postal reform. In addition, post office employees complained about outdated and dilapidated facilities and equipment, the hazards of delivering the mail in an increasingly violent society, and post office policies discriminating against regular employees. For instance, workers charged that the department had reduced overtime for regular employees and had given this work to part-timers in order to save money. The result of deteriorating conditions was that the post office has a high turnover and some unfilled jobs in large cities.

The conditions prevalent throughout the country were aggravated in New York City by the high cost of living, the relative success of municipal employees in collective bargaining, and the relative militancy of the postal unions in New York. Although inflation was a national concern, the Bureau of Labor Statistics' cost-of-living index showed that prices had increased faster in New York City than the national average; in actual dollar terms, the overall cost had always been higher in New York. The federal government's figures showed that a family of four needed $11,236 for a moderate standard of living in New York City. Meanwhile, New York City employees had managed to outstrip federal employees in economic improvements. Postal workers claimed that municipal employees such as police or sanita-

[2]Government Employee Relations Reports 304, p. A-9, and 307, p. A-8.

tion workers were receiving substantially higher pay than they were receiving, thereby completely reversing the relative financial standing of the occupations of two decades earlier. Within three years of starting, sanitation workers received $1,500 more than a postal worker could expect to receive after twenty-one years. Other benefits gained in collective bargaining gave further advantages to the municipal employees. Suggestions by New York letter carriers that the union support area wage differentials in the postal service was not accepted by the national leadership. Some members planned to depose the incumbent president at the convention in August 1970.[3] The New York City local, Branch 36, had always been considered progressive; it had led the unsuccessful attempt to change the union's no-strike provision in the 1968 convention.

Pay Raise Proposals

In the fall of 1969 the House of Representatives and the Senate considered legislation to provide pay raises for all federal employees. The House bill, passed in October, provided postal workers with a 5.4 percent increase effective October 1, 1969, and an additional 5.7 percent increase as of July 1970; it lowered the number of years required to make the top salary of a grade from twenty-one to eight years. In addition, the House bill provided for a Federal Employee Salary Commission and Board of Arbitration to determine yearly salary changes for federal employees.[4] In December 1969 the Senate approved a different bill providing for a 4 percent increase for federal workers earning under $10,000, with relatively smaller increases going to employees in the higher grades; these increases would be effective January 1, 1970. No joint conference was held on these two bills because of the pending debate on post office reform.

In the federal fiscal 1971 budget presented in January 1970, President Nixon proposed a 5.75 percent pay increase for federal employees to bring their wages in line with those paid in comparable jobs in private industry. He postponed the effective date of the increase from July 1970 to January 1971 to give evidence to the country of the administration's anti-inflationary position and to help keep the budget balanced. White House spokesmen continued to press for tying a pay raise for postal workers to passage of the administration's proposals for post office reform.

Post Office Reform Proposal

The concept of a public corporation to take over the operation of the Post Office Department had been initiated by the Johnson administration. Nevertheless, the pressures for reform were stronger in 1969 and 1970 than ever before.

The administration proposed that the Post Office Department be removed from the President's cabinet and be converted into a public corporation. The corporation would be governed by nine members, two appointed by the President. The corporation would be responsible for its own financing, including the sale of

[3]*Government Employee Relations Report 341,* A-6.
[4]*Government Employee Relations Report 319,* A-1.

bonds to raise funds, and for setting postal rates. Employees of the postal corporation would no longer be covered by Civil Service regulations and would bargain collectively for their wages and working conditions. The no-strike provision, however, would remain.

Most unions representing postal employees were opposed to the reform proposal, presumably because they would no longer have access to Congress and they doubted the effectiveness of collective bargaining without a right to strike. One exception was the president of the letter carriers, who supported the reform proposal if Congress also approved the 5.4 percent pay increase. Congressional leaders of the post office committees were also dubious about the reorganization proposal which would remove considerable power and prestige from Congress. On March 12, 1970, however, the House Post Office and Civil Service Committee approved the President's proposal for a public corporation for the postal service.

THE STRIKE

On the same day that the House Post Office and Civil Service Committee recommended the reorganization of the postal system, NALC leaders were preparing for a regular monthly membership meeting of Branch 36 in New York City to discuss the progress of wage legislation. Much to the surprise of the leadership, the members at the meeting decided to take a strike vote on March 17 to enforce a demand for a 40 percent increase in pay and a reduced-step pay scale.

Of the 6,700 members enrolled in Branch 36, 2,614 participated in the strike vote; the final tally showed the strike was approved, 1,555-1,055. As other postal unions, NALC had no strike fund. Nonetheless, the walkout started the next morning. The letter carriers in Manhattan and the Bronx were quickly joined by the letter carriers in Brooklyn. The twenty-six thousand member Manhattan-Bronx Postal Union, which represented clerks and mail handlers, respected the letter carriers' picket lines. The result was an immediate and complete disruption of mail service in New York City. The first major strike in the 195-year history of the U.S. postal service was on.

The strike caught everyone unprepared. Business, heavily dependent on mail service to transmit bills and collect receipts as well as to supply a regular stream of communications, was severely hampered. Organizations using the mails to deliver services, whether financial advice or relief checks, found they could no longer do business. A Harris poll taken after the strike showed that 61 percent of the public sympathized more with the demands of the postal employees than with the federal government, while 25 percent favored the government. The average citizen found the discomfort of not receiving personal mail mitigated by the absence of bills and "junk" mail and the unexpected extension of payment deadlines. The public press, while critical of the postal workers' tactics, generally was sympathetic to their demands.

The government followed the rhetorical and legal precedents used in previous work-stoppage situations, but the monumentality of the postal situation soon showed the traditional methods to be ineffective. Postmaster General Blount announced, "We simply cannot tolerate a mail strike in this country." At the same time he placed an embargo on all mail in New York City and adjacent areas, thereby affecting the mail service of 10 million persons. All employees absent without permission were put on nonpay status.

On the first day of the strike the government obtained from a federal district court a civil injunction ordering an end to the strike. The strike was considered a violation of the Federal Code which makes such action a criminal offense and the offender subject to a fine up to $1,000 and/or up to a year and a day in prison. Leaders of Branch 36 announced the injunction to their members and withdrew pickets to avoid charges of violating the injunction. However, the work stoppage in New York City continued and soon spread to other areas.

Other unions representing postal employees were also quick to disavow complicity and official sanction of the work stoppage. The presidents of the seven unions holding exclusive national recognition from the post office telegraphed their respective local units as follows:

> Because of the provisions of Executive Order 11491, the labor agreement existing between our organization and the Post Office Department, and the existing statutes, we cannot support or condone the service interruption which has occurred and we collectively instruct all affected postal employees to return to work immediately.
>
> We further request an immediate, full and objective congressional investigation of all the conditions and circumstances which brought this situation about.

Nevertheless, more letter carriers were going off the job, and other postal workers refused to work if the letter carriers were not.

The spread of the walkout at first represented the ripple effect of a pebble thrown into a pool. The strike spread from New York City to its suburbs, then into New Jersey and Philadelphia. But then it jumped quickly to the Midwest and West Coast. Within three days half of the country was hit by the mail strike, with major metropolitan areas from Boston to Los Angeles affected. Only the South and Southwest continued to enjoy normal mail service. At the height of the strike, four days after it had started, over two hundred thousand or 28 percent of all postal workers were off the job.

By then congressional leaders were becoming increasingly concerned with the economic impact of the strike and the futility of legal action and public appeals to end the strike. They declared that Congress would consider pay legislation only after the strike had ended. This attitude, endorsed by the administration, was also supported by the leaders of the national postal unions who felt threatened by their members' continuing refusal to follow direction. In an effort to provide a satisfactory way out of the impasse, a meeting was held on March 20 between the leaders of the postal unions with exclusive national recognition and Secretary of Labor George P. Shultz, which resulted in an agreement to discuss "the full range of issues being raised . . . as soon as we are assured that the work stoppages are ended." This agreement became the administration's position throughout the remainder of the strike.

The agreement could not be implemented. Letter carriers in one city after another rejected the agreement and voted to continue the strike. President

Rademacher of the NALC was hanged in effigy. Continuing communications between Secretary Shultz and his staff and the unions for the purpose of getting striking employees back to work failed. Pressure was mounting on the administration to take more drastic action.

On Monday, March 23, President Nixon declared a national emergency:

> What is at issue then is the survival of a government based upon law. Essential services must be maintained and, as President, I shall meet my constitutional responsibility to see that those services are maintained.

The President ordered twenty-five hundred active-duty troops to help move essential mail in New York City and called up sixteen thousand members of the National Guard to stand by. It marked the first time that troops had been used to replace workers of the federal government.

The reaction to the President's move by organized labor was predictable; George Meany, president of the AFL–CIO, declared:

> We deplore the use of military personnel to perform work of civilian employees of the post office. . . . This action will not restore mail services nor contribute to an early resolution of the problems and circumstances which caused the stoppage of those services.

At the same time he urged postal employees to return to work.

Congressional attitudes also indicated a shift. In its eagerness to see the strike end, it was reported that Congress was willing to consider an increase in wages for postal employees before the complete end of the strike.

Postal employees began to return to work. On Monday about 20 percent of those who had stayed away from work returned, principally in Pittsburgh, Milwaukee, and cities in Connecticut. On Tuesday even more returned in Boston, Buffalo, Philadelphia, Cleveland, Detroit, Chicago, and San Francisco. Although over one hundred thousand postal employees were still off the job, fifty-seven thousand in New York City, it was becoming clear that the strike was waning.

On Wednesday, March 25, the strike ended in New York City. The 10,600 troops who had been used to handle the mail had accomplished little more than indicate the administration's interest in restoring mail service. Yet local postal union leaders in New York recommended a return to work so that the promised negotiations could commence in Washington. Their action was prompted by a federal court order finding Branch 36 in contempt of court, ordering the letter carriers back to work, and levying fines against Branch 36 if the strike continued after March 25, with the fines escalating from $10,000 for the first day to $20,000 on the second day, and so on. The leaders talked of a package including a 12 percent pay increase retroactive to October 1969, a reduced longevity scale, full payment by the government of health benefits, binding arbitration of disputes, and amnesty for strikers. Moreover, if the negotiations failed to produce results in five days, they promised to recommend resumption of the strike. The membership heartily endorsed the recommendations.

THE NEGOTIATIONS

When it became obvious to the administration that the strike was crumbling, negotiations between the government and the postal unions were set to begin on March 25. The government team was composed of officials of the Post Office Department under the leadership of the deputy postmaster general. The spokesman for the seven unions was an aide of President Meany of the AFL–CIO.

The week of collective bargaining covered a range of subjects, but talks centered principally on pay, the postal authority, and amnesty for strikers. Everyone was aware of the significance of bargaining on each of these subjects. Congress, which had been impatient to settle the outstanding issues involved in the strike, was now content to await the result of negotiations before acting.

On April 2 the parties reached agreement and signed a memorandum with the following provisions:

1. A 6 percent wage increase for all postal employees retroactive to December 27, 1969.

2. A jointly bargained and sponsored reorganization of the Post Office Department to provide for:

a. collective bargaining procedures under a statutory framework establishing methods for conducting elections, providing one or more methods for resolving negotiating impasses, and requiring collective bargaining over all aspects of wages, hours, and working conditions including grievance procedures, final and binding arbitration of disputes, and in general all matters that are subject to collective bargaining in the private sector.

b. an additional 8 percent wage increase for postal workers effective as of the date the enabling legislation becomes law.

c. negotiations with the unions, to be immediately undertaken to establish a new wage schedule whereby an employee reaches the maximum step for his labor grade after no more than eight years in that grade.

d. a structure for the department so that it can operate on a self-contained basis and endow it with authority commensurate with its responsibilities to improve, manage, and maintain efficient and adequate postal services.

3. A promise of no disciplinary action "against any postal employee with respect to the events of March 1970, until discussions have taken place between the Department and such employee's union on the policy to be followed by the Department."

The government had assured the leaders of other federal unions that the results of any retroactive wage increases negotiated by the seven postal unions would be extended to cover all federal employees. The 6 percent agreed to in bargaining increased the federal budget by almost $3 billion. Despite concern about the effects of such an added expenditure on the precariously balanced budget and the economy, there was no resistance to the basic proposal. Both houses of Congress quickly held hearings and voted on the legislation to effect the increase. On April 15 President Nixon signed the implementing legislation.

The details of the independent postal service and of labor-management relations in that service were negotiated and agreed to by the parties. On April 16 President Nixon sent a message to Congress endorsing the results of that agreement:

1. An independent United States Postal Service under the direction of a nine-member bipartisan commission. The postal service would set its own rates, subject to congressional veto, and would be empowered to borrow funds.

2. Collective bargaining between the postal service and employee representatives "over wages, hours and, in general, all working conditions that are subject to collective bargaining in the private sector." The National Labor Relations Board would be given jurisdiction over unit determinations, representation issues, and unfair labor practices involving postal service employees. The ban on strikes would continue. The final step for negotiation impasses would be binding arbitration.

3. A pay raise of 8 percent when the reorganization law would be enacted, and prompt bargaining to compress pay steps to not more than eight years. The President also proposed new postal rates to reduce the amount of subsidy required by the Post Office Department. The proposal was for a 33 percent increase in first class mail, a 50 percent increase in second class mail, and a 33 percent increase in third class mail. At the same time the President proposed that the federal subsidy would decline annually until 1978 when the postal service should be self-supporting.

The heart of the reorganization proposal was similar to what President Nixon had proposed in 1969 and what the House Post Office and Civil Service Committee had approved in March 1970. The labor-management sections were more elaborate than they had originally been, but fundamentally no different. The President had been forced by political pressure to reduce his request for an increase in first class postal rates from 67 percent to 33 percent. The tie-in of an 8 percent wage increase to passage of the reorganization was undoubtedly an inducement for the postal unions to agree to the reorganization. In fact, it was the endorsement of the postal unions which marked the biggest change between the reorganization proposal of April 1970 and earlier versions.

In a joint press conference with Postmaster General Blount, George Meany commented on the reason for the changed position by the labor unions:

> This is one of the most significant events in the history of collective bargaining. This legislation which the Administration will introduce and which we will support in Congress is proof positive that collective bargaining is viable and effective.
>
> We in the AFL–CIO, quite candidly, see these negotiations as setting the stage for the future. We believe that collective bargaining can be and should be extended to all workers in the Federal Government.

OBSERVATIONS

In retrospect, it is perhaps not so surprising that the first major strike against the federal government occurred in March 1970 as that it occurred at all and that the result was not catastrophic. Contrary to the doomsayers, the nation survived and federal employee-management relations were altered to adjust to the new circumstances.

Certainly the postal workers, long well organized and closely identified with blue-collar trades because of their pay and working conditions, felt they were caught in a political squeeze by the administration's insistence that pay increases and postal reform be considered as a single package. Traditional lobbying methods with Congress were ineffective in breaking the log jam. The New York letter carriers, who were already disenchanted with national union leadership and had particular financial problems, had only to look around them to understand the role and effect of pressure activity:

> Everybody else strikes and gets a big pay increase. The teachers, sanitation men and transit workers all struck in violation of the law and got big increases. Why shouldn't we? We've been nice guys too long.[5]

But the basic issues confronting New York postal employees were common throughout the postal service. Once it became apparent that the Post Office Department could not or would not act decisively to end the walkout, strike fever spread rapidly. The spell—and the law—of not striking against the government had been broken.

While the strike had an immediate effect on business and the economy, it was apparent that a short strike did not really disturb the public. Even those who believed a strike was wrong supported the postal employees in the issues they were striking for. The government therefore could not expect public pressure to end the strike.

One of the main problems confronting the parties was how to end the strike once it had begun. Since national leaders of the postal unions immediately disavowed support of the strike, they had little control over the actions of striking employees. Moreover, the government showed that it really could not handle a major postal crisis without regular employees. The use of troops in New York City was symbolic but limited in application and ineffective in moving the mails. Perhaps major contributing factors to the end of the strike were the small size of union treasuries, the lack of personal resources by strikers, and the realization that some of the major objects of the strike had been gained. The federal court order levying fines against Branch 36 provided a timely rationale for defining the end of the walkout.

The role of George Meany, president of the AFL–CIO, was critical in the postal strike of 1970. He welded the position of the seven postal unions, became the communications link between the postal unions and the administration, pro-

[5]*New York Times,* March 19, 1970, p. 52.

vided the spokesman for labor in negotiations, and in general assumed the leadership position. In so doing, he added to his stature within the labor movement, in government circles, and with the public. His actions demonstrated the AFL–CIO's new interest in and commitment to public sector bargaining.

The repercussions of the strike were likely to continue for some time. The strike served to highlight the division between members and leaders of some of the unions; challenges to incumbent leaders and established policies were quickly forthcoming in NALC, for instance. The issue of postal reorganization was resolved, but the implementation would undoubtedly bring new problems. The most significant impact of the postal strike would concern neither the postal unions nor the postal service. The strike raised the question of the future of collective bargaining in the federal service in a new light. The existing framework and practices seemed suddenly anachronistic. Would Congress, which had the power to legislate wages and working conditions but had yielded it to the executive branch in the postal strike, insist on maintaining these rights with respect to other employees? If collective bargaining over wages and working conditions were approved for postal employees, would it not also be appropriate for other federal workers? Would compulsory arbitration become the government's response to a no-strike policy? And how would government employees regard the law forbidding strikes, once they appreciated its use by the postal workers? Perhaps the significance of the impact of the strike was best summarized in an editorial of the postal clerks:

> It was a strike.
> It was illegal.
> It had an immense impact on the nation—an impact equalled only by the enormity of the grievance which provoked it.
> It's our guess that the postal service will never be the same again—and that goes for the federal services generally.[6]

[6]*The Union Postal Clerk*, April 1970, p. 10.

CHAPTER 5

POLITICS AND PUBLIC SECTOR BARGAINING

Collective bargaining in the public sector takes place in an environment quite different from that found in the private sector. In the private sector the parameters within which the parties operate are set by economic forces—for example, product prices, competition, and profits. In the public sector, political forces are far more important. Interest group and other political pressures influence the public employer. A question frequently asked is: Will the public "buy" the tax increase necessary to implement the settlement?

Because of the close and constant relationship between politics and collective bargaining in the public sector, one would expect to find a considerable body of literature by political scientists on this topic. Unfortunately, only a small number of political scientists have written on collective bargaining in public employment. It is not surprising, then, that most of the articles in this section on "Politics and Public Sector Bargaining" have been written by industrial relations specialists and labor economists.

Derber describes the positions taken by various public employers and public employee organizations when a negotiations bill was proposed in the Illinois legislature. Moskow, Loewenberg, and Koziara develop a typology of lobbying activities of public employee organizations and the interrelationship between lobbying and collective bargaining. Nilan describes the lobbying activities of one of the largest public employee unions—the United Federation of Postal Clerks. McLennan and Moskow analyze the way in which multilateral bargaining occurs in the public sector and the topics upon which it is likely to focus. In the final article, Belasco describes and analyzes the political pressures that influence the negotiators in a municipal bargaining case study.

LABOR-MANAGEMENT POLICY
FOR PUBLIC EMPLOYEES IN ILLINOIS:
THE EXPERIENCE OF THE GOVERNOR'S COMMISSION
1966-1967

Milton Derber

APPOINTMENT OF THE GOVERNOR'S COMMISSION

The decision by Governor Otto Kerner to appoint a commission of experts to study the public employee situation and to recommend an appropriate legislative policy was made in the spring of 1966, although the commission was not formally appointed until late July of that year. A variety of factors influenced the decision. The public employee unions, particularly AFSCME and the AFT, had been pressing for legislation applying to all public employees or, at least, for an executive order covering state employees for a number of years. The neighboring states of Wisconsin, Michigan, and Missouri had recently adopted laws. The debacle of the New York City transit strike and the reports of the Rockefeller and Lindsay committees had attracted national attention.[1] Within the state, conflict situations had developed over recognition and negotiating rights of teachers, social workers, and nurses in Cook County and of institutional employees in the state's hospitals and prisons outside of Cook County. The steps taken by the public authorities to resolve these disputes had reflected uncertainty over public policy, confusion over procedures, a tendency to improvise, delay, or "pass the buck."[2] The governor decided, and so informed the labor groups, that a clear policy for the state required action by the legislature, and that he would not issue an executive order which would have dubious effects outside of the state departments directly controlled by

Milton Derber is Professor of Labor and Industrial Relations, University of Illinois. Reprinted from the *Industrial and Labor Relations Review*, XXI No. 4, July 1968. Copyright © 1968 by Cornell University. All rights reserved.

[1]New York (State). *Governor's Committee on Public Employee Relations. Final Report,* March 31, 1966 (processed); *Mayor's Tripartite Panel on Collective Bargaining Procedures in Public Employment. Report.* (New York (City): District Council 37, American Federation of State, County, and Municipal Employees, 1966).

[2]The story of public employee strikes in Illinois has not been adequately told. Even their number is unknown.

the governor. Moreover, he did not want to confine the policy solely to the employees of the state government.

The composition of the commission was characteristic of the Illinois "agreed bill" tradition, which is to involve representatives of the major interest groups in the hope that they might reach a consensus, rather than to appoint a small group of "neutral" specialists. The need for a consensus was particularly strong because both houses of the legislature were dominated by the Republicans and the governor was a Democrat. The price of achieving widespread representation was a large, seemingly unwieldy commission of twenty members. Even a body of this size did not encompass every significant interest group.

The membership of the commission reflected diverse considerations:

(1) *Occupational.* Five members, including the chairman and vice-chairman, were academicians; three of them were from state universities, the other two from private universities. Of these five, three were specialists in labor and industrial relations; one, a professor of labor law; and one, a specialist in public administration. Five members were lawyers specializing in labor relations law, three for unions and two for employers. Two members were president and vice-president respectively of two of the major industrial corporations in the state. One member was state executive secretary of a major public employee union. One member was a top school administrator. Two members represented the state executive branch. Four members were from the state legislature.

(2) *Geographical.* A majority of the members came from Cook County, which has more than half of the state's population, but downstate was represented by eight members, including the chairman and vice-chairman.

(3) *Economic.* Both employee and employer interests were represented, not by formal designation by the organizations, but with the organizations in mind. Since these are by no means homogeneous categories, however, it was necessary to reflect subgroups. On the employee side, for example, attorneys of the state federation of labor, and the building trades and an executive of the teachers' union were included. On the management side, members were associated with large private industry, school administration, the state chamber of commerce, and the state government. One legislator was legal counsel for several small cities and was active in the affairs of the municipal league.

(4) *Political.* The legislators on the commission—one from each party in each legislative house—were selected by the leaders of the Republican and Democratic parties at the request of the governor.

The commission was given broad discretion under the executive order establishing it "to consider all aspects of employee-employer relations for State and local government agencies; to recommend policies appropriate for promoting fairness, harmony, cooperation and efficiency in public employment; and to consider the need, if any, for establishing additional procedures and machinery (a) to carry out these policies, (b) to deal with issues concerning the representation of governmental employees, and (c) to provide for prompt and fair adjustment of employee grievances." This mandate, however, was understood to relate primarily to the policy on representation and negotiations and was so affirmed by the governor's office after a question about the scope of the commission's inquiry was raised at its opening meeting.

Only two constraints were placed on the commission, but these were important. The first was timing. It was essential to have the final report in the hands of the governor in time for preparation and submission of a bill to the 1967 legislature. March 1 was set as the deadline, allowing seven months from the date of the commission's appointment. Since all of the commission members were heavily involved in full-time occupations and duties and since no budget was provided for a staff, this time limitation seemed serious. As it turned out, the willingness of fourteen members of the commission to spend many hours and days of personal time and to contribute staff assistance was an impressive testimony to their interest and public spirit.

The second constraint was on content. The governor made it clear both privately and publicly that he would not recommend a bill which permitted public employees to strike. The leaders of the legislature, as well as the legislative members of the commission, adopted a similar position. Thus, from the outset the members of the commission, regardless of any personal reservations they may have had, recognized that if their recommendations were to receive serious consideration, they would have to be based on the premise of a legal prohibition of strikes, although the scope of the policy was not a closed issue. On the other hand, although it was not stated explicitly, there was also the premise that the rights of public employees to form or join organizations of their own choice and to engage in collective negotiations for economic and job benefits should be endorsed, and that public employers should be prohibited from interfering with such rights and should be required to bargain with appropriate employee representatives.

THE WORK OF THE COMMISSION

The commission had two main tasks. One was to hammer out a set of recommendations which would be acceptable overall (not necessarily in every respect) to all its members and to the interests which they represented. The other task was to set the stage for public and legislative acceptance by preparing a report which would bear the stamp of technical authority and would convey to many skeptical or even hostile leaders of public opinion (such as newspaper editors, educators, and elected public officials) that the interest of the public at large would be served well.

In preparing its recommendations, the commission was the beneficiary of the experience (both positive and negative) obtained by other states, particularly Wisconsin, Michigan, New York, and Connecticut. A group of research assistants summarized the laws in a dozen states and collected a sizable body of reports and articles on their adoption and administration. The chairman and vice-chairman, as well as other members, held informal discussions with knowledgeable individuals in several states and the commission as a whole had sessions of two to three hours each with four widely known experts: the chairman of the Michigan Labor Mediation Board, a member of the Wisconsin Employment Relations Board, an academician specializing in the public education field, and the executive director of the Public Personnel Association. A comprehensive review of data on Illinois public employee relations, including a mail survey of the municipalities and the school boards, was also undertaken.

Three subcommittees were established to develop the essential questions which the commission had to confront, and to formulate, initially, alternative proposals, and later, recommendations for their resolution. The chairman and vice-chairman coordinated the activities of the commission and one or the other attended all of the subcommittee meetings.

In order to afford all interested parties the opportunity to express their views, the commission decided to hold a series of public hearings in Chicago and Spring-field. The commission was uncertain that these hearings would yield much in the way of new facts or ideas, but it hoped that the publicity given to the hearings would generate interest in the work of the commission and would contribute to the process of educating the public. A set of key questions was sent to a large number of interested organizations which were requested to submit responses in writing, whether or not they wished to give public testimony. In general the employee organizations responded readily, a minor problem being to restrain some of the organizations from sending too many spokesmen. In contrast, the public agencies appeared reluctant to make statements at the hearings and a special effort had to be made to persuade a number of them to testify.

Contrary to expectations, the hearings proved to be of considerable educational value to the members of the commission, most of whom attended one or more of the sessions. New facts were obtained about practices which were vaguely known or completely unknown to the commission. Although some of the witnesses spoke with an eye to the press, many of them responded frankly and thoughtfully to the questions posed by the commission members. Several of the witnesses from the newer public unions displayed an aggressiveness and fervor (as well as an element of inexperience) which recalled attitudes of the early 1930s. Several of the spokesmen for public agencies reflected considerable misunderstanding of the nature of collective negotiations and a fear of its effects on the work of their agencies. On the other hand, some of the witnesses from both sides were highly sophisticated and knowledgeable.

As the subcommittees developed their thinking on the basis of the available literature, the reports from other states, the public hearings, the discussions with the invited experts, and their own experience (especially in the private sector), the main outlines of the proposed recommendations became quite distinct and the areas of doubt and debate were identified. Thus, under the heading of "coverage," there was rather rapid acceptance of the idea that any law should apply to all governmental bodies in the state and that all nonsupervisory employees should be given organizational rights and protections.

But serious questions were raised as to whether (a) supervisors should be included, and (b) policemen, firemen, and prison guards should be excluded or given special limitations. The commission was impressed by the closeness of organizational and personal relationships between supervisors and employees under them in such diverse government operations as the police and fire departments, hospitals, schools, and social work agencies. Partly these ties were professional or semiprofessional; partly they were the result of traditional practice in promotion through the ranks. The haziness of lines of authority and the reluctance to upset long-established patterns posed a serious problem. The security personnel question turned mainly on the issue of possible conflicts of interest in the performance of the police function.

The "scope" of permissible negotiations was a complex and troublesome problem throughout the inquiry and was never fully resolved. One reason for this was that on most money items the public agency must secure the approval of some superior administrative or legislative body or, in the case of many school boards, may have to win public approval through a referendum vote on raising the tax level. This is further complicated in areas like public aid where the federal government provides substantial funds and establishes rules, conditions, or criteria regarding the operations of the program. A second reason was that most state employees and many local employees are governed by civil service codes and commissions and the relationship between civil service and collective negotiations is not yet well understood.

Another commission concern was to protect the managerial function against employee "encroachment" while at the same time safeguarding the employees' interest in the effects on their job security and conditions of employment. Some employee groups, like social workers and teachers, felt that their professional interests necessitated major involvement in shaping the mission of the agency and the standards of public service. Although the commission members generally agreed that consultation with employee groups on these matters was desirable, most were unsympathetic to the idea of subjecting these functions to collective negotiations. The efforts of some groups of public-aid employees to represent the interests of their clients raised another unusual issue which the commission viewed negatively.

The need for a code of unfair practices and for administrative machinery to enforce this code and to deal with representation issues was quickly accepted in the commission. A number of the commission members were experts on the Taft-Hartley law and felt that in these areas the Taft-Hartley experience, with appropriate modifications for the public sector, should be decisive. The following issues aroused considerable debate:

(a) Should the members of the administrative Board be permitted to mediate in collective bargaining impasses as well to adjudicate unfair practice and representation cases?

(b) What criteria, if any, should be specified for appropriate units for negotiations?

(c) Should all employee organizations be required to be certified by the Board through the election process and, if not, should their signed agreements be a bar to representation proceedings initiated by others?

Although serious thought was given to the strike issue and particularly to the distinction between "critical" and "noncritical" strikes, the prohibition of strikes was accepted from the outset as a political fact of life. There was also little question in the minds of the commission members with regard to the desirability of mediation, fact-finding, and other procedures as alternatives to strikes. Three issues posed interesting questions:

(1) In the event of a strike, which official should be responsible for seeking an injunction and for initiating action for contempt in case the injunction is violated?

(2) What penalties should be assessed against strikers and should they be automatic?

(3) Should compulsory arbitration be recommended for either the resolution of grievances or the settlement of new contract terms? Would they be constitutional?

The only other issue to be seriously debated dealt with the effective date of the new law. How much lead time was necessary to get the Board organized and to educate the parties as to the procedures and rules?

The answers which the commission finally gave to the above questions are contained in the published report and recommendations of the commission, and need not be repeated here.[3] Complete agreement on each of these items was not achieved, but the commission members agreed that they could live with the predominant views and that the report as a whole provided "a sound basis for legislation on the subject." The only formal dissents came from two representatives of the legislature who wished to exclude all security personnel from the coverage of the act and to give "home rule" to local governments with more than 75,000 population—the latter provision being formulated primarily for Chicago. One of the two legislators also wanted to delay the effective date of any law for one year.

REACTIONS TO THE COMMISSION INQUIRY
AND ITS RECOMMENDATIONS

In the course of the commission's proceedings, the positions of many of the numerous interest groups began to emerge, but it was not until the end of the legislative session that the positions of some groups became known.[4] Some of these positions were fully crystallized from the start; others went through a considerable process of analysis and formulation; and a few appear to have been changed in the light of increasing political pressures. The interest groups were not only diversified on a functional basis; each of the functional groups was also extremely heterogeneous. On the employee side, for example, most of the involved organizations favored some form of legislation of the type being considered by the commission; but there were some groups which were hostile to any legislation, and among the favorable groups the differences over form were very strong, particularly in connection with the strike issue. For example,

(1) AFSCME, and AFL–CIO union most concerned with public employment outside of education, strongly supported the enactment of a law such as the commission recommended and was prepared to accept the no-strike policy if necessary to get the law. To them a law favoring organization and collective negotiations was a step in the right direction and a wedge for the future.

(2) The American Federation of Teachers seems to have started with a similar position, but during the course of the inquiry, their attitude changed. In Chicago, as in a number of other large cities throughout the country, the AFT had achieved impressive gains through strikes and strike threats, and they were reluctant to abandon what they considered a basic right even though the courts in Illinois and elsewhere had ruled such strikes illegal. During the fall and early winter of 1966-1967, the AFT had used pressure to gain agreements with the Chicago Board of Education, the Cook County Junior College Board, and the school boards in

---

[3]Governor's Advisory Commission on Labor-Management Policy for Public Employees, *Report and Recommendations* (Springfield, Ill.: State of Illinois, 1967).

[4]The session normally convenes once every two years from early January to June 30.

several smaller communities, like Joliet. They became one of the most vigorous opponents of the bill supported by the governor.

(3) Some spokesmen for the Building Service Employees Union initially left the impression that they shared AFSCME's position. In the showdown, they joined the majority of unions in opposing this stand.

(4) The building trades unions, with only a small membership in public employment, enjoyed considerable protection through the prevailing-rate policy, which made it possible for them to obtain the fruits of collective bargaining in the private sector. While symbolically concerned over the no-strike rule, they rarely, if ever, had to use the strike. Their main concern was to protect their craft jurisdiction. They also voiced to the commission some concern about what might happen if there were a change in political control in some governmental jurisdictions. They were more interested in strengthening and broadening the prevailing-wage policy than in the commission's subject. In the end, however, they, too, strongly opposed a bill with a strike ban.

(5) The Fire Fighters Union, AFL–CIO, told the commission that they were unconditionally opposed to strikes and favored a collective bargaining law with a strike ban, although nationally their historic no-strike policy was undergoing restudy and at least one small Illinois city, Danville, was faced with the threat of mass resignations by their firemen in early 1967 over salaries.

(6) The industrial unions in the AFL–CIO had no direct interest in public employment, but some of them vigorously opposed any legislation which explicitly banned public employee strikes.

(7) The collective political instrument of the AFL–CIO unions in the state, the State Federation, made the critical decision. It had historically supported legislative proposals which made no specific reference to a prohibition of strikes. Early in the 1966-1967 session, such a bill again had been introduced in the House. After considerable internal debate, the Federation leaders decided to oppose any legislation which explicitly banned strikes.

(8) Outside of the AFL–CIO, the Illinois Education Association was influenced by the successes of its sister associations in Connecticut, California, Washington, and Oregon. It too desired a law, but wanted a separate law for teachers to be administered by the state Department of Public Education. In the final critical days, however, the IEA leaders decided to support the commission's approach if that were the alternative to no law.

(9) The Illinois Nurses Association, which had become increasingly unionlike in behavior, favored a law and was willing to renounce the strike if arbitration were substituted. Like the AFT, the nurses had found it necessary to exert strike threats (usually in the form of mass resignations and absences) to gain salary increases and formal negotiating rights. During the commission's inquiry, units of the INA had applied such pressure on several occasions in Cook County hospitals. In contrast to the IEA, they did not call for special legislation for the hospitals.

(10) Certain professional groups, like the Illinois Society of Professional Engineers and the Illinois Association of Highway Engineers, opposed the idea of collective bargaining for professionals. They also stressed that if a law was passed, professionals should not be part of the same bargaining units as nonprofessionals. Not all professional groups, however, took a negative position. The Illinois Con-

ference of the American Association of University Professors, for example, saw no reason for professionals being excluded from the coverage of the proposed law.

At least one independent union, the Independent Union of Public Aid Employees, vigorously opposed the idea of a ban on strikes and indicated that they would not be sympathetic to a law containing such a ban. Later there were indications that they regretted this position.

VIEWS OF EMPLOYER ORGANIZATIONS

The diversity of views among employee organizations was matched by the diversity among employer groups. On the whole, however, it was clear that whereas most employee organizations favored legislation which encouraged collective negotiations, most employer organizations viewed the prospect of such legislation with some doubts and fears. For example:

(a) Among private employer organizations, the Illinois Manufacturers Association flatly opposed any legislation favorable to collective negotiations for public employees. The Illinois State Chamber of Commerce, while opposing private-sector collective bargaining for the public sector, appeared to accept the inevitability of some type of legislation. They called for, among other things, a strong ban on strikes with effective penalties, safeguards for professional employees, a separate law for teachers, provision for the preservation of fiscal control by the appropriate public authorities, and a year's lead time before the law took effect.

(b) The Illinois Municipal League, which represents 1,000 of the 1,200 municipalities in the state, took a position which its spokesman at the public hearing asserted to be similar to that of the Chamber of Commerce. The League's written statement was, in fact, more explicit and more positive in that it "encourages legislation which will clarify the right of municipalities to recognize and negotiate with a union of public employees." It opposed compulsory arbitration and the right to strike. It also opposed any legislative effort to impose standard working conditions on a statewide basis.

(c) The top officials of the city of Chicago and Cook County were silent throughout the commission's proceedings. Although no explanation was forthcoming, knowledgeable observers were agreed that Chicago's political leadership was satisfied with the prevailing arrangements with the unions (particularly the building trades, building service employees, and the teamsters) and saw no reason for rocking the boat. From the party standpoint, the informal tie with the unions was important. The union leaders had easy access to City Hall and any problems they had could be resolved quietly and privately. Their members had excellent employment terms and conditions in return for political loyalty. However, a few city divisions expressed views. The acting superintendent of police strongly opposed the coverage of police in a law permitting organization for the purpose of collective negotiations. The fire commissioner voiced support for continuation of the long relationship with the Fire Fighters Union. The Cook County Department of Public Aid stated that it supported the principle of collective bargaining for its employees.

(d) The Association of School Boards reversed a long-standing policy of opposition and endorsed legislation for collective negotiations by school employees; but it insisted that teachers should have their own law, separate from other public employees, and that administrative responsibility should be within the framework of the state Office of Public Instruction. It differed from the Education Association in one important respect.—It would exclude administrative or supervisory personnel, such as principals. In the end the School Board Association agreed to support a single comprehensive bill. The university administrators had been involved in collective bargaining with nonacademic employees for a long time and therefore had no objection to continuation, but they were strongly opposed to the inclusion of academic employees. As a result, they succeeded through quiet legislative discussion in obtaining an exemption of the latter from the key bill.

(e) Although the governor supported the general idea of collective negotiations by public employees, the heads of the several state departments had extremely varied views ranging from strong support to strong opposition. One department head who testified publicly before the commission noted that he had no objection to employees joining unions or to legislation providing this opportunity, but that "it is most unfortunate that a set of circumstances arises in an administrative unit . . . that produces discontent and dissatisfaction to the extent that the staff members turn to union organization."[5] A spokesman for another department felt that present arrangements were satisfactory and that there was no need for a collective bargaining law.

Apart from employee and employer groups such as the foregoing, the only organization to seek an appearance before the commission was the Civic Federation of Chicago, which expressed a strong concern over the possible effects of collective bargaining legislation on the civil service system. The Federation called for a strengthening of the merit system, especially its grievance procedure, for the requirement that all wage and salary negotiations be concluded prior to final statutory appropriation amendment dates, and for the adoption by government of a compensation system based on prevailing wage and salary rates paid in private industry.

THE LEGISLATIVE PROCESS

Even before the commission report was submitted to the governor and made public by him in early March, a number of proposals reflecting several of the above interests were submitted to the legislature for consideration. The earliest bill to be offered—by an individual senator—was concerned solely with strikes and proposed to deprive public employees of their retirement benefits if they went out on strike. It had no significant support and was not seriously considered.

A union-supported bill, H. B. 289, virtually identical with one rejected by the previous (1965) legislature, was introduced in the House by a combination of Democrats and Republicans. Although a majority of Republicans were opposed to the labor position, the State Federation of Labor had traditionally maintained close ties with some Republicans. The son of the Federation's long-time president (who had been a Republican legislator) had been elected several times to the House on the Republican ticket. In the current legislature, a counsel for a group of building trades unions had also been elected as a Republican.

[5]Transcript of hearings held in Springfield, Ill., on Dec. 8, 1966, p. 186 (processed).

In addition to affirming the rights of public employees to self-organization and collective bargaining, H. B. 289 provided for a fact-finding procedure to resolve impasses in bargaining. Strikes and lockouts were to be prohibited during a ninety day fact-finding period, although the parties could agree to an extension. The House Committee on Industry and Labor Relations voted, however, to amend H. B. 289 to include a prohibition on strikes and when it came to the House floor it was tabled.

Senate Bill 452 was introduced by a senate member of the commission who, however, had not participated in the commission's deliberations. This bill accepted the principles of employee organization and collective negotiations, but it explicitly prohibited all strikes, provided strong penalties in the event of strikes, and gave citizens the right to apply for a court injunction if the counsel for the public agency which was struck did not act promptly to do so. The bill quickly received committee approval; but since it subsequently became the vehicle for the main debate on the commission's proposals, it will be discussed in more detail later.

Two other bills were introduced in the House at the request of the Illinois Education Association to provide separate legislation for teachers in primary and secondary schools and in higher education. The first of these bills (H. B. 831) was ultimately adopted by the House but failed in the Senate. The AFT also sponsored a separate bill for teachers; it was essentially a declaration of policy favoring collective bargaining for teachers. This bill did not get out of committee.

The commission's report was well received by the governor. He informed the commission and the press that with one small qualification he supported the recommendations in the report and would have a bill introduced on the basis of it. The qualification was that prison guards would be required, like the police, to restrict their activities to those organizations which were not associated in any way with nonsecurity employees. Members of the commission worked closely with lawyers of the legislative reference bureau and the governor's office on the draft of the bill.

Despite the apparent agreement among the interest groups represented on the commission, the governor's bill, which was sent to the legislature with a message of strong endorsement on May 1, 1967, immediately found itself in troubled waters. The agreement in the commission proved not to reflect the political reality. Initially, the governor sought to have his bill substituted for House Bill 289, but the chief sponsors of that bill declined. Instead, the governor's bill was introduced in the Senate by three leading Democrats as Senate Bill 1595. There then followed an interesting and somewhat surprising compromise move. The sponsors of S.B. 452 reached an agreement with spokesmen for the governor's bill and with representatives of AFSCME to merge the two bills under the label of amended S.B. 452.

The new S.B. 452 used the governor's bill as the nucleus but contained some thirteen changes, most of which were derived from the old 452. The preamble and justification for the bill were revised and elaborated to put more emphasis than S.B. 1595 had on the obligations of public employees and less on the need to improve working conditions and correct inequities. The definition of a strike was broadened to include concerted "abstinence in whole or in part from the full, faithful and proper performance of the duties of employment. . . ." University academic employees were excluded from the new board's jurisdiction. Policemen, prison guards, and firemen were confined to separate bargaining units and to representation by local unions not admitting other employees as members, but these locals could be affiliated to national unions representing other employees as well. The union and agency shops were specifically excluded. And most serious from the standpoint of unionists, any citizen or organization could intervene in a strike situation to seek damages if an injunction was being violated and also, if the public employer did not seek an injunction within forty-eight hours after the occurrence of a strike, such citizen or organization could file such a suit in the name of the state. The amended S.B. 452 was adopted by the Senate on June 5 by a vote of 37 to 11.

When S.B. 452 was reported to the House, it was challenged by the AFL–CIO State Federation of Labor and all of the major unions except AFSCME. The House Executive Committee, however, approved the bill and referred it to the Appropriations Committee which did likewise. But the latter's vote was close, 16-13, and even more significantly, was reported to be on a straight party basis, with none of the Democrats favoring the bill despite the governor's support. This was the first open indication that the Chicago Democratic administration would support the unions which opposed the bill and was not merely seeking the exclusion of its own area from the jurisdiction of the proposed new board. When S.B. 452 came before the full House for a second reading (the amendment stage), the unions retained the virtually unanimous support of the Democrats and with a minority of Republicans were able to pass two crucial amendments, providing for the agency shop and limiting the strike ban to the lifetime of agreements. The votes on these issues were 92 to 70 and 83 to 81, respectively. The right of citizen intervention in injunction proceedings was also eliminated without challenge. The bill as amended then passed the House, 107 to 59. The final vote reflected the mixture of feelings on the bill: 75 Republicans and 32 Democrats voted in favor; 18 Republicans and 41 Democrats voted in opposition.

In the waning hours of the legislative session, the House and Senate versions of S.B. 452 went to a joint conference committee of four Republicans and two Democrats. No agreement could be reached on the key issues in dispute. The committee, by a four to two party vote, adopted essentially the Senate version with a number of minor revisions. The bill was easily approved in the Senate, 37 to 19. But in the House the labor ranks held and the bill was defeated by a vote of 73 to 82, with only four Democrats in favor.[6] Only seventeen Republicans voted against the bill, although twelve others, including the Speaker, exerted a similar effect by abstaining. Thus ended the strongest effort to enact a clear public policy on collective bargaining for Illinois public employees since the vetoed bill of 1945.

CONCLUSIONS

One might simply conclude from the failure of the legislature to enact the bill that an old maxim of Illinois politics had been reaffirmed: if a labor bill is vigorously opposed by either the main body of unions or the major management organizations, it will not pass. It is after all no accident that Illinois has less labor legislation than other important industrial states and that such meaningful legisla-

---

[6]The margin of defeat was greater than these figures reflect because under the Illinois constitution, a bill must receive a majority of all members of the House or 89 votes.

tion as it has (notably workmen's compensation and unemployment insurance) emerged out of the agreed bill process.[7]

But the 1967 legislative history suggests other conclusions as well. One is that a vigorous labor movement has autonomous sources of vitality and need not depend on a law to achieve its aims. No law may be preferred to an unsatisfactory one, especially if tight labor market conditions prevail or if a local political arrangement is favorable. The American Federation of Teachers, especially in the Chicago and East St. Louis areas, appears to have acted on the former premise; the building services and building trades unions on the latter. On the other hand, a number of the unions and associations, such as AFSCME and the Illinois Nurses Association, even with labor shortages in the latter case, considered the absence of protective legislation a serious handicap. The Cook County social workers also discovered, somewhat belatedly, that a recalcitrant public employer can pose a major obstacle.

A second important inference to be drawn from this episode is that formal collective bargaining may be viewed as a threat to political party arrangements. An informal alliance between a dominant party and various union leaders enables the party to develop and maintain a strong machine and peaceful employee relations while the involved union leaders are assured organizational stability and favorable terms for their members. If a dispute develops, the party leaders are free, in the absence of lawfully constituted dispute settlement machinery, to work out ad hoc agreements. If the party has effective leadership and strong controls, this approach can prevent most disputes from ever reaching public attention. The system encounters difficulty only if a rank-and-file rebellion occurs or the party machinery loses control in a particular sector.

A third conclusion is that legislative thinking about public employee organization and bargaining appears to focus on the important but limited issue of strikes. The governor's commission made a strong effort to set the problem of public employee relations in a broad framework of equities and responsibilities, of achieving high standards of employment and effective performance of the public service. But neither the press nor the majority of the legislature appreciated the significance of this approach. Neither realized that strikes are, in large measure, a symptom of underlying relationships, practices, and conditions and that what was of paramount importance was the establishment of rules and procedures which would encourage public managers and public employees to identify, define, and try to resolve their mutual problems in an orderly and equitable way.

[7]For an explanation of this phenomenon, see Gilbert Y. Steiner, *Legislation by Collective Bargaining* (Urbana, Ill.: Institute of Labor and Industrial Relations, University of Illinois, 1951).

LOBBYING

Michael H. Moskow

J. Joseph Loewenberg

Edward C. Koziara

Lobbying is direct representation by an interest group to the legislative branches of federal, state, or local government. A lobbying group "makes certain claims upon other groups in the society for the establishment, maintenance or enhancement of forms of behavior. . . ."

The term "lobbying" has sinister connotations; a popular conception is that lobbyists wine and dine legislators, offer bribes, and contribute to or withhold support in elections. Although such methods are used, lobbyists can more effectively influence politicians by marshaling widespread public support.

Actually, lobbyists perform an important service in a democracy. They provide legislators with important technical information and convey to legislators the implications of legislation for the voters. At the state level particularly, legislators have neither the time nor the staff to assess such implications adequately.

LOBBYING IN PUBLIC EMPLOYMENT

Lobbying activity by public employee organizations is unique, because the lobbyists are employees of the political jurisdiction or of a jurisdiction subordinate to that of the legislators. Certain advantages flow from this unique relationship. The lobbyist for the public employee is generally more sensitive to the location of power because members of his group work in close proximity with the legislators. Public employees may lobby informally with legislators directly. The constant proximity of the public employee to the employer may give disproportionate weight to the views of the public employee.

Three separate groups lobby to influence the terms and the conditions of public employment: employers, employees, and the general public. The goals of these groups do not necessarily conflict, because their goals are frequently independent of one another. For example, in the same situation a public employee organization might lobby for a better pension plan; a taxpayers group might oppose

---

Reprinted from *Collective Bargaining in Public Employment* by Michael H. Moskow, J. Joseph Loewenberg and Edward C. Koziara, Random House, 1970. Michael H. Moskow is Associate Professor of Economics, Temple University. J. Joseph Loewenberg is Associate Professor of Management, Temple University. Edward C. Koziara is Associate Professor of Economics, Drexel University.

such a plan; and a good-government group might call for higher initial salaries. In this situation the employing organization has the option of siding with one of the parties, of taking an independent course of action, or of generating no pressure whatsoever.

LOBBYING EXPENDITURES

Public employee organizations have spent considerable sums on lobbying activity. In 1966 three public employee organizations were ranked among the first twenty-five spenders in lobbying at the federal level: in first place was the United Federation of Post Office Clerks ($287,000); in fifteenth place was the National Education Association ($73,100); and in twenty-first place was the National Association of Letter Carriers ($58,500). Other large spenders among public employee organizations include the National Federation of Federal Employees, the National Rural Letter Carriers, and District Lodge 44 of the International Association of Machinists (AFL–CIO).

These lobbying expenditures were used for different purposes. The International Association of Machinists supported federal pay increases and opposed the closing of government installations. The National Association of Letter Carriers pursued federal pay increases and retirement benefits. The National Education Association spent funds to obtain federal grants for education.

No comprehensive listing of expenditures for lobbying on the state or local level is available. Where states require filing of such expenditures, state public employee organizations are prominent among reporting lobbying groups.

Expenditures are not the only effective means used in lobbying. Personal relationships can influence decision-makers. For example, fire fighters of one southern city requested the head of the state federation of labor, a former fire fighter, to plead their case to the state legislature. As a result of his lobbying efforts, and at minimal cost to the fire fighters' organization, municipal fire fighters gained increases in various state benefits.

LEVELS OF LOBBYING ACTIVITY

Public employee organizations lobby at various levels of government. Lobbying activities are directed at sources of authority where decisions over terms and conditions of employment take place. A municipal union may attempt to simultaneously persuade aldermen on the city council to act favorably on certain matters within their purview and exert pressures on the state legislature controls. In some cases, a city employee organization will engage in much greater lobbying activity at the state level than at the city level.

Despite the lobbying efforts of public employee groups at higher levels of government, a local group will probably have less success lobbying at the state level than it will have at the local level. As a general principle in lobbying, the probability of success is likely to decrease as the level of authority increases—because higher levels of authority are subject to a larger number of lobbying groups and more diversified pressures than are lower levels.

Public employee organizations composed of workers who perform essential services, such as organizations of fire fighters and policemen, are reputed to be astute lobbyists. Some observers suggest that the essential nature of the public safety services helps make their lobbying activities particularly effective. Part of the effectiveness of police and fire-fighting organizations has also resulted from the ability of these groups to wield a cohesive power block, which originates in the paramilitary nature of their occupations. Moreover, public safety personnel are more likely than any other group of public employees to be excluded from collective bargaining. When such personnel do bargain, the scope of the bargaining is often more restricted than that for employees performing nonessential services. Public safety organizations therefore have a greater propensity to turn to lobbying in order to secure benefits than do those organizations of employees performing nonessential services. In other words, public safety organizations may be more skilled at lobbying because of their greater experience with, and their greater reliance on, lobbying.

TYPOLOGY OF PUBLIC EMPLOYEE LOBBYING

Lobbying is used by public employee organizations to achieve a number of different goals, which may add or detract from viable collective bargaining in the public sector. This section presents a typology of different forms of lobbying by public employee organizations. At any particular time an employee organization may engage in one or in a number of the different lobbying techniques discussed.

Lobbying for Collective Bargaining Legislation

Public employee organizations may use lobbying to obtain or to strengthen collective bargaining legislation for public employees. In particular, public employee organizations that have difficulty securing consent recognition may lobby to secure recognition through legislation. If lobbying is undertaken to obtain collective bargaining legislation, the rules of collective bargaining are established or fortified, thereby encouraging and stabilizing bargaining. If the resulting legislation is permissive the employer legally may bargain. If the legislation is mandatory, the employer *must* bargain.

There are exceptions to the above generalization that legislation strengthens collective bargaining. Legislation allowing for proportional representation could, for instance, detract from collective bargaining.

Lobbying for Nonnegotiable Topics

Public employees may also lobby for benefits that have been excluded from negotiations either by law or by tradition. For example, after moonlighting by police was declared nonnegotiable in New York City, police lobbied with the state legislature and secured legislative permission to moonlight. Lobbying for non-bargainable issues shifts the attention of the parties from bargaining to political involvement. The total effect of such lobbying on bargaining depends upon the importance and the number of issues excluded from bargaining.

Lobbying as a Substitute for Bargaining

Lobbying may also substitute for bargaining. Rather than bargain, the organization may lobby for a wage increase with members of the finance committee, because it believes it can secure a larger wage increase. Lobbying for items that can be collectively bargained weakens the bargaining process. Every increment of such lobbying activity diminishes the importance of bargaining. The ultimate point is reached when the organization rejects bargaining completely and resorts to lobbying for all issues.

Lobbying for Limits on Working Conditions

Lobbying may establish limits on a working condition subject to bargaining and thereby affect the range of bargaining on that condition. For example, state laws often specify minimum hours teachers must teach each day for the district to qualify for state aid. The maximum number of hours that a fire fighter may work per week is also frequently legislated. These minimums and maximums affect the parties' maneuverability in collective bargaining. Whether this kind of lobbying adds to or detracts from collective bargaining depends on whether the results of the lobbying widen or narrow the range for bargaining in the specific working condition. In some cases, lobbying may have little effect on negotiations—for instance, if state legislated maximum working hours are reduced to a level above the existing negotiated schedule of hours.

"End Run" Lobbying

The employee organization may engage in "end run" lobbying while collective bargaining negotiations are in process. If the organization is dissatisfied with the progress of negotiations, it may attempt to place pressures on the negotiator through the elected officials. This type of political pressure undercuts the negotiator's position and undermines collective bargaining. Agreement is formally reached through the bargaining process, but in reality the outcome is achieved through lobbying.

"Carom" Lobbying

The employee organization may engage in "carom" lobbying if negotiations do not yield the desired result. Carom lobbying occurs after the union and the negotiator have reached agreement. The union may then attempt to improve the package by getting in touch with the chief executive or the legislative body. Carom lobbying subverts collective bargaining and affects future bargaining. It also destroys the trust of one party in the other. For example, management may have given a quid pro quo in order to induce the union to make a concession. But if the union has attempted to obtain further benefits from the legislative body, management will be reluctant to make concessions in future bargaining.

Employer Lobbying

Employer lobbying may add to or detract from collective bargaining. Management may feel that collective bargaining legislation will improve labor relations. The employer may also assist the employee organization in making a bid for increased appropriations to enhance the jurisdiction's ability to pay. On the other hand, employers may oppose legislation to establish collective bargaining or to increase the scope of bargaining.

LOBBYING OR COLLECTIVE BARGAINING?

An employee organization has certain goals that reflect the desires and needs of its leaders, its members, and the organization as an institution. Organization policies depend on the power positions of the leadership and the rank and file and on the survival and the growth requirements of the organization.

Public employee organizations often use lobbying both as an alternative and a supplement to collective bargaining. The key to the selection of tactics is the perception of the employee organization decision makers. To some extent perception will be colored by past experiences; new events and the nature of the issue may also be factors in determining the tactic to be used.

The organization will use collective bargaining when the perceived benefits per dollar of expenditure are greater than the perceived benefits per dollar of expenditure in lobbying. This decision may be represented by the formula

where: CBb = change in collective bargaining benefits
          dCBc = change in collective bargaining costs
          dLb = change in lobbying benefits
          dLc = change in lobbying costs.

As the relationship of the four factors changes, so, too, will the behavior of the employee organization. For instance, an organization that has had success with lobbying may believe that dLB>dCBb and dCBb>0 (the benefits of lobbying outweigh those of collective bargaining, and collective bargaining involves costs). In this case, the organization will continue to lobby. Where one method results in no benefits, the organization will inevitably employ the other.

The costs and benefits used in the decision whether to lobby or to bargain are largely anticipatory. The benefits may not be realized because there is no guarantee that the employee organization will win what it expects to win with either method. A certain portion of the costs may be fixed—for example, lobbyists on a retainer or professional staff preparing for collective bargaining. Other costs, however, are variable and less determinable. For example, the union may make political contributions to curry favor with certain legislators.

UNION LOBBYING AT THE FEDERAL LEVEL

Patrick J. Nilan

The right of a citizen to lobby his government is protected by the First Amendment to the Constitution of the United States. Lobbying is often regarded today as the most important expression of the right of petition. Two federal court decisions of the early 1950s cast doubt on the constitutionality of the Federal Regulation of Lobbying Act of 1946, which requires registration and financial reporting by lobbyists. In a 1954 decision, the Supreme Court limited the scope of the 1946 act by defining lobbying strictly as "direct communication with members of Congress on pending or proposed federal legislation."[1] Despite this legal tradition, public attitudes toward lobbying remain ambivalent at best.

These attitudes have been conditioned by two factors: first, widely publicized excesses in lobbying activities during the early history of this country; and, second, a general ignorance of the role of lobbying in a democracy.[2] Lobbying continues to be described today with such semantically loaded terms as "pressure group" and "special interests." If, instead, we would characterize the lobbyist as a legislative representative who alerts and directs the politician toward the desires of the people, and the people toward the politician, then perhaps the public could arrive at a better understanding of lobbying at the federal level.

This perception of lobbying as an integral part of the governmental process has been forwarded by a number of widely respected political scientists.[3] As Kelly

---

Patrick Nilan is Legislative Director, United Federation of Postal Clerks (AFL–CIO). Article prepared specifically for this volume.

[1]Corwin, Small, and Jayson, eds., *The Constitution of the United States: Analysis and Interpretation* (Washington, D.C.: Government Printing Office, 1964), p. 920. Justices Black, Douglas, and Jackson contended the act should be held void for vagueness and as violative of the First Amendment.

[2]A typical account has James Buchanan writing to Franklin Pierce in 1852: "The host of contractors, speculators, stockjobbers and lobby members which haunt the halls of Congress, all desirous . . . on any and every pretext to get their arms into the public treasury, are sufficient to alarm every friend of his country." Karl Schriftgiesser, *The Lobbyists* (New York: Atlantic-Little Brown, 1951), p. 7.

[3]"Private organizations may be regarded as links that connect the citizen and government." V. O. Key, Jr., *Public Opinion and American Democracy* (New York: Alfred A. Knopf, 1961),

suggests, government does not take place in a vacuum.[4] A legislator can neither be fully informed on the myriad number of subjects which require decisions of him nor can he be adequately aware of the opinion of his constituents on all this legislative outpouring: more than ten thousand bills and resolutions are introduced in most sessions of Congress with perhaps five hundred to one thousand enacted in some form. He needs help. The legislator also needs information and ideas which can be developed into policy proposals. This supply function is a major *raison d'etre* of the lobbyist.

There are other significant functions fulfilled by the lobbyist which have been amply discussed elsewhere.[5] These include giving representation to minority groups, implementing the democratic process through the conflict of opinion, alerting the community to proposed legislation which affects it, and helping to make the separation of powers in government workable by exerting a unifying force on both the legislative and the executive branches.

In addition to the above general functions of lobbying, the postal unions and specifically the United Federation of Postal Clerks (AFL–CIO) have another responsibility in representations to the federal government on behalf of their members, This unique role arises from the fact that members of UFPC, as employees of the government, are forbidden by law to strike. As it is Congress which determines working hours, wages, fringe benefits, job descriptions, and other work-related matters for UFPC members, lobbying of Congress takes the place of collective bargaining procedures utilized by most other workers in the United States.

Today the UFPC consists of some one hundred eighty-three thousand workers. The union's history extends back to 1890 with the formation of the National Association of Post Office Clerks. The UFPC and eight other postal employee unions represent more than six hundred fifty thousand workers in the Post Office Department or about 90 percent of the total work force. As an indication of the leadership UFPC assumes in lobbying Congress for its members, the union during 1966-1968 reported spending more on lobbying than did any other organization, according to a *Congressional Quarterly* compilation.[6] The UFPC will likely be near the top again in the 1969 reporting of lobbying spending because of the activity in the 91st Congress to reform or do away with the Post Office Department as it is known today.

The spending report forms provided by the Clerk of the House and Secretary of the Senate contain blanks for listing eight types of spending: public relations and

---

p. 500; "It is hard to imagine how committees and Congressmen would carry on without the lobbyist." William R. Young, *Introduction to American Government* (New York: Appleton-Century-Crofts, 1966), p. 281.

[4]"Any system of government, autocratic or democratic, owes its life to some kind of support in public opinion." Stanley Kelly, Jr. *Professional Public Relations and Political Power* (Baltimore: The Johns Hopkins Press, 1956), p. 3.

[5]See Norman John Powell, *Anatomy of Public Opinion* (New York: Prentice-Hall, Inc., 1951), pp. 182-188.

[6]"This ranking is probably misleading since many organizations are not required to submit lobby spending reports because of loopholes in lobby laws." *Congressional Quarterly*, XXVII, No. 25 (June 20, 1969), 1097. UFPC reported spending $170,784 in 1968, $277,524 in 1967, and $286,971 in 1966.

advertising services; wages, salaries, fees, and commissions other than public relations and advertising; gifts or contributions; printed or duplicated matter including distribution costs; office overhead; telephone and telegraph; travel, food, lodging, and entertainment; and all other expenses. No government officials check the accuracy and completeness of the reporting.

LEGISLATIVE INTERESTS

The UFPC in its lobbying interests is primarily concerned with so-called "bread and butter" issues for its members. One might conclude that such seemingly pedestrian matters as pay scales and retirement benefits respond to a routine, formalized approach which has been developed by the union over the decades of working with Congress. Nothing could be further from the truth. In reality, the "bread and butter" issues are not simple. In recent years, for example, they have been bound up with national fiscal policy, inflation, the Vietnam war, and reorganization of the Post Office Department. And Congress is not a docile old woman who responds eagerly to a compliment and the promise of a few votes. Also, as the postal unions traditionally have set the pattern of wage increases and benefits for other government employees, there exists this larger complicating factor in UFPC efforts to gain benefits for its members.

Representation of the postal clerks' interests is a highly involved and demanding responsibility. In any given session of Congress there are likely to be literally hundreds of bills introduced which are of special interest to the postal clerks union. These proposals cover salary legislation, employee-management relations, establishment of the basic work week, life insurance, sick leave credits, health matters, optional retirement, regulations for overtime, extension of rural mail delivery, protection of privacy, equality for married women employees, elimination of political influence in appointments, establishment of legal holidays, provision for mandatory retirement, cost-of-living allowances, broadening of political activities permitted federal employees, curtailment of railway post offices, provision of parking space for postal employees and patrons, improvement of reimbursement of employees' moving expenses—and many other topics! Many of the legislative proposals will be prepared by the UFPC's Legislative Department in pursuit of the union's major legislative objectives as established at its biennial convention. Some bills will be drafted by the other postal unions. Members of Congress will introduce bills. Private organizations with special interests in postal affairs, such as the American Newspaper Publishers Association or the Direct Mail Advertising Association, Inc., may seek to have bills introduced. This heavy outpouring of proposed legislation of vital interest to UFPC membership is quite ordinary and does not include the considerable workload created by special issues which may arise in Congress.

Postal reform has been a perennial concern in Congress. Some see it in financial terms and seek a solution which would make the Post Office Department self-supporting. Others stress improved service as the primary objective. The interests of the seven hundred fifty thousand persons working in the Post Office Department are deeply involved in any major change. There are political and historical influences at work.

Before discussing lobbying methods used in an issue such as the postal reform, an important point needs stressing: Many groups and individuals will have interests in the outcome of such a significant issue. While these issues may not in themselves conflict, they may ultimately result in legislative conflict. For example, the American Business Press, an organization of more than one hundred publishing companies, may favor the private corporation concept because it feels that this solution will be more efficient than the present Post Office Department. The Magazine Publishers Association, another organization of 125 firms, may weigh the merits of the two bills in terms of ultimate changes in postal rates. The postal unions see the issue as one of job security and collective bargaining rights. Some legislators may dislike the notion of giving up control over the Post Office Department. thus the range of motives aroused by significant legislative changes is complex. The lobbyist must be aware of and responsive to such conditions if he is to adequately represent his own organization.

If an organization is to operate in a reasonably efficient and rational manner in the face of this plethora of legislative proposals, there must be a system by which to focus on those objectives considered of primary importance by the group's membership. The postal clerks accomplish this by establishing at their biennial national conventions a priority list or Major Legislative Program for the United Federation of Postal Clerks. The convention also selects one of these legislative priorities as its "paramount issue." This paramount issue concerns a problem of general and overriding significance, usually a legislative objective which has been supported and sought after through several sessions of Congress. This was the case in the 1968 national convention which approved an eleven-point major legislative program with the achievement of labor-management by law as its paramount issue.

APPROACHES TO LOBBYING

There exist no pat formulas or guaranteed techniques for achieving specific objectives in the legislative environment. Competing and often conflicting interests rule out such a comforting notion. The essence of successful lobbying lies in effective communication which, in the experience of the UFPC, has three characteristics: purposeful, personal, and persistent.[7]

To be purposeful, communication whether with congressmen, UFPC membership, or the general public must be focused clearly on an objective. The language must be understandable, the message concise. And while all communication cannot be personal in nature, if there is a choice, the more personal means is desirable. Fifty union members visiting their respective congressmen in Washington have more impact than ten times that number of telegrams sent to the legislators' offices. The message needs repeating, especially if the objective is to build support among the general public for a union goal.

There are generally four communication situations involved in lobbying activities. They are as follows:

---

[7]The concept that the more personal communication is, the more effective it can be in affecting attitudes is generally accepted. See Joseph T. Klapper, *The Effects of Mass Communication* (Glencoe: Free Press, 1960), pp. 68-72, 106-110. Also see the section on repetition and variation in Wilbur Schramm, ed., *The Process and Effects of Mass Communication* (Urbana, Ill.: University of Illinois Press, p. 1954), p. 316.

The Lobbyist and the Legislator

A constellation of interests draws together the legislator and the lobbyist. The lobbyist can provide assistance by supplying information and ideas. For the congressman, there is the stark fact that the views expressed by the lobbyist represent attitudes of a certain segment of voters. It is for the congressman to weigh these opinions and to evaluate the importance of the group forwarding them.

There is another especially relevant factor: both the lobbyist and the legislator tend to develop a long-term interest and perhaps an expertise in the field of a committee's responsibility. Both have a mutual interest in the subject, for different reasons perhaps, and this mutuality of interest provides an environment in which the lobbyist may work effectively. And work he does. In any session of Congress, the UFPC legislative director and other union representatives will appear before committees twenty or more times. The many bills must be analyzed, UFPC positions prepared, and the concerned congressmen informed. The active and effective lobbyist establishes contacts in Congress and develops these relationships not only as a legislative representative of an organization but as a colleague who is part of the political process.

The Lobbyist and UFPC Members

A variety of channels are utilized for maintaining communication between the membership of UFPC and their legislative representatives. The foundation of this communication is the biennial national convention which develops and approves a legislative program. Supplementing the national conventions are UFPC Legislative Conferences held in Washington each year usually before Congress takes a mid-session recess. The Legislative Conference not only fires up the membership interest in legislation desired by UFPC, but it offers a valuable opportunity to set three thousand or more postal clerks knocking at the office doors of their congressmen, telling them face to face what they want. The conferences also give the UFPC legislative director and other union officers an excellent opportunity to canvass a wide sector of the membership, sounding out attitudes and receiving suggestions.

A series of publications keeps the membership informed of legislative developments and strategy throughout the year. These include a monthly magazine, *The Union Postal Clerk and Transport Journal,* a Biennial Report prepared for each UFPC national convention, a monthly *Washington Postal Newsletter,* and a weekly *Federation News Service Bulletin.* UFPC also distributes locally copies of news stories, columns, and magazine articles which relate to union programs and legislative objectives.

The Legislator and UFPC Members

Members of postal unions are probably more knowledgeable about the workings of Congress than most citizens of America. Their conditions of work require it. Both the UFPC leadership and members place great confidence in the principle that face-to-face contact between the union member and his congressman is the best possible means to achieve legislative objectives. This is a major function of the annual Legislative Conference, as mentioned above. Most congressmen concerned with postal matters make it a point to appear at these conferences; for them their appearance is something of a political imperative. At the June 1969 Legislative Conference, more than 3,150 UFPC delegates attended. In a series of group breakfasts and luncheons, the delegates met with the legislators and, as reported in the following month's issue of *The Union Postal Clerk,* "laid it on the line."

The UFPC members are alerted on how and where to contact their congressmen when Congress recesses and the legislators go home to campaign. The postal clerks are kept informed of the status of various congressional bills and of what to tell their congressmen. Time is taken at the Legislative Conference to review with UFPC members the art of writing to their congressmen.

There is one other vital dimension involved, especially in this situation: it is the role of the Woman's Auxiliary. Letters from the lady of the house tend to carry particular weight with members of Congress, couched as they so frequently are in the expertise of the homemaker and relating to such fundamental matters as the high cost of food, clothing, medicine, or taxes.

The letters of wives or mothers also tend to carry a greater emotional impact not only on fiscal issues but in such spheres as working conditions, fringe benefits, and generalized frustration over inadequate job satisfaction, work fulfillment, or social adjustment.

Indeed, the United Federation of Postal Clerks and the postal unions generally have been unusually sophisticated in recognizing early the validity of the latter-day injunction: Never underestimate the power of a woman! Thus the Woman's Auxiliary of the UFPC was born more than half a century ago.[8]

Another practical consideration, of course, is the fact that Auxiliary members, unlike the parent unionists, suffer no restrictions on their right of political expression. Members of Congress have found that so-called "Petticoat Brigades" prove their value in states and congressional districts in providing enthusiasm and enterprise for new voter registration, political rallies, and nose-counting chores generally.

While their husbands or fathers are sternly inhibited under the proscriptions of the federal Hatch Act, the ladies in their infinite freedom roam at will in the world of political action with talent, time, and money. The UFPC Auxiliary, for example, has maintained for many years a $10,000 legislative fund invested at from 4 1/2 to 5 percent interest from which limited funds can be withdrawn annually to help subsidize the "educational" activities of the ladies.

With sixty-five hundred active adult members in fifty states, Puerto Rico, and the District of Columbia, all devoted primarily to the welfare and needs of their menfolk, the Auxiliary constitutes a collateral legislative asset of highly useful dimensions.

For a lobbyist these varying forms of contact between voter and politician can be the most productive approach to achieving legislative objectives.

---

[8]"Wives of postal clerks fully realized that their hopes and aspirations for their families were inseparably united with the advancement of the union of their husbands." Karl Baarslag, *History of the National Federation of Post Office Clerks (Washington, D.C., 1945), p. 192.*

The Lobbyist and the General Public

A lobbyist's concern with the general public will depend on the nature of his business with Congress and the organization or individuals he represents. In any case, to neglect the work of keeping the public informed on the issues and problems of the organization one represents is to court disaster. By the nature of their employment, postal workers have continuing contact with the general public. When this exposure is reinforced with information and publicity from other channels, it is possible to build up an effective base of sympathy and support for postal workers in general and the UFPC in particular.

The lobbyist should carry out many of the standard tactics of the promotion-public relations agent. These include developing good relations with the media; systematically providing news release material to local unionists who in turn see that it gets to the area's newspaper; promptly answering newspaper and magazine articles which project distorted or unfavorable views of postal matters; providing reporters with original material for stories; and other approaches.

In the final analysis, the primary responsibility of the lobbyist is to make a strong, clear, and fair case for his client. If he does this and the case is just, the effort will generally be successful.

MULTILATERAL BARGAINING IN THE PUBLIC SECTOR

Kenneth McLennan
Michael H. Moskow

The multilateral nature of collective bargaining in the public sector has been alluded to by many commentators, but the distinction from the bilateral approach which frequently characterizes private sector bargaining has rarely been explicitly discussed.[1] By definition bargaining is multilateral when more than two groups are

Kenneth McLennan and Michael Moskow are Associate Professors of Economics, Temple University. Reprinted from 22nd *Annual Proceedings,* Industrial Relations Research Association, 1969. The Temple University Manpower Research Institutional Grant from the U.S. Department of Labor provided partial support for this study.

[1]See for example, George H. Hildebrand "The Public Sector" in John T. Dunlop and Neil W. Chamberlain (ed.) *Frontiers of Collective Bargaining,* (New York: Harper and Row, 1967), pp. 126-28.

involved in the bargaining process. It is possible for the additional parties to participate in the negotiating sessions, but typically the third party groups operate on the
fringe of the bargaining. In order for these groups to influence bargaining, they
must be in a position to impose a cost (economic, political or otherwise) on the
parties to the agreement.[2]

Under this definition of multilateral bargaining it is conceivable that bargaining
in the private sector which begins as a bilateral process may assume multilateral
dimensions. This transformation would occur if the parties thought that the federal
government intended to use its power to impose a cost on them. Only a few recent
situations have occurred, however, when such power was displayed. Examples
would include government threats to release stockpiles of raw materials such as
aluminum or reassigning federally financed construction contracts. Similarly, the
use of the Taft-Hartley eighty day injunction in some instances may have changed
bilateral bargaining to multilateral bargaining.

On the other hand, mediation and appeals for restraint without sanctions do
not constitute multilateral bargaining. The mediator's role is to secure a settlement
regardless of the impact of the terms on the parties. Any system of "wage-price
guide posts" which relies on voluntary compliance is similarly not multilateral.

Consumer groups, in some instances, may be able to impose moderate costs on
the parties in private sector negotiations. Some consumers can switch their purchases to competing products if the settlement raises prices or if a strike cuts off
the original source of supply. This transfer usually reduces profits and employment
thus negatively affecting both parties. The existence of industry-wide agreements,
pattern setting bargains, and the influence of union wage rates in the nonunionized
sector restricts incentives to transfer purchases. Nevertheless, marginal transfers of
purchases can be influential particularly in a competitive product market.

The typical multilateral nature of bargaining in the public sector is usually
attributed to the pricing characteristic of the market for a public service. Some
public services are supplied at no direct cost to the consumer as in the case of
public education and police protection; other services are provided at a price below
the average cost of providing the service. In either case consumers are to some
extent being subsidized.

The subsidy is borne out of tax revenues which are provided by both users and
nonusers of the service. Consequently, taxpayers will have an interst in any labor-
management negotiations which are likely to raise the cost of the service and which
may also increase the cost of financing the subsidy. If taxpayers are organized into
groups which represent their views to decision-makers and threaten to impose a
political cost, it is likely that there will be an indirect effect on negotiations.

VARIATIONS IN PUBLIC SECTOR MULTILATERAL BARGAINING

Multilateral bargaining varies among public employment jurisdictions and
among different services within a jurisdiction. The exact extent of multilateral
bargaining depends on the existence of an interest group structure, the scope of

---

[2]It has even been argued that bargains can frequently be struck when there is no communication between the bargainers, simply by tacit observation on the part of both parties of some

bargaining, the perceived impact of a work stoppage, and to some extent the bargaining tactics of the parties.

The interest group structure consists of a number of groups or individuals who represent sections of the community to the suppliers of the service. Well-defined interest group structures tend to develop when the public places considerable importance on the quality of the service. In general, organized interest groups at the federal and state level tend to be more permanent and have better financial backing than local groups. Many local interest groups are voluntary organizations, and their effectiveness varies to some extent with the personality and enthusiasm of their leaders. In small communities, the lack of a permanent well-defined interest group is likely to restrict the amount of communication between the parties to the negotiations and segments of the community. For this reason, the potential extent of multilateral bargaining in small communities is expected to be much less than is possible in large cities. It is possible, of course, for an individual who holds a key position in the power structure of the community to perform the same function as the interest group structure.

The scope of bargaining varies within the public sector. For example, federal employees do not bargain on wages, while some groups of social workers have attempted to bargain on aspects of their professional relationship with clients. Obviously, interest groups will be more active in negotiations if the topics being negotiated relate to their major goals. Because of the present limited scope of bargaining for federal employees, theoretical considerations suggest that multilateral bargaining is not yet present at that level.

The amount of multilateral bargaining, particularly just prior to a strike deadline and once a strike has occurred, depends greatly on the perceived impact of a work stoppage. Not all services within the public sector directly affect the public, and in some instances an acceptable alternative is available.

In part, the tactics of the parties reflect their desire to increase their relative bargaining power by gaining support of important interest groups. Since few alternative sources of supply for most services exist in the public sector, it is expected that each side will be more aware of the need for public support than is the case in the private sector.

This theoretical discussion of the variations in multilateral bargaining is illustrated in Figure I which shows expected interest group activity during negotiations for the private sector and for selected public services in urban areas. Bargaining is divided into three stages: the Initial Probing Stage (I), the Hard Bargaining Stage (II), and the Strike Stage (III). Interest group activity in the Initial Probing Stage is concerned mostly with the quality of the service. In Stage II, interest group motives begin to shift to concern over possible interruption of the service. Once a strike takes place, interest group acitivity focuses almost entirely on ending the work stoppage. These three stages, of course, represent a general statement about multilateral bargaining in the public sector. Exceptions from the general pattern may occur in some cases. For example, during the strike stage of the recent prolonged New York City teachers dispute, interest group activity was divided between those

salient feature of the situation. The same reasoning can be applied to third party involvement in the bargaining process. See: T. C. Schelling, *The Strategy of Conflict* (Cambridge: Harvard University Press, 1960), quoted in Kenneth E. Boulding, *Confict and Defense* (New York: Harper and Brothers, 1962), p. 314.

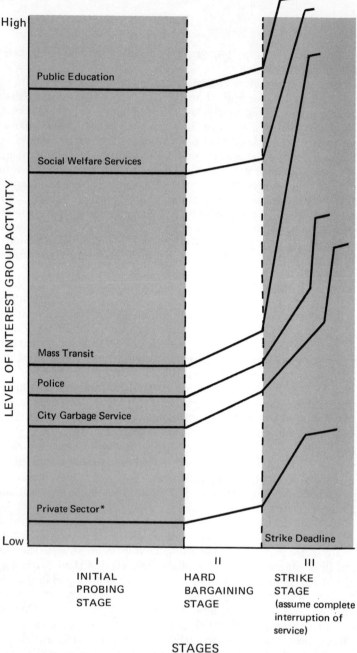

High

Public Education

Social Welfare Services

LEVEL OF INTEREST GROUP ACTIVITY

Mass Transit

Police

City Garbage Service

Private Sector*

Low

Strike Deadline

I	II	III
INITIAL PROBING STAGE	HARD BARGAINING STAGE	STRIKE STAGE (assume complete interruption of service)

STAGES

* For explanatory purposes, it is assumed that the private sector is a homogenous group of producers. In practice, the perceived inpact of an interruption of service varies among products. Consequently, it would be more accurate to represent the private sector with several different curves.

FIGURE I. Expected Interest Group Activity in Urban Areas

230

whose main concern was ending the stoppage and others who still focused primarily on the quality of the service.

The shape of the "Expected Interest Group Activity" (EIGA) line depends on the four variables discussed earlier: the interest group structure, the scope of bargaining, the perceived impact of a work stoppage, and the tactics of the parties. In the initial probing stage, the EIGA line depends primarily on the interest group structure and the scope of bargaining. In public education and social welfare services, interest groups are well organized and bargaining frequently includes topics such as class size, case load, and procedures for professional employees to participate in policy decisions. As a result, third party activity is relatively higher in the initial probing stages than in other services depicted in Figure I.

Third party activity is likely to increase slightly in the hard bargaining stage as the negotiations are given widespread publicity in the news media. Once the strike deadline is reached interest group activity then increases rapidly depending on the groups' perception of the impact of a strike. Activity continues to increase after the strike occurs, but at some point the activity will level off and possibly decrease as the public adjusts to the work stoppage or establishes substitute services. The rate at which activity levels off will vary among public services according to the difficulty involved in providing acceptable substitutes. For instance, provision of national guard troops as a substitute for striking police probably would reduce public pressure for ending such a work stoppage. Once a strike occurs, management may adopt tactics which sometimes reduces interest group pressure to end the strike and thus increases its bargaining power by trying "to keep the plant open" or provide a partial service. During a recent strike of social workers, monthly checks were still mailed to welfare recipients so that pressure from "customers" to end the strike was reduced substantially. This type of management action, which rarely occurs in the private sector, results partly from multilateral bargaining in the public sector. In addition, public sector strikes usually are illegal which gives management added incentive to attempt to provide services during a strike. A similar effect occurs when the consumers of the service try to provide a substitute service. Parents sometimes have threatened or attempted to keep schools open during teacher strikes.

The shape of the EIGA line in the hard bargaining and strike stage most likely will be different in nonurban areas. The perceived impact of a garbage strike in an urban area is depicted as relatively high in Figure I. The perceived impact of a similar strike in a rural area, however, would undoubtedly be much less since consumers often would be able to dispose of their garbage.

PRIVATE SECTOR BARGAINING

The bilateral nature of private sector bargaining generally restricts third party action particularly during the initial probing stage of negotiations when the supply of the product or service to the consumer is not interrupted. An exception to this generalization may occur during the hard bargaining stage when the strike is imminent and after the strike has occurred. The consumer then becomes aware of the likelihood of economic loss or inconvenience through the interruption of supply and he will attempt to find substitute sources of supply. As mentioned earlier, this potential loss of customers puts pressure on the negotiators.

The multilateral characteristics which sometime develop in the private sector, however, are quite different from multilateral public sector bargaining. First, as already mentioned, the timing is different since multilateral pressures in the private sector occur only in the final stages of negotiations. A second difference is in the amount of third party influence. Because virtually no market mechanism reveals immediately consumer preferences in the public sector, interest groups become the vehicle for transmitting consumer demands. In contrast, third party activity in the private sector is less prevalent since the market allows the consumer some choice in selecting the product or service.

Consumer choice in the private sector is in some instances more apparent than real. Little incentive exists for the consumer to switch to another supplier because of lower price in industries with noncompetitive product markets where oligopolistic pricing is common. In cases where the consumer may switch to avoid interruption of service, the supplier will build up inventories before the strike so that the customer will not be lost. If the product or service is perishable as, for example, in the case of transportation or newspapers, the employers will cooperate to avoid premanent loss of customers to any one employer.[3]

Finally, an important difference is that apart from the rare cases of government intervention in bargaining, the multilateral influence in the private sector is characterized by autonomous individual action. This approach is significantly different from the highly organized cooperative activity expected in many areas of public employment.

MULTILATERAL BARGAINING IN PUBLIC EDUCATION

Some support for the foregoing theoretical analysis was provided by the results of an interest group study in a large city school system. Extensive interviews were conducted with representatives of interest groups, members of the Board of Education, representatives of the Superintendent of Schools, elected city officials and the teachers' union which is the recognized bargaining agent.[4]

In conducting the interest group study, the following necessary conditions were established for demonstrating the existence of multilateral bargaining:

(1) that some of the goals of the interest groups relate to topics included in the scope of negotiations,

(2) that the interest groups pursue their goals by trying to influence the parties involved in negotiations either directly or through an intermediary,

---

[3]See the employers' agreement to use the lockout in the New York newspaper industry. Similar motivations lie behind the "Mutual Aid Pact" in the airline industry.

[4]For a detailed discussion of the methodology including the problem of identifying the interest groups within a community power structure and the characteristics of the actual groups studied, see: Kenneth McLennan and Michael H. Moskow, "Teacher Negotiations and the Public Interest" in *Emerging Sectors of Collective Bargaining,* ed. Seymour Wolfbein, forthcoming. For specific interest group studies at the community level also see: R. Dahl, *Who Governs?* (New Haven: Yale University Press, 1961), R. Presthus, *Men at the Top: A Study of Community Power* (New York: Oxford University Press, 1964), and C. E. Thometz, *The Decision Makers: The Power of Dallas* (Dallas: Methodist University Press, 1963).

(3) that at least one of the participants to the actual negotiations believes that the groups represent segments of the public and respond to the pressure from the interest group leaders.

The first necessary condition was clearly satisfied.[5] For example, the teacher transfer plan was probably the most widely discussed issue during negotiations. All community groups expressed their views about the existing teacher transfer clause. The plan provided for basically voluntary transfer and in the opinion of most local education and taypayer groups this feature of the plan was desirable. These groups were afraid that if the plan was made compulsory (i.e. the superintendent can assign teachers anywhere within the system) the best teachers in each group's neighborhood school would be reassigned to some other school. Those who favored the present plan, however, thought that some modification which would give the superintendent more control over the assignment of faculty was desirable.

The civil rights organizations and the groups representing upper income, highly educated "liberals" (classified as intellectual groups) strongly opposed the voluntary plan often viewing it in rather emotional terms. To the black community and the intellectuals, it had become a symbol of the "double standard" in education which the white establishment in the school system and the union have allowed to develop. Removal of the voluntary feature of the plan was seen as the first step toward equalizing educational opportunity in the school system. Civil rights groups thought that changing the transfer clause would improve the quality of education by allowing the superintendent to reallocate more highly qualified teachers to ghetto areas. On the other hand, the intellectuals thought that changing the transfer clause would result in faculty integration which would improve the quality of education. The possibility of loss of teachers from the system under a compulsory plan was not thought to be serious though some groups felt it might be a short run problem.

The second necessary condition (that interest groups attempt to influence the parties) was also supported. The pattern of interest group pressure was fairly complex with most groups focusing their attention on the part of the decision-making structure which was most likely to be sensitive to each particular group. Most of the pressure was directed to some part of the employer side (Board of Education, Superintendent, Mayor, and so on) with little attempt to influence the union directly. There was some evidence that the black community sought to influence the union through the local union membership.

The existence of multilateral bargaining also requires that the pressure from the community groups has some substantial effect on the bargaining stance of either the union or the employer. The case study showed that interest group activity was a major force in determining the employer's position on the transfer clause which was a crucial issue in the negotiations. Because of the community pressure, a majority of the Board of Education was prepared to bargain for a change in the transfer clause "to the point of taking a strike."[6]

[5]For a detailed description of the results of the interest group study, see McLennan and Moskow, op. cit.

[6]Of course, the case study provided other examples of the relationship between interest group goals and the scope of bargaining. The related concept of educational policy and the content of negotiation has been discussed previously in Michael H. Moskow, *Teachers and*

CONCLUSION

In this paper the authors attempted to explain and to analyze multilateral bargaining in the public sector. A case study in an urban school district tended to support the hypothesis of multilateral bargaining, but school districts, of course, are not necessarily typical of all public sector jurisdictions. School districts are governed by boards of education instead of a single individual. In addition, these governing boards frequently have power to levy their own taxes. As a result, it is concluded that further testing of the concept of multilateral bargaining is desirable in order to refine the concept and to ascertain what differences, if any, exist among various public sector jurisdictions.

A further conclusion is that interest groups in an urban school district do not appear to be concerned with all items negotiated by the board of education and teachers organization. Instead the groups tend to focus on a few issues which to them have symbolic importance.[7] As a result, if multilateral bargaining takes place in other public jurisdictions, it is predicted that it will also focus on symbolic issues because the interest groups do not have the time and resources to concentrate on the details of the agreement.

The case study also showed that the board of education attempted to legitimize its own position by obtaining support from segments of the community. The board developed procedures to increase the ease of communication with interest groups. This relationship between the community and the board led to interest group pressure on issues discussed in collective bargaining. It is predicted that in all public sector jurisdictions where government administrators or elected officials rely heavily on support from segments of the community to legitimize their positions, collective bargaining procedures established are likely to be transformed from a bilateral to a multilateral process.

Unions (Philadelphia: University of Pennsylvania Press, 1966), and Myron Lieberman and Michael H. Moskow, *Collective Negotiations for Teachers,* (Chicago: Rand McNally and Company, 1966).

[7]For a discussion of interest groups' emphasis on symbols see: M. Edelman, "Symbols and Political Quiescence." *American Political Science Review,* September 1960, p. 696. School decentralization is another issue which is likely to have increasing symbolic importance. See: Michael H. Moskow and Kenneth McLennan, "Teacher Negotiations and School Decentralization" in *The Community School* (Washington, D.C.: The Brookings Institution), forthcoming.

MUNICIPAL BARGAINING AND POLITICAL POWER

James A. Belasco

[This article analyzes the political power used in municipal collective bargaining in a medium-sized city located in upstate New York.] The city has a "strong Mayor" form of government. The Mayor is elected every four years in a general city-wide election, serves full time, and is a paid official. The Mayor appoints the Board of Estimate, all department heads, and has wide latitude in fiscal and policy matters.

The Common Council, on the other hand, is composed of part-time members elected from each of the 16 geographically determined wards. The councilmen serve for four years, though half of the Council is elected every two years.

Of the 952 full-time employees of the city in 1964, 586 were members of some employee organization. Table I details the extent to which City X employees hold membership in employee organizations. While several of the organizations have a 20-year history, their activity in City X has increased markedly since 1958. The American Federation of State, County and Municipal Employees organization, for instance, dates from 1958, when the Mayor issued an enabling statement of policy. Both the Police Benevolent Association and the International Fire Fighters Association date from approximately 1946, although their activity has increased since 1955. The Civil Service Employees Association is a relatively old organization which dates from before World War II. The newest organization, The Case Workers, emerged in 1962. . . .

Analysis of the relationship between City X and its various employee organizations reveals two interesting conclusions. In the first place, contrary to many misconceptions about how municipalities operate, the effective control in City X apparently is wielded by the Mayor. There are, of course, multiple government institutions which deal with employee relations. For instance, control over job classification is divided between the Civil Service Commission and the Common Council; responsibilities for salaries are also divided between the Controller, the Common Council, and the executive officers ranging from the Mayor to his depart-

James Belasco is Associate Professor and Chairman, Department of Organization, State University of New York at Buffalo. Reprinted by permission of the Public Personnel Association from *Government Labor Relations in Transition*, Personnel Report 662.

**table 1   Extent of Affiliation with Employee
Organizations, City X, 1964**

Name of Organization	Total Members	Percentage of Department Organized
American Federation of State, County, Municipal Employees, AFL-CIO	221	75
Police Benevolent Association	140	70
International Fire Fighters Association, AFL-CIO	140	70
Welfare Case Workers Association	25	30
Civil Service Employees Association	60	40
Total in all employee organizations	586	61

Source: AFSCME figures were taken from the checkoff list as compiled by the City Controller March 15, 1965. The other information
was secured by interviews with the leaders of the various employee
organizations, March, 1965.

ment heads. Behind all of this local governmental structure stands the New York
State Legislature empowered to act on any of these matters.

Yet, beneath this facade of overlapping bureaucracies, the strings of effective
control in the city originate from the Mayor's office. For instance, even though the
Civil Service Commission and the Common Council are independent bodies, neither
has turned down a request from the Mayor in the employee relations area during
the past 10 years. Since this spans the terms of three mayors, it appears that this
control adheres to the office and not just the incumbent. Despite heated discussions
and very close budget votes, the Mayor's salary proposals have always been
approved. Similarly, any request for reclassification has always been approved by
the Civil Service Commission.

This highly concentrated control over employee relations matters on the
employer's side means that the employer is capable of coordinated action in
employee relations matters. Therefore, meaningful collective bargaining can take
place between an employee organization and the Mayor, with both sides capable of
carrying out what has been agreed to in the bargaining sessions.

A second interesting conclusion . . . concerns the diversity of bargaining
structures. Professor John Commons points out in Chapter XIV of *Labor and
Administration* (New York, Macmillan, 1913), that union seek to negotiate with

the major source of power on the employer's side. In City X, while it is very apparent that the Mayor is the focal point of power in the city, the strategy employed and the bargaining structure which emerges varies with the employee organization. The Welfare Case Workers, the PBA, and the IFFA all attempt to influence the Mayor through their department heads. These organizations believe that their department head will be more able to secure concessions from the Mayor than if they approached the Mayor alone.

The organizations of policemen and firemen also present a unique study in bargaining structure. The matter of wages is the only question discussed on the local level. On all other matters, these organizations bargain with the New York State Legislature. Contrasting with this bargaining structure, AFSCME deals directly with the Mayor and the City Council. This may be due in part to the fact that AFSCME's membership cuts across department lines. Thus, the bargaining structure which emerges varies with the nature of the employee organization, its perception of how it can best manipulate its power to attain its ends, the issue under discussion, and the structure of power on the employer's side.

The unique organization of the municipal employer into overlapping areas of jurisdiction enables the employee organization, on any issue, to choose the form in which it will seek to exert influence. For instance, if the municipality is unwilling to grant the employee organization's demands, the employee organization can frequently go to the State Legislature and have the same demands mandated into law. While somewhat of a parallel exists in the private sector where unions can win concessions from Congress that they may be unable to win from private employers, the range of issues on which this "going to Congress" strategy is possible is very limited. In a real sense, the multi-level power structure on the employer's side provides more than one opportunity for the municipal employee organization to attain its ends.

This option of going to the State Legislature may be more real for the PBA, IFFA, and CSEA than for AFSCME. These previous organizations have well-organized lobbies in Albany and can exert significant pressure. AFSCME, on the other hand, is somewhat of a novice in the lobbying arena and may not do as well. However, AFSCME's attempt to secure a collective bargaining bill has been through the State Legislature. So on some issues, this option must be a real one for AFSCME.

In summation, it appears that power is highly centralized in the municipal employer thus permitting effective collective bargaining to take place. The structure of bargaining which emerges and the scope of bargaining will vary with the employee organization, the issue involved, and the employee organization's perception of how it can best maximize its power.

POWER

Crucial to any discussion of collective bargaining relationships is the concept of power. As pointed out previously, efforts to maximize the employee organization's power are likely to determine what and where issues are discussed. The following study is an analysis of the power relationships as they exist in City X.

Bargaining power (or power), as used in this paper, is defined as: (1) the control over desirable resources or desired outcomes (these are power assets); and (2) the ability to utilize these assets to achieve desired ends. In essence, bargaining power has at least two dimensions: First, the different elements of power assets which might be called potential power, and second the situational circumstances which enable either party to utilize these assets.

POWER ASSETS

A power asset, as used here, is anything which one party controls which is of value to or is sought after by the other party. For example, in the private sector control over labor force participation is one of the power assets of the union. In the public sector, it will be shown that control over votes is a power asset for the employee organization.

Power assets, which may or may not be used in any given situation, may be classified as political, social, organization, or economic. Because of the nature of the arena within which bargaining takes place in the public service, the key controlling assets in this relationship would appear to be political in nature.

This discussion will revolve mainly about AFSCME since this is the organization that was studied most intensively. However, fragmentary evidence does indicate that the same power assets would apply to all employee organizations.

Political Power Assets

One of the most potent power assets of a political nature which the employee organization possesses is the voting strength of its members, families and relatives of its members, and friends. It is estimated that AFSCME alone can influence between 2,000 to 3,000 votes. These 2,000 to 3,000 votes are normally the margin of victory in a Mayoralty campaign. Furthermore, unlike other voting groups whose interests tend to be diverse, the public employee group would most likely vote as a bloc. They have a clearly definable, simple economic interest which is almost totally dependent upon the Mayor for satisfaction. The employee organization, through its channels of communication, provides a means of influencing this voting bloc. Therefore, since election to office is the objective of the Mayor, and the employee organization can deliver votes which could result in this election, this control constitutes one of the most potent power assets of the employee organization.

While no such evidence of bloc voting exists in City X (because no study has been made) the following empirical evidence can support the inference that public employees vote as a bloc. AFSCME conducts an analysis of the registrations of their members. While registrations may not indicate how people vote, 92 percent of all AFSCME members are registered in the same party as the Mayor. Other employee organizations do not maintain such systematic records, though I was assured by PBA, IFFA and Case Workers Association leaders, that the vast majority of their members voted for the Mayor and his party. Political scientists have discovered that politicians seek out public employee groups and attempt to persuade them to swap support for special favors simply because the popular myth is that public employees vote as a bloc. See particularly Robert A. Dahl, *Who Governs* (New Haven: Yale University Press, 1961), pp. 160, 250-54. While the evidence is far from conclusive, the fact remains that politicians in City X believed that bloc voting exists and acted accordingly.

The same power asset, the control over 2,000 to 3,000 votes, also is potent when dealing with the City Council. The public employee group holds the balance of effective political control in three wards of the city. While public employees do not represent a majority of voters in any one ward, they do represent up to one-third of the total voters. This fact, combined with their bloc voting pattern, gives the public employee group the balance of effective control in the three wards. The ability to elect councilmen provides the employee organization with a potent power asset when dealing with the Council.

Optimizing Political Assets

To maximize the potency of this political power asset, the AFSCME group has been very active in registering public employees and their families and getting them out to vote. In 1957, before the formation of AFSCME, only 22 percent of the employees of the Public Works Department voted in the Mayoralty election. In 1963, the last time Council members were elected, almost 80 percent of the same group cast ballots. AFSCME efforts to get out the public employee vote obviously augments its political power assets.

To enhance these political power assets, the employee organizations, especially AFSCME, are active in political party affairs. Through the union, the local AFSCME people have contacts with other party officials throughout the state. The present Mayor, on more than one occasion, has requested that AFSCME arrange speaking engagements for him in other cities. These connections throughout the political party serve as another power asset for which AFSCME can extract a price.

In addition to the special interest group of public employees, AFSCME seeks to identify its objectives with the objectives of the broader labor movement in the city. To accomplish this, AFSCME is urging participation of the leaders of the Central Trades and Labor Council in the budget hearings with the Mayor and the handling of final step grievances. ' The presence of these local labor leaders serves to remind the Mayor of the support of organized labor for AFSCME's program and thus increases the possible vote which AFSCME, through the Central Labor Trades Council, might be able to influence. The endorsement of the Central Labor Trades Council, for instance, is a much sought after political prize, and one which AFSCME has a large voice in awarding. This access to the votes of persons in the labor movement in City X provides another power asset for AFSCME.

Another political power asset which AFSCME controls is its support for the Mayor's budget. In essence, the Mayor grants AFSCME a portion of its requests, in return for which AFSCME uses its influence to support the entire budget including some key projects of the Mayor. For instance, AFSCME actively supported the Mayor's urban renewal program and was influential in security passage of the bill. This support of the Mayor's budget and legislative program is another vital power asset for the employee organization.

Another power asset of a political nature is AFSCME's almost absolute control over the grievance procedure. This control over the grievance procedure and the application of peer and union pressure to disgruntled employees is useful politically to the Mayor in two ways. In the first place, the union does not grieve when the Mayor makes appointments which do not follow the standard policy. For instance, to pay off a political debt the Mayor may appoint a person, out of seniority order, to a job as foreman. The union will refuse to process the grievance, thus making it extremely difficult for the aggrieved employee to have his case heard. The union also applies pressure on the aggrieved employee to drop the case "for the good of all." In the four cases where this occurred, the employee dropped his grievance.

In the second place, the union thoroughly investigates and screens all grievances. Previously, the Mayor or his Executive Assistant were forced to perform this function. With the union assuming this investigatory function, the Mayor and his Assistant are freed for other duties. Since time is one of the most precious of all political assets, releasing the Mayor's time is particularly valuable. Thus, the union controls, to some extent, the Mayor's ability to make political payoffs and the release of his time from grievance matters. This represents another power asset.

In short, the employee organization's political power assets are its supposed control over the votes of both public employees and some members of the general labor class, contacts within the political party, support of the Mayor's legislative program, and domination of the grievance procedure.

Social Power Assets

The employee organization also possesses certain social power assets. For one, the Secretary-Treasurer of AFSCME is recognized by members of the City Council as an expert on the budget. The Secretary-Treasurer is relied upon quite extensively by several councilmen to give them information not only on the technical points but also about what is going on in the city. Even the city hall newspaper reporter thought highly of the Secretary-Treasurer's ability to understand and reliably communicate the budget contents. By being accepted as an expert, the AFSCME Secretary-Treasurer places himself in control of a considerable flow of information, both to the city councilmen and the press. The high reliability rating and the expert stature of this individual, is one of the most potent social power assets possessed by the union.

David B. Truman points out in *The Governmental Process: Political Interests and Public Opinion* (New York, Alfred Knopf, 1951), that the assumption of this expert information giving role is one of the most effective devices utilized by lobbyists. When the legislator cannot possibly study the situation thoroughly, which is true of the budget deliberations, he may be influenced by anyone who supplies him with reliable information. The AFSCME Secretary–Treasurer supplies this information—a potent social power asset for the union.

In addition, because of his access to the press and his high believability rating, the AFSCME Secretary-Treasurer has a potent power asset which is particularly useful in grievance handling. Through access to the press the union can make the actions of various department heads very visible to the general public. Such visibility could be embarrassing politically for the department head involved.

This power asset was invoked only once when the union could no longer tolerate the anti-union actions of the Water Commissioner. By threatening to go to the newspaper, the union precipitated a crisis and succeeded in having the Commissioner appointed to another post. This access to the newspaper combined with the Secretary-Treasurer's expertness is usually enough to convince the department head of the wisdom of at least minimum cooperation.

Organizational Power Assets

In addition to the social assets and political assets mentioned previously, there are also certain power assets which are organizational in nature. For instance, through the Mayor the union has applied organizational pressure on department heads to cooperate. Immediately after the union was recognized it encountered harassment from several department heads, such as stewards who suddenly became too busy to be released for union duty. The Secretary–Treasurer prevailed upon the Mayor to exert his organizational pressure to counter this harassment activity. The access of AFSCME to the chief executive and the threat that through this channel might flow information unfavorable to the department head are the main organizational power assets of the union.

A second power asset of an organizational nature is the union's ability to slow things to a standstill by obeying all of the rules in the book. While this asset has never been utilized, it has been frequently mentioned in the bargaining sessions with the Mayor. In many ways, this is similar to the private sector where one of the union's principle assets is its ability to control the work force.

Because of the nature of the relationship, economic power assets do not play a major role. Since the right to strike is prohibited, and the employee organizations seem uninterested in the strike weapon, economic considerations do not enter in at this time. This is not to say, however, that economic considerations will not enter into the relationship in the future or do not play a role in other collective bargaining relationships.

The Mayor's Power Assets

The Mayor is not without his own power assets. Perhaps the most potent asset at his command is the status, prestige, and legitimacy of his office. As Mayor, he has a very high believability rating in the press and with the general public. This gives him effective access to many of the communication channels in the city. In addition, since he has the stamp of legitimacy in what he says, it would be very difficult to refute him. This is true especially since he will probably be able to have his side of any controversy told first.

In addition, of course, the Mayor controls a considerable amount of patronage. Through patronage he has effective control over many persons including several on the City Council. This patronage enables the Mayor to extract political favors in return; and in turn, can reduce the Mayor's dependence upon AFSCME. Thus, this political control over patronage is a political asset for the Mayor.

In total, and without exploring them in depth, it would appear that the executive arm of the municipal employer is endowed with significant power assets. The political assets of the Mayor include control over patronage; social assets include the status, prestige, and legitimacy of the Mayor's office and his access to communications media; organizational assets include control over job assignments and the climate of cooperation or non-cooperation; economic assets include the ability to terminate employees either directly or through reorganization.

SITUATIONAL CONSIDERATIONS

In short, the first major conclusion which emerges from an analysis of this data is that the major power assets on both sides appear to be political in nature. Though power assets exist on both sides, situational factors determine the ability of either side to utilize these assets. These situational determinants seem to revolve about the nature of the issue involved. In turn, at least four separate situational aspects of the issue can be identified.

First, the legitimacy of the issue is one of the situational determinants. All employee organizations believed that they had more power (were better able to influence outcomes) if they bargained for a $150 per year increase than if they bargained for $1,000 per year increase. The reason given is that most people, both in the city administration and in the general population, were committed to increasing city employees' salaries to keep pace with the increases in the cost of living. A $150 increase per year is about the increase in the cost of living. Thus, this request is viewed as being legitimate. However, a $1,000 per year increase would involve changing the relationship which exists between city employees and other employees in the local area. Such a request would be viewed as non-legitimate. Thus, the legitimacy of the request is one of the situational determinants which flow from the nature of the issue involved.

Second, the visibility of the issue is another situational determinant. The more visible an issue is, the more power assets are necessary to attain the employee organization's objective. For instance, it is easier to get the Mayor to approve an extra holiday than to get the same holiday approved by the City Council. The basic reason for this difference is that the issue is far less visible when the Mayor grants the holiday than when it goes before the Council and is debated in the public press.

A third characteristic of the issue involved is the degree to which it is threatening to administration prerogatives. It would be far easier to win a wage increase than it would be to win a contract or binding arbitration. The former concession by the city does not threaten any of the established management prerogatives, while the latter proposal would evoke strong feelings surrounding the issue of sovereignty.

A fourth characteristic is the prestige which accrued to the granting agency. Thus, it is a relatively easy matter to convince the Mayor and the City Council to provide uniforms for city employees. These uniforms dress up the employees and reflect prestige back on the city administration. Uniforms would be far easier to obtain than a wage increase principally because of the visible symbols which reflect back on the city administration.

In addition to these four characteristics of the issue, other situational factors which seem to influence the ability of one side or another to utilize its power assets include: structure of the decision-making process in the municipality; cohesiveness of the union group; previous tax history; proximity to election time; and circumstances surrounding the election. The existence of these situational determinants which influence the exercise of power assets form the second major conclusion of this study of power.

RESTRAINT IN USE OF POWER

The third major conclusion concerning the power relations in City X is that both sides have been very cautious in exercising their power assets. The employee organizations, for instance, have concentrated their efforts on the "bread and butter matters" of wages and benefits and have not emphasized the union security matters of a binding contract or grievance arbitration. In the employee organization's opinion the cost of demanding these union security provisions would be too great. Thus, the employee organizations refrain from mounting a major attack in these sensitive areas.

AFSCME also is cautious in its exercise of its grievance rights. Rather than lose a case, the union drops it. Also, matters have to become extremely serious before the union threatens to use its power assets of appeal to the newspaper. It took the union three years to finally bring the matter of the Water Commissioner to a head. In addition, AFSCME is very conscious of the Mayor's limitations in preparing a budget. Rather than ask for a large increase and settle for significantly less, AFSCME gears its requests to approximately what they believe the Mayor can grant.

The same cautiousness is expressed by the Mayor as well. For instance, he prepares the budget knowing almost exactly how much the Council will approve. Part of the reason that his budget has never been turned down is because it has been checked informally with key members of the Council and consensus had been achieved before the budget was ever formally submitted. In addition, the Mayor is well aware of the strong economy minded group on the Council. A study of the Council votes indicates that every budget motion is passed by a close vote—8 to 7, or 7 to 6, or 8 to 6. The defection of even one councilman could be disastrous to the budget. Thus, the Mayor prepares the budget with the Council in mind and tries to submit what he knows will be accepted

The Mayor has been reluctant to employ the power assets at his disposal in dealing with the union. He has relied upon persuasion rather than coercion. His handling of one particularly difficult steward problem is an excellent example of the Mayor's cautiousness in the employee relations area. A union steward was discovered drinking on the job. In fact, even the Secretary-Treasurer was convinced that the steward was intoxicated. Rather than firing him, the Mayor insisted that the employee be returned to his job. The Mayor stated that if he "was good enough to be chosen Steward we ought to give him another chance." The Mayor could have used this incident to discredit the union. His action can be interpreted as cautiousness in the exercise of his power.

David Truman outlines an excellent reason why this cautiousness may be very important to both sides. According to Truman, many interest groups form as a reaction against the activities and successes of a counter group. Thus, AFSCME may exercise restraint in its demands for money and union security matters to prevent formation of vociferous business or taxpayer groups which would fight to slash the budget. The union has said, "Better to ask for half a loaf, upset no one and get it, than to ask for two loaves, arouse significant opposition and get nothing."

The Mayor may submit reasonable budgets to prevent strengthening the economy minded group on the Council and he may cooperate with the union to forestall the formation of a more militant group. In any event, restraint in the use of power assets on both sides is a third major conclusion.

DEFENSIVE USE OF POWER

As a natural outgrowth of the above, the fourth major conclusion readily apparent from this study is that the exercise of power assets can be defensive as well as offensive. The public hearing is the best example of the defensive exercise of power assets. Public hearings are commonly thought of as a means of transmitting information. However, even though this is the most familiar use of the hearing, it is also the least important. Evidence indicates that most important decisions have already been made concerning the budget before the hearing ever takes place. The AFSCME Secretary-Treasurer has already agreed with the Mayor and the key members of the City Council to the increases included in the budget. (Truman points out that the real function of a public hearing is to consolidate the interest groups' position and generate a broadly based interest in the group's program.) So, the public hearing informs no one except the public and in the last six years only four people have ever attended the hearing.

Rather than providing information, this hearing provides a forum in which the ritual of collective bargaining can take place. The AFSCME Secretary-Treasurer, along with the President of the local Central Labor Trades Council appear and request several hundred dollars a year more than they have already tacitly agreed to accept. This appearance serves three functions. First, the appearance serves as a means of keeping potentially errant councilmen in line. With the organization's potent political assets on display, this is presumed to convince any wavering councilman of the need to approve the budget at the lower figure. Second, this appearance serves to prove to the AFSCME members the value of membership in the AFSCME organization. Third, these appearances are useful in organization efforts among non-union personnel. This use of power assets to minimize the possibility of loss clearly emerges as the fourth major conclusion.

The fifth major conclusion is that power assets are differentially employed. For instance, in dealing with the Mayor during budget negotiations, the major power assets employed are political in nature. Involvement of the Central Labor Trades Council President is an example of the use of political assets at this point. Contrasting with this, is the use of social and organizational assets in dealing with the department heads over grievances. Both social and political assets are employed in dealing with the City Council. In short, the power assets utilized at any given point are likely to be determined partially by the individual over whom the influence is being exerted. . . .

THE PUBLIC INTEREST

If one general conclusion emerges from this study it is that collective bargaining can and does work within the confines of a political system. However, many scholars are concerned that, in such a collective bargaining relationship, the public interest will not be adequately protected. The basic question they raise "Who (or what) protects the public interest?" is germane at this juncture.

A priori there appear to be three public interests. These are: economy, efficiency, and continuity of operations. In the private sector of the economy, collective bargaining is encouraged as one means to accomplish the public interest. The private marketplace and the price mechanism are the regulators that protect the public. In the private marketplace price is determined, thus placing a ceiling beyond which the costs of any firm cannot go. This market pressure on price is matched by an upward pressure on wages and costs by the union. To meet both the price and wage pressures and still function, management must become more efficient. The essence, then, of the regulator in the private sector are the opposing pressures of price and performance.

It is often stated that nothing equivalent to the price pressure is present in the public service. It is argued that strengthening the union through the imposition of a collective bargaining system can result in exploitation of the taxpayer because of the lack of a marketplace imposed ceiling. The heart of the argument rests on the absence of a mechanism to prevent indiscriminate wage increases to public employees. If, therefore, such a mechanism could be found, collective bargaining might be a viable alternative. At the onset, it is recognized that collective bargaining might be desirable for other reasons. However, these other reasons have been set aside for the moment and attention will be focused on the exploitation argument outlined above.

Budget Control

As mentioned previously, there are two separate opposing pressures: the pressures on price and the pressures on performance. In the public service the pressure on price becomes the pressure on the budget. Analysis reveals that there are five pressures that tend to restrict the number of dollars available in the budget. The first, and most important, downward pressure on the budget comes from the legislature. As illustrated in City X, the legislator tends to be very economy-minded and extremely responsive to the wishes of the relatively small electorate he represents. Reading of the Council proceedings in City X clearly indicates that any major fiscal change comes in for extremely close and unfriendly scrutiny.

However, the legislature is limited in its ability to control fiscal matters in the municipality. The budget has become so complex that it is almost impossible for a part-time councilman to fully comprehend all of its nuances. It is ludicrous to believe that a councilman working four or five evenings for several hours each evening can understand a budget that took three city bureaucrats two months to prepare. Because of this, and the confusing way in which the budget is presented, the councilman has almost no effective control over individual items in the budget. Councilmen are forced to push for "across-the-board cuts" rather than a more meaningful selective reduction of expenditures which are out of line. The inherent injustice in such a move is recognized by the councilmen. Yet in the same breath the councilman will probably shrug his shoulders and say, "But what else am I to do?"

Given this inability of the legislative arm to exercise effective control over individual items in the budget, the mere threat of a general across-the-board slash places an upper limit on the city administration's total budget proposal. The Mayor recognizes that any budget that is too big is likely to be cut. Thus, even in this gross way the budget approval of the legislature acts as a constraint on the upper limits of the budget request.

The second major limiting factor on the budget is the existence of the taxpayer-voter. While it is true that many people do not vote, and many of those who do vote pay little attention to the affairs of government, taxpayers have been known to rise in revolt and "throw the rascals out." It is a popular myth, shared by many municipal officials, that the revolution is just around the corner. While no evidence of such a popular uprising exists in City X, the Executive Assistant and many councilmen speak as if it is just a matter of time. This myth tends to restrict the Mayor's budget proposal and thus exerts one additional downward pressure on the number of available dollars.

The third factor limiting the budget is the political competition ready to capitalize on spending errors of the administration. In the competition for votes, the public employees, while a significant group, are a minority. A far broader political bloc would include all taxpayers. If the opposing party could whip up enough sentiment among this latter group, the public employees could be outvoted. While it is true that any person's vote is likely to be the result of several conflicting forces, only one of which is the spending pattern of the current administration, it is also true that most voters probably are accustomed to rising taxes. The central fact remains, however, that if taxes rise quickly the opposition political party may seize upon the tax increases as a campaign issue and use it to arouse voter antagonism against the current administration. The existence of a competing party serves as a third limiting factor.

The fourth limiting factor arises out of the nature of interest group formation. Some people are active in several interest groups, but the vast bulk of persons in the society tend to hold only nominal membership in any voting interest group. David B. Truman points out that gains won by one interest group encourage the formation of a counter interest group dedicated to holding the first group in check. The threat of this rival balancing interest group emerging is one additional downward pressure on budgetary systems designated for public employees.

A fifth downward pressure on budgetary items for public employees arises out of the nature of the bureaucratic structure. It is a truism that bureaucrats can always spend money, and giving more money to present employees is one of the poorest ways to spend money from the viewpoint of a bureaucrat. A good bureaucrat would rather build more buildings or hire more employees than pay his current employees more. These competing uses for the money in the budget exert another pressure limiting the wages and benefits of public employees.

In addition to these five limitations on the number of dollars available for salaries for public employees, there are also two pressures for performance regardless of the salaries paid. First, there is the professional identification with doing a good job. Many of the administrators consider themselves "professionals" with a dedication to public service. This self-generated professional drive to accomplish the job exerts one pressure for performance.

Mayor's Influence

Second, the Mayor exerts considerable pressure on his department heads to accomplish the city's business. The streets must be cleaned, the garbage collected, crimes must be prevented, and fires must be extinguished. In each of these ways, and the hundreds of others in which municipal services touch the lives of the voting public, the Mayor has a vital political stake. The Mayor is well aware that voters tend to evaluate him on the basis of their contact with city employees and city services. Thus, the Mayor, in an effort to project a favorable political image, exerts strong pressure to get the work done as quickly as possible. This pressure constitutes the major performance pressure in the city.

On the balance, there would appear to be little to prevent "creeping exploitation." None of the mechanisms outlined above are capable of preventing the slow inflation of wages for city employees. Many of the mechanisms outlined only work after the excess has occurred. In this sense, political democracy would appear to be as imperfect an instrument as market competition in preventing some form of consumer exploitation in the short run. However, as with competition, there would appear to be a good deal of pressure, both potential and current, to prevent long-run exploitation.

Legal Devices

In addition to the natural mechanisms which were outlined above, two other "artificial" legal devices might be adopted to prevent exploitation. The first of these devices would be the extension of the "prevailing wage" concept to all city employees. This concept now applies to laborers in the city and state service and apparently is working successfully. There appears to be little disagreement that the city employee is entitled to wages which are equal to those of other employees performing similar tasks. Yet, the prevailing wage concept would prevent escalation of wages beyond the average paid in other industries and thus provide protection for the taxpayer. This approach also provides room for negotiation over the local area to be considered. A built-in means of resolving disputes is also provided through court review of any prevailing wage ruling. The extension of the prevailing wage concept to all city employees would appear to provide protection of both the city employee and the taxpayer.

Second, provision could be made for local political approval of any collective bargaining agreement. Such approval should be preceded by a public hearing on the contract. The public hearing provides a forum at which any exploitative aspects of the contract could be brought to light. The public hearing also provides the opportunity for the formation of an opposition group, should it appear that the administration is too lax with the taxpayers' dollars.

In short, the public interest seems adequately protected, and with the adoption of the two suggestions made above, this protection could be increased. The fear of inadequate protection of the public interest appears groundless and one which should not be used as an argument against collective bargaining in the municipal service.

In the final analysis, whether collective bargaining is a desirable alternative in the municipal service becomes a question of values. This paper, rather than proving a case for or against collective bargaining has sought to present the facts surrounding a given collective bargaining relationship. The reader is left to weigh these facts and reach his own conclusions.

SUMMARY

Rather than become involved in the hurly-burly of argument over the "values" of collective bargaining, this paper has sought to present and analyze the facts and circumstances surrounding a particular collective bargaining relationship in one municipality. Five main threads seem to run through the analysis. First, collective bargaining can and does function in a municipality. Arguments over its legality or morality do not erase the fact that collective bargaining exists as an on-going process in City X. Second, it is impossible to separate collective bargaining from politics.

The collective bargaining relationship is a swapping of political power assets. The Mayor grants salary and benefits to the employee organization in return for their support in a variety of political activities. The trading of votes and support for salaries and benefits is the heart of the negotiation process. Third, each side possesses significant power assets. Unlike the commonly accepted view of employee organizations in government, the organizations in City X were strong and potent. Fourth, there appear to be many factors which limit the potential exploitation of the taxpayer by the union and management combination. These factors may be strengthened by the addition of the prevailing wage concept to all city employees and the strengthening of local political control over any agreement. Fifth, the character of the collective bargaining relationship varies widely with the employee organization involved.

As stated in the introduction, these conclusions are based on a case study approach. Whether they represent a general trend or an isolated event is a matter for future research. . . .

CHAPTER 6

STRIKES IN THE PUBLIC SECTOR

Strikes in the public sector have captured the main focus of public attention to developments in this field. The reason for the public's concern is quite simple— services performed by public employees affect the daily lives of large groups of citizens. When a strike occurs among police, fire fighters, teachers, postal employees, or sanitation workers, people are, to say the least, inconvenienced.

The reader can see that the arguments regarding public employee strikes are far from settled and that they involve fundamental questions of public policy. In fact, some of the differences between those favoring and those opposing the legalization of public employee strikes can be traced to conflicting goals of public policy. There are at least four "public interests" which relate to this question: (1) maintaining our system of government under which the elected officials represent the wishes of the majority of the electorate; (2) assuring that wages of public employees do not increase excessively because of the lack of market constraints, (3) permitting government employees some say in the determination of their wages and working conditions; and (4) minimizing strikes by public employees.

To some extent these goals of public policy are contradictory, and one's answer to the question of whether public employee strikes should be legalized rests on which goals he believes to be most important. The objective of public policy is not to achieve any of the above goals perfectly if that means forfeiting one of the others. Rather, it is to maximize all four goals to the fullest extent possible. It is within this framework that our public policy must be shaped.

After an analysis of statistics in public employee strikes, the next two articles in this section are by George W. Taylor and Theodore Kheel. Taylor was chairman of the "Taylor Committee," consisting of five outstanding authorities on labor relations, which recommended the continued prohibition of public employee strikes to New York State's Governor Rockefeller. Kheel, also an authority on labor relations, is the most well-known critic of this part of the Taylor Committee report. The articles by Wellington and Winter and Burton and Krider provide an in-depth analysis of the two points of view, reaching different conclusions. Fowler analyzes the problem from the political scientist's point of view. The articles by Stieber,

Doherty and Oberer, Kilberg, and Fusilier and Steinmetz present alternative ways of giving public employees a limited right to strike. Rains discusses the "final offer selection procedure" as a means for resolving impasses in public employment. This procedure was recommended by President Nixon in 1970 as one of the options to be given the President as a means for resolving impasses in the transportation industry.

WORK STOPPAGES OF GOVERNMENT EMPLOYEES

Sheila C. White

Labor-management relations in government service have changed dramatically in the past decade. A system administered solely by management has given way to one in which officials negotiate with employee representatives on wages and working conditions, at times even on the operations and functions of the public agency. Underlying this marked change is a new outlook of government workers. In addition to the security provided by merit systems, public employees now seek compensation equal to that received by their counterparts in private industry, comparable fringe benefits and working conditions, and procedures to ensure that grievances will be seriously considered and fairly settled.

The new aspirations of government employees received legal recognition in Executive Order 10988 on employee-management cooperation in Federal service, issued by President Kennedy in January 1962,[1] and in an increasing number of State laws and municipal ordinances enacted to permit or require negotiation between managers and public employee organizations.[2] As a result of the changing attitudes toward collective bargaining in government service, public employee unions have become the fastest growing labor organizations in the country.

The recognition of bargaining rights, in conjunction with the desire of public employees to attain comparability of wages and benefits with those in the private sector, has brought with it an increased number of work stoppages.[3] While the constitutions of some public employee unions include clauses banning strikes, others make no reference to the issue; some unions have recently removed the ban. Proponents of the public employees' right to strike believe that this weapon is necessary to ensure that bargaining is conducted effectively and in good faith.

Sheila C. White, formerly in the Division of Industrial Relations, Bureau of Labor Statistics, is an economist in the Bureau's Office of Manpower Employment Statistics. Reprinted from the *Monthly Labor Review*, December 1969.

[1]Executive Order 11491, revising the original order, was signed by President Richard Nixon on October 29, 1969.

[2]See Joseph P. Goldberg, "Labor-Management Relations Laws in Public Service," *Monthly Labor Review*, June 1968, pp. 48-55.

[3]For statistical purposes, the situations reported in this article have been deemed to fall within the Bureau's definition of a work stoppage. This decision does not constitute a legal determination that a work stoppage has taken place in violation of any law or public policy.

Executive Order 10988, however, denies recognition to unions that claim the right to strike; and Public Law 330 (1955), as amended, imposes a $1,000 fine and a year and a day in jail for Federal employees who strike, assert the right to strike, or knowingly belong to an organization which asserts that right. At the State and local level, the laws and court decisions of 35 States prohibit strikes. Many of these do not set forth specific penalties, leaving public officials free to take whatever action they deem necessary, including court action. Others require dismissal or fines for the employees or their organizations.[4] But many jurisdictions find these sanctions inexpedient or difficult to enforce. As a result, government workers are rapidly discovering that their goals can be achieved by exerting political and social pressure on their employers through work stoppages.

RISE OF DISCONTENT

Statistics on stoppages by government employees during the past 11 years suggest that public employees are no longer willing to wait patiently for that to which they believe they are entitled—collective bargaining and the benefits derived from it. Between 1958 and 1968, the number of government employee strikes per year rose from 15 to 254 and the number of workers involved from 1,700 to 202,000; the man-days of idleness increased from 7,500 to 2.5 million. These strikes included eight Federal stoppages involving 5,870 employees. (See table 1.)

In the private sector the number of work stoppages in this period also increased significantly, but not at the same rate as in government. In 1958 public employee strikes constituted four-tenths of 1 percent of all strikes, eight one-hundredths of a percent of the workers involved, and three one-hundredths of a percent of total idleness. By 1968 these ratios had risen to 5.0 percent, 76 percent, and 5.2 percent, respectively.

The change of attitudes among public employees from emphasis on security to demands for recognition and comparability in wages and working conditions with the private sector has not occurred suddenly. From 1958 to 1965 there was a gradual, though erratic, increase in government work stoppages. The number of workers involved and the resulting idleness fluctuated greatly from year to year. In 1966, however, public employee strikes and man-days of time lost were more than 3 times as high as the year before, and the number of workers involved was almost 9 times as great. The large increase in government strikes that began in 1966, and which still continues, coincided with the start of the current inflation. Most of these stoppages arose from disputes over wages and union recognition.

All measures of dispute activity in this sector rose substantially between 1965 and 1966 and continued to increase in 1967 and 1968. Since 1966 the rate of increase has accelerated. Between 1966 and 1967, the number of work stoppages and of the workers involved rose somewhat more than one-fourth. In 1968, the number of strikes exceeded that of the previous year by 40 percent and the number of workers involved increased by 50 percent. The proportionate rise in idleness followed a different pattern, a deviation attributable to the low 1966 base. Man-

[4]See Goldberg, op. cit.; see also Anne M. Ross, "Public Employee Unions and the Right to Strike," *Monthly Labor Review*, March 1969, pp. 14-18.

table 1 Work Stoppages in Government, 1958-68*

Year	Total			State government			Local government		
	Stoppages	Workers involved	Man-days idle	Stoppages	Workers involved	Man-days idle	Stoppages	Workers involved	Man-days idle
1958	15	1,720	7,510	1	30	60	14	1,690	7,450
1959	26	2,240	11,500	4	410	1,650	22	1,830	9,850
1960	36	28,600	58,400	3	970	1,170	33	27,600	57,200
1961	28	6,610	15,300				28	6,610	15,300
1962	+28	31,100	79,100	2	1,660	2,260	21	25,300	43,100
1963	29	4,840	15,400	2	280	2,160	27	4,560	13,300
1964	41	22,700	70,800	4	280	3,170	37	22,500	67,700
1965	42	11,900	146,000			+1,280	42	11,900	145,000
1966	142	105,000	455,000	9	3,090	6,010	133	102,000	449,000
1967	181	132,000	1,250,000	12	4,670	16,300	169	127,000	1,230,000
1968	o254	201,800	2,545,200	16	9,300	42,800	235	190,900	2,492,800

*Includes stoppages lasting a full day or shift or longer and involving at least 6 workers.
+Includes 5 stoppages of Federal employees, affecting 4,190 workers, resulting in 33,800 man-days of idleness.

‡Idleness in 1965 resulting from a stoppage that began in 1964.
oIncludes 3 stoppages of Federal employees, affecting 1,680 workers, resulting in 9,600 man-days of idleness.

days lost rose by almost 800,000 between 1966 and 1967, and an increase of 175 percent. A 1.3-million increase between 1967 and 1968, however, represented only a 100-percent rise.

Despite the large increase in work stoppages by government employees in the past 3 years, strike activity in the public sector still is low relative to the private sector. In 1968, a larger number of government employees were involved in stoppages than in any previous year, but these workers represented only 1.65 percent of total government employment. Workers involved in all strikes during that year represented 3.8 percent of total employment, a rate more than twice that in government service.

In terms of man-days of idleness as a percent of estimated total working time, government employees also are far behind the workers in the private sector. In 1968 strike idleness represented 0.08 percent of man-days worked by government employees; for the economy as a whole, this figure was 0.28 percent.

Work stoppages directed against public agencies often are of greater magnitude than those involving private firms. This has been true during 6 out of the past 11 years. The main reason for this is that strikes in government service usually involve the large employee units found in metropolitan centers.

MAJOR ISSUES

The issues that prompted government workers to leave their jobs during the past decade were generally similar to strike issues in private industry. In both sectors higher wages and supplementary benefits are the most frequent cause of striking, while job security is least likely to induce action. Government employees, however, are more likely to strike to secure official recognition of their unions than are their counterparts in private industry. Employees in the private sector, many of whom work for firms that have recognized and bargained with unions for decades, strike over matters of administration as frequently as they do over union organization. From 1962 through 1968, in just under 14 percent of all private sector strikes, union organization was the major issue, while the matters of administration were the immediate cause in slightly more than 15 percent of the disputes. During the same period, almost 22 percent of the walkouts in government involved problems of union organization and security, while administration matters accounted for only about 13 percent of the total.

Wage issues have become even more important in government in recent years. (See table 2.) From 1962 to 1965, this issue accounted for 54 percent of government stoppages and somewhat higher proportions of workers and man-days of idleness. In the last 3 years of the period studied, 61 percent of the government walkouts, excluding the 1968 New York City teachers' strike,[5] arose from the parties' inability to reach an agreement on wage and fringe benefit changes. These stoppages accounted for 73 percent of all workers and 83 percent of the resulting idleness.

At least part of the increase in economic stoppages in public service is attribut-

---

[5]This strike, called over matters of administration, involved 47,000 employees and resulted in 1,645,000 man-days of lost time (65 percent of total idleness in government service for 1968).

table 2   Work Stoppages in Government, by Major Issue, 1958-68*

Year	General wage changes and supplementary benefits			Union organization and security			Job security†			Administration matters‡			Interunion and intraunion matters			Other working conditions		
	Stop-pages	Workers involved	Man-days idle	Stop-pages	Workers involved	Man-days idle	Stop-pages	Workers involved	Man-days idle	Stop-pages	Workers involved	Man-days idle	Stop-pages	Workers involved	Man-days idle	Stop-pages	Workers involved	Man-days idle
1958	8	1,130	4,760	2	340	1,990	...	...	...	...	...	...	...	...	§60	5	250	700
1959	7	950	2,640	9	820	4,580	...	...	...	...	...	...	2	40	180	8	430	4,060
1960	19	16,600	40,800	8	6,220	9,610	...	...	...	...	...	...	1	10	10	8	5,770	8,010
1961	22	5,970	13,600	1	20	20	...	...	...	...	...	...	1	10	20	4	610	1,640
1962	10	25,500	40,300	5	380	840	2	30	200	8	2,380	6,100	3	2,870	31,700	...	...	...
1963	15	1,700	8,350	5	2,750	6,060	2	90	170	5	170	340	1	30	120	1	100	400
1964	26	9,620	37,300	8	2,550	7,680	...	...	...	7	10,600	25,900	...	...	...	...	...	...
1965‡	25	9,830	128,000	12	850	11,500	1	80	80	1	10	50	2	980	6,160	...	...	...
1966	78	58,200	355,000	36	11,600	45,600	2	170	1,680	21	33,300	46,500	5	1,760	5,840	...	...	...
1967	128	118,000	1,040,000	29	6,670	99,300	2	730	1,430	19	2,670	5,630	1	90	360	2	4,030	99,900
1968‡	146	110,300	759,200	60	33,600	90,100	2	90	200	33	53,200	1,684,200	5	2,700	4,900	5	1,700	6,200

*See footnote 1, table 1.
†Job security and administration matters were included in "other working conditions," 1958-61.

‡The issues involved were not reported in 1 stoppage in 1965 and 3 in 1968.
§Idleness resulting from stoppages that began in previous year.

255

able to the growing demands of teachers and other school employees for higher pay. Over the past decade, strikes by these employees represented two-fifths of all government strikes in which wages were the principal issue. Almost three-fifths of the workers involved and two-thirds of the time lost because of wage disputes arose from public school stoppages. Most of the school strikes have occurred in the past 3 years.

Union organization and security, the second most common cause of public employees' stoppages, has been the major issue in about 20 percent of disputes in the 1958-68 period. Public school and library employees accounted for about 26 percent of the union organization strikes and 73 percent of the workers involved during the first 8 years of the period. In 1966-68, the proportion of union organization strikes attributable to public school stoppages increased to 38 percent but numbers of workers involved decreased to 66 percent.

TYPE OF WORK

Government employee stoppages in education and in sanitation and health services have received most public attention in recent years. Teachers' strikes have aroused interest because white-collar employees had rarely withheld their services in the past. Stoppages in sanitation and health services attracted attention because of the hazards to public health they can pose, and because several major disputes have had the militant support of civil rights organizations.

Schools and Libraries

During the past 3 years, nearly half (44 percent) of all stoppages by government employees have involved teachers and other employees of public schools and libraries. Teachers have sought not only higher salaries but also the right to participate in decisions on how, what, and where they were to teach, and in determining the best allocation of usually limited school budgets. The majority of the workers involved and most of the time lost because of disputes over matters of administration from 1966 to 1968 is attributable to teachers' stoppages. In 1958 no work stoppages in this sector of public service were reported; in 1968, there were 112 stoppages in public schools and libraries, involving 148,000 employees and resulting in 2,194,000 man-days of idleness. These strikes accounted for 86 percent of the man-days of idleness in the public sector.

The high level of strike activity in public education began in 1966, when the number of such strikes increased sixfold from the previous year—from 9 to 54. In fact, the 3 years of 1966-68 accounted for 5 times as many school strikes, involving 5 times as many workers and resulting in 28 times as many man-days of idleness, as did such stoppages in the preceding 8 years.

During the first 6 years of the 1958-68 period, teachers were less likely to leave their jobs than were other school employees. When they did, their walkouts tended to involve more workers than did those of the nonteaching staff (largely because teachers form the majority of a school's employees). But teacher strikes tended to end sooner and thus result in fewer man-days of idleness. In each year since 1964, the majority of all public school stoppages have involved teachers. The latter have constituted over 75 percent or more of the idleness in public schools.

Throughout the 11-year period school strikes have been most frequent in the Midwestern States. However, these stoppages have typically involved fewer workers and resulted in fewer days of idleness than those in either the Northeast or the South. One 2-day teacher "protest" in Utah in 1964 involving 10,000 workers, and a 1968 New Mexico teacher stoppage, together accounted for well over half of the workers involved and man-days lost in school stoppages in the Far West during the past 11 years.

Sanitation Services

Usually among the lowest paid public workers in a community, sanitation department employees have been demanding recognition of their unions, wage increases, and improved supplementary benefits. In many parts of the country most of them are black and are actively supported by civil rights organizations. The 1968 sanitation strike in Memphis, Tenn., was a case at hand. Between 1966 and 1968, 41 percent of the stoppages, resulting in 48 percent of idleness in the sanitation services, occurred in the South.

In the 11 years covered by the study, sanitation services accounted for the second largest number of public employee stoppages. The upward trend of strike activity in this area has been quite erratic. In 1960, for example, there were 12 sanitation strikes involving over 8,000 workers and resulting in more than 21,000 man-days of idleness; in 1966 the number of such strikes was 3 times as large and the idleness they caused 15 percent greater, yet the number of workers involved was lower than in 1960. After a drop in 1967, there was a large increase in all three measures of dispute activity in sanitation services in 1968.

Health Services

During 1968 most work stoppages in hospitals and other health services involved semiprofessional and nonprofessional employees. As in the sanitation field, the nonprofessional hospital employee is often a member of a minority group and, until recently, usually not covered by minimum wage laws. Typically he is at or near the lowest rung of the wage ladder. Along with wages and union organization, civil rights issues have also figured in many hospital disputes, as in the 1969 strike of nonprofessional employees in Columbia, S.C. In 1966 and 1967, however, it was the nurses and other professional health workers who participated in most of the hospital strikes; the racial issue was absent.

There has been a remarkable change in labor-management relations climate in hospitals from the 1958-65 period to the past 3 years. Few strikes occurred through 1965, but the years 1966-68 were marked by 57 stoppages of 20,000 hospital and health service employees, resulting in almost 135,000 man-days of idleness.

LEVEL OF GOVERNMENT

Since municipalities employ more workers than do States, most public work stoppages occur at the local level. Although the increases in idleness have been highest at the local level, the percentage divisions between State and local governments have remained steady. Strikes at the State level have occurred in 9 of the past 11 years, ranging from 6 to 8 percent of all the strikes in government. They have involved 2 to 6 percent of all workers and resulted in 1 to 5 percent of idleness, with no significant trend apparent.

For the Federal Government, Bureau of Labor Statistics data indicate eight strikes during the past 11 years: five stoppages in 1962, involving 4,190 workers and resulting in 33,800 man-days of idleness, and three stoppages in 1968, affecting 1,680 workers and resulting in 9,600 man-days of lost time. The majority of these eight stoppages in Federal Government occurred at Tennessee Valley Authority construction sites.

UNION INVOLVEMENT

For the purposes of this discussion, public workers' stoppages were divided into categories based on the extent of union involvement. Thus the division was according to situations in which (1) the unions or other formal associations involved are made up entirely or predominantly of public employees (called here "public" or "government" unions); (2) the unions involved are made up of employees from both public and private sectors, primarily the latter ("mixed" unions); (3) two unions or more with bases in different sectors are involved ("other" unions); and (4) no unions or other formal associations are involved. (See table 3.)

As already indicated, the number of government stoppages has increased substantially over the last 3 years. And as unions have come to represent larger proportions of public servants, the percentage of walkouts led by "public" unions has also increased. From 1966 to 1968 the number of workers involved in all public disputes almost doubled; for public employee unions the increase was 227 percent. In 1966, only 28 percent of man-days of idleness resulting from government stoppages were attributable to public unions; by 1968 the figure climbed to 94 percent, 34 percentage points higher than the average for 1958-65.

The proportion of stoppages which do not involve any union or formal association has ranged from 7 percent in 1962 to 31 percent in 1963. Unions whose membership is predominantly in the private sector were involved in fewer strikes than those with government base in only 1 of the first 8 years (1959). In the past 3 years, however, private sector unions were involved in fewer than one-third as many government disputes as were public unions; this ratio declined from 49 percent in 1966 to 26 percent in 1968. The high rates for private union participation in government walkouts in the earlier period and the low level of participation during the past 3 years, suggest that much of the initial impetus for organizing was provided by this group. Now that public unions have established a strong and growing

table 3   **Work Stoppages in Government by Type of Union Involvement, 1958-68**

Year	Public unions			Mixed unions			Other*			No union involved		
	Stoppages	Workers Involved	Man-days idle	Stoppages	Workers involved	Man-days idle	Stoppages	Workers involved	Man-days idle	Stoppages	Workers involved	Man-days idle
1958	5	980	4,170	7	670	3,160	....	....	....	3	70	130
1959	12	1,570	8,040	10	470	2,950	....	....	....	4	210	470
1960	11	7,070	10,500	19	21,200	47,200	....	....	....	6	290	770
1961	7	1,050	3,440	12	5,090	8,880	....	....	....	9	470	3,000
1962	5	24,300	38,600	21	6,820	40,260	....	....	....	2	30	150
1963	10	4,000	11,800	10	600	3,260	....	....	....	9	250	420
1964	16	16,500	36,800	17	5,440	27,100	....	....	....	8	800	6,800
1965	16	9,890	131,000	18	1,340	13,800	....	....	....	8	640	1,040
1966	78	54,300	128,700	38	49,000	322,000	3	840	940	23	940	3,740
1967	116	118,000	1,182,000	37	10,400	57,200	....	....	....	28	2,930	6,970
1968	177	177,600	2,398,000	46	21,900	120,200	1	123	246	30	2,150	26,600

*Stoppages involving more than 1 union, with 1 predominantly in the public sector and the other with members in the public and private sectors.

259

membership, they have assumed the leadership of the rapidly growing union activity in the public sector.

Collective bargaining in the public sector at the present time is a relatively new phenomenon. Neither managers nor employees have yet had time to learn how to negotiate. They have also found it difficult to apply the experience gained in private situations to their situation. As both parties experiment with and develop patterns of bargaining, they will become more proficient at negotiating on a give-and-take basis. And as parity with the private sector is approached, a major cause of work stoppages in government service will be removed.

USING "FACTFINDING AND RECOMMENDATIONS" IN IMPASSES

George W. Taylor

The right to strike has not been accorded to employees in the public sector. The wherewithal to pay wages does not derive from a competitive marketplace, but through taxes levied and budgets enacted by elected government officials. In a representative government the elected officials are responsible for determining the amount of taxes we are to pay and how the total revenue is to be allocated among claimants so as to maintain a viable society. In some respects, the legislative body may be looked upon as the counterpart of competitive forces of the market in private industry. The refusal or the inability of some people to recognize this evident difference has resulted in proposals for public employee relations that are impractical and unreasoned.

In public employment, boards responsible for factfinding and the making of recommendations in particular negotiating impasses have the function of insuring that, in the budgetmaking process, the claims of public employees do not become inequitably subordinated to the myriad other claims for public funds. Nevertheless, some public employees and their unions—by no means all of them—insist that a strike, or at least the threat of a strike, is essential to insure their fair treatment. Nearly everybody else holds the conviction that such strikes seriously impair their fundamental rights and equities.

This is the crucial conflict of interests which the so-called experts and the mediators should seek to accommodate. Avoiding this difficult but underlying issue is scarcely professional. Maybe it is sometimes merely adopting a partisan position.

George Taylor is Harnwell Professor of Industry, University of Pennsylvania. Reprinted from *Monthly Labor Review,* July 1969.

For, unless ways and means other than the strike can be developed to provide equitable terms and conditions of employment, we face a cycle of futility: Illegal strikes followed by legislative imposition of increasingly harsh penalties. This cycle has to be broken as one of the important steps for reestablishing social stability. Factfinding and recommendations offer some promise of breaking the cycle. I eagerly await the advancement of other proposals.

Factfinding and recommendations in impasse cases should be made on the basis of labor relations criteria applied to the particular case. If rejected by either party to the negotiations, the recommendations should nevertheless be presented to the legislative body along with the positions of the parties. The objective is to insure that employee claims be carefully evalued in the competition for funds that occurs in the formulation of taxing and budget policies. The final decision, however, must remain with the legislative and executive officials who have a constitutional duty to carry out these formulations. Considering all the demands for public funds, these officials are responsible for deciding whether there are, on balance, sound reasons to modify, upward or downward, factfinders' recommendations.

There is an additional reason for placing such a responsibility upon elected government officials. Since negotiations are fragmented when public employees are accorded the right to have representatives of their own choosing, no board in a particular case is in a position to appraise the claims of other public employees who also want to be first.

It should be noted that the factfinding and recommendations approach adopted by the Taylor Law has produced highly encouraging initial results in New York State outside of New York City. A number of critical strikes there have obscured the successes of the Office of Collective Bargaining. Outside of New York City, the Taylor Law accorded rights to public employees long withheld. New York City practices, however, are a different matter. The threat of an illegal strike in New York City had become virtually standard negotiation practice despite the provisions of the Condin-Wadlin Act. A major effect of the Taylor Law, as originally enacted, was to change those penalties of the Condin-Wadlin Act from ones which experience had shown could not be invoked to penalties which can be imposed. This doubtless accounts for many of the most vociferous attacks on the law, which have contributed much to the cycle of futility mentioned earlier.

However, let me make it clear that there is nothing in the Taylor Law requiring the imprisonment of union officials as a penalty in the event of an illegal strike. In its January 23, 1969 report the Governor's Committee observed: "From the standpoint of sound government-employee relations alone, we are convinced that the possibility of such imprisonment is not an effective deterrent against engaging in illegal strikes. We have never recommended it. Nor is it a part of the Taylor Law. Indeed, achievement of the objectives of the Taylor Law could very well be enhanced if an imposition of this penalty was not a possibility. On the other hand, whether or not such a penalty is deemed by the courts to be essential for the preservation of the judicial process, upon which all of us depend for the protection of our basic rights, is a question which goes far beyond the matter of government-employee relations with which we are here particularly concerned. This is a matter, therefore, for courts to determine."

Now, what about the constructive results of that law? Without work stoppages, teachers in scores of school districts have, for the first time, organized for collective negotiations. So have thousands of employees in towns, cities, and counties. They have begun the establishment of formalized relationship with the appropriate administrative agencies. Over 1,000 agreements have been consummated, most of them without outside assistance. The Public Employment Relations Board has settled, or is in the process of settling, nearly 400 representation disputes. Approximately 400 disputes over the terms of agreements were brought to PERB during 1968, and by the end of the year most of them were settled and a relatively few were in the process of settlement. Through 1968, 125 factfinding panels were appointed. Eight of them were three-member panels and the balance were single-member panels. Through 1968, five brief work stoppages occurred as a result of disputes arising within PERB's initial jurisdiction. They involved 1,700 employees. There were nine other stoppages in which the law's impasse procedures were not utilized.

To be sure, a final testing has yet to be made and modifications in the procedures will doubtless be made as experience is gained. On the record, it seems to me, strong reasons can be advanced to support the proposition that while strikes and compulsory arbitration are not proper pressures on representative government, factfinding and recommendations can be developed to enhance the status of public employee claims. A failure of this proposition would give credence to the view that the important item of wages should be excluded from negotiations with public employees, as is the case in the Federal Government.

RESOLVING DEADLOCKS WITHOUT BANNING STRIKES

Theodore W. Kheel

For better or worse, the conclusion is inescapable that collective bargaining cannot exist if employees may not withdraw their services or employers discontinue them. This is not a statement of preference, but a statement of fact. But it is now also evident that collective bargaining is the best way of composing differences between workers and their employers in a democratic society even though there is much room for improvement in the process. So, if we believe public employees should have bargaining rights, we must accept the possibility of a strike and consider how best to guard against it. If we believe the case against strikes by public employees is so overwhelming that all such strikes must be prohibited, let us then say frankly that public employees cannot be given bargaining rights and that the use of such euphemisms as collective negotiations cannot alter the basic structural differences the strike ban entails.

Theodore Kheel is a member of the law firm of Battle, Fowler, Stokes, and Kheel. Reprinted from *Monthly Labor Review*, July 1969.

But if we believe that the case for collective bargaining even for public workers is as persuasive as most commentators including the Taylor Committee believe it to be, then we should try, it seems to me, to grant public workers bargaining rights while still protecting the public at least as much as it is protected in the private sector against strikes that threaten health or safety. I think this can be done by using the formula of the Taft-Hartley Law for emergency disputes. But let us not deceive ourselves. When all strikes are barred, collective bargaining or joint determination is out except to the extent that express or implied threats to violate the law create a bargaining atmosphere which is hardly the way to encourage respect for law.

There are only two real substitutes for bargaining: either the employer makes the final determination or it is made by a third party, an arbitrator. The procedures of the Taylor Law called collective negotiations are long and complex but at their end the final decision is made by the employer.

I believe that the time has come for us to forego the view that all strikes by all public workers under all circumstances and for all time must be considered illegal. I do not mean by this to suggest that the right to strike is sacrosanct. On the contrary, it is a right like all other rights that must be weighed against the larger public interest, and it must be subordinated where necessary to the superior right of the public to protection against injury to health or safety. There is also the right to bargain collectively, which most of us would like to extend to public workers, and it depends on the possibility that a strike or lockout may take place. This right to collective bargaining is likewise subordinate to other rights as the circumstances arise.

These principles, in my judgment, apply to the private sector as well as the public sector. Moreover, their application cannot be determined in advance. The strike of Consolidated Edison employees might have been the most calamitous New York City has ever seen. But the company kept its plants operating with supervisory help, and as a result there was little public inconvenience. I assume that if the strike had closed down the operations, the President might have obtained an injunction under Taft-Hartley. That would have foreclosed a strike for 80 days, not for all time as does an injunction under the Taylor Law. It leaves the door open to bargaining during the 80-day period. If the prospect of a renewal of the strike loomed ominously ahead, the Congress (or the State Legislature) might have imposed arbitration on the specific issues remaining in dispute as Congress did in the railroad disputes in 1964 and 1967.

Why cannot a similar system be used in public employment? Would it not make better sense to save the awesome power of government for those few instances where its strength is really needed, instead of dissipating it in a complicated system of procedures and a set of ambivalent penalties that may or may not work but do make a process we endorse as beneficial in the private sector subversive in the public sector? If the Governor was able to halt a strike for a period of time, alternative solutions could be found, including the imposition of arbitration on the unresolved issues if no other alternative remained. In this way collective bargaining would be encouraged in practically all instances, practitioners would learn better how to use the process in the public service, as they have in the private sector, and the complicated procedures and penalties the strike ban makes necessary could be discarded.

THE LIMITS OF COLLECTIVE BARGAINING
IN PUBLIC EMPLOYMENT

Harry H. Wellington
Ralph K. Winter, Jr.

THE CLAIMS FOR COLLECTIVE BARGAINING IN THE PRIVATE SECTOR

Those who deny the validity of the claims for collective bargaining in the private sector will surely not find those claims to have merit in the public. We do not intend to debate the merits of these claims. We must, however, if we are fully to test our thesis that a full transplant of collective bargaining to the public sector is inappropriate, assume a minimal validity of the claims that are made for it in the private.

Four claims then, are made for a private-sector collective bargaining. First, it is a way to achieve industrial peace. The point was put as early as 1902 by the Industrial Commission:

> The chief advantage which comes from the practice of periodically determining the conditions of labor by collective bargaining directly between employers and employees is that thereby each side obtains a better understanding of the actual state of the industry, of the conditions which confront the other side, and of the motives which influence it. Most strikes and lockouts would not occur if each party understood exactly the position of the other.

Second, collective bargaining is a way of achieving industrial democracy—that is, participation by workers in their own governance. It is the industrial counterpart of the contemporary demand for community participation.

Third, unions that bargain collectively with employers represent workers in the political arena as well. And political representation through interest groups is one of the most important types of political representation that the individual can have. Government at all levels acts in large part in response to the demands made upon it by the groups to which its citizens belong.

Fourth, and most important, as a result of a belief in the unequal bargaining

Harry Wellington and Ralph Winter are Edward J. Phelps Professor of Law, Yale University, and Professor of Law, Yale University, respectively. Reprinted from *The Yale Law Journal* LXXVII, No. 7, June 1969. Most footnote references have been deleted.

power of employers and employees, collective bargaining is claimed to be a needed substitute for individual bargaining. Monopsony—a buyer's monopoly, in this case a buyer of labor—is alleged to exist in many situations and to create unfair contracts of labor as a result of individual bargaining. While this, in turn, may not mean that workers as a class and over time get significantly less than they should—because monopsony is surely not a general condition but is alleged to exist only in a number of particular circumstances—it may mean that the terms and conditions of employment for an individual or group of workers at a given period of time and in given circumstances may be unfair. What tends to insure fairness in the aggregate and over the long run is the discipline of the market. But monopsony, if it exists, can work substantial injustice to individuals. Governmental support of collective bargaining represents the nation's response to a belief that such injustice occurs. Fairness between employee and employer in wages, hours, and terms and conditions of employment is thought more likely to be ensured where private ordering takes the collective form.

There are, however, generally recognized social costs resulting from this resort to collectivism. In the private sector these costs are primarily economic, and the question is, given the benefits of collective bargaining as an institution, what is the nature of the economic costs? Economists who have turned their attention to this question are legion, and disagreement among them monumental. The principal concerns are of two intertwined sorts. One is summarized by Professor Albert Rees of Princeton:

> If the union is viewed solely in terms of its effect on the economy, it must in my opinion be considered an obstacle to the optimum performance of our economic system. It alters the wage structure in a way that impedes the growth of employment in sectors of the economy where productivity and income are naturally high and that leaves too much labor in low-income sectors of the economy like southern agriculture and the least skilled trades. It benefits most those workers who would in any case be relatively well off, and while some of this gain may be at the expense of the owners of capital, most of it must be at the expense of consumers and the lower-paid workers. Unions interfere blatantly with the use of the most productive techniques in some industries, and this effect is probably not offset by the stimulus to higher productivity furnished by some other unions.

The other concern is stated in the 1967 Report of the Council of Economic Advisors:

> Vigorous competition is essential to price stability in a high employment economy. But competitive forces do not and cannot operate with equal strength in every sector of the economy. In industries where the number of competitors is limited, business firms have a substantial measure of discretion in setting prices. In many sectors of the labor market, unions and managements together have a substantial measure of discretion in setting wages. The responsible exercise of discretionary power over wages and prices can help to maintain general price stability. Its irresponsible use can make full employment and price stability incompatible.

And the claim is that this "discretionary power" too often is exercised "irresponsibly."

Disagreement among economists extends to the quantity as well as to the fact of economic malfunctioning that properly is attributable to collective bargaining. But there is no disagreement that at some point the market disciplines or delimits union power. As we shall see in more detail below, union power is frequently constrained by the fact that consumers react to a relative increase in the price of a product by purchasing less of it. As a result any significant real financial benefit, beyond that justified by an increase in productivity, which accrued to workers through collective bargaining, may well cause significant unemployment among union members. Because of this employment-benefit relationship, the economic costs imposed by collective bargaining as it presently exists in the private sector seem inherently limited.

THE CLAIMS FOR COLLECTIVE BARGAINING IN THE PUBLIC SECTOR

In the area of public employment the claims upon public policy made by the need for industrial peace, industrial democracy and effective political representation point toward collective bargaining. This is to say that three of the four arguments that support bargaining in the private sector—to some extent, at least—press for similar arrangements in the public sector. . . .

The pressures thus generated by size and bureaucracy lead inescapably to disruption—to labor unrest—unless these pressures are recognized and unless existing decision-making procedures are accommodated to them. Peace in government employment too, the argument runs, can best be established by making union recognition and collective bargaining accepted public policy.

Much less clearly analogous to the private model, however, is the unequal bargaining power argument. In the private sector that argument really has two aspects. The first, which we have just adumbrated, is affirmative in nature. Monopsony is believed sometimes to result in unfair individual contracts of employment. The unfairness may be reflected in wages, which are less than they would be if the market were more nearly perfect, or in working arrangements which may lodge arbitrary power in a foreman, i.e., power to hire, fire, promote, assign or discipline without respect to substantive or procedural rules. A persistent assertion, generating much heat, relates to the arbitrary exercise of managerial power in individual cases. This assertion goes far to explain the insistence of unions on the establishment in the labor contract of rules, with an accompanying adjudicatory procedure, to govern industrial life.

Judgments about the fairness of the financial terms of the public employee's individual contract of employment are even harder to make than for private sector workers. The case for the existence of private employer monopsony, disputed as it is, asserts only that some private sector employers in some circumstances have too much bargaining power. In the public sector, the case to be proven is that the governmental employer ever has such power. But even if this case could be proven, market norms are at best attenuated guides to questions of fairness. In employment as in all other areas, governmental decisions are properly political decisions, and economic considerations are but one criterion among many. Questions of fairness do not centrally relate to how much imperfection one sees in the market, but more to how much imperfection one sees in the political process. "Low" pay for teachers may be merely a decision—right or wrong, resulting from the pressure of special interests or from a desire to promote the general welfare—to exchange a reduction in the quality or quantity of teachers for higher welfare payments, a domed stadium, etc. And we are limited in our ability to make informed judgments about such political decision because of the understandable but unfortunate fact that the science of politics has failed to supply us with either as elegant or as reliable a theoretical model as has its sister discipline.

Nevertheless, employment benefits in the public sector may have improved relatively more slowly than in the private sector during the last three decades. An economy with a persistent inflationary bias probably works to the disadvantage of those who must rely on legislation for wage adjustments. Moreover, while public employment was once attractive for the greater job security and retirement benefits it provided, quite similar protection is now available in many areas of the private sector. On the other hand, to the extent that civil service, or merit, systems exist in public employment and these laws are obeyed, the arbitrary exercise of managerial power is substantially reduced. Where it is reduced, a labor policy that relies on the individual employment contract must seem less unacceptable.

The second, or negative aspect of the unequal bargaining power argument, relates to the social costs of collective bargaining. As we have seen, the social costs of collective bargaining in the private sector are principally economic, and seem inherently limited by market forces. In the public sector, however, the costs seem to us economic only in a very narrow sense and are on the whole political. It further seems to us that, to the extent union power is delimited by market or other forces in the public sector, these constraints do not come into play nearly as quickly as in the private. An understanding of why this is so requires further comparison between collective bargaining in the two sectors.

THE PRIVATE SECTOR MODEL

While the private sector is, of course, extraordinarily diverse, the paradigm case is an industry which produces a product that is not particularly essential to those who buy it and for which dissimilar products can be substituted. Within the market or markets for this product, most—but not all—of the producers must bargain with a union representing their employees, and this union is generally the same through the industry. A price rise of this product relative to others will result in a decrease in the number of units of the product sold. This in turn will result in a cutback in employment. And an increase in price would be dictated by an increase in labor cost relative to output, at least in most situations. Thus, the union is faced with some sort of rough trade-off between, on the one hand, larger benefits for some employees and unemployment for others, and on the other hand, smaller benefits and more employment. Because unions are political organizations, with a legal duty to represent *all* employees fairly, and with a treasury that comes from per capita dues, there is pressure on the union to avoid the road that leads to unemployment.

This picture of the restraints that the market imposes on collective bargaining settlements undergoes change as the variables change. On the one hand, to the extent that there are non-union firms within a product market, the impact of union pressure will be diminished by the ability of consumers to purchase identical products from nonunion and, presumably, less expensive sources. On the other hand, to the extent that union organization of competitors within the product market is complete, there will be no such restraint and the principal barriers to union bargaining goals will be the ability of a number of consumers to react to a price change by turning to dissimilar but nevertheless substitutable products.

Two additional variables must be noted. First, where the demand for an industry's product is rather insensitive to price—*i.e.*, relatively inelastic—and where all the firms in a product market are organized, the union need fear less the employment-benefit trade-off, for the employer is less concerned about raising prices in response to increased costs. By hypothesis, a price rise affects unit sales of such an employer only minimally. Second, in an expanding industry, wage settlements which exceed increases in productivity may not reduce union employment. They will reduce expansion, hence the employment effect will be experienced only by workers who do not belong to the union. This means that in the short run the politics of the employment-benefit trade-off do not restrain the union in its bargaining demands.

In both of these cases, however, there are at least two restraints on the union. One is the employer's increased incentive to substitute machines for labor, a factor present in the paradigm case and all other cases as well. The other restraint stems from the fact that large sections of the nation are unorganized and highly resistant to unionization. Accordingly, capital will seek non-union labor, and in this way the market will discipline the organized sector.

The employer, in the paradigm case and in all variations of it, is motivated primarily by the necessity to maximize profits (and this is so no matter how political a corporation may seem to be). He therefore is not inclined (absent an increase in demand for his product) to raise prices and thereby suffer a loss in profits, and he is organized to transmit and represent the market pressures described above. Generally he will resist, and resist hard, union demands that exceed increases in productivity, for if he accepts such demands he may be forced to raise prices. Should he be unsuccessful in his resistance too often, and should it cost him too much, he can be expected to put his money and energy elsewhere.

What all this means is that the social costs imposed by collective bargaining are economic costs; that usually they are limited by powerful market restraints; and that these restraints are visible to anyone who is able to see the forest for the trees.

THE PUBLIC SECTOR MODEL

The paradigm case in the public sector is a municipality with an elected board of aldermen, and an elected mayor who bargains (through others) with unions representing the employees of the city. He bargains also, of course, with other permanent and *ad hoc* interest groups making claims upon government (business groups, save-the-park committees, neighborhood groups, etc.). Indeed, the decisions that are made may be thought of roughly as a result of interactions and accommodations among these interest groups, as influenced by perceptions about the attitudes of the electorate, and by the goals and programs of the mayor and his aldermanic board.

Decisions that cost the city money are generally paid for from taxes and, less often, by borrowing. Not only are there many types of taxes, but also there are several layers of government which may make tax revenue available to the city; federal and state as well as local funds may be employed for some purposes. Formal allocation of money for particular uses is made through the city's budget, which may have within it considerable room for adjustments. Thus, a union will bargain hard for as large a share of the budget as it thinks it possibly can obtain, and beyond this to force a tax increase if it deems that possible.

In the public sector too, the market operates. In the long run, the supply of labor is a function of the price paid for labor by the public employer relative to what workers earn elsewhere. This is some assurance that public employees in the aggregate—with or without collective bargaining—are not paid too little. The case for employer monopsony, moreover, may be much weaker in the public sector than it is in the private. First, to the extent that most public employees work in urban areas, as they probably do, there may often be a number of substitutable and competing private and public employers in the labor market. When that is the case, there can be little monopsony power. Second, even if public employers occasionally have monopsony power, governmental policy is determined only in part by economic criteria, and there is no assurance, as there is in the private sector where the profit motive prevails, that the power will be exploited.

As we have seen, market-imposed unemployment is an important restraint on unions in the private sector. In the public sector, the trade-off between benefits and employment seems much less important. Government does not generally sell a product the demand for which is closely related to price. There usually are not close substitutes for the products and services provided by government and the demand for them is inelastic. Such market conditions are, as we have seen, favorable to unions in the private sector because they permit the acquisition of benefits without the penalty of unemployment, subject to the restraint of non-union competitors, actual or potential. But no such restraint limits the demands of public employee unions. Because much government activity is, and must be, a monopoly, product competition, non-union or otherwise, does not exert a down-ward pressure on prices and wages. Nor will the existence of a pool of labor ready to work for a wage below union scale attract new capital and create a new, and competitively less expensive, governmental enterprise. The fear of unemployment, however, can serve as something of a restraining force in two situations. First, if the cost of labor increases, the city may reduce the quality of the service it furnishes by reducing employment. For example, if teachers' salaries are increased, it may decrease the number of teachers and increase class size. However, the ability of city government to accomplish such a change is limited not only by union pressure, but also by the pressure of other affected interest groups in the community. Political considerations, therefore, may cause either no reduction in employment or services, or a reduction in an area other than that in which the union members work. Both the political power exerted by the beneficiaries of the services, who are also voters, and the power of the public employee union as a labor organization, then, combine to create great pressure on political leaders either to seek new funds or to reduce municipal services of another kind. Second, if labor costs increase, the city may, even as a private employer would, seek to replace labor with machines. The absence of a profit motive, and a political concern for unemployment, however, may be a deterrent in addition to the deterrent of union resistance. The public employer which decides it must limit employment because of unit labor costs will likely find that the politically easiest decision is to restrict new hires, rather than to lay off current employees.

Even if we are right that a close relationship between increased economic benefits and unemployment does not exist as a significant deterrent to unions in the public sector, might not the argument be made that in some sense the taxpayer is the public sector's functional equivalent of the consumer? If taxes become too high, the taxpayer can move to another community. While it is generally much easier for a consumer to substitute products than for a taxpayer to substitute communities, is it not fair to say that, at the point at which a tax increase will cause so many taxpayers to move that it will produce less total revenue, the market disciplines or restrains union and public employer in the same way and for the same reasons that the market disciplines parties in the private sector? Moreover, does not the analogy to the private sector suggest that it is legitimate in an economic sense for unions to push government to the point of substitutability?

Several factors suggest that the answer to this latter question is at best indeterminate, and that the question of legitimacy must be judged not by economic, but by political criteria.

In the first place, there is no theoretical reason—economic or political—to suppose that it is desirable for a governmental entity to liquidate its taxing power, to tax up to the point where another tax increase will produce less revenue because of the number of people it drives to different communities. In the private area, profit maximization is a complex concept, but its approximation generally is both a legal requirement and socially useful as a means of allocating resources. The liquidation of taxing power seems neither imperative nor useful.

Second, consider the complexity of the tax structure and the way in which different kinds of taxes (property, sales, income) fall differently upon a given population. Consider, moreover, that the taxing authority of a particular governmental entity may be limited (a municipality may not have the power to impose an income tax). What is necessarily involved, then, is principally the redistribution of income by government rather than resource allocation,[1] and questions of income redistribution surely are essentially political questions.

For his part, the mayor in our paradigm case will be disciplined not by a desire to maximize profits, but by a desire—in some cases at least—to do a good job (to effectuate his programs), and in virtually all cases either to be reelected or to move to a better elective office. What he gives to the union must be taken from some other interest group or from taxpayers. His is the job of coordinating these competing claims while remaining politically viable. And that coordination will be governed by the relative power of the competing interest groups. Our inquiry, therefore, must turn to the question of how much power public employee unions will exercise if the full private model of collective bargaining is adopted in the public sector.

[1] In the private sector what is involved is principally resource allocation rather than income redistribution. Income redistribution occurs to the extent that unions are able to increase wages at the expense of profits, but the extent to which this actually happens would seem to be limited. It also occurs to the extent that unions, by limiting employment in the union sector through maintenance of wages above a competitive level, increase the supply of labor in the non-union sector and thereby depress wages there.

PUBLIC EMPLOYEE STRIKES AND THE POLITICAL PROCESS

Although the market does not discipline the union in the public sector to the extent that it does in the private, the paradigm case, nevertheless, would seem to be consistent with what Robert A. Dahl has called the "'normal' American political process," which is "one in which there is a high probability that an active and legitimate group in the population can make itself heard effectively at some crucial stage in the process of decision," for the union may be seen as little more than an "active and legitimate group in the population." With elections in the background to perform, as Mr. Dahl tells us, "the critical role . . . in maximizing political equality and popular sovereignty," all seems well, at least theoretically, with collective bargaining and public employment.

But there is trouble even in the house of theory if collective bargaining in the public sector means what it does in the private. The trouble is that if unions are able to withhold labor—to strike—as well as to employ the usual methods of political pressure, they may possess a disproportionate share of effective power in the process of decision. Collective bargaining would then be so effective a pressure as to skew the results of the "'normal' American political process."

One should straightway make plain that the strike issue is not *simply* the essentiality of public services as contrasted with services or products produced in the private sector. This is only half of the issue, and in the past the half truth has beclouded analysis. The services performed by a private transit authority are neither less nor more essential to the public than those that would be performed if the transit authority were owned by a municipality. A railroad or a dock strike may be much more damaging to a community than "job action" by teachers. This is not to say that governmental services are not essential. They are, both because the demand for them is inelastic and because their disruption may seriously injure a city's economy and occasionally the physical welfare of its citizens. Nevertheless, essentiality of governmental services is only a necessary part of, rather than a complete answer to, the question: What is wrong with strikes in public employment?

What is wrong with strikes in public employment is that because they disrupt essential services, a large part of a mayor's political constituency will press for a quick end to the strike with little concern for the cost of settlement. The problem is that because market restraints are attenuated and because public employee strikes cause inconvenience to voters, such strikes too often succeed. Since other interest groups with conflicting claims on municipal government do not, as a general proposition, have anything approaching the effectiveness of this union technique—or at least cannot maintain this relative degree of power over the long run—they are put at a significant competitive disadvantage in the political process. Where this is the case, it must be said that the political process has been radically altered. And because of the deceptive simplicity of the analogy to collective bargaining in the private sector, the alteration may take place without anyone realizing what has happened.

Therefore, while the purpose and effect of strikes by public employees may seem in the beginning merely designed to establish collective bargaining or to "catch up" with wages and fringe benefits in the private sector, in the long run strikes must be seen as a means to redistribute income, or, put another way, to gain a subsidy for union members,[2] not through the employment of the usual types of political pressure, but through the employment of what might appropriately be called political force.

As is often the case when one generalizes, this picture may be thought to be overdrawn. In order to refine analysis, it will be helpful to distinguish between strikes that occur over monetary issues and strikes involving non-monetary issues. The generalized picture sketched above is essentially valid as to the former. Because there is usually no substitute for governmental services, the citizen-consumer faced with a strike of teachers, or garbage men, or social workers is likely to be seriously inconvenienced. This in turn places enormous pressure on the mayor, who is apt to find it difficult to look to the long-run balance sheet of the municipality. Most citizens are directly affected by a strike of sanitation workers. Few, however, can decipher a municipal budget or trace the relationship between today's labor settlement and next year's increase in the mill rate. Thus, in the typical case the impact of a settlement is less visible—or can more often be concealed—than the impact of a disruption of services. Moreover, the cost of settlement may be borne by a constituency much larger—the whole state or nation—than that represented by the mayor. It follows that the mayor usually will look to the electorate which is clamoring for a settlement, and in these circumstances, the union's fear of a long strike, a major check on its power in the private sector, is not a consideration. In the face of all of these factors other interest groups with priorities different from the union's are apt to be much less successful in their pursuit of scarce tax dollars than is the union with power to withhold services.

With respect to strikes over some non-monetary issues—decentralization of the governance of schools might be an example—the intensity of concern on the part of well-organized interest groups opposed to the union's position would support the mayor in his resistance to union demands. But even here, if union rank-and-file back their leadership, the pressures for settlement from the general public, which may be largely indifferent as to the underlying issue, would in time become irresistible.

SOVEREIGNTY AND DELEGATION REVISITED

As applied to public employment, there is a concept of sovereignty entitled to count as a reason for making strikes by public employees illegal. For what sovereignty should mean in this field is not the location of ultimate authority—on that the critics are dead right—but the right of government, through its laws, to ensure the survival of the "'normal' American political process." As hard as it may

[2]Strikes in some areas of the private sector may have this effect, too. The difference in the impact of collective bargaining in the two sectors should be seen as a continuum. Thus, for example, it may be that market restraints do not sufficiently discipline strike settlements in some regulated industries, or in industries that rely mainly on government contracts. If this is so—and we do not know that it is—perhaps there should be tighter restraints on the use of the strike in those areas.

be for some to accept, strikes by public employees may, as a long run proposition, threaten that process.[3]

Moreover, it is our view—although this would seem to be much less clear—that the public stake in some issues makes it appropriate for government either not to have to bargain with its employees on these issues at all or to follow bargaining procedures radically different from those of the private sector. It is in this respect that the judicial doctrine of illegal delegation of power should have relevance.

Consider, for example, the question of a public review board for police; or, for that matter, the question of school decentralization. These issues, viewed by the unions involved primarily as questions of job security, engage the interest of so many disparate groups in a relevant population, that it may be thought unfair to allow one group—the police, the teachers—to exert pressure through collective bargaining (quite apart from the strike) in which competing groups do not directly participate as well as through the channels (e.g., lobbying) open to other interest groups.

Our hesitation in this area is caused by two factors. First, models of the political process have trouble with fine-grained distinctions about too much power. Given the vulnerability of most municipal employers, one can say with some confidence that the strike imparts too much power to an interest group only because the distinction addressed there is not fine-grained at all. Second, it is difficult indeed for any governmental institution to make judgments about the issues that should be included in the non-bargainable class. The courts are badly suited to this task; and the legislature is not well constituted to come in after the fact and effect a change. Nevertheless, limits will have to be set or bargaining procedures radically changed, and this will in a sense be giving content to the doctrine of delegation as it bears upon the subject of public employment.

While there is increasing advocacy for expanding the scope of bargaining in public employment and in favor of giving public employees the right to strike—advocacy not just by unionists but by disinterested experts as well—the law generally limits the scope of bargaining and forbids strikes. This is often done with little attention to supporting reasons. Ours has been an attempt to supply these reasons and thereby to give some legitimate content to sovereignty and delegation.

We do not, however, mean to suggest that legislatures should abdicate to the courts the task of constructing a new system of collective bargaining for the public sector through the elaboration of sovereignty and delegation. Legislation is needed, for the problems we have explored require solutions beyond the power of the courts to fashion. In the future, if strikes are to be barred, sophisticated impasse procedures must be established. If, on the other hand, some strikes are to be tolerated, changes in the political structure which will make the municipal employer less vulnerable to work stoppages must be developed. And, in any event, legislative action will be necessary either to separate out these non-monetary issues which might not be decided solely through collective bargaining, or to change

---

[3]It should be understood that this claim is with respect to the employment of the strike once collective bargaining is established. In our opinion the opportunity for public employees to organize and bargain through a union is compelled by the private sector analogy and is consistent with the survival of the "normal American political process."

bargaining procedures so that all interested groups may participate in the resolution of such issues. These legislative choices and legal procedures will be the subject of a forthcoming article.

THE ROLE AND CONSEQUENCES OF STRIKES
BY PUBLIC EMPLOYEES

John F. Burton, Jr.
Charles Krider

The vexing problem of strikes by public employees has generated a number of assertions based largely on logical analysis. One common theme is that strikes fulfill a useful function in the private sector, but are inappropriate in the public sector, because they distort the political decision-making process. Another is that strikes in nonessential government services should not be permitted because it is administratively infeasible to distinguish among the various government services on the basis of their essentiality. The present article attempts to evaluate these assertions in terms of labor relations experience at the local level of government.

The assertions concerning strikes by public employees which we shall discuss have been drawn mainly from *The Taylor Report*, a report on public employee labor relations submitted to the Governor of New York State and "The Limits of Collective Bargaining in Public Employment," a recent article by Harry Wellington and Ralph Winter. Most of the evidence used to evaluate these assertions has been gathered in connection with the Brookings Institution *Study of Unionism and Collective Bargaining in the Public Sector*. Statistical information on all local public employee strikes which have occurred between 1965 and 1968 has been provided by the Bureau of Labor Statistics. Because education is outside the scope of our portion of the Brookings study, the data used in this article primarily relate to strikes by groups other than teachers.

John F. Burton is Associate Professor of Industrial Relations and Public Policy, Graduate School of Business, University of Chicago.

Charles Krider is a graduate student, University of Chicago; and Research Assistant, Brookings Institution.

This paper was prepared as part of a *Study of Unionism and Collective Bargaining in the Public Sector* which is being conducted by the Brookings Institution with financial support from the Ford Foundation. The views are the authors' and are not presented as those of the officers, trustees, or staff members of the Brookings Institution or of the Ford Foundation. [Footnote references have been deleted.]

The section entitled "The Role of Strikes in the Public Sector" has been omitted.

THE ROLE OF STRIKES IN THE PRIVATE SECTOR

Wellington and Winter have catalogued four claims which are made to justify collective bargaining in the private sector. First, collective bargaining is a way to achieve industrial peace. Second, it is a way of achieving industrial democracy. Third, unions that bargain collectively with employers also represent workers in the political arena. Fourth, and in their view the most important reason, collective bargaining compensates for the unequal bargaining power which is believed to result from individual bargaining. Wellington and Winter recognize that the gains to employees from collective bargaining, such as protection from monopsony power, are to be balanced against the social costs resulting from the resort to collectivism, such as distortion of the wage structure. While noting that considerable disagreement exists among economists concerning the extent of the benefits and costs, they stress the fact that costs are limited by economic constraints. Unions can displace their members from jobs by ignoring the discipline of the market. These four justifications for private sector collective bargaining are presumably relevant to some degree whether or not strikes are permitted. Nonetheless, one can conceptualize two models of collective bargaining—the Strike Model, which would normally treat strikes as legal, and the No-Strike Model, which would make all strikes illegal—and evaluate whether, in terms of the above justifications, society benefits from permitting strikes.

Most scholars of industrial relations accept the view that the right to strike is desirable in the private sector. Chamberlain and Kuhn assert, "[T]he possibility or ultimate threat of strikes is a necessary condition for collective bargaining." The distinguished scholars who comprised the Taylor Committee asserted similarly, "[T]he right to strike remains an integral part of the collective bargaining process in the private enterprise sector and this will unquestionably continue to be the case." One reason for this endorsement of the strike is that its availability is often essential to the union in its bid for recognition by the employer. In addition, once the bargaining relationship is established, the possibility that work may be interrupted forces the parties to bargain seriously. The possibility of a strike thus increases the likelihood that the parties will reach an agreement without third-party intervention. More important, the ability to strike increases the bargaining power of employees and their union so that, unlike the No-Strike Model, the employer cannot dominate the employer-employee relationship.

Use of the Strike Model instead of the No-Strike Model appears to enhance all but the third of the four claims for private sector collective bargaining offered by Wellington and Winter. While they do not provide a claim by claim analysis of the consequences of permitting strikes, their endorsement of strikes in the private sector must indicate that they believe the Strike Model preferable to the No-Strike Model. . . .

CONSEQUENCES OF STRIKES IN THE PUBLIC SECTOR*

The best procedure for evaluating public sector strikes would be to investigate the respective impacts of the Strike Model and the No-Strike Model on each of the claims made for collective bargaining. Such an analysis should consider the economic, political, and social effects produced. An inquiry into these effects is particularly important since several authors who have implicitly endorsed the Strike Model in the private sector have done so more on the basis of noneconomic reasons than economic reasons. Nonetheless, the attack on the Strike Model in the *public* sector has been based largely on the evaluation of the fourth claim for collective bargaining, that relating to unequal bargaining power. We will attempt to meet this attack by confining our discussion to the economic consequences of collective bargaining with and without strikes.

Even an examination confined to economic consequences is difficult. The most desirable economic data, which would measure the impact of unions on wages and other benefits, is unavailable. A major examination of the relative wage impact of public sector unions is now being conducted by Paul Hartman, but pending the outcome of his study we have to base our evaluation on less direct evidence. Our approach will be to review carefully the various steps in the analytical model developed by Wellington and Winter by which they arrive at the notion of sovereignty. If we find that the evidence available on public sector strikes contradicts this model, we shall conclude that the differential assessment they provide for public and private strikes is unwarranted.

Benefits of Collective Bargaining

Wellington and Winter believe the benefits of collective action, including strikes, are less in the public sector than in the private sector since (1) the problem of employer monopsony is less serious, and (2) any use of monopsony power in the public sector which results in certain groups, such as teachers, receiving low pay may reflect, not a misallocation of resources, bur rather a political determination of the desired use of resources.

Wellington and Winter assert that employer monopsony is less likely to exist or be used in the public than in the private sector. But as they concede, referring to Bunting, monopsony is not widespread in the private sector and, except for a few instances, cannot be used as a rationale for trade unions. They provide no evidence that monopsony is less prevalent in the public than in the private sector. Moreover, other labor market inefficiencies, common to the public and private sectors, are probably more important than monopsony in providing an economic justification for unions. For example, the deficiencies of labor market information are to some extent overcome by union activities, and there is no reason to assume that this benefit differs between the public and private sectors.

Assuming there is monopsony power, Wellington and Winter believe that collective bargaining in the private sector can eliminate unfair wages "which are less than they would be if the market were more nearly perfect." They assert, however, that low pay for an occupation in the public sector may reflect a political judgment which ought not to be countered by pressures resulting from a strike. To say, however, that the pay for an occupation would be higher if the employees had the right to strike than if they did not is not independent proof that strikes are inappropriate. The same criticism could be made of any activity by a public employee group which affects its pay. An independent rationale must be provided to explain why some means which are effective in raising wages (strikes) are inappropriate while other means which are also effective (lobbying) are appropriate. Whether the Wellington and Winter discussion of the politically based decision-making model for the public sector provides this rationale will be discussed in more detail subsequently.

Costs of Collective Bargaining

Wellington and Winter's discussion of the cost of substituting collective for individual bargaining in the public sector includes a chain of causation which runs from (1) an allegation that market restraints are weak in the public sector, largely because the services are essential; to (2) an assertion that the public puts pressure on civic officials to arrive at a quick settlement; to (3) a statement that other pressure groups have no weapons comparable to a strike; to (4) a conclusion that the strike thus imposes a high cost since the political process is distorted.

Let us discuss these steps in order:

(1) Market Restraints: A key argument in the case for the inappropriateness of public sector strikes is that economic constraints are not present to any meaningful degree in the public sector. This argument is not entirely convincing. First, wages lost due to strikes are as important to public employees as they are to employees in the private sector. Second, the public's concern over increasing tax rates may prevent the decision-making process from being dominated by political instead of economic considerations. The development of multilateral bargaining in the public sector is an example of how the concern over taxes may result in a close substitute for market constraints. In San Francisco, for example, the Chamber of Commerce has participated in negotiations between the city and public employee unions and has had some success in limiting the economic gains of the unions. A third and related economic constraint arises for such services as water, sewage and, in some instances, sanitation, where explicit prices are charged. Even if representatives of groups other than employees and the employer do not enter the bargaining process, both union and local government are aware of the economic implications of bargaining which leads to higher prices which are clearly visible to the public. A fourth economic constraint on employees exists in those services where subcontracting to the private sector is a realistic alternative. Warren, Michigan, resolved a bargaining impasse with an American Federation of State, County and Municipal Employees (AFSCME) local by subcontracting its entire sanitation service; Santa Monica, California, ended a strike of city employees by threatening to subcontract its sanitation operations. If the subcontracting option is preserved, wages in the public sector need not exceed the rate at which subcontracting becomes a realistic alternative.

An aspect of the lack-of-market-restraints argument is that public services are essential. Even at the analytical level, Wellington and Winter's case for essentiality is not convincing. They argue:

> The Services performed by a private transit authority are neither less nor more essential to the public than those that would be performed if the transit authority were owned by a municipality. A railroad or a dock strike may be much more damaging to a community than "job action" by teachers. This is not to say that government

services are not essential. They are both because they may seriously injure a city's economy and occasionally the physical welfare of its citizens.

This is a troublesome passage. It ends with the implicit conclusion that all government services are essential. This conclusion is important in Wellington and Winter's analysis because it is a step in their demonstration that strikes are inappropriate in all governmental services. But the beginning of the passage, with its example of "job action" by teachers, suggests that essentiality is not an *inherent* characteristic of government services but depends on the specific service being evaluated. Furthermore the transit authority example suggests that many services are interchangeable between the public and private sectors. The view that various government services are not of equal essentiality and that there is considerable overlap between the kinds of services provided in the public and private sectors is reinforced by our field work and strike data from the Bureau of Labor Statistics. Examples include:

1. Where sanitation services are provided by a municipality, such as Cleveland, sanitationmen are prohibited from striking. Yet, sanitationmen in Philadelphia, Portland, and San Francisco are presumably free to strike since they are employed by private contractors rather than by the cities.

2. There were 25 local government strikes by the Teamsters in 1965-68, most involving truck drivers and all presumably illegal. Yet the Teamsters' strike involving fuel oil truck drivers in New York City last winter was legal even though the interruption of fuel oil service was believed to have caused the death of several people.

(2) Public Pressure: The second argument in the Wellington and Winter analysis is that public pressure on city officials forces them to make quick settlements. The validity of this argument depends on whether the service is essential. Using as a criterion whether the service is essential in the short run, we believe a priori that services can be divided into three categories: (1) essential services—police and fire—where strikes immediately endanger public health and safety; (2) intermediate services—sanitation, hospitals, transit, water, and sewage—where strikes of a few days might be tolerated; (3) nonessential services—streets, parks, education, housing, welfare and general administration—where strikes of indefinite duration could be tolerated. These categories are not exact since essentiality depends on the size of the city. Sanitation strikes will be critical in large cities such as New York but will not cause much inconvenience in smaller cities where there are meaningful alternatives to governmental operation of sanitation services.

Statistics on the duration of strikes which occurred in the public sector between 1965 and 1968 provide evidence not only that public services are of unequal essentiality, but also that the a priori categories which we have used have some validity. As can be seen from Table 1, strikes in the essential services (police and fire) had an average duration of 4.7 days, while both the intermediate and the nonessential services had an average duration of approximately 10.5 days. It is true that the duration of strikes in the intermediate and nonessential services is only half the average duration of strikes in the private sector during these years. However, this comparison is somewhat misleading since all of the public sector strikes were illegal, and many were ended by injunction, while presumably a vast majority of the private sector strikes did not suffer from these constraints. It would appear that

table 1   Duration of Strikes by Essentiality of Function*

	Average Duration in Days	*Standard Deviation† in Days*
Essential	4.7	7.9
Intermediate	10.3	18.5
Nonessential	10.6	20.1
Education	7.2	8.9

*Based on data collected by the Bureau of Labor Statistics on strikes during 1965-68 involving employees of local government.

†Standard deviation is a measure of dispersion around the average or the mean.

with the exception of police and fire protection, public officials are, to some degree, able to accept long strikes. The ability of governments to so choose indicates that political pressures generated by strikes are not so strong as to undesirably distort the entire decision-making process of government. City officials in Kalamazoo, Michigan, were able to accept a forty-eight day strike by sanitationmen and laborers; Sacramento County, California survived an eighty-seven day strike by welfare workers. A three month strike of hospital workers has occurred in Cuyahoga County (Cleveland), Ohio.

(3) The Strike as a Unique Weapon: The third objection to the strike is that it provides workers with a weapon unavailable to the employing agency or to other pressure groups. Thus, unions have a superior arsenal. The Taylor Committee Report opposes strikes for this reason, among others, arguing that "there can scarcely be a countervailing lockout." Conceptually, we see no reason why lockouts are less feasible in the public than in the private sector. Legally, public sector lockouts are now forbidden, but so are strikes; presumably both could be legalized. Actually, public sector lockouts have occurred. The Social Service Employees Union (SSEU) of New York City sponsored a "work-in" in 1967 during which all of the caseworkers went to their office but refused to work. Instead, union-sponsored lectures were given by representatives of organizations such as CORE, and symposia were held on the problems of welfare workers and clients. The work-in lasted for one week, after which the City locked out the caseworkers.

A similar assertion is made by Wellington and Winter, who claim that no pressure group other than unions has a weapon comparable to the strike. But this argument raises a number of questions. Is the distinctive characteristic of an inappropriate method of influencing decisions by public officials that it is economic as opposed to political? If this is so, then presumably the threat of the New York Stock Exchange to move to New Jersey unless New York City taxes on stock transfers were lowered and similar devices should be outlawed along with the strike.

(4) Distortion of the Political Process: The ultimate concern of both the Taylor Committee and Wellington and Winter is that "a strike of government employees ... introduces an alien force in the legislative process." It is "alien" because, in the words of the Taylor Committee Report:

> Careful thought about the matter shows conclusively, we believe, that while the right to strike normally performs a useful function in the private enterprise sector (where relative economic power is the final determinant in the making of private agreements), it is not compatible with the orderly functioning of our democratic form of representative government (in which relative political power is the final determinant).

The essence of this analysis appears to be that certain means used to influence the decision-making process in the public sector—those which are political—are legitimate, while other—those which are economic—are not. For several reasons, we believe that such distinctions among means are tenuous.

First, any scheme which differentiates economic power from political power faces a perplexing definitional task. The *International Encyclopedia of the Social Sciences* defines the political process as "the activities of people in various groups as they struggle for—and use—power to achieve personal and group purposes." And what is power?

> Power in use invariably involves a mixture of many different forms sometimes mutually reinforcing—of persuasion and pressure. . . .
>
> Persuasion takes place when A influences B to adopt a course of action without A's promising or threatening any reward or punishment. It may take the form of example, expectation, proposals, information, education, or propaganda. . . .
>
> Pressure is applied by A upon B whenever A tries to make a course of action more desirable by promising or threatening contingent rewards or punishments. It may take the form of force, commands, manipulation, or bargaining. . . .
>
> Physical force is a blunt instrument. . . .Besides, more flexible and reliable modes of pressure are available. Rewards, in the form of monetary payments, new positions, higher status, support, favorable votes, cooperation, approval, or the withdrawal of any anticipated punishment, may be bestowed or promised. Punishment, in the form of fines, firing, reduction in status, unfavorable votes, noncooperation, rejection, disapproval, or withdrawal of any anticipated reward, may be given or threatened. . . .
>
> Bargaining is a still more fluid—and far more persuasive—form of using pressure. In bargaining, all sides exercise power upon each other through reciprocal promises or threats. . . .Indeed, force, command, and manipulation tend to become enveloped in the broader and more subtle processes of bargaining.

We have quoted at length from this discussion of the political process because we believe it illustrates the futility of attempting to distinguish between economic and political power. The former concept would seem to be encompassed by the latter. The degree of overlap is problematical since there can be economic aspects to many forms of persuasion and pressure. It may be possible to provide an operational distinction between economic power and political power, but we do not believe that those who would rely on this distinction have fulfilled their task.

Second, even assuming it is possible to operationally distinguish economic power and political power, a rationale for utilizing the distinction must be provided. Such a rationale would have to distinguish between the categories either on the basis of characteristics inherent in them as a means of action or on the basis of the ends to which the means are directed. Surely an analysis of ends does not provide a meaningful distinction. The objectives of groups using economic pressure are of the same character as those of groups using political pressure—both seek to influence executive and legislative determinations such as the allocation of funds and the tax rate. If it is impossible effectively to distinguish economic from political pressure groups in terms of their ends, and it is desirable to free the political process from the influence of all pressure groups, then effective lobbying and petitioning should be as illegal as strikes.

If the normative distinction between economic and political power is based, not on the ends desired, but on the nature of the means, our skepticism remains undiminished. Are all forms of political pressure legitimate? Then consider the range of political activity observed in the public sector. Is lobbying by public sector unions to be approved? Presumably it is. What then of participation in partisan political activity? On city time? Should we question the use of campaign contributions or kickbacks from public employees to public officials as a means of influencing public sector decisions? These questions suggest that political pressures, as opposed to economic pressures, cannot *as a class* be considered more desirable.

Our antagonism toward a distinction based on means does not rest solely on a condemnation of political pressures which violate statutory provisions. We believe that perfectly legal forms of political pressure have no automatic superiority over economic pressure. In this regard, the evidence from our field work is particularly enlightening. First, we have found that the availability of political power varies among groups of employees within a given city. Most public administrators have respect for groups which can deliver votes at strategic times. Because of their links to private sector unions, craft unions are invariably in a better position to play this political role than a union confined to the public sector, such as AFSCME. In Chicago, Cleveland and San Francisco, the public sector craft unions are closely allied with the building trades council and play a key role in labor relations with the city. Prior to the passage of state collective bargaining laws such unions also played the key role in Detroit and New York City. In the No-Strike Model, craft unions clearly have the comparative advantage because of their superior political power.

Second, the range of issues pursued by unions relying on political power tends to be narrow. The unions which prosper by eschewing economic power and exercising political power are often found in cities, such as Chicago, with a flourishing patronage system. These unions gain much of their political power by cooperating with the political administration. This source of political power would vanish if the unions were assiduously to pursue a goal of providing job security for their members since this goal would undermine the patronage system. In Rochester, for example, a union made no effort to protect one of its members who was fired for political reasons. For the union to have opposed the city administration at that time on an issue of job security would substantially have reduced the union's influence on other issues. In Chicago, where public sector strikes are rare (except for education) but political considerations are not, the unions have made little effort to establish a grievance procedure to protect their members from arbitrary treatment.

Third, a labor relations system built on political power tends to be unstable since some groups of employees, often a substantial number, are invariably left out of the system. They receive no representation either through patronage or through the union. In Memphis, the craft unions had for many years enjoyed a "working relationship" with the city which assured the payment of the rates that prevailed in the private sector and some control over jobs. The sanitation laborers, however, were not part of the system and were able to obtain effective representation only after a violent confrontation with the city in 1968. Having been denied representation through the political process, they had no choice but to accept a subordinate position in the city or to initiate a strike to change the system. Racial barriers were an important factor in the isolation of the Memphis sanitation laborers. Similar distinctions in racial balance among functions and occupations appear in most of the cities we visited.

Conclusions in Regard to Strikes and Political Process

Wellington and Winter and the Taylor Committee reject the use of the Strike Model in the public sector. They have endorsed the No-Strike Model in order "to ensure the survival of the 'normal' American political process." Our field work suggests that unions which have actually helped their members either have made the strike threat a viable weapon despite its illegality or have intertwined themselves closely with their nominal employer through patronage-political support arrangements. If this assessment is correct, choice of the No-Strike Model is likely to lead to patterns of decision making which will subvert, if not the "normal" American political process, at least the political process which the Taylor Committee and Wellington and Winter meant to embrace. We would not argue that the misuse of political power will be eliminated by legalizing the strike; on balance, however, we believe that, in regard to most governmental functions, the Strike Model has more virtues than the No-Strike Model. Whether strikes are an appropriate weapon for all groups of public employees is our next topic.

DIFFERENTIATION AMONG PUBLIC SECTOR FUNCTIONS

The most important union for local government employees, The American Federation of State, County, and Municipal Employees (AFSCME), issued a policy statement in 1966 claiming the right of public employees to strike:

> AFSCME insists upon the right of public employees . . . to strike. To forestall this right is to handicap free collective bargaining process [sic]. Wherever legal barriers to the exercise of this right exist, it shall be our policy to seek the removal of such barriers. Where one party at the bargaining table possesses all the power and authority, the bargaining becomes no more than formalized petitioning.

Significantly, AFSCME specifically excluded police and other law enforcement officers from this right. Any local of police officers that engages in a strike or other concerted refusal to perform duties will have its charter revoked.

Can a distinction among functions, such as is envisioned by AFSCME, be justified? In view of the high costs associated with the suppression of strikes, could each stoppage be dealt with, as Theodore Kheel suggests, only when and if it becomes an emergency?

Despite arguments to the contrary, we feel that strikes in some essential services, such as fire and police, would immediately endanger the public health and safety and should be presumed illegal. We have no evidence from our field work to support our fears that any disruption of essential services will quickly result in an emergency. But the events which occurred on September 9, 1919, during a strike by Boston policemen provide strong proof; those which occurred on October 7, 1969, following a strike by Montreal policemen would appear to make the argument conclusive. Contemporary accounts amply describe the holocausts:

> About me milled a crowd of aimless men and women, just seeing what they could see. . . . There was an air of expectancy without knowing what was expected.
> Then came the sound of two hard substances in sharp impact, followed a second later by a louder one and the thrilling crash of falling splintering glass. A plate show-window had been shattered. Instantly the window and its immediate vicinity were filled with struggling men, a mass of action, from which emerged from time to time bearers of shirts, neckties, collars, hats. In a few seconds the window was bare. Some with loot vanished; others lingered.
> Lootless ones were attacking the next window. Nothing happened. That is, the fear of arrest abated after the first shock of the lawless acts. I saw men exchanging new shirts each with the other, to get their sizes . . . good-looking men, mature in years, bearing all the earmarks of a lifetime of sane observance of property rights.

Montreal, 1969

> "You've never seen the city like this," said the owner of a big women's clothing store surveying his premises, strewn with dummies from which the clothing had been torn. "It's like the war."
> A taxi driver carrying a passenger up Sherbrooke Street in Montreal today blamed the police for "not knowing the effect their absence would have on people." He continued: "I don't mean hoodlums and habitual lawbreakers, I mean just plain people committed offenses they would not dream of trying if there was a policeman standing on the corner. I saw cars driven through red lights. Drivers shot up the wrong side of the street because they realized no one would catch them."

In the case of strikes by essential employees, such as policemen, the deterioration of public order occurs almost immediately. During the first few hours of the police walkout in Montreal, robberies occurred at eight banks, one finance company, two groceries, a jewelry store and a private bank. In the case of the Boston police strike of 1919, outbreaks began within four hours after the strike had commenced. Such consequences require that strikes by police and other essential services be outlawed in advance. There is simply no time to seek an injunction.

Even if a distinction in the right to strike can be made among government functions on the basis of essentiality, is such a distinction possible to implement? The Taylor Committee based their argument against prohibiting strikes in essential functions but allowing them elsewhere on this difficulty:

> We come to this conclusion [to prohibit all strikes] after a full consideration of the views . . . that public employees in nonessential government services, at least, should have the same right to strike as has been accorded to employees in private industry. We realize, moreover, that the work performed in both sectors is sometimes comparable or identical. Why, then, should an interruption of non-essential governmental services be prohibited?

To begin with, a differentiation between essential and nonessential governmental services would be the subject of such intense and never ending controversy as to be administratively impossible.

Despite the conclusion of the Taylor Committee it appears that in practice a distinction is emerging between strikes in essential services and strikes in other services. Employee organizations and public officials do in fact treat some strikes as critical, while other strikes cause no undue concern.

Our analysis of the Bureau of Labor Statistics strike data pertaining to the last four years suggests that it is possible to devise an operational definition of essential service. First, as we have indicated above, strike duration was considerably shorter in the essential services than in the intermediate or nonessential services [see Table 1]. These data suggest that, except in police and fire services, public officials have some discretion in choosing to accept long strikes. Second, the statistics reveal that managers have been able to distinguish between essential and non-essential services in their use of counter sanctions. In strikes involving essential services, injunctions were sought more frequently and employees, because of their short run indispensability, were fired less frequently. Injunctions were granted in 35% of the essential strikes, and in 25% of the intermediate, but only in 19 % of the nonessential strikes. Third, partial operation was attempted more frequently in essential services [see Table 2]. By using nonstrikers, supervisors, replacements or volunteers, local governments were able to continue partial operation during 92% of the essential strikes, but in only 80% of the intermediate, and 77% of the nonessential strikes. Such data suggest that it may be administratively feasible to differentiate among public services so as to permit some, but not all, public employees to strike. Indeed, public administrators already seem to be making such distinctions.

The idea that distinctions among functions are appropriate is also beginning to emerge among legislators. The first state to move in this direction has been Vermont, which apparently restricts municipal employee strikes only if they endanger the health, safety, or welfare of the public. Unfortunately—at least from the viewpoint of researchers—there has been no experience under the statute. Montana prohibits strikes in private or public hospitals only if there is another strike in effect in a hospital within a radius of 150 miles. Study commissions in other states have accepted the distinction between essential and non-essential services. In 1968, the Governor's Commission in Pennsylvania recommended a limited right to strike for all public employees except police and firemen. In 1969, the Labor Law Committee of the Ohio State Bar Association recommended repeal of the Ferguson Act, which prohibits strikes by public employees. They proposed a Public Employment Relations Act which would permit strikes by recognized employee organizations in nonessential occupations following mandatory use of fact-finding procedures. The proposed statute states:

[I] n the event a public employer and a certified labor organization are unable to reach an agreement within forty-five days following the date of the receipt of the recommendation of the fact-finding board, the public employees in the bargaining unit . . . and/or the labor organization shall not thereafter be prohibited from engaging in any strike until such time as the labor organization and the public employer reach agreement on a collective bargaining agreement.

table 2 Partial Operation by Essentiality of Function*
(Noneducation)

	Essential		Intermediate		Nonessential		Total†	
	Number	Percentage	Number	Percentage	Number	Percentage	Number	Percentage
Total Number of Strikes	37	100.0	221	100.0	43	100.0	301	100.0
Partial Operation‡	34	91.9	175	79.2	33	76.7	242	80.4
Supervisors	(28)	(75.7)	(154)	(69.7)	(29)	(67.4)	(211)	(70.1)
Nonstrikers	(27)	(73.0)	(137)	(62.0)	(28)	(65.1)	(192)	(63.8)
Replacements	(3)	(9.1)	(34)	(15.4)	(4)	(9.3)	(41)	(13.6)
Volunteers	(5)	(13.5)	(16)	(7.2)	–	–	(21)	(7.0)
No Partial Operation	3	8.1	46	20.8	10	23.3	59	19.6

*Based on data collected by the Bureau of Labor Statistics on strikes during 1965-68 involving employees of local governments.
†Twenty-eight strikes in such miscellaneous functions as libraries, museums, and electric or gas utilities were not classified. There was partial operation in 18 (64.3%) of these strikes.
‡The sub-totals for partial operation do not add to 100% because more than one method may have been used in each strike.

285

IMPLICATIONS FOR PUBLIC POLICY

We have expressed our views on the market restraints that exist in the public sector, the extent of the public pressure on public officials to reach quick settlements, the likely methods by which decisions would be made in the No-Strike Model, and the desirability and feasibility of differentiating among government services on the basis of essentiality. In this light, what public policy seems appropriate for strikes at the local government level?

In general, we believe that strikes in the public sector should be legalized for the same reasons they are legal in the private sector. For some public sector services, however—namely, police and fire protection—the probability that a strike will result in immediate danger to public health and safety is so substantial that strikes are almost invariably inappropriate. In these essential functions, the strike should be presumed illegal; the state should not be burdened with the requirement of seeking an injunction. We would, however, permit employees in a service considered essential to strike if they could demonstrate to a court that a disruption of service would not endanger the public. Likewise, we would permit the government to obtain an injunction against a strike in a service presumed nonessential if a nontrivial danger to the public could be shown.

The decision to permit some, but no all, public employee strikes cannot, of course, take place in *vaccus publicum jus.* Mediation, fact finding, or advisory arbitration may be appropriate for those functions where strikes are permitted. Where strikes are illegal because of the essential nature of the service, it may be necessary to institute compulsory arbitration. The choice of a proper role for third parties in the public sector is difficult, and we do not wish to leave the impression that we are unaware of the problem. In our portion of the Brookings Institution study, we will examine the experience which many cities have had in the use of neutral third parties. Our initial reaction is that such experience does not undermine the feasibility of a public policy which would permit some, but not all, public employees the right to strike, and include that decision in a comprehensive public policy for collective bargaining.

While we have indicated our support for the right of public employees to strike, we do not mean to suggest that all strikes are desirable. In particular, strikes which are necessary solely because the employer refuses to establish a bargaining relationship seem anachronous. The right of employees to deal with their employer through a representative of their choosing should be reflected in our public policy. The obligation on employers to recognize and to bargain with properly certified unions has eliminated many strikes in the private sector. The evidence in Table 3 suggests that, in the public sector, strikes on such issues can be sharply reduced. In those states in which local governments are required to recognize and to bargain with unions representing a majority of their employees, strikes to establish the bargaining relationship have been virtually eliminated. States with permissive laws, which require minimal recognition of unions and which require only that employers

table 3   Local Government Strikes by Public Policy and Issue*

	Noneducation Strikes		Education Strikes	
	Number	Duration in Days	Number	Duration in Days
Mandatory Law				
Strikes to establish bargaining relationship†	1	10.0	5	3.4
Other strikes	56	6.7	104	8.7
Permissive Law				
Strikes to establish bargaining relationship	20	19.6	2	7.0
Other strikes	34	10.4	16	6.5
No Law				
Strikes to establish bargaining relationship	68	21.6	29	5.9
Other strikes	150	5.8	93	6.2

*Based on data collected by the Bureau of Labor Statistics on strikes during 1965-68 involving employees of local governments.

†Includes strikes where union was demanding recognition as well as strikes where union was demanding bona fide collective bargaining.

"meet and confer," as opposed to "bargain," with these unions, have perhaps aggravated the strike problem.

Similarly, our general endorsement of public sector strikes does not mean that we are unconcerned about the circumstances under which such strikes take place. Public policy has an important role to play in shaping the structure and, hence, influencing the outcome of collective bargaining. An example is the inclusion or exclusion of supervisors in the bargaining unit. As indicated in Table 2, supervisors are often used during strikes to provide partial operation. Presumably, this enhances the ability of local governments to resist union demands. Some states, such as Wisconsin, have wisely stipulated that supervisors are to be excluded from bargaining units, while other states, such as New York, have not. A supervisor who belongs to a striking union is likely to be of limited usefulness to management in attempting to counteract the strike. Another way in which a state's public policy could enhance local government's ability to resist strikes would be to enact a statute prohibiting public employers from signing away their right to subcontract. The absolute right to subcontract operations would thereby be preserved. While it is unlikely that some services, such as police and fire protection, will ever be placed under private management, other services can be subcontracted if union demands raise the cost of a public service to a level at which private service becomes competitive. Excluding the education sector, subcontracting was threatened by management in 16 local government strikes and implemented in five between 1965 and 1968.

CONCLUSIONS

This article has offered a policy to deal with public sector strikes. It has also examined several propositions concerning public sector strikes which have been based largely on logical analysis. The assertions that strikes by public employees inevitably distort the decision-making process in the public sector and that differential treatment of public employees in their right to strike would be infeasible have been found to be wanting when evaluated in the light of our actual experience with public sector strikes. This evaluation suggests that logic alone is an inadequate basis for public policy in this area. Yet we would not want to suggest that a literal interpretation of Holmes' view on the relative merits of logic and experience is appropriate. If we were forced to choose a mentor in any debate concerning the proper bases for law, we endorse Cardozo:

> My analysis of the judicial process comes then to this, and little more: logic, and history, and custom, and utility, and the accepted standards of right conduct, are the forces which singly or in combination shape the progress of the law.

MORE ON STRIKES BY PUBLIC EMPLOYEES

Harry H. Wellington
Ralph K. Winter, Jr.

We have two brief observations on the paper by Messrs. Burton and Krider. First, we suggest that society is not limited to a choice between their strike and no-strike alternatives. Our earlier article argued that the typical municipal political structure is vulnerable to strikes by well entrenched public employee unions, and that, given this existing political structure, the no-strike model is preferable to the strike model. We stated, however, that changes in the political structure which reduce the vulnerability of municipal employers to strikes by public employees can

Harry Wellington is the Edward J. Phelps Professor of Law at Yale University and Ralph Winter is Professor of Law, Yale University. Reprinted from the *Yale Law Journal*, LXXIX (1970), 441-43. Most footnotes deleted from edited version.

be made and that we intended (and we still do intend) to explore these possibilities in a future article. There is, therefore, a third model—one which permits some strikes in conjunction with various changes in municipal political structures.

Second, we wish to define what seems to be the principal area of our disagreement with Messrs. Burton and Krider. All agree that the services performed by some public employees are in one way or another "essential" and that this "essentiality" is in some sense related to society's ability to tolerate strikes. However, which employees under the Burton-Krider strike model are to have union activities limited depends very much on one's view of essentiality. It is now clear that our vision is different from theirs.

For them, the essentiality of the service depends on the extent to which disruption of the service by a strike would "immediately endanger public health and safety." They limit the concept to situations creating an immediate danger to the public health and safety and, therefore, advocate a prohibition on strikes affecting municipal police and fire functions. They would permit strikes in other areas, such as education. We agree that strikes which create an immediate danger to public health and welfare cannot be tolerated, and that any concept of essentiality must, at a minimum, embrace such situations.

We claim more for the concept, however.[1] Many government services are essential in two additional senses, senses which are of critical importance to the issues before us. First, the demand for numerous governmental services is relatively inelastic; that is, relatively insensitive to changes in price. Indeed, the lack of close substitutes is typical of many governmental endeavors.[2] And, since at least the time of Marshall's *Principles of Economics,* the elasticity of demand for the final service or product has been considered a major determinant of union power. Because the demand for labor is derived from the demand for the product, inelasticity on the product side tends to reduce the employment-benefit trade-off unions face. As our earlier article noted, this is as much the case in the private as in the public sector. But, in the private sector product inelasticity is not typical. Moreover, there is the further restraint on union power created by the real possibility of non-union entrants into the product market. In the public sector, inelasticity of demand seems to us more the rule than the exception, and non-union rivals are not generally a serious problem.

Consider education. A strike by teachers may never create an immediate danger to public health and welfare. Nevertheless, teachers rarely need fear unemployment as a result of union-induced wage increases, and the threat of an important non-union rival (competitive private schools) is not to be taken seriously so long as potential consumers of private education must pay taxes to support the public school system.

The third sense in which the concept of essentiality has significance is the extent to which the disruption of a government service inconveniences municipal voters. A teachers' strike may not endanger public health or welfare. It may, how-

[1] If one were using "essentiality" in merely a descriptive sense, the Burton-Krider definition might well be satisfactory. They employ this concept, however, as the touchstone for resolving the strike question. When so used, their definition is totally inadequate.

[2] Sometimes this is so because of the nature of the endeavor, national defense, for example, and sometimes because of the existence of the governmental operation necessarily inhibits entry by private entities, as in the case of elementary education.

ever, seriously inconvenience parents and other citizens who, as voters, have the power to punish one of the parties—and always the same party, the political leadership—to the dispute. How can anyone any longer doubt the vulnerability of a municipal employer to this sort of pressure? Was it simply a matter of indifference to Mayor Lindsay in September, 1969, whether another teachers' strike occurred on the eve of a municipal election? Did the size and the speed of the settlement with the U.F.T. suggest nothing about one first-rate politician's estimate of his vulnerability?

Messrs. Burton and Krider's disagreement with us on this point seems based principally on their conviction that anticipation of increased taxes as the result of a large labor settlement will countervail the felt inconvenience of a strike, and that municipalities are not, therefore, overly vulnerable to strikes by public employees. We remain convinced, however, that governmental budgets are so complex that the effect of any particular labor settlement on the typical municipal budget is a matter of very low visibility. It will not, therefore, significantly deter voters, inconvenienced by a strike, from compelling political leaders to settle quickly. Moreover, as we noted in our earlier article, municipalities are often subsidized by other political entities—the nation or state—and the cost of a strike settlement may not be borne by those demanding an end to the strike. Surely Mayor Lindsay's pleas for federal and state aid because of the increased cost of municipal services are not totally unrelated to his labor problems.

The sum of our position then is—given today's typical municipal structure—that once public employee unions become well established, they will, if they are allowed to strike, have too much power. For the effect of the strike weapon[3] is to put competing claimants in the political process (at all levels of government) at a disadvantage substantial enough for us to insist that it constitutes, what in our earlier article we called, a "distortion" of the "'normal' American political process."[4] This distortion, moreover, may make everyone from large taxpayers to welfare recipients poorer than they are, and the cities less livable, but more volatile, than they have become.

[3] Our convictions remain unshaken in the face of Messrs. Burton and Krider's argument that the threat of the New York Stock Exchange to move to New Jersey is analogous to a public employee strike. When teachers strike, education ceases. If the Stock Exchange moved, citizens of New York would continue to buy and sell stock. New York City might get less tax revenue, to be sure, but it also might get more, depending on what kind of business takes the Exchange's place.

[4] Indeed, we suggest that this distortion, as much as anything else, accounts for the socialist planner's aversion to strikes. Such strikes, after all, cannot help but "distort the 'plan.'"

PUBLIC EMPLOYEE STRIKES AND POLITICAL THEORY

Robert Booth Fowler

Normative political theory cannot answer the question of whether public employees ought to have the legal right to strike in a political system like ours with constitutional, representative government. Political theory can never provide definite universal answers to such questions. All a normative theorist can do is present the best answer he can to value questions, employing reasoned argument. In my view, the reasons supporting the proposition that government workers ought to be given the legal right to strike are convincing. This view I shall argue in this essay.

To begin to make this case, we must get out of several of the highly dubious rhetorical thickets into which proponents and opponents of public employee strikes so often lead us. We need, first, to dismiss those enthusiasts of guaranteed access to the strike weapon for government workers who talk grandly of the public employee's "right" to strike.[1] They offer us no help.

Their argument is generally phrased as if to imply an abstract right, suggesting that this alleged right is a natural right. About such a notion one ought to raise certain immediate objections. Highly abstract claims like natural rights always require close scrutiny since they are never demonstrable and often appear to be somebody's private value reified into an absolute claim. Moreover, they bear close scrutiny especially when, like the "right" to strike, they turn out to be newly discovered, never part of the traditional notion of natural rights; not unreasonably, the skeptical will ask why such rights were not previously uncovered.

In any case, natural rights claims need not be allowed by any political community whose leaders are ultimately responsible to that community. For representative government implies the idea that in the end right will be decided on and legally defined by the political community as a whole or by its agents. Some individual rights may be created or ratified in a fundamental constitution; but this is a decision for the political community to make, and ours certainly did not include the right to strike by government employees in the Bill of Rights.

On the other hand, justification by tradition is an equally dubious way to

Robert Fowler is Assistant Professor of Political Science, University of Wisconsin. Article prepared specifically for this volume.
[1]For example, see David Siskind, *One Thousand Strikes of Government Employees* (New York: Columbia University Press, 1940), pp. 232, 258-59.

proceed. Specifically, just because the right of government workers to strike has traditionally been denied in the American political experience does not enlighten us at all as to the normative merits of the question. This is sometimes forgotten by opponents of the right to strike. The real question is always not whether policy or values are traditional or not, but whether they are normatively justifiable.

So what is needed from the perspective of at least one political theorist in considering the issue of whether or not government workers ought to be legally allowed to strike is reasoned normative argument, not citations of traditionalist and natural rights claims. Unfortunately, too much of the argument has not yet gotten off these wrong tracks and onto more useful ones.

Needed too is an eye toward reality. The growth of strikes at the local and state governmental level is a well-known phenomenon. And the trend is clear.[2] In the face of it, the normative political theorist ought to raise one basic question: Are there any convincing normative reasons why we ought not to accept and legalize this coming social reality? Surely in the face of the increasing recourse to strikes by public workers the burden of justification must fall upon those who would oppose evolving social change with positive law.

In fact, there are now many normative reasons argued in opposition to legalizing the right to strike just as there have been in the past. And they are arguments that must be given serious consideration. Unquestionably the most important of these in terms of political theory has been the contention that if strikes by public employees are permitted, the result will be to threaten the sovereignty of the general political community or its agents, its governments.[3] This is a crucial matter in both theoretical and practical terms. By no means ought it to be patronizingly dismissed as irrelevant because of the growing recourse to strikes, unless one wishes to accept the implication that whatever is ought to be.[4]

Those who fear public employee strikes' effects upon sovereignty have a solid point. A political community cannot permit its authority or that of its agents to be transferred away to special parts of the community, such as public employee unions, without being alerted to the danger of surrendering its final sovereignty. Surely no democrat can argue otherwise. Thus there is reason for suspicion of those enthusiasts for public unionism who praise bilateralism, co-decision-making by management and unions, as something glorious and worth seeking as an end in government.[5] Clearly, bilateralism could easily infringe upon the sovereignty of the political community.

Indeed, far short of bilateralism, one wonders whether government-union settlements would be more likely to involve sacrifice of basic authority of the political community or its governmental agents if striking was legalized as a means.

---

[2]Gordon Nesvig in Felix A. Nigro, ed., "Collective Negotiations in the Public Service: A Symposium," *Public Administration Review,* XXVIII, 2 (March/April 1968), 126; Frederick Mosher, *Democracy and the Public Service* (New York: Oxford University Press, 1968), p. 190; Wilson Hart, *Collective Bargaining in the Federal Civil Service* (New York: Harper & Brothers, 1961), p. 25.

[3]For example, see Morton Godine, *The Labor Problem in the Public Service* (Cambridge: Harvard University Press, 1951), p. 172.

[4]As does Mosher, *op. cit.,* p. 178.

[5]Felix Nigro in Nigro, ed., *op. cit.,* p. 143.

With some government functions a strike by government workers can place the government institution at a decisive bargaining disadvantage, so pressed might it be to end a strike in an essential area of activity. The result might be a fatal delegation of final authority out of the hands of the political community, or its responsible governmental agents, into some irresponsible part of it, such as a public employee union.

All this is possible, but not a matter on which normative argument is as yet decisive. These are concerns for empirical investigation first. The sovereignty of the political community might indeed be threatened by strikes of government workers. But it is precisely the question of whether "might" will in fact work out to be a false fear or a correct one that remains to be seen. France, for example, permits strikes by public employee unions; life goes on, and sovereignty does not seem diminished.[6] Nor is the evidence, such as it is, from the United States different.[7] But mostly the jury is still out.

Probably the day-to-day practical power, if not necessarily ultimate authority, of administrators will be limited by strike-armed government worker unions. Administrators' lives may become less happy. But the great gain from a normative perspective will be that public employees will at last be treated as equal citizens within their political community. This is essential in every democratic community, but is seriously impaired when some citizens are denied an otherwise general legal right, here the right to strike, today widely and properly taken to be an important right of citizenship. Indeed, the fear of those concerned about dimunition of public sovereignty through the ceding of the authority of the whole to an irresponsible part must be matched by the reality of today when a part of the community, government workers, is clearly treated as a part who may be discriminated against in terms of full citizenship by the whole community.[8]

Another normative objection that is offered contends that strikes by public employees may substantially damage the "public interest," either in terms of the contents of the strike settlement or because of the nonperformance of essential tasks during the strike.[9] This second argument usually recognizes that the sovereignty matter is one that remains to be substantiated empirically and that were a threat to basic sovereignty of the political community to arise out of a legal strike both democratic theory and the United States Constitution provide that the general political community always has residual authority to take action to preserve itself.

If we take the public interest to mean the expressed will of the general political community, of course strikes might seriously damage the public interest. In that case they would indeed be unacceptable in a democracy. But this argument does not get us as far along as one might think. For it usually ends up as either a rhetorical or an empirical claim. If a rhetorical claim, it is worthless, for it is no argument at all, but rather amounts to the expression of highly emotional, vague sentiments about the public interest and strikes. If the argument, on the other hand, is meant as a serious claim, then at the moment it too needs empirical

[6]Paul P. Van Riper, *History of the United States Civil Service* (Evanston: Row, Peterson & Co., 1958), p. 352.

[7]Ziskind, *op. cit.,* pp. 190-91.

[8]*Ibid.,* p. 250.

[9]A good argument around this view is presented in Mosher, *op. cit.,* pp. 199-200.

support. And data would be needed for the general proposition that strikes threaten the public interest, as defined, as well as for any given strike by a union of government workers.

If such evidence could be marshalled regarding any strike by public employees, then the agents of the political community, government at the level affected, must take action to block this threat. Democratic values require that in the end the will of the community must not be thwarted by self-seeking minorities, as long as minorities have equal political rights.

At the same time one must keep in mind the developing reality of recourse to strikes by public workers. For attempts to fulfill the public interest demand that public officials or normative theorists attune themselves to reality.[10] It is very possible that simply dismissing any efforts to legalize the right to strike by public employees will lead only to increasingly divisive and uncontrolled splits within the political community as strikes occur.

My proposal would be to create a Taft-Hartley law for public employee unions, allowing them to strike, but also allowing governments to block a strike for a specified period of time while negotiations are undertaken or, in emergencies, permanently until the end of the emergency. After all, it is true that strikes or the outcomes of strikes by public workers might be terribly dangerous in their consequences to the expressed will of the political community.

But needed are specific methods and means to make sure that such temporary provisions for halting strikes are not easily available to public administrators. Perhaps the courts or independent boards might be the answer; certainly administrators will tend to see threats to the public interest on every hand and will justify stopping of strikes perhaps too frequently. On the other hand, there must be a willingness for public employee unions to act responsibly once they are granted the legal right to strike so that the reasonable normative fears of the opponents of legalizing public strikes do not become empirical realities. "Responsibly" here means that public employee unions must remember that there is indeed something besides their own selfish interests; they must remember that they are employees of the whole political community; and they should not, therefore, resort often to strikes or exact exorbitant settlements from strike-bound governments. And in case they "forget," my Taft-Hartley law will be brought into action.

Now there seems to be no good normative basis for justifying the extension of the right to strike to public employees on any selective basis with regard to the level of government or the type of work or workers involved. To be selective here would be to deny citizen equality. A better approach would be to invoke the Taft-Hartley law for public employee strikes whenever the public interest is seriously threatened, whatever the level of government, whatever type of work or whatever kind of workers are involved. We may guess that this law would be invoked much more quickly if a local police force struck than if the local public health nurses did and much more quickly if the Secret Service agents of the Treasury Department struck than if a local police force did, and so on.

But the decisions must be based on the consequences of individual strikes, not on illusions about different levels or different workers. Much done on the federal level is clearly less essential to the political community than are, for example, many

[10]Godine, *op. cit.*, p. 169.

local police forces, and the truth is that most government jobs at every level are not essential to their respective political communities either in the short or the long run. Indeed, many jobs in the "private" sector of our economy are more essential than many in the public realm; railroad workers are far more important than street cleaners or lifeguards. This is so complex a business that the arbitrary drawing of lines over jobs and levels makes no sense; a test of consequences appears to be the only practical way out.

At least one other significant normative qualm about public employee strikes is frequently expressed. This is the possibility that the merit system, widespread in several forms in American public bureaucracy, with its values of individualism and equality of opportunity, will be killed off intentionally by strike-armed unions of government workers hostile to the merit system; that is, that accepting strikes will be choosing the value of equal citizen rights over the merit system norms.[11]

This is the possibility that astute politicians like Governor Knowles of Wisconsin cite today when they make their case against public union strikes. They point up a possibility which is real and which emphasizes that policy choices may indeed have substantial and deep-reaching costs in terms of one set of values as opposed to another.[12]

Certainly a loss of the merit system in the face of strike-armed union pressure would be a heavy loss. First of all, however, it is not clear how this particularly refers to strikes per se so much as it does to the general question of public unions and collective bargaining by public workers. Strikes may magnify the threat posed by public unions to the merit system, if there is such a threat, but they are not at the base of this hypothetical problem.

Second, the challenge in question is so far mostly a theoretical one. As usual, a hypothesis, a possibility, has been transformed in some hands into a certainty. It is easy to understand how this has happened, and I too have suspicions that the merit system may become a casualty. But the fact is that analysis to deal with these suspicions awaits the gathering of substantial empirical evidence.

In any case, why should we always assume that governments are powerless and that public employees are bent on striking to destroy the merit system? Governments at all levels can and ought to resist attempts to abolish the merit system and they have the means to do so; moreover, if necessary, federal and state law can be written in a form which will place the basic principles of the merit system beyond strike-based settlements. This must be done, however—if done at all—with care so that the outcome does not turn a genuine, if inevitably uneasy, attempt to balance several sets of values into simply a backdoor way of legislating strikes out of existence. Third, most government unions do not want to strike about anything and never have. Some even go so far as to incorporate into their own constitutions antistrike provisions.[13] Still fewer have appeared to want to strike in order to end the merit system. Why should we assume that the future will be different?

It may well be that a nice balance between the right to strike and merit system values may not work out in practice. I am not without pessimism. But only if this starts to happen in fact will we have to ask ourselves about hard value choices. Then

[11] Ziskind, *op. cit.*, p. 257, is convincing here.

[12] A good discussion of this is in Mosher, *op. cit.*, pp. 198-200.

[13] Hart, *op. cit.*, pp. 24-25.

one may have to accept the reality that these systems of values may not be reconcilable and to make one's choice. But even then all may not be hopeless. Even if conflict is real, compromise is not impossible. Perhaps the merit system may be preserved in a weakened form or at entrance only,[14] or some other compromise may be worked out. Such a compromise would probably not be easy or satisfactory to all. Yet it might work well enough to preserve both sets of values to some substantial degree. There is still nothing wrong with compromise in politics or, sometimes, the compromise in politics that touches deep values.

On this dimension of the problem, as with all the serious normative issues regarding the strike issue, there seems to be a tremendous gap between the fears of the opponents to government worker strikes and the confidence of proponents of this "right." The relative lack of empirical evidence has not helped close this gap. As of now, we really have no basis for broad assertions about the consequences of the use of strikes by public employees.

Since we have little information, positive or negative, and yet a growing experience of strikes, why should we not move to legalize and thus control them? This seems a sound strategy as long as we remain aware of the substantial normative dangers that may arise from public worker strikes: the possible threat to the sovereignty of the political community, the possible threat to the "public interest" of the political community, and the possible threat to the values of the merit system. This awareness could be incorporated into the proposed Taft-Hartley Act for public employee unions.

All this will entail certain risks. We should understand that. But if we are democrats, we need to be prepared to take chances on ourselves and on our fellow citizens. We ought to be prepared to do so without further delay for those of our fellow citizens who are public employees.

A NEW APPROACH TO STRIKES IN PUBLIC EMPLOYMENT

Jack Stieber

. . . While still insignificant in number of strikes, workers involved, and days lost as compared with any other industry, strikes in public employment pose a major

---

Jack Stieber is Director of the School of Labor and Industrial Relations and Professor, Department of Economics, Graduate School of Business Administration, Michigan State University. Jack Stieber, "A New Approach to Strikes in Public Employment," *MSU Business Topics,* Autumn 1967, pp. 67-71. Reprinted by permission of the publisher, The Bureau of Business and Economic Research, Division of Research, Graduate School of Business Administration, Michigan State University.

[14] An idea suggested in the discussion of Paul Camp and W. Richard Lomax in Nigro, ed., *op. cit.,* pp. 134-37.

problem in labor-management relations in the United States today. There are several reasons why so few strikes should occasion so much concern.

First, all strikes in government are in violation of the law. They are specifically prohibited by the Taft-Hartley Act, by all states which have public employment relations law, and by numerous court decisions. The willingness of so many otherwise law-abiding citizens to violate and defy the law poses a moral issue as well as a practical problem of how to deal with such stoppages.

Second, many government services are vital to the normal functioning of the community. Strikes by policemen, fire fighters, and prison guards are intolerable and even the organizations to which these employees belong do not assert the right to strike. Strikes in hospitals, sanitation, and public utilities may present a threat to health or safety if they last more than a few days. Public transit, especially in a few large cities, is so important to the convenience and economic well-being of the people that many would classify it as an essential service. And strikes which close schools disrupt the social, economic, and emotional lives of more people than almost any other kind of work stoppage.

Third, strikes in public employment are bound to increase because government is the largest and fastest-growing industry in the United States and public employees are joining unions at a rapid rate. . . . In the AFL–CIO, almost the only unions which are growing rapidly are those operating in government. . . . Equally important are professional associations which, under pressure from union competition, act more and more like unions. . . . It is the belief of most people that employee organization and strikes go together, and there is nothing in the record of recent years to dissuade them from this belief. . . .

NEGOTIATION PROCEDURES

. . . Most negotiations, in public as in private employment, are resolved by the parties with or without the assistance of government mediators. The use of fact-finding—a procedure that is reserved for emergency disputes in private industry but that is available in even the smallest and most inconsequential public dispute under most state laws—will result in settlement of all but a few really hardcore disputes. But what about impasses after all efforts to resolve the dispute have failed? Should public employee organizations be denied the ultimate weapon which is available to unions in private industry? What should be done about employees who strike in violation of the law? These questions have aroused great passions among some public employee unions and have led to considerable disagreement among impartial experts in the industrial relations field.

With respect to the second question, the trend is away from laws calling for automatic dismissal or other severe penalties, including re-employment only under extremely harsh conditions, for striking public employees. Experience has shown such laws to be ineffective because elected public officials will almost never invoke them. This was the case in New York under the Conlin-Wadlin Act and in Michigan under the old Hutchinson Act. Most states with statutes governing labor relations in public employment do not specify automatic penalties for employees who violate the law by striking. However, the 1965 Michigan law states that a public employer may discipline a striking employee up to and including discharge, and the New York State law, passed in 1967 over bitter union opposition, provides penalties against unions rather than employees. The New York law calls for injunctions to halt public employee strikes and prescribes fines against unions that disobey such court orders, equal to one week's membership dues or $10,000, whichever is less, for each day that the strike continues.

Some of those who oppose a blanket prohibition on strikes in government argue that there cannot be genuine collective bargaining without the right to strike. Take away the strike threat and employers, public and private alike, will realize that they have the upper hand and will not engage in real collective bargaining. Unions can cite case after case in which a government employer contended he could not negotiate certain issues, but when a strike was threatened or actually called he quickly changed his tune. Under these circumstances, apparently unsurmountable obstacles to negotiation seemed to fade away and an agreement was reached in short order.

Others consider it illogical and inequitable to deny the right to strike to government employees when it is not denied to employees doing the same work in private industry. For example, at one level or another the government owns and operates printing plants, electric utilities, transit facilities, hospitals, cafeterias, liquor stores, and other establishments that are indistinguishable in almost every way from similar facilities in the private sector. In some cases, direct public employment shades over into government-owned but privately-operated enterprises. In atomic installations, for example, although the operation is wholly financed with public funds, collective bargaining modeled on the private sector (including strikes) has been permitted. Looking at the problem in another way, one may ask why clerks and office workers in the state capitol or in the highway authority should be prohibited from striking, when electric utility, transit or even hospital employees may strike as long as they work for private employers. Surely, the services supplied by the first group of public employees are less essential to the community than those furnished by the second group of private employees.

Those who support the prohibition against all government strikes do so primarily on three grounds: 1) fear that the principle of sovereignty will be imperiled by legalizing any strikes in government, 2) difficulty in differentiating between essential and nonessential activities, and 3) belief that the strike is an economic weapon which, in government, is not matched by countervailing power normally available in private industry.

The sovereignty doctrine holds that any strike of public employees is an attack upon the state and a challenge to government authority. It has been used for many years and is still cited in some states to deny government employees the right to bargain collectively. However meaningful state sovereignty may be to political scientists, it carries little weight with government employees when it comes to their relationship to the state as employer. Secretary of Labor Wirtz put it succinctly when he said: "This doctrine is wrong in theory; what's more, it won't work." It is interesting to note that other countries do not regard all strikes by government employees as a threat to state sovereignty. Most West European countries limit but do not prohibit all public employee strikes, and, in 1966, Canada passed a law which expressly permits federal employees to strike. The Canadian statute gives unions of government employees a choice between compulsory arbitration or strike action in the event of an impasse in negotiations. The union must indicate which course it will follow at the beginning of each negotiation and may not alter its choice throughout that negotiation.

The essential versus nonessential services approach to government employee stoppages has usually been rejected because of the difficulty of classifying activities in each category. Furthermore, this approach would have to take into account the distribution of employment at the local level, where almost all government strikes have occurred. Of the 6.4 million local government employees, more than 3.5 million are employed in schools—2.3 million as teachers and 1.2 million in non-instructional activities. An additional 1.6 million are employed in police and fire protection, public welfare, hospitals and health, sanitation, correctional institutions, and public utilities. Only 1.3 million are engaged in activities that are clearly nonessential in the sense that interruption of service could be endured for an extended period without posing a threat to the health, safety, or welfare of the populace. The employment distribution will, of course, vary from one community to another. It is clear from these statistics that, if it is to be meaningful, any law which limits the prohibition of strikes to essential government services would have to be narrowly construed and would certainly have to exclude schools, where more than half of all local government employees are concentrated. A law which extended the right to strike only to a small minority of all public employees, most of them unorganized and without the power to carry out a successful strike, would be a hoax.

While the classification of essential and nonessential services would be difficult, I am not convinced that it represents an insurmountable obstacle to legislation that would distinguish between prohibited and permissible stoppages in government employment. This is an administrative problem no more difficult than many others handled by government agencies, and particularly by the National Labor Relations Board in its day-to-day administration of the Taft-Hartley Act.

RECIPROCAL PRESSURES

The third argument against relaxing the prohibition on government strikes is that public employers cannot long withstand stoppages that victimize the community. It is argued that private employers may resort to a variety of weapons to combat strikes: they may lock out their employees, try to operate with other workers, or suspend operations, secure in the knowledge that pent-up demand or strike insurance will mitigate economic losses; or they may even go out of business entirely. The knowledge that potent weapons are available to the opposing sides exerts reciprocal pressures upon the parties to modify their positions to the extent necessary to bring about a settlement. Both unions and employers know from experience that jobs can and have been lost and markets seriously depleted as a result of strikes or settlements leading to noncompetitive price increases.

The government employer is in an entirely different position. He cannot lock out his employees or decide to go out of business. Extended suspension of government services is not politically feasible. While government may, in an emergency, call upon the National Guard or the Army to perform certain essential services, this solution does not lend itself, even on a temporary basis, to such public services as education and hospital care. Besides, such action involves political risks which elected officials would be reluctant to take.

The economic and market pressures that operate upon unions and private employers do not usually exist in the public sector. Competitors will not teach children, write relief checks, or provide case work services to welfare clients; consumers will not find ready substitutes or learn to do without garbage collection or medical care; excessive settlements will not price most government services out of the market, although the resulting tax increase may drive elected officials out of office.

Certainly there are important differences between strikes in government and work stoppages in private industry. At the same time, strikes by public and private employees have the same economic objectives—the improvement of wages, hours, and working conditions. Given the low salaries and poor conditions that often characterize employment in our schools, hospitals, social agencies, and other public services, one is loath to deprive these employees of any legitimate weapon to improve their situation, unless it is clear that irreparable injury may result to the community at large.

LESSONS FROM EXPERIENCE

The United States has come a long way in dealing with public employee-management relations during the last few years. Future progress will depend, in part, upon how we handle the difficult problem of public employee strikes. What are the lessons of past experience for future policy on this issue?

1. The right to join employee organizations and to negotiate with their employers through representatives of their own choosing should be guaranteed to all public employees at all levels of government, by federal legislation, if necessary. Government employees in backward states should not be denied these fundamental rights.

2. Governments have a responsibility to promote settlements without interruption of public services. This includes provision for mediation and fact-finding with recommendations in all disputes in which an impasse has been reached in negotiations.

3. Employee organizations and public employers in all government services should be encouraged to develop their own procedures to resolve disputes without interruption of work (including the use of voluntary arbitration). Long experience in private industry has demonstrated that the parties are usually better satisfied with their own solutions than with those imposed from the outside.

4. Regardless of preventive measures or prohibitions and penalties provided by law, strikes in government will occur. Government policy toward such stoppages should take into account the nature of the service provided and the impact upon the public. There is no more reason to treat all strikes in government alike than there is to apply the same yardstick to all stoppages in private industry. Just as a work stoppage on the railroads or waterfront is handled differently from a strike in a widget factory, so should a strike of policemen or fire fighters be regarded differently from an interruption of service in state liquor stores.

5. Public services should be classified into three categories: those which cannot be given up for even the shortest period of time, those which can be interrupted for a limited period but not indefinitely, and those services in which work stoppages can be sustained for extended periods without serious effects on the community.

With respect to the first category, which in my opinion would include only police and fire protection and prisons, compulsory arbitration should be used to resolve negotiation impasses but only after all other methods have failed.

Strikes in the second group of services, which would include hospitals, public utilities, sanitation and schools, should not be prohibited but should be made subject to injunctive relief through the courts when they begin to threaten the health, safety or welfare of the community. The courts, in deciding whether or not to issue injunctions, should consider the total equities in the particular case and should utilize their traditional right to adapt sanctions against those violating injunctions to the particular situation, as recommended in the report of the Advisory Committee on Public Employee Relations to Michigan Governor George Romney. The term "total equities" includes not only the impact of a strike on the public but also the extent to which employee organizations and public employers have met their statutory obligations.

Work stoppages in government activities which do not fall into either of the above classifications should be permitted on the same basis as in private industry.

These changes in public policy will come slowly, if at all. Experimentation with different approaches in the states is desirable and should be encouraged. Eventually, however, I believe that laws dealing with employee-management relations in government will tend toward greater uniformity because the nature of public employment differs little among states, and employee organizations, which are national in scope, will insist on equality of treatment for all government employees.

THE LIMITED RIGHT TO STRIKE IN TEACHER NEGOTIATIONS

Robert E. Doherty

Walter E. Oberer

The real dilemma of collective bargaining in public employment, as we have seen, is the absence of any effective means or incentive for the parties to avoid a stalemate. The employees cannot strike, and therefore should not threaten to

Robert Doherty and Walther Oberer are Professor Industrial Relations, Cornell University, and Professor of Law and Industrial Relations, Cornell University, respectively. Reprinted from *Teachers, School Board and Collective Bargaining: A Changing of the Guard,* Copyright · 1967, Cornell University, which was published by Cornell University, Ithaca, New York, for the New York State School of Industrial and Labor Relations.

strike. The employer cannot lock out. The parties can, of course, continue to talk, to reason, but it may be accepted as axiomatic that each side considers its position reasonable and the other's unreasonable. Moreover, the budgetary deadline looms nearer and nearer.

Obviously, outsiders must be brought in as catalysts or arbiters. The full panoply of uses to which these outsiders may be put is as follows: (1) mediation; (2) fact finding; (3) non-binding recommendations for settlement (advisory arbitration); (4) binding recommendations (binding arbitration).

All of the eight statutes prescribing teacher negotiations provide some impasse-resolving procedures through the use of outsiders, with the sole exception of California. While the language of the statutes is not always explicit as to the precise function and powers of the outsiders, a fair reading indicates that mediation, fact finding, and non-binding recommendations are available under all seven. The Rhode Island statute is the only one of these which takes the next and final step of binding arbitration, but the range of issues subjected to binding arbitration is narrow. The Rhode Island statute reads: "The decision of the arbitrators shall be made public and shall be binding upon the certified public school teachers and their representative and the school committee on all matters not involving the expenditure of money."[1]

The reluctance to subject the resolution of bargaining impasses to a binding arbitration, the most obvious substitute for the strike from a lay standpoint, is the product of two fears. The first is the old bugaboo of sovereignty. The second is the concern that this would destroy collective bargaining.

The sovereignty argument we have already explored elsewhere. In the immediate context, it consists of the idea that the superintendence of school affairs is entrusted under the law to school boards, and that this power cannot be delegated to a board of arbitrators. In the words of the Taylor Report to Governor Rockefeller: "Compulsory arbitration is not recommended. There is serious doubt whether it would be legal because of the obligation of the designated executive heads of government departments or agencies not to delegate certain fiscal and other duties."[2] Curiously, however, the Taylor Report immediately adds: "Voluntary arbitration on an ad hoc basis is a desirable course, on the other hand, *although it also leads to binding decisions.*"[3] The Report argues strenuously the wisdom of a *contractual* commitment by the public employer and the employee representative to submit a dispute over wages and other conditions of employment to "arbitration" or to "fact-finding with recommendations, with or without the advance commitment by one or both parties to accept the recommendations. The procedures may provide a number of variants. The negotiators may jointly agree in advance to accept the recommendations of the fact-finders and to urge their acceptance upon their principals. They may jointly agree in advance to take the recommendations to the appropriate legislative body to advocate jointly the requisite appropriation or change in regulations, recognizing the authority of such legislative body."[4]

[1] *Gen. Laws of R.I.* title 28 sec. 28-9. 3-12.

[2] *Governor's Committee on Public Employee Relations, Final Report,* March 31, 1966, p. 46.

[3] *ibid.* (italics added).

[4] *ibid.* pp. 35-36.

The wisdom of impasse-resolution contractually agreed upon is clear, and legislation encouraging it is strongly to be commended. But, on the *sovereignty* front, what magic is there in distinguishing between legislative *permission* being given to public employers to contract in advance for binding arbitration of bargaining disputes and a legislative *mandate* that such impasses be resolved by binding arbitration *whether or not there has been any prior voluntary contractual commitment to that effect?* Is it the point of the Taylor Report that while the public employer may *itself* delegate its "fiscal and other duties," the legislature may not do the delegating for it? If so, this is a curious position, at least in the case of school boards, since the latter are creatures of the legislature and have only the powers legislatively bestowed upon them. If the legislature can give a school board the power unilaterally to determine conditions of employment and the power to contract away this power to an arbitrator, why cannot the legislature bestow the power of such determination, in the case of an impasse, *directly* upon an arbitrator or board of arbitrators, or, indeed, upon a fact finder"?

It is not necessary to belabor this legal question, however, because a closer reading of the Report makes it clear that the real concern of the Taylor Committee is that compulsory (i.e. legislatively directed) arbitration is incompatible with collective bargaining. The Report states:

> The Committee has rejected the proposal for compulsory arbitration not merely because there may be serious questions as to its legality but because of the conviction that impasse disputes may arise less frequently and be settled more equitably by the procedures outlined in this report. In our judgment, the requirement for binding arbitration would likely reduce the prospects of settlement at earlier stages closer to the problems, the employees and the agency; it would tend to frustrate the participation of employees in the determination of compensation and conditions of employment and tend to encourage arbitrary and extreme positions on both sides.[5]

This is an admirable statement of the classic view of the effect of compulsory arbitration in the area of private employment, where collective bargaining is, at base, a test of economic strength, the weapons of strike and lockout hovering over the bargaining table. But does it follow that the same is true in public employment, where these weapons, the Taylor Report agrees, should not be available? Our guess is that, as applied to school teachers in a district where NEA and AFT afiliates are in strong competition, the school board and teacher representative are going to bargain to impasse, conservatively stated, more often than not, largely over money issues. If they have seen fit to agree upon impasse procedures entailing more than mere mediation, the likelihood may be strong that the recommendations resulting, binding or not, will be honored. The reason for this is that these procedures, being the product of mutual agreement, carry with them an implied, if not express, obligation of good-faith observance by the parties. This is, of course, the strength of contractually created impasse procedures.

But what if the parties do not so agree? If the school board is jealous of its

[5]*ibid.,* pp. 37-38.

prerogatives, as many are, why should it so agree? Theoretically, it has no strike to fear. Why should it place itself under even an *implied* obligation of good-faith adherence to an arbitrator's award or a fact-finder's recommendations? And if the teacher representative is an AFT affiliate, sold on the righteousness of the strike, legal or illegal, why should it commit itself in any way to arbitration or fact finding with recommendations? To so do would be to derogate from the righteousness of its strike threat, however unspoken the latter may be. Indeed, if the teacher representative is an NEA affiliate and therefore, at best, a reluctant convert to the cause of teacher strikes, why should it prejudice itself in the continuing competition with the AFT by restricting in any degree its freedom of action? The willingness of an NEA affiliate to make this concession where the right of collective bargaining is bestowed upon it by the grace of a progressive school board (as happened in Rochester, New York[6]) is hardly demonstrative of a similar willingness where the right is a product of state law, as would be the case under the Taylor Bill. Perhaps we are unduly Machiavellian, but we are not as sanguine as the Taylor Committee about contractually based impasse resolution in the teacher area.

We must turn, therefore, to an examination of the Taylor Bill's non-contractual—i.e. statutory—impasse procedures. These are: (1) Mediation under the guidance of the Public Employment Relations Board, which the bill would create. (2) Appointment of a fact-finding board by the PERB to consist of "not more than three members, each representative of the public, from a list of qualified persons maintained by the board, which fact-finding board shall have . . . the power to make public recommendations for the resolution of the dispute."[7] (3) Further recommendations by the PERB. (4) A submission by "the chief executive officer of the government involved [chairman of the school board?]" of the fact-finding board's findings of fact and recommendations "to the legislative body of the government involved [school board?]," "together with his recommendations for settling the dispute; and the employee organization may submit to such legislative body its recommendations for settling the dispute."[8]

Whatever may be said of the first three steps, the fourth leaves considerable to be desired as applied to school teacher bargaining. Ostensibly, it leaves to the school board the final resolution of the bargaining dispute between that school board and the teachers it employs! It would seem that the Taylor Committee did not have *independent* school districts in mind when it framed these procedures, despite the fact that these outnumber the half-dozen dependent districts in the State of New York many times over. But the six dependent school districts do include the most populous cities of the state, and in these the "legislative body of the government involved" would apparently be the city council. In such districts, the Taylor Bill provisions would, in effect, result .in a kind of state-legislature mandated "binding arbitration" by the city council. This, too leaves something to be desired, however, from the standpoint of the teachers, since on the core money issues the city council's niggardliness, as viewed by the teachers, is apt to be what produced the bargaining impasse in the first place—the dependent school board being a captive

---

[6]See *Section of Labor Relations Law—1966, American Bar Association*, pp. 168-169.

[7]S. Int. No. 4784. Pr. No. 5689 (1966), sec. 209(3) (b).

[8]*ibid.*, sec. 209(3) (e).

ultimately of the council's budget. One may be forgiven a little pessimism as to whether such a procedure is well calculated to stave off strikes.

Preferable in the view of the authors would be a scheme which provided the teachers with the lawful right to strike if, but only if, the recommendations of the fact-finding body appointed by the PERB were not honored by the purse-controlling authority, be it an independent school district or, where dependent, the city council. This alternative seems preferable to completely binding arbitration since it provides an escape for the school board where the fact finders are deemed by it to have gone "haywire." The public interest, as viewed by the school board would be protected to this extent. Conversely, the refusal of the school board to accept the recommendations would trigger the offsetting rights of the teachers to strike. If this were the law, there might be more likelihood of the parties contractually committing themselves to arbitration of the bargaining dispute because of the greater control this would give them over the constituency of the impasse-resolving body. Moreover, teachers would be less likely to strike illegally under such a scheme—i.e. in defiance of the fact-finders' recommendations—and if they did so strike, the climate of public opinion would be the best possible for enforcement of the statutory sanctions against such a strike.

A LIMITED RIGHT TO STRIKE FOR PUBLIC EMPLOYEES

William J. Kilberg

As part of the new approach to labor relations in the municipal service, *the total ban on strikes ought to be eliminated. It is an unworkable device.* Psychologically, municipal employee unions are geared to strike. Their members have felt harassed for too long and are anxious to redress past grievances in one fell swoop. Moreover, they see what a strike can bring; the 1967 teachers strike in New York netted an average increase of well over 20 per cent in pay and benefits in a 26-month contract, a settlement three times larger than anything granted before.[1] Unions in most major cities are a potent political force, and the newly organized public employee organizations are willing to share in the power without having to taste the responsibility. Public unions have a strategic and tactical need to strike.

William Kilberg is General Counsel of the Federal Mediation and Conciliation Service. Reprinted from the *Harvard Journal on Legislation,* November 1969.

[1]Kilberg, *Limiting Public Strikes,* Ripon Forum 5 (March, 1968).

The municipal political process is a slow one. The institutional and procedural differences between the public and the private sectors prevent a government from acting with the speed and efficacy with which a corporation may act. A strike may be what is required to stir lethargic elected and administrative officials into action. A ban on strikes is, in itself, an inducement to strike. The pressure of the strike mechanism is reintroduced by the threat of unions to violate it.

Mediator Theodore W. Kheel has asked: "Is it socially desirable to create a circumstance in which the wish of the union to bargain collectively is achieved through the violation of the law rather than the prospect of a legal strike?"[2] This total strike ban, Kheel argues, "eliminates collective bargaining, which implies the right of the buyer or seller to refuse to buy or sell by a strike or a lockout."[3]

The formulation of sanctions in the public strike area is a delicate proposition. If sanctions are imposed too harshly on a striking union, they become ineffective. One cannot throw an entire employee organization into prison and still expect the city's vital services to continue functioning. On the other hand, if sanctions are too mild, they will simply have no deterrent value. The solution is not to forbid all strikes but to give a public employee union a way to demonstrate its grievance without endangering the entire fabric of a metropolitan community.

Aids to contract settlement have slowly been evolving in the private sector. Fact finding, mediation and voluntary arbitration are all common mechanisms for labor peace in the industrial world. In the public sector, however, only a handful of states have seen fit to authorize their state and local officials to use these devices. Most states simply forbid strikes by public employees and are then powerless when they occur. Any collective bargaining scenario envisioned in the public sector must provide for adequate procedures to aid the parties in reaching agreement. The one procedure which ought not to be on the agenda is compulsory arbitration. There are serious questions as to the legality of a procedure which purports to impose a binding settlement upon a city government.[4] A procedure which allows collective bargaining participants to forego good faith bargaining in the expectation that a third party will settle their disputes for them should be avoided.

Mechanisms for the resolution of collective bargaining impasses, however, are not enough. As we have seen, employers in the public sector lack the discipline which the profit motive supplies to employers bargaining process in the private sphere.[5] Means must be developed to unify the municipal bureaucracy into a bargaining force which can approach the union's demands with acceptable counteroffers. Municipal unions must be given a legal weapon which will impress all city officials with the importance of reaching a settlement. There is a need for political confrontation in the public sector, moreover, which is absent in the private. The voting public is a more potent force in municipal bargaining than it is in corporate labor relations. Any weapon which the union is given must allow it to bring its case to the public.

[2] N.Y. Times, Jan. 7, 1969, at 1.

[3] Id.

[4] Cf. Everett Fire Fighters Assoc. v. Johnson, 46 Wash. 2d 114, 278 P.2d 662 (1955) (compulsory arbitration held invalid as an illegal delegation of governmental authority).

The danger, of course, is that of a crippling confrontation. Too much power in the hands of a striking union may endanger the health and safety of the city and lead to repressive counter-measures by the municipality, such as the jailing of union officials or the calling out of the National Guard. In vital employment areas to be determined by each city individually through the use of a committee made up of representatives of government, labor and the public, no strike should be permitted. Two such areas would be the police and fire departments. Only one "bright line" would, therefore, have to be drawn, between essential and unessential community services. In all other sectors of the municipal service, a restricted strike schedule should be devised. This schedule would set a number of hours that a union would be allowed to strike once a contract deadline has been reached without agreement and all mediation, factfinding and conciliation procedures are exhausted. The independent committee might, for example, settle on four hours a week as allowable strike time, to be used when and how the union sees fit. Transit workers might then choose to go out on Friday evening from 3 to 7 p.m. This would produce a great public inconvenience and would give the union the attention it needs to put pressure on a political entity like a city government. But it would not paralyze the community. The problem of defining an "essential" service would thus be greatly minimized; only those services which a city could not forego for the briefest moment would be deemed "essential" and not subject to a work stoppage.[5]

If a four-hour strike would not be enough to impress the city's negotiators with the union's legitimate claims, the independent commission might allow a longer work stoppage period. However, this probably would not be necessary. The point of the restricted strike schedule is one of inconvenience—to inconvenience the public enough so that a union will feel that its claims will be heard. The news media tend to detail the issues of a collective bargaining dispute only when there is confrontation between the parties, no matter how brief. The necessary inconvenience of even a short work stoppage would have its desirable impact. Inconveniencing the public is the only way the necessary confrontation may take place in the public sector. The cab drivers in New York City made this plain when they staged a one-day work stoppage and successfully influenced the city's decision to permit an increase in taxicab fares. Collective bargaining on the municipal level is basically a political struggle involving the use of power. But it is not the use of power, per se, that should be objected to: it is wanton destructiveness that ought to be deplored. The restricted strike schedule is a means of halting that destructiveness.

A restricted strike schedule is a weapon that can be accepted by cities because it would allow normal negotiations to continue without a major disruption of the life of the city. For the union it presents a step forward, a legal means for bringing

[5]*But cf.* Letter to the author from Professor Eric Polisar, Nov. 8, 1967: "What, for example, are the market pressures on utilities? What are the market pressures on private hospitals as distinct from publicly owned hospitals? In practical, as distinct from theoretical or philosophical terms, what is the difference between aerospace production in Huntsville, Alabama and the production of similar and occasionally identical items by North American Aviation on the West Coast? The illustrations could be extended almost indefinitely." Professor Polisar was, up until the time of his death in July, 1968, Associate Professor of Industrial and Labor Relations at Cornell University.

grievances to the public without facing fines, jail sentences or worse. Were the union to take undue advantage of the restricted strike, strong sanctions would be appropriate including suspension of the union's certification as a representative of its members. Yet one would expect public employee unions, once their right to strike is accepted, to obey limitations on this right, much as unions in the private sector obey artificially contrived limitations on picketing and boycott procedures. The supreme art in the field of labor relations is to develop rules that both permit struggle and control it. A restricted strike schedule may be such a rule.

PUBLIC EMPLOYEE STRIKES: AN OPERATIONAL SOLUTION

H. L. Fusilier
Lawrence L. Steinmetz

Public employee strikes are often in the news. Their frequency is surprising in view of the fact that there are laws prohibiting such strikes, which the courts have emphatically upheld. Yet, they continue to occur. ... These strikes certainly present a strong challenge to the claims that public officials, as opposed to private employers, do not have the need or the desire to oppress the worker because the profit system is absent, and that fair treatment of public employees is assured by law and regulation (for example, civil service rules on promotions, public retirement and pension plans, and tenure programs).

In addition to bona fide strikes, public employees leave their jobs for a few hours or for a day to dramatize their complaints, to win popular support for their cause, and to avoid the public wrath that withholding their services for a long period might bring. Policemen have protested by refusing to issue traffic tickets. Firemen have gone to their stations to be available in case of fire but have refused to perform any other duties. There have also been severe work slowdowns.

Thus, there appears to be ample evidence that public employees feel the need for additional procedures to achieve what they deem to be fair and equitable working conditions. The laws and regulations established for the benefit of the employees and the absence of the profit motive do not seem sufficient. Therefore, the authors would like to explore a proposal that might reconcile the need felt by public employees to organize and to strike with the need of the public to have uninterrupted public service . . . .

The authors are members of the faculty of the Graduate School of Business Administration, University of Colorado. Reprinted from the *Quarterly Review of Economics and Business,* Autumn 1967.

THE VALUE OF STRIKES

Whether public employees should be allowed to strike is, of course, a value judgment based on considerations which weight the value of work stoppage as an ingredient of meaningful negotiation and agreement against the potentially harmful effects on public health and safety, national defense, and the essentiality of orderliness and continuity of governmental activities. Smith, in his article "Are Public Service Strikes Necessary?"[1] takes a firm stand against such strikes and supports his position well. We disagree with his position, at least to the extent that *all* government employees should be denied the right to strike. Our position is based on the beliefs (1) that the strike power is a most effective and forceful device in producing meaningful agreement which should not be denied workers except for the most compelling reasons and (2) that our lawmakers can effectively distinguish between public employees who can be allowed to strike and those who cannot, thus protecting the public health and safety.

The value and desirability of the strike has been supported on various grounds. It is said that the strike power is consistent with our democratic concepts of equality, freedom, and the dignity of man. With the ability to strike, the worker can resist the unilateral power of the employer—be it dictatorial or paternalistic—and can achieve a sense of dignity, of worth, and of freedom consistent with the highest ideals of our democratic society. It is also asserted that the workers' capacity to successfully resist unsatisfactory conditions provides employers with the incentive for more efficient management, thereby benefiting the total economy. A strike potential also forces both sides to consider not only their own selfish wishes and demands but also those of their opponents—each must weigh the possibility of gain against the possibility of loss and attempt to produce a reasonable, meaningful bilateral agreement which will benefit both labor and management.

DISTINGUISHING BETWEEN FUNCTIONS

The present concept of the sovereign's power and immunity stands as a solid roadblock to strikes by public employees. However, the sovereign authority rests with the public and they, through their elected representatives, have the power to modify this concept. We believe that the concept should be modified to permit some government employees to strike and to provide an effective strike substitute for the others. As stated by Professor Leonard D. White, the criterion should be strike consequences.[2] The public, through their elected representatives (municipal, county, state, or federal), can distinguish between their primary and secondary interests—forbidding strikes affecting the first but allowing those affecting the second. For example, strikes by policemen, firemen, sanitation and utility workers,

---

[1]Oscar S. Smith, "Are Public Service Strikes Necessary?" *Public Personnel Review*, Vol. 21, No. 3 (July, 1960), pp. 169-73.

[2]Leonard D. White, "Strikes in the Public Service," *Public Personnel Review*, Vol. 10, No. 1 (January, 1949), pp. 3-10. Professor White would allow or prohibit strikes by either public or private employees according to the strike consequences.

and hospital employees can be prohibited as detrimental to the *primary interests* of the public because they do constitute an immediate and serious danger to the public health and safety. Strikes involving *secondary functions,* although inconvenient and injurious to some extent, could be permitted because they would not constitute an immediate and serious threat to the public health and safety—for example, strikes by employees of a government-owned barge line, employees of public-owned liquor stores, maintenance crews, teachers, and office workers.

A basic problem is finding an effective strike substitute for government employees in the primary function areas. It is no secret that a government official can be as high-handed, ill-tempered, and grossly unfair as any corporate official. In his excellent article reviewing the program of employee-management cooperation in the federal civil service, initiated by Executive Order 10988, Wilson Hart makes the statement that without the right to strike

> Management representatives at the bargaining table are subject to no compulsion to make concessions or compromises leading to meaningful agreements, comparable to the threat of a crippling strike, which hangs over the heads of their counterparts in industry in comparable circumstances.[3]

THE NONSTOPPAGE STRIKE

Government employees engaged in the primary function areas could be given the right to engage in a nonstoppage strike, similar to that proposed for private industry by Professor George W. Goble and others.[4] In such a plan, the work continues but both sides suffer economic loss. Goble, for example, recommends that during the nonstoppage strike, 25 percent of the wages of the workers, 25 percent of the salaries of management, and the net earnings of the company be withheld. If the nonstoppage strike is resolved within 90 days, the money withheld would be returned to those who contributed it. If no agreement is reached within this period, all funds would be forfeited to the United States government. The same procedure would then be repeated for an additional 90 days, and repeated again, if need be, until an agreement is effected. As Goble states:

> ... it is the intent that the very threat of this forfeiture shall cause both parties to exert every effort toward a settlement. ... [The plan] makes possible the building up of a heavy penalty which will drop suddenly on the parties on the ninety-first day. ... This feature of the plan, it is be-

---

[3]Wilson R. Hart, "The Impasse in Labor Relations in the Federal Civil Service," *Industrial and Labor Relations Review,* Vol. 19, No. 2 (January, 1966), pp. 175-99. Hart finds that there is much evidence of refusal to bargain in good faith on the part of government. His recommendations do not include giving public employees the right to strike.

[4]George W. Goble, "The Nonstoppage Strike," *Labor Law Journal,* Vol. 2, No. 1 (February, 1951), pp. 105-14; David B. McCalmont, "The Semi-Strike," *Industrial and Labor Relations Review,* Vol. 15, No. 2 (January, 1962), pp. 191-208; and Stephen H. Sosnick, "Non-Stoppage Strikes: A New Approach," *Industrial and Labor Relations Review,* Vol. 18, No. 1 (October, 1964), pp. 73-80.

lieved, introduces a powerful psychological factor in favor of early settlement. . . . [5]

And, needless to say, promotes much reasonableness about the 89th day.

PUBLIC EMPLOYEE NONSTOPPAGE STRIKE

Applying Goble's nonstoppage strike to a government agency presents many difficulties. Such an application must begin with at least a minimum of specifics. A nonstoppage strike plan for government employees involved in primary functions is proposed in this paper as follows: That a union or an organization representing a majority of the employees of a government agency or department may, upon vote of its members, declare that a nonstoppage strike exists. Upon such declaration, the agency would withhold 30 percent of the workers' wages and 30 percent of the agency's management salaries, and the agency or department would commit from its budget an amount equal to the first two.[6] Such sums would be held in trust by the agency or other designated party. If agreement were reached within 90 days, all funds would be returned to the parties who contributed them. If no agreement were reached within that period, all funds would be forfeited, and the same procedure would be repeated until an agreement could be effected. Forfeited funds would be given to support research conducted by a private university or other private nonprofit research organization as determined by a board appointed by the mayor, governor, or president. The enabling ordinance or statute could broadly specify research areas of public concern, such as cancer, heart, or educational programs.

As in an actual strike, the nonstoppage strike would have to be accompanied by sufficient penalties to labor; otherwise it might be used for petty grievances and would not produce sincere efforts at prompt settlement. It seems that 30 percent of each worker's wage would be an amount substantial enough to avoid this problem.

The workers are not angered at an abstract thing or symbol such as the "agency" or "department." They are upset by lack of effort to raise pay and by specific conditions that exist because of rules, decisions, or policies established by the management of the agency. Therefore, the management, having had a large part in producing or allowing the problem to exist, should also be made to bear an economic burden. It would seem fair that their burden should be in proportion to that of their employees. If the amount is large enough to prevent petty grievances and to produce earnest efforts on the part of the workers, the same proportion should be large enough to prevent obstinacy and lack of good faith on the part of management.

For more effective economic pressure, the agency or department should contribute a sum from its budget. Since it is on a fixed annual budget, the agency—in order to prevent current loss of service—would be committed to contribute funds the following year to cover its share of any forfeited funds. The purpose would be to bring economic pressure to bear on the governmental unit as a whole—that is, the

---

[5]Goble, *loc. cit.*, pp. 107-9.

[6]Various percentages have been recommended. No figure is magic, of course; experience would indicate whether the percentage would be more effective if it were larger or smaller.

municipal, state, or federal government. The agency officials would have to explain and justify the request for additional funds to their superiors, who, in turn, would have to do the same to the municipal council, legislature, or other superior body. Such pressure would ensure sincere consideration and good faith on the part of agency officials. Furthermore, knowing that the additional sums might not be granted or might be granted only in part, and thus that some jobs might have to be eliminated, the employees would also be constrained to act in good faith. This pressure should also be felt indirectly from the top downward. The mayor, governor, or other superior would become much more concerned in the selection of able management and less inclined to political favoritism. Again, in this way, the voters themselves would be made to recognize that they must bear part of the responsibility for the working conditions existing in government.

Forfeited funds must go to something other than the general funds of the governmental unit. Otherwise, such forfeiture would merely constitute moving money from one pocket to another and the funds would be used to alleviate some need which must be attended to anyway. Objection might be raised against giving public money to a private organization, but there appears to be sufficient precedent—especially in the field of public grants to private research.

The majority of government employee strikes concern salaries and other basic conditions of employment often set by law. It could be objected that since the agency managers cannot be held responsible for this, it would be unfair to penalize them. On the other hand, it can be argued that many agency heads are more interested in empire-building than in improving the lot of present employees and that they could do much to improve these basic conditions if they really tried.

Perhaps this problem could be resolved in one of two ways. If the employees were shown that management had made real efforts to improve salaries and other basic conditions set by law, they certainly would not want to penalize the management for something beyond its control. Therefore, when the nonstoppage strike vote was taken, the employees could also vote whether or not to include management in the salary penalty.

A more direct solution might be to tie, by law, the salaries, hours, and fringe benefits of public employees to the average of their private, union counterparts. The nonstoppage strike plan would then apply only to other conditions of public employment and would also assure an adequate grievance procedure. . . .

THE FINAL OFFER SELECTION PROCEDURE

Harry H. Rains

. . . Many proposals have been offered to solve the problems arising in public sector dispute settlement. Some involve major changes in the present system, while others entail only minor modifications. In the opinion of the author, none of them fully copes with the problems.

One partial solution which has been proposed to encourage more meaningful bargaining at the initial stage, is to make the negotiating team's settlement binding on the union membership. Negotiators would be able to reach the best possible settlement without having to be concerned about crumbling support from the ranks.

This solution is probably unworkable, however, for at least two reasons. First, the union negotiator is still subject to eventual ouster from office and, if he senses a militant posture among the members, he will continue to be inflexible at the bargaining table for fear of binding the membership to a much resented package. Second, at least in the case of teacher disputes, this solution does nothing to prevent the negotiator from attempting to save his demands for the fact finder. The negotiator might still believe that his best course of conduct would be to hope that the school board would accept recommendations in the fact finder's report which had previously been rejected in negotiations.

A more elaborate proposal has been advanced by Theodore Kheel. Kheel would allow public employees the right to strike, with more troublesome strikes subject to an eighty day cooling off period before a work stoppage could begin. This limited strike concept has been proposed in various forms by many prestigious groups, but the proposal has serious problems. The determination of which strikes are to be permitted without the cooling off period could become a political issue. Also, some strikes which appear tolerable could, as time passed, become intolerable. Who could decide at what point the damage becomes intolerable?

The concept of a cooling off period raises problems in its own right. The main purpose of the cooling off period is the continuation of normal operations after the old contract has expired. In the case of public employment, however, the contract expiration date normally will occur long after the budget submission date. This

Harry Rains is a partner in the law firm of Rains, Pogrebin and Scher. Reprinted from *Buffalo Law Review*, XIX, No. 2 (1969-70).

submission date, according to the Taylor Act, is the time at which a government's proposed budget must be submitted to the "legislative body" for final action. An extended cooling off period may bring the parties beyond this budget submission date. After the budget has been submitted, negotiations tend to become somewhat strained, since the manager has already estimated his expenditures for the year, and any concession to the union which brings costs above the employer's estimation would have to be reallocated from another source. The limits already set on the budget would make the negotiations somewhat inflexible. Ill feeling on all sides would result.

The system of public expenditures and budget preparation is not consonant with the concept of the cooling off period which follows the expiration of a contract. Furthermore, present impasse procedures are, in effect, a public sector version of the cooling off period, with due regard to timing before budget vote dates. At a specified period before the budget submissions date, intensive negotiations begin, and impartial government mediators can be called in. As time begins to run out, successive emergency procedures may be invoked.

The cooling off period concept is also a psychological handicap to bona fide bargaining. The negotiators feel that they have more time in which to bargain and they hold on to extreme positions for a longer period, thus pushing the crisis up to the end of the cooling off period. We should try to prevent strikes by improving the quality of collective bargaining. It will serve no purpose to increase merely the quantity of such negotiating sessions. . . .

Still another solution to the current system of final submission has been championed by advocates of a "Labor Court." It would seem this solution has little of substance to offer. Is the labor court merely a method of institutionalizing binding arbitration, of giving such arbitration the trappings of judicial majesty? Is there really any power that this court would have that ordinary courts could not have under a revised Taylor Act? If the previous answer is no, might this not be an ostentatious method of simply giving labor disputes their own decongested court calendar?

While none of the suggestions is bad, each (binding arbitration, arbitration with judicial safeguards, increased power of courts, more practical court calendars for labor cases) should be dealt with on its own merits and not under the vague blanket heading of "Labor Court." Most important, the court cannot act in a vacuum and without legislative guidelines. Therefore, to give even a modicum of effectiveness to this proposal, other approaches, such as unfair labor practice provisions, would first have to be considered.

NEW SOLUTIONS TO PUBLIC EMPLOYEE DISPUTE PROBLEMS

. . . The penalty system, the limited right to strike and the cooling off period have all been criticized for the same reason—none of them gives to the negotiators an incentive to bargain more maturely and more realistically. They do nothing to create a situation in which both parties feel the urgent need, above all else, to be "reasonable" for their own immediate personal gain. In order to achieve this goal, it is suggested that the fact-finder be called in when an impasse has developed, and that he be empowered to arrive at one of two binding recommendations: that the last firm counterproposal of the employer is the more reasonable when compared with the last firm demand of the union, or vice versa. It is recommended that the fact-finder's conclusion be phrased in the form of a binding decision, thus, in effect, ending the dispute by irrevocably choosing one side over the other. The effect of this proposal would be felt at every bargaining table. It is reasonable to assume that each side will trim its unrealistic positions and speak not to mollify its extreme factions, for it can no longer afford that luxury, but to state a position at the point of submission to fact finding which may reasonably be acceptable to an impartial party. If both parties are moved to such point of reason they can at that point resolve their differences voluntarily.

Throughout the short life-span of public bargaining, it has been the practice of both parties—whether because of amateurism, volatile rank and file, ill will or other factors—to short circuit the whole negotiating process and proceed right to the fact finder with positions virtually as rigid as they were at the very first meeting. Each side has seemed incapable or unwilling to give an inch, and each proposal and counterproposal has emerged sounding like just so much grist for the propaganda mill. When the problem has come before the fact finder, he has found himself confronted with two totally divergent extreme and unrealistic positions, irreconcilable and immovable, and totally incapable of mutually satisfying resolution. The fact finder's frequent answer has been to compromise, by recommending a course of action that proceeds directly down the middle road. This type of recommendation has had no relevance to the equities of the situation, since the two positions are so polarized and since there are so many unnecessary side demands and rejections. The confused fact finder must choose in a vacuum, unaware of what the parties really need or desire. The parties, aware of this situation, have done everything within their power to maintain the most extreme position possible, believing that the fact finder will come to rest closer to their position if their demands remain far afield.

The parties must be discouraged from substituting this "stalemate" settlement mechanism for bona fide collective bargaining. Both sides must be forced to "put their cards on the table," instead of waiting until the final step to wrest an extra measure of victory from the chaos of exaggerated demands and unreasonable confrontation. A logical method of achieving this is one which would limit the fact finder to the last firm proposal of either party. It is hoped that the onus thus placed upon each party to arrive at a position more reasonable and acceptable than his adversary's will result in the positions of the parties actually meeting on some middle ground, eliminating the need for impasse procedures and thus demonstrating the value of good faith negotiations.

Even if the psychological atmosphere created by this step does not prevent an impasse from arising, the resolution of such impasse will be simpler and more meaningful as a result of the constructive talks that have already paved the way. The fact finder, or arbitrator, will have a clear idea of what is really essential to the parties and of what each can forego with impunity. He will be faced with a clear choice, and his choice will be final.

The main drawback to this recommendation is the binding arbitration feature of the fact finder's decision. There has been much criticism of the concept of binding arbitration by those who imply that it faces insurmountable legal and constitutional obstacles. If there are any legal obstacles to compulsory arbitration, they have been greatly overstated.

The old cases, which held that governmental bodies could not delegate their decision making functions to any private board, have been rejected in the more forward looking cases. Although there is a strong chance that the present state of the law might allow arbitrators the leeway to resolve even non-monetary issues, for the purpose of furthering general acceptance of this proposal only purely monetary disputes need be subject to binding fact finding. Specifically, the fact finder would have the power, in matters of purely financial import only, to reach a final determination by choosing the last offer of the more reasonable side.

Criticism of the concept of binding arbitration has proved incorrect. It was suggested that compulsory arbitration would result in the hardening of partisan positions and the substitution of arbitration for any sort of collective bargaining. We now know that this has happened anyway. The type of restricted compulsory arbitration suggested is specifically designed to eliminate the problem that its detractors thought it might cause.

Professor Taylor's more recent analysis of arbitration attacks the policy of submitting disputes to a board which acts without the checks and balances of elected government, and which spends the public's funds without considering the broad effect of its decision on the entire financial structure of the state or city. These arguments are far from overriding. While the arbitrator's discretion is limited to a simple choice between two alternatives, the result is extremely effective arbitration, the mere threat of which will advance the objectives of good faith bargaining. The benefit to the parties and to the public which would result from the encouragement of good faith bargaining in the public sector would more than outweigh the possible harm which might result if the arbitrator is infrequently forced to decide between two extreme alternatives.

CHAPTER 7

IMPASSE PROCEDURES

One of the major innovations in public sector bargaining has been the introduction and widespread use of procedures for resolving impasses in negotiations. The objectives of these procedures has been to minimize the need for or provide alternatives to the strike. In the private sector mediation is the only procedure used extensively because the strike or threat of a strike almost always induces the parties to reach agreement without any further assistance from neutrals. Thus the strike performs an important role in collective bargaining; when the strike is prohibited, settlements become more difficult to achieve. In practice, collective bargaining in the public sector seems to drag on longer because the lack of a strike threat permits the parties to negotiate beyond the expiration date of the existing contract without the threat of sanctions.

The impasse procedures used in the public sector to help the parties reach agreement are mediation, fact finding, and compulsory binding arbitration. Under mediation, a neutral enters the negotiations and attempts to help the parties reach agreement. Mediation is a very personal process and varies with the mediator. Usually the mediator tries to clarify issues and opens up channels of discussion. He rarely makes recommendations unless he is confident that they will be accepted by the parties. In this section, Moffett describes the experience of the Federal Mediation and Conciliation Service in the public sector, and Robins compares the process of mediation in the private and public sectors.

Fact finding, which begins after an impasse is declared, is a procedure whereby a neutral listens to the proposals and supporting evidence of each party and then issues a report summarizing the "facts" in the dispute and almost always including recommendations for settlement. The parties are not obliged to accept the recommendations, but it is hoped that they will help form the basis for a settlement. McKelvey summarizes the varied experience with fact finding in the public sector.

Compulsory binding arbitration is quite similar to fact finding with recommendations except that the parties are required by law to accept the award. This

317

procedure is used in four states for police and/or fire fighters, and it promises to increase in importance in future years. Arbitration of new contract terms raises many questions about collective bargaining and decision making in the public sector. Will the parties be willing to bargain and make concessions if they know that an impasse will result in a binding award of a neutral? Does arbitration give too much power to persons who are not responsive to the electorate? And, finally, will arbitration lead to excessive settlements which are higher than would have been achieved through collective bargaining with or without the right to strike? In other words, how is the public to be protected from government officials and unions passing on high settlements which interfere with other goals of public policy? In the final group of articles Chamberlain discusses arbitration and suggests that wages of public employees must be tied to wages in the private sector through the use of comparability surveys, and Loewenberg describes the initial year's experience under the Pennsylvania compulsory arbitration statute.

THE FEDERAL MEDIATION AND CONCILIATION SERVICE EXPERIENCE IN THE PUBLIC SECTOR 1965-1969

Kenneth E. Moffett

The signing of Executive Order 11491, Labor-Management Relations in the Federal Service, projected the Federal Mediation and Conciliation Service (FMCS) into the forefront, as the Order specifically names the agency as a source of assistance in resolving disputes between federal employers and federal employee unions.

Although the FMCS involvement in public sector disputes has been brief, it has also been successful. The period of the Service's assistance to the parties has been less than five years. During that period ninety-five contracts were mutually agreed to through collective bargaining, with FMCS assistance. By way of background and prior to reviewing some recent experiences, the history of the FMCS in public and federal disputes will be briefly traced.

Following issuance of Executive Order 10988 in January 1962 and for sometime thereafter, the official view in government did not encourage the use of mediation as a vehicle for assisting the parties in their collective bargaining negotia-

Kenneth Moffett is Special Assistant to the Director, Federal Mediation and Conciliation Service. Article prepared specifically for this volume.

tions. In April 1962 this policy was reflected when the Civil Service Commission issued Bulletin No. 700-5, which underscored that the new Executive Order 10988 did not assign any responsibility to the FMCS; consequently, this bulletin acted as a deterrent to the parties in their desire for FMCS assistance.

By 1965 it was obvious that public employees were on the march in state and local governments to organize and demand recognition rights. The federal service concurrently experienced acceleration in union growth and activity. The problems attendant to such growth and organization initiated requests by union representatives and some agency managers that the FMCS make its services available in dispute situations.

Late in 1965 a series of discussions were held with representatives of the Civil Service Commission, Department of Labor, certain federal agencies, federal employee unions, and the FMCS. These representatives decided to take another look at the possible use of the mediation process in governmental labor-management relationships. It was generally recognized, however, that additional information was needed and that such information should be based on actual dispute mediation experience in the public sector in order to determine the extent of FMCS involvement.

As a result of the deliberations, the Service adopted an in-house policy for the consideration of mediation requests in the federal service as well as in state and municipal disputes. This policy provided that:

1. Requests for mediation had to be screened and decided at the FMCS National Office in Washington, D.C.
2. Requests would not be considered unless made by both parties.
3. Requests would not be considered unless both parties certified an impasse had been reached following genuine bargaining efforts.
4. Requests which were approved stipulated that the Service would select and assign a mediator.
5. Mediators assigned would be available only for a limited period of time and/or a limited number of joint meetings as the situation dictated.

It should be noted that this policy was designed to restrict the consideration of mediation requests. This approach was dictated by staff limitations, budget considerations, and the fact that the Service's authority to act in these situations had not been specifically granted.

From late 1965 to July 1968 the Service was involved in thirty-four dispute assignments. Using the mediation techniques which have proved successful in the private sector, FMCS mediators were able to assist the parties to reach a settlement in thirty of the thirty-four cases. In the four cases which were not successfully concluded at the bargaining table, all were referred to higher authority. The parties involved with these cases had been bargaining in most instances for many months. In several cases bargaining extended for two and three years.

During fiscal year 1969 the FMCS participated in thirty dispute cases. This year, after the special request of employee organizations or administrators, the Service became involved in seventy preventive mediation or training assignments.

Because of the lack of experience and skill at the bargaining table, it had become apparent that both labor and the agencies need training.

Steward-foreman training programs, joint labor-management committees, and, at the special request of the parties, continuing liaison and consultation were maintained after the contract was negotiated.

It is difficult to measure the value of preventive mediation. However, it is immensely popular, and the number of requests received outstrip the available mediators.

From July to December 1969 the dispute caseload equaled the output for the previous year—thirty-five dispute assignments and forty preventive programs. FMCS involvement in this type of bargaining was definitely on the upswing.

The Service decided that it had gained hard facts from experience in both the dispute and training areas and continued to evaluate and reexamine its procedures and techniques in this arena. This information was shared with the Labor Department and the Civil Service Commission Task Force as they were preparing Executive Order 11491, Labor-Management Relations in the Federal Service.

In another effort to glean additional information and experience, the Service became active in a number of cases at municipal, state and local levels where no mediation services were available to the parties and an immediate crisis situation was present.

In 1966-67 mediators worked with four local disputes, most in the northeast Ohio area—a strike of nurses at Youngstown and of employees at three Cleveland hospitals.

In fiscal year 1968 the Service was involved in local municipal disputes in New Orleans, Louisiana; Memphis, Tennessee; and Cincinnati, Akron, Columbus, Dayton, and Mansfield, Ohio. These cases were highly charged from an economic standpoint as well as involving a social issue. In some cases public employees such as firemen and police sought economic benefits; in others these issues were present and entangled with civil rights issues.

Some of the more prominent municipal disputes handled this year were the Charleston, South Carolina hospital strike, Johns Hopkins Hospital, Memphis, Indianapolis, and Charlotte, North Carolina sanitation disputes, and the four Illinois state university system disputes.

In terms of employees affected, mediated settlements ranged from a relatively small number of employees to the seven hundred thousand employees of the Post Office Department. In addition to the Post Office Department, other federal departments and agencies involved included the Army, Navy, Air Force, Commerce, Interior, Social Security Administration (HEW), Veterans Administration, and the Tennessee Valley Authority. The unions involved were the seven national AFL—CIO postal unions, several AFGE and Machinists lodges, many local metal trades councils, NAGE, Federation of College Teachers, Pattern Makers, Military Sea Transport Union, and the National Maritime Union.

Some of the disputed contract issues mediated by the FMCS were comparable to those in the private sector and generated the same degree of intense bargaining. Among the issues were overtime distribution and assignment, work week and night shift schedules, recall procedures, layoff procedures, journeyman-apprentice ratio, apprentice programs and training, union representation in adverse actions, and paid time for authorized union business.

The number of unresolved issues successfully mediated by the Service in any one case has ranged from a single issue to as high as fifty.

With the realization that a new executive order was to be signed, the Service decided to evaluate in depth its experiences and summarize its findings on public sector and federal service disputes since 1965. An intensive one-week seminar was conducted on that subject with sixteen of the Service's most experienced and competent mediators from the seven regions of the country. To give direction to the deliberations, authorities in the field from other interested agencies,—both inside and outside government—participated in an effort to determine more precisely the FMCS role in public employee disputes.

The results were very illuminating and encouraging and indicate a rapidly expanding role for mediation in the public sector—local, state, and federal. Conclusions based on experience is that voluntary mediation works equally as well in the public sector as it does in the private sector.

Experience also indicates that the most significant difference between mediating a dispute in the public sector, as opposed to the private sector, stems from the environmental and structural differences between the two areas. Said another way, the ability to provide benefits and to improve working conditions in the public sector does not stem from the free enterprise or profit system but is derived almost totally from the tax or regulatory structure, which is essentially political in nature.

The authorities and the mediators agreed that the procedures and techniques used by the Service in settling public and private disputes are essentially the same. There are, however, many important differences between the two sectors. The knowledge of these differences can be most helpful in resolving disputes.

One difference is the lack of experience or sophistication on the part of the representatives of the parties. Collective bargaining in the public sector is relatively new and, while there are knowledgeable practitioners in the field, these are relatively few.

For example, the negotiating responsibility may be given to the head of the Department of Sanitation or to the agency's attorney in addition to his other responsibilities. In one recent bargaining situation involving an educational establishment, the representative of the administrators was the football coach. While no offense is meant to football coaches, it is most unlikely that such individuals have the training and experience required to handle bargaining matters. The lack of experience can result in the creation of unnecessary issues which serve to impede the discussion process and hamper the resolution of basic disputes.

Another problem peculiar to the public sector is the absence of dispute settlement procedures, including mediation. The ability to resolve impasse situations through well-structured and considered procedures is generally absent. The parties move from crisis to crisis and finally settle for ad hoc or "one shot" settlement procedures.

In most situations the parties are without the right to strike or lock out. The pressures accompanying a deadline and crisis bargaining are missing. To overcome this handicap, the Service has been forced to create pressures on the parties to keep them bargaining. Such was the situation where the mediator found the parties had been bargaining for many months without progress. To stimulate movement, the mediator set a reasonable time limit for his availability, thus creating a sense of urgency. As a result of his imposing such a restriction, the agreement was reached within the time limits he created.

Although budget deadlines, legislative sessions, and pending elections may create pressures for settlements in the public sector, the lack of the strike deadlines of the private sector tends to unnecessarily prolong discussions, particularly with respect to collateral or non-key issues.

Parenthetically, one requirement of the new executive order may help create a sense of urgency toward impelling settlement. This is the proviso which requires that employer-employee negotiations be conducted outside of normal working hours. Heretofore, federal employee bargaining has been during working hours.

Additionally, parties in the public sector usually seem willing to submit their problems to a third party. An overriding reason may be the apparent need for an endorsement of a mediator, arbitrator, or fact finder for their constituency—which may be their fellow employees or the voters who elected the official. Fact finding, tripartite panels, boards of inquiry with powers of recommendation, impasse panels, and advisory or binding arbitration are procedures most often used to satisfy this need.

In the deliberations there was a consensus that, because of the highly visible and political nature of public sector disputes, the parties often find themselves negotiating in a veritable fishbowl. One of the participants of the workshop reported that he found himself chairing a negotiating session between a striking city social workers' union and the city fathers. In the room with him were the city council, the invited public, the press, and the live microphone of a local radio station. Understandably, the result of the first day's negotiations was no progress. Both sides were talking for the record and to the public—they were making speeches, not negotiating. It was not until subsequent negotiations were held behind closed doors that progress and an eventual settlement were made.

Aside from the lack of experience of bargainers, one of the glaring faults of public employers is the lack of authority granted to their representatives. This unquestionably contributes to long delays in obtaining responses to proposals and offering of counterproposals.

When faced with this dilemma, most mediators will seek out a person who can speak with authority. The scheme is to get him to the bargaining table or close enough to it so he will have a positive impact on the proceedings.

A companion problem we have been frequently faced with in dealing in federal employee negotiations is the reversal by a higher-up of bargaining-table decisions made by local management negotiators. It is hoped that this practice will cease under the new executive order. Repudiation of agreements made between the parties obviously creates distrust.

Another problem is the group or organization that "forum shops." Since the public sector is basically unstructured and for the most part without viable laws, we find some parties come to the FMCS to see what arrangement can be made. If dissatisfied with the refusal of the FMCS to participate in fact finding or arbitration, they move on to a settlement procedure that will perform such functions.

The general consensus of the FMCS professional staff is that a panel of two mediators on a case is more effective in municipal disputes than a single mediator. Particularly if there is more than one bargaining agent and bargaining unit involved, or if the dispute is complicated by social issues.

Also the parties are more accustomed to dealing with boards and commissions and thus a team of mediators adds a sense of familiarity and prestige to the situation.

It was determined that the manner in which a mediator conducts himself is dependent largely on the issues, parties, and conditions surrounding the case. The situation may call for him to practically direct every move by both parties, including submission of contract provisions. The reverse may find him doing little more than chairing the meeting and keeping the parties separated.

It is in separate caucuses that meaningful progress and groundwork can be achieved. During the caucus confidential and privileged information is related to the mediator, and positions can be reexamined without embarrassment to the party. The mediator utilizes the separate session to suggest alternative ideas or procedures and at times makes recommendations to the parties.

Usually the mediator only suggests optional positions, but on rare occasions he may be forced to make formal recommendations as a last resort or in an exceptional type of circumstance. Formal recommendations are very rare. Most of the time the bargaining process is adversely affected through the use of formal recommendations.

Surely the parties would be less inclined to bargain if there were an awareness that the mediator intended to make recommendations. Positions would understandably be less flexible and bargaining more stilted.

The FMCS is convinced that, as limited as the experience has been, it has demonstrated that labor-management disputes within the public sector can and will be successfully mediated.

SOME COMPARISONS OF MEDIATION
IN THE PUBLIC AND PRIVATE SECTOR

Eva Robins

As public employee collective bargaining becomes more widespread, undoubtedly there will be an increase in the use of mediation as a tool of bargaining impasse resolution. In many instances the use of mediation will be required by statute. In many others, it will be initiated by the political head of a government because of the need to satisfy the public that every meaningful effort is being made to resolve the impasse. It has been and will be invoked at the request of public

Eva Robins is associated with the Office of Collective Bargaining, New York City. Article prepared specifically for this volume.

employee organizations which are learning the value of working with a mediator. The quality of the mediators, the characteristics of the public sector in which the mediator serves tend at this time to make public sector mediation a somewhat different process than the classic private sector mediation. It is important that private sector mediators recognize the similarities and differences, so that they may remain flexible and accommodate their mediatory activities to the peculiar needs of the new situations into which they are thrust. It is also important that new mediators understand the unique nature of the undertaking.

WHO ARE THE MEDIATORS?

Mediators come from a variety of sources and backgrounds. They do not come into the public sector equally equipped either with mediation experience and skills or with knowledge of the process of collective bargaining. Briefly, the following are the major sources and some of the problems in their use:

1. Mediators on the permanent staffs of the Federal Mediation and Conciliation Service, various state mediation agencies and of the public employment relations boards and commissions. These are mostly skilled mediators, with experience in private sector negotiations. They represent the largest single source of mediators transferrable from private to public sector disputes. It is very clear that there are not enough staff mediators employed by federal and state agencies to handle the thousands of contract negotiations which require mediation, generally at approximately the same time. Too, the private sector will have first call on the services of staff mediators, at least for the foreseeable future and only the public employment relations board staff mediators will devote themselves exclusively to public sector mediation. It is a very limited source.

2. Private mediators, generally men and women who have had considerable experience as grievance arbitrators in private sector labor disputes. There is a growing utilization of such people, but some arbitrators do not wish to mediate, partly because they do not profess to have the skills, patience, or temperament and partly because the uncertain hours and duration of the mediation process play havoc with the orderly scheduling of arbitration hearings. This, too, is a limited source, but its use probably will increase substantially.

3. The new mediators: Advocates who have had much experience representing management or unions in labor relations matters in the private sector, but who have had no experience in the neutral role; or educators, lawyers, business executives, retired civil servants, all of whom have a vast interest in the process of collective bargaining in the public sector but no first-hand experience. Some of the new mediators have a background in labor relations, others do not. Unhappily, because of a growing need for mediators, some of these are serving without any preparation or training. Some, obviously, will attain the skills in time and have substantial acceptability; others will not. This, however, is the most promising source for the new mediators; further, this group welcomes training and guidance from the skilled mediators and appears to have a love for the work without which no mediator can function.

4. A growing number of persons with no background in labor relations, either academic or practical, and with no claimed expertise, but who apparently see a

possibility of developing a sideline. Whether they achieve inclusion on the mediator lists maintained by the designating agencies through political push or because of the acute need, this is the group which seems least likely to survive; most of its members appear to take no interest in training sessions or in the guidance of skilled mediators.

5. The "public figure" mediators, some with and some without knowledge of labor relations, are utilized sometimes when the public interest is so great that the head of government—mayor, governor, county executive—feels it essential to enlist a respected "name" to achieve acceptability to both parties. Though generally knowledgeable and immensely capable people, of integrity and reputation, they usually are not mediators and more often serve in a fact-finding capacity, making very public recommendations for settlement rather than mediating the parties into their own settlement.

These, then, are the mediators who are being used in public sector labor disputes. The wide variations in skill and interest have an effect on the mediation process and its success, and on its acceptability to public employers and public employee unions.

METHODS OF SELECTION AND PAY

It is still very unusual for public employee organizations to join in the selection of the mediator and to share the cost of mediation. In the private sector, the mediators on the staffs of government mediation agencies are assigned to cases, and neither party pays for their services. In the public sector, government staff mediators are assigned when available, but this is extremely limited. When private mediators are named, in the vast majority of cases they are designated and paid by the state or city. Under most such arrangements, if the designation is made by a public employment relations board or commission, neither the public employer nor the union has a voice in the selection. In the private sector, when government appoints and pays for mediation services, it acts in a neutral role. But in the public sector, government agencies which appoint and pay the mediator act in their capacities as an arm of the employer. Hence the mediation process and the mediator sometimes are suspect to the unions involved and this has an influence on the mediator's ability to function.

SIMILARITIES AND DIFFERENCES—
PUBLIC AND PRIVATE MEDIATION

In addition to the variations in the quality of the mediator and the effect of the method of appointment on the mediator's effectiveness, public sector mediation varies from that of the private sector in other meaningful ways.

Obviously, the aim is the same: to assist the parties in arriving at a settlement. The skills employed are the same: identifying the decision makers, narrowing the gap between the positions of the parties, earning their confidence, maintaining communications at various levels between and with the parties, setting a balanced pace for the negotiations, getting some understanding of the esoteric language of public employment negotiations, keeping movement going, and developing and achieving—at the appropriate time—a mutual will and push to settle.

The practice of public sector mediation is different from private sector mediation, however, in several significant ways. A mere listing is inadequate, but space limitations do not allow for more than a cursory explanation of only a few major differences.

The mediator may not assume—as he does in private mediation—that the decision makers, the people who can make binding and effective offers and counteroffers, are at the bargaining table or within easy reach of the bargainers. Thus, in conveying offers or positions of the parties at various times or in obtaining guidance from the parties on potentially fruitful areas of exploration, the mediator must exercise great care. He must be sure that he knows the extent of the parties' authority and what strings are attached. Is an offer firm if the budget people have final say and may not approve? Who has power to veto a settlement? Does the union's bargaining committee have authority to act, subject to membership ratification, or is there no ratification vote unless the executive board of the union first approves the settlement? What are the political and power structure problems on both sides? These and similar questions are constantly with the mediator and he is foolish, indeed, if he does not have a clear understanding of the problems before he attempts to interpret the position of one side to the other.

Until such time as the bargainers understand the bargaining process for what it is, the mediator in the public sector will continue to function as a teacher. Rarely is there the need today to so function in private industry mediation. But in an area in which there heretofore has been unilateral determination by the employer of wages, hours, and working conditions, the obligation for joint determination of terms does not achieve ready acceptance in practice simply by passage of a law. Too, where unions and individual employees formerly sought benefits, rights, and change through the legislative process or through the courts, they now must learn that the utilization of collective bargaining takes the place of the individual's petitioning of government and of recourse to the legislature. These are hard lessons to learn. Until they are learned, the mediator is the teacher, the guide the parties need to help them through the first several years of this unfamiliar ground. He is leading the parties to a recognition of their obligation to bargain and teaching them how to bargain responsibly.

Subjects for bargaining in the public sector frequently differ substantially from those accepted as bargainable in the private sector. Many of the conditions of employment applicable to public employees are provided for by statute and modification would require statutory amendment. Some place in the hands of other agencies or commissions the authority over certain aspects of the employment. Thus a demand for the establishment of a new job classification might be outside the power of the public employer to agree to, though he could agree to join the union in a petition to the Civil Service Commission which has jurisdiction over establishing job classifications. This particular aspect of public employee bargaining has no counterpart in private sector bargaining.

Countless disputes arise over the demands which allegedly invade the managerial prerogative. The practice in a particular area of the public sector may be to allow joint negotiation on such items, while in other areas there is steadfast refusal even to discuss them. For the mediator in public sector bargaining, presented with the initial proposals for contract terms made by the union and the employer (sometimes as many as seven hundred individual demands), on which little progress has been made, the problem can be staggering enough without the added problem of a dispute on the obligation to bargain. When discussion on a particular subject which is clearly outside the scope of bargaining is essential if a settlement is to be reached, all the skills of the mediator may be required to encourage and channel the dialogue, while preserving the legal positions of the parties. Scope of bargaining disputes are acrimonious and emotional. They can bring negotiations to a dead stop unless the mediator can, with ingenuity and imaginative suggestions, remove the roadblock. The mediator cannot, of course, decide which subjects are within the scope of bargaining. But free and productive exchanges of opinions and positions often remove the roadblock if the legal positions of the parties are protected. It is the mediator's function to keep such discussion, communication, and movement going as productively as possible.

It is widely believed that the tension of a no-contract, no-work deadline is necessary for real collective bargaining, and that the process cannot exist without the right and potential to strike. That right is not unlimited in the private sector; it is prohibited in the public sector. Thus, in private sector negotiations, if a union has the capacity to strike, and if strike is a possibility, the strike threat itself impels the parties to take a realistic look at the issues. But with or without strike talk, the existence of a deadline and the tension generated by it as the deadline approaches very often produce a settlement psychology which the mediator must be quick to recognize and use.

Deadlines and tension are present in the public sector as they are in the private sector, although the characteristics are different. Each situation, each negotiation, has within it the potential for generating, on both sides, a pressure to settle. At some time in each neogtiation the mediator can recognize and utilize the tension and pressure to settle, provided he is sensitive to the timing of such pressure. If it exists, the mediator can change the quality of the talks, make them more intensive, and generate the excitement and the mood of settlement. This may be no substitute for the right to strike, but is a perfectly viable substitute for the kinds of settlement deadlines and tensions found in the private sector.

The push to settle may come from the desire of one or both parties to avoid fact finding, or from budget submission date considerations, although the latter is realized more in concept and statutes than it is in practice. The public sector mediator should avoid placing too much value on the potential pressure of budget submission dates. One has only to look at the large number of local school board cases remaining unresolved long after the budget submission date has come and gone, to know that budget submission date does not serve effectively to create deadline pressure or to result in timely settlement.

Pressure to settle comes from other causes as well: from the anxiety of the membership for money, benefits, or just a terminal point; from the limited time available to a particularly acceptable mediator; from a desire of one side or the other quickly to establish a "pattern"; from the plan of a principal negotiator to go on vacation; from the imminence of a political or union election; or from causes so obscure as almost to defy identification. It is the mediator's job to try to identify and evaluate pressures when they are present, and to use them to achieve settlement.

Fiscal and taxing power considerations make public sector bargaining and negotiations different from the private sector. An employer in private industry or in the
nonprofit field has decisions to make which are almost entirely economic. Where
must the price line be held? At what point must services to a community be
reduced? At what point is a strike more acceptable than increased labor cost? The
luxury of choice is not available in the public sector. The public expects the
continuation of government services. Public sector employers and employee organizations are aware of the intricacies of taxing power and fiscal problems, but it is not
much discussed in negotiations. Partly this is due to the fact that public employers
seem reluctant to talk of fiscal matters with unions much as private employers
hesitate about claiming inability to pay, lest they must open their books to examination. But the private sector concept of "ability to pay" does not, at least in the
view of this observer, apply to the public sector. It translates into the public sector
as "ability and willingness to tax," a thoroughly different notion.

But whether or not discussed in direct across-the-table negotiations, clearly the
mediator must not ignore fiscal considerations and problems if he expects to shep-
herd the parties through to settlement. Fiscal and taxing power problems are
present at the bargaining table and do not involve the employer only. There are an
increasing number of settlements which put larger portions of the economic
package into second and third years, giving the employer an opportunity to
accommodate, by taxing and otherwise, to the increased costs. The mediator must
be alert to these considerations.

Public sector bargaining is excessively "public." It is a fact that many negotiators and as many mediators cannot resist the television camera and microphone
or the public press. The experienced interviewer or reporter can, if he works at it,
get from them conjectures and statements about a strike, possibilities of ratification, movement in the negotiations, and intransigence of the parties. Excessive
publicity sometimes provides an urgency and pressure to the negotiations which is
frequently untimely and even may be harmful.

Obviously, the public is entitled to know if a strike in a vital service (legal or
not) is imminent, just as it has a right to know the dimensions of a settlement. But
there is damage to the process of bargaining if the negotiators try to negotiate
through the public press and other news media. So, too, there is danger if the
mediator tries to make himself a public figure through his frequent appearances on
news broadcasts, unless the situation itself calls for it. If it is agreed by the parties
that only the mediator makes public statements (generally a wise move) and, if such
statements are carefully structured, no harm is done. Damage could be done, however, by the very few mediators who ignore and do not consider the needs of the
process in which they are engaged and think only of their own images. It may be
tempting, but it is a temptation one learns to resist. The foot-in-mouth club will
survive without the mediator.

One last point of difference: The public sector is a political arena. As a particularly sticky negotiation goes through its crises, it is not unusual for a public figure
to volunteer his services, publicly, as mediator, even though a professional mediator
is currently engaged in assisting the parties. This does not refer to those in political
office charged with the responsibility for continuation of government services, nor
does it apply to specialists named by such officials. But in every community and
certainly in every large city there are persons whose names are fairly well known

and who feel impelled publicly to volunteer to help. The mediator in public sector bargaining must learn to accommodate to this. It may be cynical to point this out, but these efforts to intervene, *pro bono publico,* usually involve no more than the initial announcement to the press of the offer to serve, a fairly public briefing by both sides, and an innocuous statement (usually that the situation is serious, but in good hands). A professional mediator learns to ride with the punches.

The skills of the mediator remain the same—whether he serves in the public or private sector. He must have patience, the personality for this work, power of analysis, sensitivity to what is meaningful to others, and no burning desire to dictate terms of settlement. But though the skills of the mediator are the same, the environment, the attitudes, the issues, and the legal considerations in public sector bargaining differ substantially from those in the private sector. If the process of mediation is to be acceptable to the parties in the public sector, this must be understood by the public sector mediator.

FACT FINDING IN PUBLIC EMPLOYMENT DISPUTES: PROMISE OR ILLUSION?

Jean T. McKelvey

This article proposes to examine the process of fact finding at this relatively early stage of its development in the hope of raising some questions as to the conditions under which fact finding may be a promising procedure for settling disputes in the public sector, as distinguished from those situations where its invocation may prove to be only a snare and a delusion. Hence, it should be obvious at the outset that the question posed in the subtitle: "Promise or Illusion?" can have only one answer: "It depends."

THE PRIVATE SECTOR

Although the "name of the game" is fact finding, this is a misnomer since the sport itself has little to do with fact finding in the literal sense of determining objective facts through the judicial process of trial and proof to provide evidentiary

Jean McKelvey is Professor of Industrial and Labor Relations, Cornell University. Reprinted from *Industrial and Labor Relations Review,* XXII, No. 4, July 1969. Copyright ©1969 by Cornell University. All rights reserved.

answers to the resolution of impasses. Even so eminent a practitioner and pragmatist as the late William H. Davis was guilty of a lapse into simplistic reasoning when, in response to a question from Senator Taft during the 1945-1946 hearings on the proposed Labor Fact-Finding Boards Act, he said: "As to fact-finding, we cannot disagree about a fact; we can only be ignorant about it."[1] A more realistic description of the process was offered by Labor Secretary Schwellenbach in opening the same hearings:

> S. 1661 would provide for the appointment of fact-finding boards consisting of persons who have no pecuniary or other private interest in the matter, to investigate labor disputes which seriously affect the national interest and to make a report containing their findings of fact and recommendations with respect to such disputes. This provision recognizes clearly the general public concern in both the prevention of work stoppages which seriously affect the national public interest and in being informed with respect to issues involved in such controversies.[2]

Examining the essential elements of this description of the game, one finds that it involves two groups of contestants, labor and management; a board of neutral or disinterested referees, called fact finders; formal rules of procedure under which the game is to be played (for a period not to exceed thirty days); and a definition of the goal—to win the acclaim of the spectators (i.e., the public) in order to convince the players they should accept the verdict of the umpire. Should this goal fail to be achieved, the parties are then left free to "slug it out," or in the more contemporary idiom, to "sock it to" each other and to the public. This particular design of the game of fact finding, modeled upon the Emergency Board procedures of the Railway Labor Act, was subsequently modified by the Taft-Hartley Act in 1947 which eliminated the recommendatory powers of the neutrals and extended the length of the playing period to eighty days. The neutrals were commissioned to inquire into the causes and circumstances of the dispute, and in some instances they even have engaged in mediation during the cooling-off period. Thus it can be seen that in the private sector statutory fact finding, at least on the federal level, has been conceived as a step between the breakdown of collective bargaining and the onset of a legal strike or lockout in essential industries. Whether the process is, or should be, one of mediation or of adjudication has provoked endless debate among academicians and practitioners alike.[3] These uncertainties have multiplied as the fact-finding process has been transposed to the public sector where the rules of the game are somewhat different.

---

[1]U.S. Congress, Senate, Committee on Education and Labor. *Hearings on S. 1661,* 79th Cong., 1st and 2nd sess., Part I (Washington: G.P.O., 1946), p. 133. . . .

[2]*Ibid.,* p. 7.

[3]For an excellent example of this controversy, see "Procedures under the Railway Labor Act: A Panel Discussion," in *Proceedings of the Eighteenth Annual Meeting of the National Academy of Arbitrators, 1965,* Dallas Jones, ed. (Washington: B.N.A., Inc. 1965), chap. 2.

THE PUBLIC SECTOR

In the public sector there are, according to conventional theory, three sets of players all competing for the acclaim of the public or the electorate: public management, the employee organization, and the legislative body or budgetary authority. There are also two sets of referees: the fact-finding body which renders the initial opinion and the legislative body which delivers the final verdict. Public management and employee organizations are regarded as adversaries. In the first round of the game, the task of the referee (or fact finder) is to determine the positions of the players and to recommend what, in his judgment, would be a fair outcome of the game in order to persuade the ultimate umpire (the legislative body) to accept his verdict. The goal here is not primarily one of using public opinion to influence the parties, but rather to enlighten the public so that it, in turn, can bring pressure on the lawmakers to adopt the recommendations. As George Hildebrand puts it: "Fact finding with recommendations is a way to redirect the pressure of opinion and to economize on the legislators' time, while providing them the guidance they need. In these respects, a fact-finding tribunal can play a role much like that of a parliamentary select committee in England."[4] In this model of the game, the role of the neutral is primarily adjudicatory in nature: one of determining on the basis of facts, evidence, and argument what the "correct" settlement should be. Since recourse to economic action or strikes is unlawful, or outside the boundaries of the game, the final decision is to be reached by what Hildebrand terms "straight political bargaining involving diverse interest groups."[5]

The model described above has a number of variants, however, which may change the role of the neutral. In some instances, the public management and the employee organization may not be antagonists. Instead, they may have common goals such as improving education or enhancing the efficiency of the public service. Where this is the case, their common adversary may be the legislative or budgetary authority, and the purpose of fact finding, to which they may readily (even enthusiastically) agree, is to gain an ally who may be able to persuade the public and the legislature to accept the terms on which they are tacitly in accord. Here the goal is exactly the reverse of that of fact finding in the private sector; it is to exert the pressure of the parties on the public. The role of the fact finder in this situation is similar to that of the arbitrator in making a consent award. A minor variant of the game just described is one in which the public employer, the employee organization, and the legislative body are all in accord. Here the fact-finder's report is required to "save face" for the negotiators and the legislative body. In other words, the game is merely a sham.

In another situation, the fact finder may act initially as a mediator to bring the adversaries to agreement. In order to persuade the principals, the rank and file, or the legislators to accept the settlement, the fact finder must issue recommendations

[4]George H. Hildebrand, "The Public Sector," in J. T. Dunlop and N. W. Chamberlain, eds., *Frontiers of Collective Bargaining* (New York: Harper and Row, 1967), chap. 5, p. 147.

[5]*Ibid.* See also George H. Hildebrand, "The Resolution of Impasses," in *Proceedings of the 20th Annual Meeting of the National Academy of Arbitrators,* 1967, D. Jones, ed., pp. 287-297.

embodying the agreed-upon terms in his report. Here his primary function is one of mediation not adjudication, despite appearances to the contrary.

Many variants come to mind; one final one follows. Where the legislative body and the public employer are identical, as in the case of the independent school board or the town council, the conventional model breaks down completely. For here there is no independent legislative body to consider the merits of the fact-finder's recommendations. In this situation, the fact finder may play a role similar to the one he occupies in private-sector bargaining. His goal is to influence the public to bring pressure for settlement on the parties.

Moreover, in this version of the game, fact finding cannot have the finality which is built into the model design. There is no second referee or umpire. Hence, resort to economic warfare or strikes may become more common in those situations where the final decision can be imposed unilaterally by a public employer who rejects the recommendations of the fact finder. In this situation, the fact finder has no alternative other than that of striving for the accommodation of competing interests. His primary role is that of mediator.

This excursion into model building primarily has been to make one point. It is that the fact finder in the public sector must understand that his role or function will vary according to the circumstances in which he finds himself. Fact finding is not necessarily adjustment or adjudication. It may often be a mixture of both with a large infusion of political and strategic considerations. Let us move now from the theory of fact finding to examination of its practice in the public sector.

FACT FINDING IN THE PUBLIC SECTOR

Broadly speaking, fact finding in the public sector has been designed as a procedural substitute for strikes and lockouts, which currently are prohibited by law. Of the seventeen states which have enacted comprehensive labor relations laws governing the public service, nine provide for fact finding if collective bargaining and mediation are unsuccessful in resolving impasses.[6] Five of these nine states, Connecticut, Massachusetts, Michigan, New York, and Wisconsin have had more extensive experience with fact finding to date than the others. With the exception of Wisconsin, however, little or no research has been published, either on a state-by-state or on a comparative basis, so that any evaluation of fact-finding experience must await the completion of more systematic studies. Fortunately, just as Wisconsin has served as the pioneer in the enactment of public employment legislation (its laws date back to 1959 and 1962), so the successive studies of fact finding in Wisconsin by James L. Stern, Edward B. Krinsky, and Jeffery B. Tener are proto-types of the kind of research which needs to be undertaken elsewhere.[7] A few

[6]These states are Connecticut, Massachusetts, Michigan, Minnesota, New York, Rhode Island, Vermont, Wisconsin, and, most recently, New Jersey. . . .

[7]L. Stern, E. B. Krinsky, and J. B. Tener, *Factfinding Under Wisconsin Law,* 3rd ed., 1966 (Madison, Wis.: University of Wisconsin, University Extention, 1966). See also J. L. Stern, "The Wisconsin Public Employee Fact-Finding Procedure," *Industrial and Labor Relations Review,* Vol. 20, No. 1 (October 1966), pp. 3-29. An interesting analysis of the school dispute cases in Wisconsin through December 1967 has been made by Zel S. Rice II, Commissioner, Wisconsin Employment Relations Board, in an unpublished speech, "Reaching Impasses—Mediation and Fact Finding," 1968.

studies on a more limited basis have been made or are in progress in Michigan, New York, Connecticut, and Massachusetts. A major inter-urban comparison of municipal collective bargaining by Arnold Weber and his associates promises to yield substantial insights into the processes of impasse resolution.

There is, of course, no dearth of published raw material in this field. Fact-finders' reports are flooding the market, making available rich sources for studying substantive matters such as major issues, criteria and standards, reasoning, and conclusions. ... On the basis of this author's fragmentary survey of the field, the following research questions are tentatively suggested. Hypotheses for testing will be presented at a later point.

1. Why is fact finding apparently more successful in resolving impasses in some states than in others? Is the difference to be explained in terms of such variables as the type of legislation, its administration, the economic climate, the stage of management and union organization, union rivalry, the influence of the private sector, politics, or the skills of practitioners—to mention only a few of the possible determinants?
2. Is fact finding more or less successful in urban areas than in small towns and rural sections?
3. Is fact finding more or less successful in resolving teacher disputes than those involving firemen, police, and other types of municipal employees?
4. Are the parties more likely to accept the fact-finder's recommendations on certain issues than on others? Why?
5. What variations in procedure are significant, for example, the composition of fact-finding bodies, the imposition of costs, the timing of intervention, the choice of neutrals, etc.?
6. To what extent has fact finding in practice been mediatory or adjudicatory in nature? Under what circumstances?
7. What standards of decision making have emerged from the reports?
8. In those instances where strikes have occurred or where the fact-finder's report has not been accepted, does the final settlement exceed his recommendations?

This article addresses only the first question posed above, namely, the extent to which fact finding has been successful or unsuccessful in achieving the strikeless resolution of impasses in public employment in the four states for which some data are currently available: Wisconsin, Michigan, Connecticut, and New York.

WISCONSIN

Stern, Krinsky, and Tener[8] have used four criteria for measuring the success of fact finding:

1. The results of the procedure, i.e., whether the disputes sent to fact finding were successfully resolved.
2. The opinions of the parties involved toward the process.
3. The frequency of its utilization and its impact on collective bargaining.
4. Whether the procedure has reduced conflict and served as a substitute for strike.

[8] *Op. cit.*

According to information made available by Krinsky as of February 1968 (some six years after the effective date of the Wisconsin statute), there had been 135 petitions for fact finding in munciipal and county employment. Over one half of these cases had been resolved through mediation and informal investigation by the staff of the Wisconsin Employment Relations Board. Fifty cases had resulted in the issuance of formal fact-finding reports, of which 90 percent had been accepted in whole or in part. There were three strikes after fact finding, a rejection rate of 6 percent. In one instance the union rejected the findings; in the other two, where the employer refused to accept the report, the unions involved were weak. Fears that fact finding might become an automatic step in the bargaining process were not borne out by the experience noted above. Nor had there been a noticeable reuse of the process by the same parties, perhaps because in Wisconsin the statutory requirement that the parties share the costs of fact finding has served as a constraint on overuse of the process. These findings are consistent with those of an earlier study of the first three years of experience under the Law:

> In conclusion, it appears that the Wisconsin procedure is working well. It moves slowly, but when the occasion demands and the parties permit, it functions rapidly and at a cost which does not seem to stimulate over- or under-utilization. Awards have a high rate of acceptance. A few have been rejected in rural areas where unions are weak and managements do not recognize collective bargaining. The process is still too new to make a definitive evaluation. In the future, strong unions in the big cities may tend to overuse the procedure and then tire of it. In the first three years, this has not happened, and the law has been a substantial contribution to the improvement of collective bargaining among public employees in Wisconsin.[9]

Some changes in the law to increase its effectiveness have been suggested to the Wisconsin legislature by Nathan Feinsinger. These include recommendations that the statute explicitly authorize the fact finder to engage in mediation and that each party advise the other in writing as to its acceptance or nonacceptance of the fact-finders' recommendations, with a copy to the board. In the event of rejection, the Employment Relations Board would be authorized to conduct a show-cause hearing to determine why the dispute had not been resolved and why the remaining issues should not be submitted to a procedure which would finally dispose of them.[10]

MICHIGAN

In contrast to the successful use of fact finding in public employment disputes in Wisconsin, such studies and reports as are available on Michigan's experience

[9]Stern, *loc. cit.*, p. 19.

[10]Wisconsin Legislature, Assembly Bill 866 (1968): Municipal Employment Labor Relations Act.

indicate a somewhat different result.[11] Russell Allen's investigation of 36 teachers strikes in Michigan in the summer of 1967 showed that there were 28 fact-finding reports issued by 23 different fact finders—a usage rate of 80 percent.[12] Because of the urgency of the strike situation, the fact finders engaged in what has been termed "instant fact finding," issuing their reports within an average of 26 calendar days from the date the initial request for fact finding was made. Since Allen's study was limited to strike situations, it is obvious that the fourth criterion employed by Stern, Krinsky, and Tener has no application in terms of the contribution of fact finding to the *strikeless* resolution of the disputes. In 12 of the cases where fact finding was invoked, strikes were in progress before the issuance of the report. Allen made a more intensive study of the utility of fact finding by conducting interviews in 9 of the 36 school districts where strikes occurred, including 8 in which fact finding had been employed. In 6 of these 8, the reports had been issued after the commencement of the strike. As far as the reactions and perceptions of the parties were concerned, in 6 out of 8 cases one or both parties expressed strong negative reactions, especially to the efforts of the fact finders to engage in mediation. In the 6 cases where a full report was issued, the final settlement was close to the recommendations in 4 instances. In terms of the impact on collective bargaining, Allen noted that the fact finder "raised the ante" above the final offer of the employer in 20 out of 25 cases for which data were available—a consequence which led Allen to conclude that in the future the parties might engage only in sham bargaining in order to "save something for the fact finder."

Allen's criticisms of fact finding as practiced in Michigan were that the parties were too inexperienced to present their cases properly, that there was insufficient time for the procedure to work effectively, that fact finding was too easily available to the parties because the state bore the costs, that the criteria used by the fact finders were idiosyncratic and inconsistent, and that the process had an adverse impact on collective bargaining. These criticisms led Allen to propose that the Michigan statute be amended to incorporate criteria to govern fact-finding recommendations or that a panel of experts develop such criteria.[13]

[11]Russell Allen, "1967 School Disputes in Michigan," paper delivered at the Joint Conference of the Association of Labor Mediation Agencies and the National Association of State Labor Relations Agencies in Puerto Rico, Aug. 19-24, 1968, published by the Bureau of National Affairs in *Public Employee Organization and Bargaining* (Washington: BNA, 1968), chap. 9. For a lively personal account and appraisal of the Michigan experience, see Charles T. Schmidt, "Observations on the Process of Fact- Finding in Michigan Public Education Teacher-School Board Contract Disputes." Schmidt observes that in his experience the typical role played by the fact finder in Michigan was not exclusively judicial in nature. The fact finder might assume several different roles besides that of judge: a mediator, "a bargaining consultant, an educator, a scapegoat, a disciplinarian, an informed (or perhaps uninformed neutral) and certainly as far as some of the parties were concerned, a potential 'executioner.'" *Ibid.,* p. 84.

[12]Robert G. Howlett, chairman of the Michigan Labor Mediation Board, has reported that in all teacher disputes in August and September 1967 (not just those involving strikes) fact finders were appointed in 81 cases, with 35 reports being issued. Howlett, "Experiences with Current Substantive Practices in Public Employee Labor Relations," *Ibid.,* p. 50.

[13]In one of his concluding paragraphs, Allen expressed fear that resort to fact finding might become a fairly routine matter, displacing collective bargaining. "At this point in time," he observed, "I would opt for more experimentation with bargaining, whatever the risks." *Ibid.,* p. 78.

Other groups have also made proposals for improving the fact-finding process in Michigan. The Advisory Committee on Public Employee Relations appointed by Governor Romney issued reports in February and December 1967 suggesting that a time table related to budget submission dates be established in order to permit more orderly fact finding. It also proposed that all fact finding be conducted by members of a permanent "blue-ribbon" panel of twelve experts and that the panel itself be empowered to conduct "show-cause" public hearings and make a report to the governor assessing blame for the failure to reach agreement on the recalcitrant party or parties.[14]

The Michigan Labor Mediation Board, which administers the statute, has also made suggestions for improvement. Among these are the divorce of mediation from fact finding, the requirement that mediation be exhausted before fact finding is invoked, and the imposition on the parties of the responsibility for framing the issues in advance of the hearing.

Unlike Wisconsin, which is emphasizing the mediation aspect of fact finding, the Michigan critics seem to be moving in the opposite direction to make fact finding a more formal procedure, stressing its kinship with arbitration. Thus the emphasis on the formal submission, the development of consistent criteria, and the use of a professional body (or court) of fact finders all suggest that in Michigan the fact-finding process is viewed as one of adjudication, rather than as one of adjustment.

CONNECTICUT

Experience in Connecticut, on the other hand, shows that mediation has been the principal method of resolving disputes both under the education act and the municipal statute. Of the 57 impasses reached in teacher negotiations from 1965 to June 1968, 39 (70 percent) were resolved through mediation, 12 (20 percent) were resolved through advisory arbitration, and 6 (10 percent) were reported as unresolved.

During the first three years (from July 1, 1965 through June 30, 1968) of fact-finding experience under the Connecticut Municipal Employees Act, there were 57 petitions for fact finding filed with the Connecticut Board of Mediation and Arbitration. In 25 (almost 45 percent) of these cases, settlements were reached through mediation without recourse to the appointment of a fact finder. There were 32 fact finders appointed, of whom 11 settled their cases by mediation. In 21 disputes, formal fact-finding reports were issued. In summary, mediation either by the staff of the board or by the designated fact finder settled two thirds of the disputes without the need for formal fact finding. In the 21 cases in which reports were issued, there were different parties involved in every instance, indicating that in Connecticut, as in Wisconsin, fact finding has not proved to be addictive.[15]

[14] Advisory Committee on Public Employee Relations, composed of Russell A. Smith, Chairman, Gabriel N. Alexander, Edward L. Cushman, Ronald W. Haughton, and Charles C. Killingsworth, "Report," Feb. 15, 1967 in Bureau of National Affairs, *Government Employees Relations Report*, No. 181, Feb. 27, 1967, pp. F 1-12.

[15] The data from which these figures were compiled were supplied by the Connecticut State Department of Education and by Robert L. Stutz, chairman of the Connecticut Board of Mediation and Arbitration on Nov. 1, 1968. . . .

NEW YORK: "WHERE THE ACTION IS"

Among all the state laboratories, New York provides the greatest opportunities for the dissection of fact-finding experiences in the public sector. This is true because of the sheer volume of cases processed during the first year of the Taylor Act, and also because the whole question of procedural substitutes for the strike was thoroughly examined by the Taylor Committee in its original report on March 31, 1966[16] and reviewed in its interim report of June 17, 1968.[17]

Section 209 of the Taylor Law provides two routes for dealing with impasses in the course of collective negotiations. One is the authorization given to the parties to enter into written agreements setting forth procedures to be followed in the event an impasse is reached. These are commonly referred to as contractual impasse procedures. The second consists of state statutory procedures administered by the Public Employment Relations Board (PERB); local laws and ordinances in substantial conformity with the state law and administered by what are colloquially known as Mini-PERBs; or in the special case of the mayoral agencies of New York City, administered by the Office of Collective Bargaining.

The statutory procedures empower PERB on the request of either party or on its own motion in the event of an impasse (which is deemed to exist if the parties have failed to reach agreement at least sixty days prior to the budget submission date of the employer) to appoint a mediator from a list of qualified persons maintained by the board. If mediation is unsuccessful, the board is directed to appoint a fact-finding board of not more than three members. If the dispute is not resolved at least fifteen days prior to the budgetary submission date, the fact-finding board is directed to transmit its findings of fact and recommendations to the chief executive officer of the government involved and to the employee organization "and shall simultaneously make public such findings and recommendations."

In the event that findings of fact and recommendations are made public by a board established under contractual procedures, but the impasse continues, the state board is empowered "to take whatever steps it deems appropriate to resolve the dispute." These include the making of recommendations, after giving due consideration to the report of the fact-finding board. No further fact-finding board may be appointed, however. The intent of this prohibition obviously is to discourage the escalation of the fact-finding process by the creation of additional boards.[18]

If the recommendations of a statutory fact-finding board are not acceptable in whole or in part to either or both parties, the law *directs* the chief executive officer of the government involved to submit to the appropriate legislative body (within five days after receipt of the report) a copy of the report, together with his recommendations for settling the dispute, and *permits* the employee organization to

---

[16]Governor's Committee on Public Employee Relations, *Final Report,* March 31, 1966.

[17]Governor's Committee on Public Employee Relations, *Interim Report,* June 17, 1968.

[18]In the dispute involving the Transit Supervisors in New York City in late August and early September 1968, PERB itself conducted a showcause hearing subsequent to the issuance of a formal mediation proposal, and issued recommendations which led to the settlement of the dispute. The Transit Authority is not a mayoral agency, and hence its labor relations are subject to the jurisdiction of PERB.

submit its recommendations for settling the dispute to the same body. In the statutory design the legislative body has the final voice in determining how the dispute is to be resolved. This indicates, of course, that the statute was based solely on the conventional model of fact finding described earlier, without taking into account any of the possible variants. . . .

THE TAYLOR ACT IN OPERATION

Concerning the statutory impasse procedures, the record for the first year of operation under the Taylor Act is an impressive one. Some 316 impasses were referred to PERB, 80 percent of them involving disputes between school boards and their employees. Over one half (155) of the impasses were resolved by mediation without the necessity of appointing a statutory fact-finding board. Some 150 disputes were referred to formal fact finding. Of these, 22 percent were settled by mediation and 45 percent by the acceptance of the fact-finder's report. In 33 percent of the cases, however, the report was not fully accepted. In one third of these, the recommendations were modified by the employer. In the remaining two thirds, settlement was achieved through "super-mediation" after the fact-finder's report had been issued. There was a total of 9 strikes, 2 of them in New York City and 7 outside. [19]

In its first annual report, PERB concluded that "the overall picture for Year One was bright despite the fact that nine strikes occurred." [20] A similarly favorable evaluation was made by the Taylor Committee in its June 17, 1968 interim report.

The reaction of some of the parties has not been as favorable. Thus Donald H. Wollett, an attorney for many of the National Education Association affiliated teacher organizations in New York State, while conceding that "the record thus far supports the conclusion that the Taylor Law, measured quantitatively, has worked reasonably well," went on to say that it was too early for a qualitative analysis. [21] In the hard cases which really test the effectiveness of the procedures, Wollett was skeptical, if not cynical, as to the promise of fact finding as an alternative to the strike.

"What can be learned, for example," he asked, "from the protracted dispute and nine days teachers' strike in Huntington, Long Island, or from the experience in Plattsburgh, New York, where the school board rejected the settlement worked out

---

[19] The 2 in New York City were the strikes of teachers in September 1967 and of the sanitation workers in February 1968. There were 3 school district strikes outside of New York City, all involving affiliates of the New York State Teachers Association.

For further appraisals of the Taylor Act, see the summary of Governor Rockefeller's Conference on Public Employment Relations held in New York City on Oct. 14-16, 1968 in Bureau of National Affairs, *Government Employment Relations Report*, No. 267 (AA-1-9), Oct. 21, 1968.

[20] Public Employment Relations Board, *Year One of the Taylor Law, September 1, 1967-August 31, 1968*, p. 17.

[21] D. H. Wollett, "The Taylor Law and the Strike Ban," paper delivered at the Association of Labor Mediation Agencies meeting in Puerto Rico, Aug. 20, 1968, published in BNA, *Public Employee Organization and Bargaining*, chap. 4, p. 30.

in mediation and agreed to by its negotiators, insisted on going to fact-finding, and then rejected the recommendations of the fact-finder?"[22]

His answer was that the procedure is inequitable and unbalanced, weighted unfairly in favor of the employer. The risks of fact finding are, in his view, greater for the employee organization than for the employer since the employer is free to reject or accept the recommendations of a fact finder while the employee organization is barred from striking. "Thus the employer risks little and may gain much from pushing a dispute into fact-finding."[23] . . .

A review of this record in terms of the criteria employed by Stern, Krinsky, and Tener indicates that in New York fact finding apparently has been more successful than in Michigan, but less successful than in Wisconsin. Since the New York experience is so recent, it is obviously too early to reach any firm conclusions as to the reasons for these apparent differences. Some tentative hypotheses may, nevertheless, be advanced.

HYPOTHESES ON RESULTS OF FACT FINDING

Fact finding seems to be more effective in smaller communities and rural areas than in large urban centers, where strong and militant labor organizations exist in both the private and public sectors, and where both sides have had more experience in collective bargaining, have more sophisticated practitioners, or have a longer history of joint dealings. This hypothesis may help to explain why in New York City, unlike the upstate areas, public employees have not been reluctant to engage in job actions and strikes, notwithstanding the alternative procedures provided by statute.

Another variable may be the frequency and cost of fact finding. Where fact finding is provided without cost to the parties, and where its invocation is fairly automatic under the statutory procedures, the parties may have less incentive to accept the results than where the procedure is one of their own choosing and their own financing. One could test this hypothesis by comparing the results of statutory and contractual impasse procedures in New York once the data become more available.

Still another variable may be differences in the statutes and in their administration, though these may turn out to be less significant than differences in economic, political, and organizational factors. Whether the supply of expert neutrals skilled in the management of conflict is another determinant remains a question for further study, although the wealth of talent available in New York City suggests that talent alone, while a necessary, is not a sufficient condition for resolving intractable disputes in the public sector.

Instead of limiting inquiries to the causes of failure, however, it might be more pertinent to ask why impasse procedures have been as successful as the record indicates. The orthodox view is that impasse procedures cannot be expected to work equitably, if at all, in the absence of the ultimate right to engage in economic warfare. What is to provide the substitute deadline for the eleventh hour before a

[22]*Ibid.*, p. 31.
[23]*Ibid.*, p. 33.

strike? Absent a legal right to strike, how can impasse procedures assure any measure of justice for employees when the employer has the final right of unilateral determination of the conditions of employment? As far as deadlines are concerned, the substitution of budgetary for strike deadlines has provided a useful pressure level for settlement. The ingenuity of the neutral may also be helpful here in creating artificial deadlines, such as asserting limits on his own continuing availability.

The more difficult question, however, is the one posed by Wollett: "What is the substitute for the strike?"[24] Since the employer or his alter ego, the legislative body, has the final voice, why should he make *any* concessions to his adversary on the other side of the table? Yet those who have been active as neutrals in this field have seen countless instances where such concessions have been made, in some instances even beyond those demanded by the employee organization! What forces prevent the lion's share from going to the lion?

One explanation lies in the inexperience of many of the parties—their collective bargaining illiteracy which will diminish as they gain competence in negotiations. Even some experienced advocates practicing in the public sector have been under the impression that fact finding is the same as arbitration, and that the fact-finder's report and recommendations must be accepted—an illusion that no intelligent neutral cares to dispel! Moreover, many employers now recognize with increasing frequency (as New York City preempts the headlines) that in rejecting a fact-finder's report they may run the risk of an illegal strike—a prospect which may be as coercive in the public as in the private sector. In fact, some representatives of public management recently have been arguing that it might be easier to reach agreements if employees had to face the reality of a strike, and that some settlements might be lower if strikes were not illegal.

Another reason is that the threat of fact finding is in many instances equivalent to the threat of a strike in inducing agreement. Why this should be so is an intriguing question to which a number of answers are possible. Like their counterparts in the private sector, government employers are sometimes reluctant "to open the books," which although a matter of public record, often conceal fiscal juggling and hidden items which may not bear public scrutiny or explanation. Local government and union officials often fear the time and expense involved in formal fact finding, and a skillful neutral will emphasize (or even exaggerate) these costs, just as he stresses the costs of economic conflict in private-sector mediation. The threat of public exposure of unreasonable positions works as effectively (perhaps more effectively) in the public sector as in the private sector because of the potential risk of political retaliation.

Finally, the mediator's argument that the parties run a risk as to the possible outcome of fact finding is not too different from his warnings as to the possible costs of disagreement in private-sector negotiations. In other words, the threat of fact finding, like the threat of a strike, may serve as a powerful inducement to agreement. Even Wollett recognizes this possibility when he says:

> If fact-finding is to serve as an adequate substitute for the strike, it
> must be sufficiently unattractive that employers and employees will usu-

[24]Wollett, *loc, cit.*, p. 31.

ally find it preferable to make their own agreements. Thus, theoretically, both parties should be motivated to reach agreement without outside intervention because of the risks inherent in the fact-finding process. [25] . . .

PROPOSALS FOR CHANGE

A number of other proposals for legislative and administrative changes have been made in recent months for redressing the imbalances and presumed inequities of fact finding in public sector disputes without going to the extreme of legalizing strikes.

One is compulsory arbitration, already enacted into law for police and firemen in Pennsylvania.[26] Another is the recognition by the Taylor committee itself of the need to develop more "effective procedures for achieving finality in the resolution of differences when an impasse occurs."[27] What the committee had in mind was its original recommendation that the legislative body, before acting on a fact-finder's recommendations, conduct a show-cause hearing at which the parties would be directed to appear. The presumption would be that the report should be adopted unless the parties could show that the recommendations were "patently unjust and arbitrary."[28] This proposal might have merit in those instances where the legislative body is not identical with the negotiating team for the employer, as in state and city governments. In the vast majority of cases in New York State, however, this separation of functions is a fiction in most school boards, towns, villages, and counties. As Wollett puts it, "Why should a school board, sitting as a legislative body on the rectitude of its own cause, change the position it has taken at the bargaining table or decide that perhaps there is some merit in the position of the fact finder?"[29] Even where the legislative body is not represented at the bargaining table, it has in many instances laid down the guidelines and fiscal constraints within which the public administrator must bargain.

In this search for a real rather than an illusory forum, some have proposed that the show-cause hearing be conducted by a judge, by an administrative agency (such as PERB), or even by another neutral![30] It has also been suggested that under some

[25]*Ibid.,* p. 32.

[26]Rhode Island has recently amended its law to provide for compulsory arbitration in police and firemen's disputes. The Wyoming Supreme Court has upheld the constitutionality of the Wyoming Fire Department Collective Bargaining Act providing for binding arbitration of disputes concerning wages and conditions of employment.

[27]*Interim Report,* June 17, 1968, p. 41.

[28]*Ibid.,* p. 42.

[29]Wollett, *loc. cit.*, p. 34.

[30]An interesting procedure has been set forth in the "Fact-Finding Rules" adopted by the Massachusetts Board of Conciliation and Arbitration on Apr. 3, 1968. These include the requirement that the fact finder number or letter each of his recommendations. Within 30 days after receipt of the report, each party is required to advise the board in writing as to what action, if any, it has taken with respect to each recommendation contained in the report. Obviously, the intent here is to bring pressure on the parties to consider and respond to the recommendations of the fact finder. The text of the rules can be found in Bureau of National Affairs, *Government Employment Relations Report,* No. 240 (D-1), Apr. 15, 1968.

circumstances an employer's rejection of a fact-finding report might constitute a refusal to bargain so seriously provocative as to free the employee organization from the statutory penalties for striking.[31]

All of these proposals, which fall somewhere between compulsory arbitration and the granting to public employees of the right to strike, suggest a significant shift in public opinion. . . .

As indicated above, under some circumstances, especially for unsophisticated and inexperienced public bargainers, fact finding has performed both an educational and a dispute-resolving function well beyond what the precepts of orthodox teaching would lead one to expect. In this sense it has shown promise. It has been useful, if not entirely successful. In another and more profound sense, however, it may prove ultimately to be not only an illusion, but what is worse, an exercise in futility.

COMPARABILITY PAY AND COMPULSORY ARBITRATION IN MUNICIPAL BARGAINING

Neil W. Chamberlain

Municipal bargaining has its own special complications. It can perhaps be wrapped up in a phrase which has gained currency and credibility—"the sickness of the cities". When we catalogue our major social ills, most of them are traceable to the urban condition. And inevitably these social ills have their impact on the working conditions of city employees, whether we are talking about teachers confronting unruly students or perhaps equally unruly parents, or policemen and firemen called on to meet the desparate conditions created by civil disorders, or welfare workers whose duties take them into the worst of slum areas, or sanitation workers and bus drivers who must fight the almost impossible traffic congestion of

---

Neil Chamberlain is Professor, Graduate School of Business, Columbia University. Reprinted from the *Proceedings* of the 5th Annual Orvil Dryfoos Conference on Public Affairs, Dartmouth College.

[31]This is the argument made in the brief of Associated Teachers of Huntington, Inc., in support of their appeal from the report and recommendation of the hearing officer to the Public Employment Relations Board, Sept. 15, 1968. Case No. D-0003. Of course, if the statute contains explicit unfair labor practice provisions, including the refusal to bargain in good faith, might not the rejection of a fact-finder's report evoke a different administrative and judicial

the central city. The plight of our cities has made working conditions for such as these so miserable that it is small wonder they are driven to seek more of a voice concerning programs to ameliorate their lot and more remuneration for what they are called on to do.

Indeed, I am inclined to think we would make more progress in resolving problems of collective bargaining in the public sector if we concentrated first on municipal or local employment, and tried to see this less as a problem of public service generally than as part of the problem of the cities. In the remainder of my remarks I shall proceed on that basis.

If I may simply summarize now the thesis which I intend to develop a little more fully, it would take this form. A solution to how city employees can be fairly dealt with is not to be found in trying to untie, one by one, all the knots which entangle that issue—the knots of sovereignty and exclusive representation and political constraints and right of strike—but rather by cutting through that whole inherited snarl and trying to devise freshly a feasible and functional system of urban labor relations which falls into place alongside other urban programs. For it is clear that our cities are in need of drastic treatment, and the forms the treatment takes are bound to affect their pattern of labor relations.

To begin with, despite all the traditional American regard for home rule and despite the current renewed emphasis on decentralization as a means of focusing affirmative responsibility on those who are quick to be negatively critical, a revitalization of metropolitan civil service will not prove possible without some federal leadership. We are faced here with something which, like civil rights, so blankets the nation that to hope its massive problems can be solved by dozens of disjointed and unrelated efforts is quixotic. The federal government is needed not to impose solutions on the cities or even to assume a dominant role; it is needed chiefly as the natural governmental unit capable of coordinating the otherwise fragmented urban efforts.

It is now abundantly clear that the problems of our cities are no longer local problems. To cope with the mounting pressures that come from urban congestion, racial unrest, unwelcome technical fallout, social welfare programs with rising case loads, and all the other manifestations of urban blight, requires a nationally coordinate program. Local leadership, drive, and imagination are indispensable, but they are not enough. To meet the demands which the times place upon us we cannot do without national leadership, drive, and imagination in impelling and propelling the local effort.

I will confine myself principally to labor relations aspects of the matter, even though I emphasize the holistic nature of the urban condition. Let me begin at a simple, indeed, elemental level—the necessity for providing some standards for adequate remuneration for the various occupational groupings common to cities. Whether by some agency within the federal Department of Housing and Urban Development or by some independent commission, there is a role to be played by some small body of experts which could collect and compare data from all the cities relating to pay scales, and which can compare such data with comparable jobs

---

response? Case law on this subject is not yet sufficiently well developed to answer this question. See, however, School District for City of Holland, etc. v. Holland Education Association, *et al,* 380 Mich. 314 (1968).

in private industry taking into account differences in job advantages and responsibilities. In effect, this would constitute something of a national job evaluation for the common municipal occupations.

Such a continuing survey would have several benefits. It would set meaningful benchmarks which would at least partially outflank the problem of the political unpalatability of tax increase to raise pay scales, It would expose more vividly to the citizens of any community how the remuneration which they offer their public employees compares with remuneration elsewhere, and put pressure on them to raise their sights where that is called for. That pressure comes from outside the jurisdiction, in the form of what Arthur Ross once called "coercive comparisons." And how can a municipal administration be condemned for conceding to its organized workers increases which are designed to bring them up to a standard?

The kinds of job evaluation or rate ranges of which I am talking would not constitute a substitute for collective bargaining, but standards around which bargaining can take place. There would be no expectation of national uniformity to city pay scales, but at least an informed sense of the range within which remuneration could be expected to fall. By linking such scales to comparable private employments, with adjustments, provision would also be made for more orderly upward movement.

But this is only the start. Earlier I commented that governments, unlike business, cannot rely on increased productivity to finance higher pay scales, since governments deal chiefly in services. But that is at best a half truth. The efficiency of services can be improved, perhaps not as easily as can the manufacture of goods but enough to warrant more effort in this direction. And municipal administrations, again with appropriate federal coordination, can pool experience and research results in a continuing push to upgrade their operations. Here the coordinated effort is more likely to put pressure on the unions which may be expected to fight changes in working practices, but will find resistance less easy if there is a nationally coordinated effort to introduce changes, especially if this is accompanied by improvement in remuneration.

Who would doubt, for example, that our sorely pressed police forces around the country would benefit from a good deal more experimentation and innovation? But changes, particularly in organization, sometimes come with difficulty when a Policeman's Benevolent Association, understandably concerned with the welfare of its members, sees this as resting on the preservation of forms and traditions. With the prod of a federally coordinated national program, led by experts, it would be less easy for the local PBA to resist changes which are entitled to more serious consideration by charging the local administration with being uninformed or with playing political football with public safety.

With an impartial, objective, but concerned search for standards both of performance and remuneration, it would be an act of folly to allow an inherited dogma of governmental sovereignty to stand in the way of realizing their full potential. Leaving to one side the question of applicability to all municipal employees, I see no reason why arbitration should not serve as an appropriate means of resolving disputes which city authorities and unions cannot settle by negotiation. Surely one can question whether the sovereign city of, say, Cincinnati or Detroit or Seattle (I pick the names at random) should be privileged to pay its employees as little as they can get away with, regardless of how this deteriorates the quality of their services or leads to labor embroilments. Surely it needs no argument in these days that what happens in any major city is of importance to all cities. Arbitration with the benefit of carefully researched standards to determine what a city should pay and what it should expect for its payment scarcely impugns the sovereignty of a city in any essential respect.

There is not the slightest prospect—I say this categorically—that any city can withdraw from its employees the right to strike, and fail to put in its place a meaningful substitute, and expect to preserve a system of orderly labor relations. The last few years have demonstrated that the consequence can only be illegal strikes and disrespect for law. Is the city more sovereign when it presides over anti-strike ordinances which are ignored than when it joins in an initiative to establish a well-founded arbitration procedure?

But—a cautious voice may well inquire—suppose we do provide national standards guiding arbitration decisions in municipal settlements, where do the cities obtain the financing to underwrite the higher awards? Can there be any doubt that the cities' payrolls would swell enormously if they were to pay salaries commensurate with the upgraded quality of performance which is needed if they are to remain afloat?

The fact is that the tax base of the cities is woefully inadequate to their fiscal needs. The property tax which is their chief resort is too limited a support. The Pechman task force appointed by President Johnson recognized that the federal government is the great revenue producer with its prior accessibility to the income tax, which even with a steady rate structure produces a heavier flow of funds as incomes rise and move into higher brackets. Out of that recognition emerged the Heller-Pechman plan for redistributing funds from federal government to the states. In its original formulation there was no restriction on the uses to which such funds could be put. The assumption was made that the states would of their own accord channel the federal bonus to their most pressing needs. As others latched on to the idea, variant versions appeared. Some wanted to tie the allocations to specific uses. One interesting variation would have funneled the funds directly to cities, bypassing the state administration, on the premise that here is where the financial need is greatest.

At the moment the war in Vietnam has effectively dampened any interest in the Heller-Pechman proposal. Rising military outlays pose a need for new sources of revenue rather than for means of their effective disbursement. But the war will not go on forever, and the time will come soon enough for us to be thinking of it now, when the efficient tax collection machinery of the federal government can be put in the service of the cities, whether or not through the states as intermediaries.

It is here that the importance of a fresh new approach to the problems of collective bargaining in the public service becomes evident. Instead of relating it to questions of strike and sovereignty and the like, we relate it to needed standards of performance and remuneration consonant with performance, and we recognize the national character of the urban crisis by effective federal coordination of municipal initiatives, and we provide—through the Heller-Pechman mechanism—the financial means of backing up the negotiated settlements and arbitral awards which are linked to federal fact-finding.

To encourage local initiative and at the same time to set some constraint on local awards, some sort of local matching of federal assistance would probably be required. Perhaps the federal treasury would underwrite one-third of municipal wage and salary awards when these were specifically linked to standards for scales and performances. I do not propose any particular formula since this would have to be fitted within the overall framework of Heller-Pechman federal disbursements.

Obviously some such financial bolstering of the cities is absolutely essential if they are to survive, and it should be equally obvious that the cities' problems of labor relations are directly linked to their financial problems. Unless there is some orderly mechanism for an upward adjustment of salary scales in keeping with the private sector, we can expect continued labor unrest in the cities, bubbling up into recurrent illegal strikes as the only means of forcing attention to need and providing the rationale for some kind of settlement, political or otherwise. I do not think an orderly system can be devised separately by each city out of the resources available to them. It will require a federal coordinating initiative supplemented by federal fiscal power.

But I do not want to stress too singly the financial aspect. Performance in the public sector is also of the highest importance. The quality of the cities' services, from education to sanitation, is much in need of improvement. But tied in with the quality of performance is a variety of matters which might also be labelled working conditions. Questions such as moonlighting by policemen and firemen, the hours of rubbish pickup in residential and commercial areas, teachers' extracurricular requirements, and so on in a seemingly endless list involve at one and the same time performance and working conditions. Such double-interest issues cannot be discussed as though the issues were separable. It is here that continuing discussions with representative unions in a nonbargaining atmosphere can be fruitful, but they are likely to be most fruitful if the cities can move such discussions on to a professional plane. Most of the services a city supplies can be converted into professional services, standards of performance can then be examined in terms of professional standards, and working conditions in terms of professional practice.

This may seem excessively optimistic, but I would prefer to set my sights higher than lower. I see no reason why we should conceive of collective bargaining in the public service as involving only or even primarily a transfer of experience from the private sector. Some experience is extremely relevant, as I indicated at the start of my remarks, but other facets of the process may be remarkable different. If we see the present as a time of opportunity, when we can newly fashion a system of public collective bargaining responsive to its peculiar needs, and do it with whatever innovative mechanisms give promise of help, we are likely to achieve a better result than if we attempt to tailor the public garment by alterations on the private pattern.

I have confined the burden of my comments to labor relations in the cities, barely touching on the federal government and the states. These latter, I think, present more tractable problems. Our greatest need at the moment is in the cities, and I urge that we think of collective bargaining there not as presenting just one more nearly insuperable problem but as something which itself can contribute to a better society.

COMPULSORY ARBITRATION FOR POLICE
AND FIRE FIGHTERS IN PENNSYLVANIA
IN 1968

J. Joseph Loewenberg

The role of compulsory arbitration in collective bargaining has long been controversial.[1] In the past, the argument has been largely theoretical because compulsory arbitration was invoked only on an ad hoc basis on a few occasions. Now compulsory arbitration has moved from academic polemics to bargaining reality. Four states have legislated compulsory arbitration as the final step to impasses in collective bargaining negotiations between public employers and certain groups of public employees: Michigan (1969), Pennsylvania (1968), Rhode Island (1968), and Wyoming (1965). The Wyoming statute applies to fire fighters, while those of the other three states cover impasses involving police and fire fighters. Legal challenges to the Pennsylvania, Rhode Island, and Wyoming statutes have been denied by the respective state supreme courts. The experience under these statutes permits examination of the questions long raised about compulsory arbitration. This article will deal with the experience of Pennsylvania in the first year of the statute's operation.

Pennsylvania Act III of 1968 permits police and fire fighters employed by the state or local governments to (1) designate representatives if 50 percent or more of the employees favor such representation, (2) bargain collectively with employers concerning the terms and conditions of employment, and (3) enter into written agreements with employers. In case of impasses in bargaining due to either inability to reach settlement or failure of the appropriate lawmaking body to approve the agreement, arbitration may be implemented. A majority of the tripartite board of arbitration—which consists of one employer representative, one employee representative, and a neutral member selected by the two representatives—determines the

Joseph Loewenberg is Associate Professor of Management, Temple University. Reprinted from *Industrial and Labor Relations Review*, XXIII, No. 3, April 1970. Copyright©1970 by Cornell University. All rights reserved.

[1] See, for instance, Herbert R. Northrup, *Compulsory Arbitration and Government Intervention in Labor Disputes* (Washington: Labor Policy Association, Inc., 1966); Orme W. Phelps, "Compulsory Arbitration: Some Perspectives," *Industrial and Labor Relations Review*, Vol. 18, No. 1 (October 1964) pp. 81-91; Carl M. Stevens, "Is Compulsory Arbitration Compatible with Bargaining?" *Industrial Relations*, Vol. 5, No. 2 (February 1966), pp. 38-52; and the Governor's Committee on Public Employee Relations, State of New York, *Final Report* (March 31, 1966), pp. 15-16.

binding award. Excluding costs of the employee representative and of the employees' presentation, all expenses of the arbitration proceedings are to be paid by the public employer. The act also contains a tight time schedule for various steps in the bargaining process. Negotiations must be initiated at least six months prior to the start of the fiscal year; a declaration of a bargaining impasse must be made thirty days after bargaining commences; arbitration must be initiated at least 110 days before the start of the fiscal year; and the arbitration award must be determined within 30 days after the third member has been named to the arbitration board.

Pennsylvania Act III of 1968 was signed on June 24, 1968. Since most political jurisdictions have a fiscal year corresponding to the calendar year and since the act required the start of collective bargaining at least six months prior to the start of the fiscal year, considerable confusion accompanied the implementation of the act.

Unfortunately, the Pennsylvania legislature made no provision for compiling information on the initial experience under the act. To help fill this gap, the author undertook to find out what happened in Pennsylvania in 1968. The research included a survey of major municipalities and a review of secondary sources (the results are described in this article), and the case studies of particular situations. This information should assist Pennsylvania municipalities and employee representatives to prepare for future bargaining as well as aid others in assessing the value and the effects of compulsory arbitration. While the information answers some existing questions about compulsory arbitration, it also raises unexpected new issues which require further research.

SURVEY OF MAJOR MUNICIPALITIES

The questionnaire survey included all municipalities designated as major municipalities and townships in the *Pennsylvania Abstract for 1968*.[2] Data were obtained from 156 of the 171 municipalities; some information about the non-respondents was available from other sources. The characteristics of the non-respondents were representative of the entire population; therefore, any conclusions may be attributed to the entire survey group.

The closed-end, check-off questionnaire asked if the respondent negotiated wages, hours, and working conditions with policemen for 1969; if so, were compulsory arbitration proceedings instituted at any time in the negotiations; and if the municipality and the police arrived at an agreement, what method determined its terms. The same questions were asked about the municipality's fire fighters, once it was established that the municipality employed paid fire fighters.

The municipalities were analyzed by three characteristics: size of population, type of government, and geographic location. The survey group of 171 municipalities may be described in terms of these characteristics:

[2]Table 162, pp. 237-239.

Characteristic	Number
Population	
Less than 10,000	7
10,000-19,999	110
20,000-49,999	36
50,000-99,999	12
100,000-499,999	4
500,000 and over	2
Government	
City	47
Township	54
Borough	70
Location	
Philadelphia SMSA	42
Pittsburgh SMSA	51
Other SMSA	44
Other areas	34

All the municipalities surveyed, except five townships with populations ranging from 10,000 to 20,000, had police forces, their size generally varying in proportion to population. Twenty-six police departments numbered 50 or more employees and 135 departments had fewer than 50 members. No information on size was obtained for five departments.

Altogether, three fifths of the communities surveyed engaged in negotiations with representatives of their police forces in 1968. Almost half of those involved in negotiations, as may be seen in Table 1, had some experience with arbitration proceedings. Of the 103 cases in which bargaining occurred, the parties reached a negotiated settlement in 67 instances. In the other 36 cases, impasses occurred which were resolved by arbitration awards. In 12 of the cases settled by negotiation, however, arbitration proceedings were initiated in the course of negotiations,

table 1 Collective Bargaining Experience of Major Municipalities in Pennsylvania with Police in 1968

Experience	Number of Municipalities
No negotiations	51
Engaged in negotiations	103
Negotiated settlement*	67
Arbitration award	36
Insufficient information	12
No police force	5
Total	171

*Arbitration proceedings initiated in 12 cases.

although the parties resolved their differences without an award. In several cases the parties never chose an arbitrator; in other instances they were able to notify the arbitrator before the start of hearings that they were in the process of settling; and in some cases the arbitrator suggested the parties bargain further before they submit the unresolved issues to arbitration.

The likelihood of negotiations, it is suggested by Table 2, is related to size of community. While only three of the seven municipalities under 10,000 population were involved in negotiations, two thirds of the communities between 10,000 and

table 2   Collective Bargaining Experience of Major Municipalities
in Pennsylvania with Police in 1968 by Population of Municipality

Experience	Less than 10,000	10,000- 19,999	20,000- 49,999	Population 50,000- 99,999	100,000- 499,999	500,000- 1,000,000	Total
No negotiations	4	39	5	3	0	0	51
Negotiations	3	56	30	8	4	2	103
Negotiated settlement*	3	37	18	6	2	1	67
Arbitration award	0	19	12	2	2	1	36
Insufficient information	0	10	1	1	0	0	12
No police force	0	5	0	0	0	0	5
Total	7	110	36	12	4	2	171
*Arbitration initiated during negotiations .	1	4	4	1	2	0	12

50,000 persons and four fifths of the municipalities with over 50,000 people engaged in collective bargaining with their police forces in 1968. Negotiations were most likely to occur in communities located in the Pittsburgh and Philadelphia regions, somewhat less likely in other metropolitan areas of the state, and least likely in nonmetropolitan areas (see Table 3).

Whether impasses in negotiations were resolved by bargaining or by arbitration does not, according to the data in Tables 2 and 3, seem to be related to size of city or size of police force, but some variation is apparent by locality and type of government. Only 18 of 39 municipalities in the Pittsburgh SMSA reached agreements with their police forces by negotiation, compared with 23 of 27 municipalities in the Philadelphia area. Elsewhere in the state about seven out of ten settlements were through collective bargaining. About half of the cities concluded agreements through negotiation, compared to two thirds of the boroughs and nearly four fifths of the townships.

table 3   Collective Bargaining Experience of Major Municipalities in Pennsylvania with Police in 1968 by Geographic Location

Experience	Philadelphia SMSA	Pittsburgh SMSA	Location Other SMSA	Other Areas	Total
No negotiations	10	8	16	17	51
Negotiations	27	39	23	14	103
Negotiated settlement*	23	18	16	10	67
Arbitration award	4	21	7	4	36
Insufficient information	4	2	4	2	12
No police force	1	2	1	1	5
Total	42	51	44	34	171
*Arbitration initiated during negotiations	7	1	2	2	12

POLICE SALARY AND BARGAINING ACTIVITY

Total compensation for public safety employees consists of a number of factors, of which salary is one. Other items, including fringe benefits and premium pay, vary from municipality to municipality, but wages are the largest component in compensation and played a significant part in 1968 collective bargaining in Pennsylvania police and fire departments. In some cases, the only real topic for discussion was wages. It is therefore pertinent to analyze collective bargaining developments by 1968 salaries and increases gained for 1969.

In 1968, maximum basic salaries for patrolmen in Pennsylvania ranged from less than $5,200 to $7,000. Salary levels correlated with both the size of a municipality and its location. Median salary ranges of municipalities by population sizes were as follows:

Population	Median Salaries
10,000-19,999	$5,800-6,099
20,000-49,999	6,100-6,399
50,000-499,999	6,400-6,699
500,000 and over	7,000 and over

The median police salary in the Philadelphia SMSA ranged from $6,700 to $6,999; in Pittsburgh and other SMSA's it varied from $5,800 to $6,099; and in other areas it was between $5,500 and $5,799.

Information on 1968 police salaries and bargaining experience was available in 112 cases (see Table 4). Bargaining activity was somewhat related to median salary

Table 4   Collective Bargaining Experience of Major Municipalities in Pennsylvania with Police in 1968 by Salary Range of Patrolmen in 1968.

Experience	Salary Range (dollars)								NA*	Total
	Under 5,200	5,200–5,499	5,500–5,799	5,800–6,099	6,100–6,399	6,400–6,699	6,700–6,999	7,000–and up		
No negotiations	6	7	3	3	4	4	3	1	20	51
Negotiations	3	8	11	15	12	12	9	11	22	103
Negotiated settlement†	2	6	7	5	9	8	7	9	14	67
Arbitration award	1	2	4	10	3	4	2	2	8	36
Insufficient information	1	2	1	0	1	0	1	1	5	12
Total	10	17	15	18	17	16	13	13	47	166
†Arbitration initiated during negotiations	0	1	1	1	0	1	3	2	3	12

*Not available.

in 1968. The median salary range of police departments where negotiations did not occur ($5,500-5,799) was substantially below the median salary range where negotiations were conducted ($6,100-6,399). Likewise, an analysis of collective bargaining experience within the Pittsburgh and the Philadelphia areas shows that two thirds of the police forces with salaries in the lower half of the scale for their respective region did not participate in collective bargaining negotiations in 1968, whereas the majority of those in the upper half of the salary range were involved in negotiations.

Where negotiations occurred, the 1968 salary range was typically higher among police who settled by negotiation ($6,100-6,399) than among police who pressed for an arbitration award ($5,800-6,099). Those situations which involved a demand for arbitration but were concluded with a settlement were typically in the highest range of all $6,700-6,999). These data may be explained in terms of the preponderance of negotiations in larger municipalities, of arbitration in the Pittsburgh area, and of demand for arbitration but eventual settlement in the Philadelphia SMSA.

The amounts of increase in salary gained by police between 1968 and 1969 were available in 91 cases. The median salary gain was in the range of $600 to $799, with the extremes of less than $200 in five cases and more than $1,400 in six others. These increases were for the year beginning January 1, 1969, although some police received increases covering 1970 as well as 1969. Neither size of muncipality nor 1968 salary had much relationship to the amount of salary increase awarded for 1969. Increases at the upper end of the range were given in smaller- and larger-sized municipalities and in lower- and higher-paying police forces. On the other hand, police in metropolitan areas gained substantially more in salary increases than those in other areas; and the police in the Pittsburgh region received slightly more, on the average, than those in Philadelphia and other SMSA's.

Area	Number of Cases	Median Salary Increase for 1969
Philadelphia SMSA	19	$600-799
Pittsburgh SMSA	28	800-1,199
Other SMSA's	23	600-799
Other areas	21	200-399

When viewed in terms of methods of settlement, salary increases for 1969 reveal broad dispersion, but a pattern is evident (see Table 5). Overall, it appears that an arbitration decision resulted in higher salary increase than where there was no negotiation or where the parties negotiated a settlement.

Method of Settlement	Number of Cases	Median Salary Increase, 1968-1969
No negotiation	24	$600-799
Settlement by negotiation	39	600-799
Arbitration award	24	800-999

table 5   Collective Bargaining Experience of Major Municipalities
in Pennsylvania with Police in 1968
by Salary Increase for Patrolmen in 1969

Experience	Amount of Salary Increase (dollars)								NA*	Total
	0-199	200-399	400-599	600-799	800-999	1,000-1,199	1,200-1,399	1,400-and up		
No negotiations	3	7	0	6	3	3	1	1	27	51
Negotiations	1	9	9	13	7	8	11	4	41	103
Negotiated settlement†	0	8	5	10	4	6	4	2	28	67
Arbitration award	1	1	4	3	3	2	7	2	13	36
Insufficient information	1	0	1	1	0	1	1	0	7	12
Total	5	16	10	20	10	12	13	5	75	166
†Arbitration initiated during negotiations.	0	0	1	2	1	1	1	0	6	12

*Not available

Although the 1968 median salary range for police who negotiated a settlement
was higher than that of police who received an arbitration award, the differential in
1968 does not account for the variance in the salary increases received for 1969.
The Pittsburgh region data illustrate the point. The 1968 median salary range for
Pittsburgh police who negotiated a settlement was $6,100-6,399 and for those who
received an arbitration award, $5,800-6,099; salary data for police who did not
negotiate are too sparse to be meaningful. Information on salary increases by collective bargaining experience is presented in Table 6. The median increase in the
case of both "no negotiations" and "negotiated settlement" was $600-799, but the
median increase in the case of "arbitration award" was $1,200-1,399. In general,
the police who received an arbitration award received a higher salary in 1969 than

table 6   Collective Bargaining Experience of Major Municipalities
in Pittsburgh SMSA with Police
in 1968 by Salary Increase for Patrolmen in 1969

Experience	Salary Increase (dollars)							Total
	200-399	400-599	600-799	800-999	1,000-1,199	1,200-1,399	1,400-and up	
No negotiations	0	0	2	1	0	0	0	3
Negotiations	2	1	6	2	4	7	2	24
Negotiated settlement	2	1	4	1	2	1	0	11
Arbitration award	0	0	2	1	2	6	2	13
Total	2	1	8	3	4	7	2	27

other groups, although they had been receiving less in 1968 than those who nego-tiated a settlement in 1968.

Analysis of the 1968 salaries for police, the increases secured for 1969, and the method by which these increases were secured show that police who received higher salaries in 1968 did not necessarily gain larger increases than those at the lower end of the scale, regardless of method used. Nor was there a perfect relationship within a salary range between the size of salary increase for 1969 and the collective bargaining experience in 1968. For instance, when considering the forty-two police departments with 1968 median salaries above $6,400 per annum, the median increase for 1969 for those which did not negotiate was $1,000 to $1,119; for those which negotiated a settlement, $600 to $799; for those which arbitrated, $400 to $599. No evidence exists, however, to support the hypothesis that police chose not to negotiate because unilateral employer offers tended to be higher than salary increases gained through bargaining and arbitration. In fact, the Pittsburgh area data reveal that in every salary category the median increases received in arbitration awards were higher than those gained through negotiated settlements. But, even here, no consistent pattern developed of larger salary increases at either the upper or the lower end of the salary scale.

FIRE FIGHTERS

Of the 171 communities in the survey, over three fifths had no professional fire-fighting department. Although sixty-two municipalities employed full-time members in their fire departments, only fifty-four employed professional fire fighters. In the remaining eight cases, which will be discussed separately, the employees were truck drivers. The majority of municipalities with population over 50,000 had professional fire fighters, but several communities with population under 10,000 also employed professional fire fighters. The size of the fire depart-ment generally related, however, to the size of the municipality. By far the lowest incidence of municipal professional fire departments was in the Philadelphia area, where only 10 percent of the municipalities reported such a department. On the other hand, in the Pittsburgh region, other SMSA's, and other areas of the state, 38 to 45 percent of the municipalities had a fire department with professional fire-fighting employees. Eighty percent of the cities had professional fire fighters, compared to 31 percent of the boroughs and 5 percent of the townships. Thus, professional fire fighters could be found most typically in a city outside the Phila-delphia SMSA.

Where a municipality employed professional fire fighters, collective bargaining probably took place in 1968 (see Table 7). Bargaining occurred in forty of the fifty-four municipalities employing professional fire fighters. The parties negotiated settlements in twenty-five municipalities, although in four cases arbitration pro-ceedings were initiated prior to the reaching of agreement. In fifteen other muni-cipalities, terms were set by an aribtration award. Thus in nearly half the munici-palities in which bargaining occurred between the public employer and the professional fire fighters, some use was made of compulsory arbitration. A final binding award was made in approximately three fourths of the situations in which compulsory arbitration proceedings were instituted.

table 7　Summary of Collective Bargaining Experience of Major Municipalities in Pennsylvania with Fire Fighters in 1968

Experience	Number
No negotiations	14
Negotiations	40
*Negotiated settlement**	*25*
Arbitration award	*15*
Insufficient information	11
No fire fighters	106
Total	171

*Arbitration proceedings initiated during negotiations in 4 cases.

CHARACTERISTICS OF COLLECTIVE BARGAINING ACTIVITY WITH FIRE FIGHTERS

The probability of collective bargaining was somewhat higher in larger municipalities than in smaller ones, in cities than in boroughs and townships, and in the Pittsburgh and the Philadelphia regions than in other SMSA's and other areas of the state. In no grouping by size or area, however, did the proportion of municipalities engaging in bargaining fall below 50 percent. There was a marked differentiation, however, as to the resolution of negotiations (see Tables 8 and 9). Municipalities under 20,000 in population which bargained with their fire fighters negotiated an agreement 80 percent of the time, while larger municipalities negotiated a settlement with their professional fire fighters in only 45 percent of the cases. Arbitration procedures were more likely to be initiated in metropolitan areas than elsewhere, but the incidence of arbitration awards was exceptionally high in the Pittsburgh area. Municipalities in the Pittsburgh area were involved in over half the compulsory arbitration awards to fire fighters but in only three eighths of the bargaining situations in 1968.

Data on wages of fire fighters in 1968 and salary increases for 1969 were spotty, and therefore, the following analysis is suggestive rather than definitive. The 1968 wages of fire fighters were generally in proportion to the population of the municipalities, with a median salary range of $5,200 to $5,499 for fire fighters in municipalities under 20,000 population to a salary range of over $6,700 in cities over 500,000 population. Annual salaries were generally highest in the Philadelphia area and lowest in non-metropolitan areas. No clear distinction in 1968 salaries was apparent between municipalities which negotiated and those which did not nego-

table 8   Collective Bargaining Experience of Major Municipalities
             in Pennsylvania with Fire Fighters in 1968
             by Population of Municipality

Experience	Less than 10,000	10,000- 19,999	20,000- 49,999	Population 50,000- 99,999	100,000- 499,999	500,000 and over	Total
No negotiations	1	10	1	2	0	0	14
Negotiations	1	19	11	5	2	2	40
Negotiated settlement*	1	15	3	4	1	1	25
Arbitration award	0	4	8	1	1	1	15
Insufficient information	0	6	3	1	1	0	11
No fire fighters	5	75	21	4	1	0	106
Total	7	110	36	12	4	2	171
*Arbitration initiated during negotiations .	0	1	1	1	1	0	4

tiate with fire fighters. Where negotiations did occur, however, arbitration was
initiated more often in municipalities which were paying higher salaries. As far as
salary increases for 1969 were concerned, the median range in situations where no
bargaining occurred was slightly lower than where the parties did bargain. The
median salary increase awarded in arbitration was identical to that negotiated by
the parties.

Eight communities in the survey indicated they employed only fire drivers, as
distinguished from fire fighters. Presumably the fire fighters in these communities,

table 9   Collective Bargaining Experience of Major Municipalities
           in Pennsylvania with Fire Fighters in 1968, by Geographic Location

Experience	Philadelphia SMSA	Location Pittsburgh SMSA	Other SMSA	Other Areas	Total
No negotiations	0	3	5	6	14
Negotiations	4	15	12	9	40
Negotiated settlement*	3	7	8	7	25
Arbitration award	1	8	4	2	15
Insufficient information	3	3	4	1	11
No fire fighters	35	30	23	18	106
Total	42	51	44	34	171
*Arbitration initiated during negotiations	1	0	2	1	4

which ranged in population from 10,000 to 50,000 persons, were volunteers. Whether other respondents in the survey considered fire drivers to be fire fighters cannot be determined.

Collective bargaining negotiations between public employers and representatives of the fire drivers took place in four of the eight municipalities; no negotiations occurred in three other municipalities; and no information was available on the remaining municipality. In all four cases where bargaining occurred, a settlement was negotiated by the parties. Coincidentally, the municipality in each of these four cases also negotiated a settlement with the police.

COMPARISON OF POLICE AND FIRE-FIGHTER EXPERIENCE

In Pennsylvania in 1968, collective bargaining negotiations were slightly more common among fire departments than among police departments. Approximately 67 percent of the police departments in the survey (103 of 154) negotiated with the municipal employer, whereas about 74 percent of the fire departments (40 of 54) were involved in collective bargaining negotiations with fire fighters. The somewhat higher incidence of bargaining among fire fighters may be explained by the concentration of fire departments in larger communities. Once negotiations began, however, the chances of requests for arbitration were almost identical: 48 of 103 police negotiations and 19 of 40 fire-fighter negotiations included initiation of arbitration. Likewise, the proportion of arbitration proceedings ending in an award was similar for police and fire-fighter negotiations: 36 of 48 arbitration proceedings involving police and 15 of 19 involving fire fighters.

Among the survey group, seventy municipalities employed both police and professional fire fighters and thus provided an opportunity to study similarities and differences in bargaining patterns among public safety forces in the same government jurisdiction. In thirteen cases, however, there was insufficient information about collective bargaining in 1968 for one or both of the groups to permit a comparison. Two thirds of the fifty-seven communities where useable data were available were cities; almost all had populations above 10,000. An identical pattern of bargaining activity occurred for both police and fire fighters in forty-three of the fifty-seven communities.

In fourteen municipalities, however, bargaining experience with police and fire fighters differed. The police received an arbitration award in eight communities, while the fire fighters settled in five of these municipalities, did not negotiate in another, and provided no information in two others. The fire fighters received an arbitration award in three communities, while the police settled in two (one after the initiation of arbitration) and did not negotiate in the third. The other three community situations involved one in which the police alone negotiated a settlement, a second one in which the fire fighters alone negotiated a settlement, and a third in which the police did not negotiate and no information was provided on the fire fighters.

In seven situations in which the police and fire fighters reached agreement by the same process with their municipal employer, the amount of the salary increase gained by the two groups differed. In three of these communities the fire fighters gained the larger increases; in the other four the police received the larger increases.

Arbitration awards figured in four of the seven cases. In four additional situations, which also include one arbitration award, the police and the fire fighters received the same amount of salary increase for 1969.

OTHER INFORMATION

At least fifty-four municipalities other than those in the survey bargained collectively with their police and/or fire fighters in 1968. Information on their experience was obtained from newspapers, the files of the American Arbitration Association, municipal organizations in Pennsylvania, and the Pennsylvania State Mediation Service. While these data indicate the existence of collective bargaining outside the survey group, they are not intended to be either a complete listing or representative of the situation in the 2,394 nonmajor municipalities in Pennsylvania.

The fifty-four municipalities not included in the survey included five cities, thirty-six boroughs, and thirteen townships. With one exception, all contained less than 10,000 inhabitants. Forty two of these municipalities were in the Pittsburgh SMSA, two in the Philadelphia SMSA, three in other SMSA's, and seven in other areas.

A summary of the 1968 collective bargaining experience of the fifty-four municipalities is presented in Table 10. Considering the size of the municipalities, it is probable that most of them did not employ paid fire fighters. Unlike fire fighters in the survey group, all the fire fighters outside the survey who bargained reached a negotiated settlement. Among police, too, the incidence of arbitration awards was somewhat lower among those not in the survey group (29 percent) than among

table 10 Summary of Collective Bargaining Experience in 1968 in Fifty-four Nonmajor Municipalities in Pennsylvania.

Experience	Police	Fire Fighters
Negotiated settlement	37	3
Without arbitration	20	0
With arbitration	4	0
No information on arbitration	13	3
Arbitration award	15	0
No information on bargaining	2	51
Total	54	54

those included in the survey (35 percent). The largest number of arbitration awards, eleven, was made in the Pittsburgh SMSA, but a higher proportion of arbitration awards to municipalities which entered collective bargaining with their police occurred in the Philadelphia SMSA and other areas. It is also interesting to note that six of the arbitration decisions affected municipalities of less than 5,000 in population and that arbitration occurred in towns, boroughs, and cities.

CONCLUSIONS

Compulsory arbitration played a prominent role in collective bargaining between local governments and their police and fire fighters in 1968. At least sixty-six arbitration awards covering conditions of employment for Pennsylvania police and fire fighters resulted from compulsory arbitration proceedings implemented during the first year in which Act III of 1968 was in operation. In a minimum of twenty additional cases, arbitration proceedings were initiated but suspended because the parties were able to negotiate an agreement. Among major municipalities, arbitration was invoked in almost half the municipalities which bargained.

The availability of compulsory arbitration did not terminate collective bargaining activity among police and fire fighters in Pennsylvania. Two thirds (132 of 198) of the municipalities discussed in this article which negotiated with their police or fire fighters arrived at a negotiated settlement.

The advent of compulsory arbitration did not bring collective bargaining to all. In major municipalities, about one third of all police departments and one fourth of all fire departments did not engage in collective bargaining in 1968. Probably a much higher proportion of nonmajor municipalities did not bargain with their public safety employees in 1968. There is consensus, however, that the provision of Act III providing for the compulsory arbitration feature encouraged more collective bargaining than had existed previously.

A strong regional bias was evident in the use of compulsory arbitration. The Pittsburgh SMSA accounted for 57 percent of arbitration cases in major municipalities, although the area accounted for only 38 percent of the bargaining situations.

Larger municipalities were more likely to become involved in arbitration than smaller ones. Once so involved, however, the chances of settlement were higher in bargaining between larger municipalities and their police than between smaller municipalities and their police.

Arbitration was invariably invoked by employee representatives on the ground that employers were not bargaining in good faith. Evidence exists, however, that arbitration was used at times as a tactical weapon by both sides, rather than as a court of last resort to resolve a deadlock in bargaining. First, of the ninety-two negotiated settlements reported in the survey, sixteen involved formal initiation of arbitration proceedings at some point during negotiations. It is likely that the threat of arbitration was used in other cases, even though no formal steps were taken to implement arbitration. Second, some public employers preferred to have the wages and working conditions of public safety employees decided by an arbitrator in order to avoid responsibility for making decisions which might be unpopular with the electorate. In the same fashion, representatives of employees chose to go to arbitration to prove their militancy and fortitude to members. In a few cases, the parties agreed to submit negotiated settlements to arbitration for their mutual benefit.

The principal—and in some cases the only—subject for arbitration was wages.

Economic benefits with cost implications for municipalities but with few operating repercussions for departments were also raised. The 1968 salaries of police who reached a settlement with their employers tended to be higher than the salaries of police who received an arbitration award. The opposite was true for fire fighters, however. Perhaps these differences provide a clue (although it by no means accounts fully) for the fact that the median increase in salary for 1969 was similar for fire fighters whether the increase was negotiated or determined by an arbitration award, whereas arbitration decisions in police cases resulted in larger salary increases than did negotiated settlements or employer determinations.

Compulsory arbitration and the resulting awards were resisted by public employers in the form of court suits and escrow payments. In June 1969, the Pennsylvania Supreme Court upheld the constitutionality of Act III in *Harney v. Russo et al.*[3] The decision ended the primary legal basis for employer opposition to compulsory arbitration and noncompliance with arbitration awards.

Despite employer objections to arbitration awards and some employee unhappiness with particular awards, compulsory arbitration seemed to fulfill its main purpose in 1968, i.e., to provide an alternative to strike action as a terminal point in collective bargaining. So far as is known, no form of organized work stoppage, slowdown, or sick call occurred among police or fire fighters in Pennsylvania during the first six months after Act III went into effect.

QUESTIONS FOR THE FUTURE

The 1968 experience with compulsory arbitration in Pennsylvania is important, not only in its own right, but also because it suggests the climate for the future. While providing interesting and heretofore unavailable data, however, the experience cannot answer many questions which concern those who oppose the use of compulsory arbitration in collective bargaining. At the same time, the experience to date poses some additional questions which deserve long-run attention.

Experience with Collective Bargaining	Number of Municipalities
Engaged in negotiations	31
*Negotiated settlement**	*18*
Arbitration award	*13*
No negotiations	12
Total	43

*Arbitration initiated during negotiations in four cases.

What will be the long-term effects of compulsory arbitration on collective bargaining? Will some or all of the parties come to view it as a substitute for bargaining or will they prefer to use it sparingly in extreme situations? Do parties not involved in arbitration proceedings become dependent on arbitration awards elsewhere as a

[3]435 Pa. 183 (1969).

guide to determining their own settlements, thereby permitting the arbitration award to set the pattern?

What will be the effects of compulsory arbitration on maintaining labor peace? Will the parties be satisfied with compulsory arbitration procedures and be willing to accept the awards? Certainly, some of the spectacular increases awarded in 1968 on the basis of relatively low salaries cannot be duplicated in each succeeding round.

What will be other effects of arbitration? Parity in salary between police and fire fighters was broken by separate arbitration awards in some communities. Will this lead to demands for joint arbitration sessions in the future? What will be the repercussions for other municipal employees, whose salaries traditionally have been related to those of police and fire fighters? Will they demand the right to compulsory arbitration, or will they try to support police and fire fighters and hope for a "trickle-down" effect? What will be the effect on public safety department administration if nonwage matters become the subject of arbitration? What tax reforms or supplements will be necessary to permit municipalities to pay for cost increases determined by an arbitration award? Does the state legislature, which mandated the availability of compulsory arbitration, have an obligation to make it fiscally feasible? If the costs imposed by arbitration become prohibitive, will municipalities seek other ways of reducing or spreading the burden, such as consolidation of departments within a region or "contracting out" of public safety services?

These questions are not simple ones. Their answers will come from detailed, complex research over a period of years. But if the true impact of compulsory arbitration is ever to be learned, these are the types of questions which will need answers before the theoretical discussions will be substantiated or disproved.